RECONSTRUCTING THE CORPORATION

From Shareholder Primacy to Shared Governance

MW00626291

Modern corporations contribute to a wide range of contemporary problems, including income inequality, global warming, and the influence of money in politics. Their relentless pursuit of profits, though, is the natural outcome of the doctrine of shareholder primacy. As the consensus around this doctrine crumbles, it has become increasingly clear that the prerogatives of corporate governance have been improperly limited to shareholders. It is time to examine shareholder primacy and its attendant governance features anew, and reorient the literature around the basic purpose of corporations. This book critically examines the current state of corporate governance law and provides decisive rebuttals to long-standing arguments for the exclusive shareholder franchise. *Reconstructing the Corporation* presents a new model of corporate governance – one that builds on the theory of the firm as well as a novel theory of democratic participation – to support the extension of the corporate franchise to employees.

GRANT M. HAYDEN is Professor of Law at Southern Methodist University Dedman School of Law. He writes and teaches in the areas of voting rights, labor law, and corporate governance. He is also the author of *American Law: An Introduction*, 3rd edition (with Lawrence M. Friedman, 2017).

MATTHEW T. BODIE is Callis Family Professor at Saint Louis University School of Law and Co-Director of the William C. Wefel Center for Employment Law. He served as a reporter for the Restatement of Employment Law (American Law Institute, 2015) and chair of the business associations section of the Association of American Law Schools.

RECONSTRUCTING THE CORPORATION

From Shareholder Primacy to Shared Governance

GRANT M. HAYDEN

MATTHEW T. BODIE

CAMBRIDGE
UNIVERSITY PRESS

CAMBRIDGE
UNIVERSITY PRESS

University Printing House, Cambridge CB2 8BS, United Kingdom

One Liberty Plaza, 20th Floor, New York, NY 10006, USA

477 Williamstown Road, Port Melbourne, VIC 3207, Australia

314–321, 3rd Floor, Plot 3, Splendor Forum, Jasola District Centre, New Delhi – 110025, India

79 Anson Road, #06–04/06, Singapore 079906

Cambridge University Press is part of the University of Cambridge.

It furthers the University's mission by disseminating knowledge in the pursuit of education, learning, and research at the highest international levels of excellence.

www.cambridge.org
Information on this title: www.cambridge.org/9781107138322
DOI: 10.1017/9781316481325

© Grant M. Hayden and Matthew T. Bodie 2020

First published 2020
Reprinted 2021

Printed in the United Kingdom by TJ Books Ltd, Padstow Cornwall

A catalogue record for this publication is available from the British Library.

Library of Congress Cataloging-in-Publication Data
Names: Hayden, Grant M. author. | Bodie, Matthew T. author.
Title: Reconstructing the Corporation: From Shareholder Primacy to Shared Governance / Grant M. Hayden, SMU-Dedman School of Law; Matthew T. Bodie, Saint Louis University School of Law.
Description: Cambridge, United Kingdom; New York, NY, USA: Cambridge University Press, 2020. | Includes index. | Summary: This book critically examines shareholder primacy and its principal manifestation in corporate law: the exclusive shareholder franchise. It presents a new model of corporate governance, fully consistent with the economic theory of the firm and democratic participation theory, that supports shared board representation between shareholders and employees. – Provided by publisher.
Identifiers: LCCN 2020006022 | ISBN 9781107138322 (hardback) | ISBN 9781316502914 (epub)
Subjects: LCSH: Corporation law – United States.
Classification: LCC KF1414 .H378 2020 | DDC 346.73/066–dc23
LC record available at https://lccn.loc.gov/2020006022

ISBN 978-1-107-13832-2 Hardback
ISBN 978-1-316-50291-4 Paperback

To my mom, Julie Hayden, who is probably embarrassed to be associated with someone who writes about corporate governance.
G.M.H.

To my parents Joan and Tom Bodie, who taught me the importance of fairness and a love of the underdog.
M.T.B.

CONTENTS

PREFACE

It is a remarkable moment in corporate law. Everything is about to change. The status quo of shareholder primacy clings stubbornly on, full of its old power in appearance, and yet it is a façade. It is the Soviet Union after the fall of the Berlin Wall. It is Persia after Thermopylae, Napoleonic France after Leipzig, the British Raj after the Salt March, disco after the Ramones. We are at the beginning of the end.

This claim may seem absurd in light of the current reign of shareholder primacy throughout the United States, the European Union, and developing nations. The academic network behind shareholder primacy remains resolute; almost all corporate law scholarship pivots around the central idea of shareholder control. Shareholder wealth maximization is so firmly ensconced as the governing norm that some scholars have declared the end of corporate law history.[1]

But underneath the superficial agreement is a roiling mass of disputes and divisions. The field is more fractured than ever before. The prospect of real shareholder empowerment, through proxy access or shareholder bylaws, has split the academy into subgroups that advocate for divergent approaches. Activist investors have gone from the saviors of shareholder rights to short-term opportunists who should be marginalized. Money is being shoveled like never before into passive index funds and exchange-traded funds – the absentee landlords of stock ownership. Recent corporate law scholarship focuses on the problems of "principal costs" generated by investor governance and even touts the advantages of nonvoting shares.[2] Corporate and economic luminaries such as the Nobel laureate Oliver Hart, Michael Jensen, and Delaware Chief Justice Leo Strine are questioning the stability of shareholder primacy as a regulatory norm.[3] Even the Business Roundtable – an organization of CEOs at major U.S. companies – proclaimed that every group of stakeholders is "essential," while committing to "deliver value to all of them, for the future success of our companies, our communities and our country."[4]

This shift away from shareholder primacy follows a set of problematic trends that corporations have created or exacerbated. Climate change continues unabated, with market economies failing to deliver the crisis-level change in energy production and consumption that is necessary to stem disastrous warming. Income inequality has reached staggering levels – the gap between the middle class and the 1 percent, 0.1 percent, and 0.01 percent is reminiscent of the Roaring Twenties or the Gilded Age. Workers' wages have remained largely stagnant, while executive compensation and corporate profits continue their climb. Rather than going into workers' pockets, the vast majority of the 2018 corporate tax cuts were plowed into stock buybacks.[5] And the millennial generation has still not economically recovered from the financial crisis a decade ago – a crisis that left Alan Greenspan in a state of "shocked disbelief" at the banks' failure to protect shareholder equity.[6]

With the standard economic approaches on the ropes, we'd expect to see alternatives rise to fill the gaps in corporate governance theory. But there is a dearth of such alternatives. Advocates of stakeholder theory have provided the consistent yin to the yang of shareholder primacy (or, perhaps more accurately, have played the Generals to shareholder primacy's Globetrotters). They reject the idea that the corporation should maximize shareholder wealth and instead argue that it should promote the interests of all corporate participants: shareholders, customers, employees, suppliers, and communities alike. But turning stakeholder theory into governance reality has long proven to be an intractable puzzle. To date, stakeholder theorists have left the shareholder franchise alone and crossed their fingers for more ecumenical firm decision-making, which makes the Business Roundtable's proposal look a little less radical (and a little more self-serving).

So we find ourselves at a curious point in the history of the corporation. Shareholder primacy is well entrenched in law and in practice, but its intellectual foundations do not stand up to scrutiny. In particular, the main arguments for the exclusive shareholder franchise have been exposed: they are riddled with faulty assumptions about the nature of shareholder preferences and are oftentimes inconsistent with the basic economic principles thought to underlay them. But most corporate law scholars, rather than develop new arguments or at least rehabilitate the old ones, have been content to place those difficulties to one side and attend to the finer details of corporate governance. And, when pressed, the scholars who do address these issues tend to move, somewhat opportunistically, between one or more of the several justifications for the current corporate voting scheme.

For this reason, one of the principal tasks in this book is to pin down and scrutinize in one place all of the main arguments for the shareholder franchise. That is, we need to start with a thorough assessment of the state of the arguments for the exclusive shareholder franchise. The corporate form, at bottom, is a legal mechanism that allows a variety of groups – shareholders, employees, suppliers, and others – to coordinate their activities in a process of joint production. As we reconstruct corporate governance, we need to, at a minimum, reassess which of these stakeholders should have their preferences captured through voting – the most powerful feature of corporate control – and which through contract.

As part of this undertaking, we will be setting forth a new model of corporate governance that synthesizes our understandings of business organizations derived from the economic theory of the firm and from democratic participation theory. Building on eighty years of research into the nature of the firm, we derive a governance model based on joint production, in which the participants within the firm have a right to participate in the governance of the firm. In assessing the appropriate governance responsibilities, we will look to democratic participation theory to calculate the preferences of the participants in the enterprise through markers that are accurate and manageable. Together, both economic and democratic theories support a model for corporate theory that incorporates employees and shareholders expressly into the inner sanctum of corporate governance, while leaving other stakeholders to manage their interests through contract and regulation.

Reconsideration of shareholder primacy and the exclusive shareholder franchise is long overdue. We hope that this contribution to the corporate law literature will provide a base for others exploring the foundational questions of the field, as we unsettle established doctrines and propose a new way of thinking about these legal engines for our economy.

ACKNOWLEDGMENTS

This book, like all books, owes its existence to a large number of people who have helped us over the years. Many people have provided feedback during conferences or other presentations. Some have provided commentary that's been particularly helpful on one aspect or another of this project, including Margaret Blair, Ron Colombo, Stephen Ellis, Dan Greenwood, Summer Kim, Brett McDonnell, Ewan McGaughey, Elizabeth Pollman, Larry Ribstein, and Emily Winston. The project couldn't have been completed without the help of research assistants Victoria Petty and Jase Carter, who helped with some of the earlier chapters, and Hallie Dunlap, who was invaluable toward the end of this process. We'd also like to thank our original editor at Cambridge University Press, the ever-patient John Berger, who helped us through the peer review process and got us a book contract. Thanks as well to Jackie Grant, Becky Jackaman, Anjana Karikal Cholan, and Virginia Hamilton, who all helped bring the book to fruition.

Earlier versions of some portions of this book were first worked out in some of the law review articles we've written over the last decade. Those articles include: *One Share, One Vote and the False Promise of Shareholder Homogeneity*, 30 *Cardozo Law Review* 445 (2008); *Arrow's Theorem and the Exclusive Shareholder Franchise*, 62 *Vanderbilt Law Review* 1217 (2009); *Shareholder Democracy and the Curious Turn Toward Board Primacy*, 51 *William and Mary Law Review* 2071 (2010); *The Uncorporation and the Unraveling of "Nexus of Contract" Theory*, 109 *Michigan Law Review* 1127 (2011); *The Bizarre Law and Economics of Business Roundtable v. SEC*, 38 *Journal of Corporation Law* 101 (2012); *Larry from the Left: An Appreciation*, 8 *Virginia Law & Business Review* 121 (2014); *Shareholder Voting and the Symbolic Politics of Corporation as Contract*, 53 *Wake Forest Law Review* 511 (2018); *The Corporation Reborn: From Shareholder Primacy to Shared Governance*, 61 *Boston College Law Review* (forthcoming 2020); and *Codetermination in Theory and Practice*, 73 *Florida Law Review* (forthcoming 2021). We'd like to thank the many student editors of those journals for their hard work and their ultimate acquiescence to our view that law review articles could use a few more contractions.

We'd also like to thank our families. For Grant, that's Joanna Grossman, who told him to write books instead of articles, and their tolerant children Luke, Ben, and Milo. Matt thanks his children Teddy, Julius, and Benjamin for their support for and interest in the project, as well as Rebecca Hollander-Blumoff, his partner in all things.

1

Introduction

In the United States, our large-scale economic enterprises are almost always conducted by corporations. Although a variety of legal options for organizations exist – such as the partnership, the limited liability company (LLC), and the sole proprietorship – the corporation dominates the economic landscape.[1] The corporation (or company) has been described as the "most important organization in the world" and "the basis of the prosperity of the West and the best hope for the future of the rest of the world."[2] When we think of businesses, we think of corporations.

And corporations are booming. Corporate profits have hovered between 9 and 11 percent of the U.S. gross domestic product, the highest sustained average percentage on record.[3] The Tax Cuts and Jobs Act of 2017 dramatically slashed corporate tax bills and funneled billions of additional dollars into corporate coffers.[4] By providing corporations with individualized constitutional and statutory rights of expression, the Supreme Court's decisions in *Citizens United*[5] and *Hobby Lobby*[6] have extended the corporation's powers even more deeply into politics, religion, and culture.

So, what exactly are corporations, and where do they come from? Under our federalized system, corporations are creatures of state law. To form a corporation, the incorporating individuals must file a corporate charter, also known as the articles or certificate of incorporation.[7] Once a corporation is established, control shifts from the entity's incorporators to its board of directors.[8] The board controls the firm and has the ability to legally bind the corporation to its decisions.[9] Shareholders elect the directors at the annual general meeting by in-person voting or the use of proxies.[10] Directors must act in the corporation's interests and are bound by certain fiduciary duties, primarily good faith, care, and loyalty.[11] However, directors generally delegate the actual job of running the business to the officers, who act through a hierarchy of employees headed by the chief executive officer (CEO).[12]

Even though state corporate law allows for a great deal of organizational flexibility, actual governance structures are remarkably uniform. Delaware corporate law, for example, does not even require a corporation to have a board,[13] and yet all corporations have one. And the basic structure – where shareholders elect the directors, who in turn select the officers to run the corporation – replicates itself in corporations from every state. While there are some variations in governance structures, both among actual corporations and in the guise of potential reforms, the corporate form has remained relatively stable over the last century. And the critical features of corporate governance – who gets to vote, about what, and under what circumstances – have also been settled: the corporate franchise belongs to shareholders and shareholders alone.

Over time, scholars have worked to develop an intellectual framework that supports this central role of shareholders in corporate governance. In the course of their doing so, the role of shareholders within the corporation has evolved from that of absentee landlords to the center of the entire enterprise. The resulting theory of shareholder primacy redesigned the purpose and function of the corporation to revolve around shareholder wealth maximization.[14] And the shareholder primacy norm, a familiar notion even to nonlawyers, now has wide acceptance in both theory and practice.

Along with the shareholder primacy norm, the "nexus of contracts" theory of the corporation is also popular among legal academics.[15] This theory rejects the notion that the corporation is a separate entity and describes it instead as a set of voluntary contractual relationships with the corporation at the center. Under this theory, the corporation does not really exist and is best thought of as a cluster of commercial agreements among a variety of parties. The nexus of contracts framework counsels for a "hands-off" or default-rule approach to corporate law, as the corporation itself is conceived of as a set of voluntarily chosen relationships between different parties.[16]

Although these pillars of modern corporate law theory are both associated with the law and economics movement, their relationship has always been, at best, an uneasy one.[17] Shareholder primacy focuses on the importance of shareholders to the corporation and often trades on the notion that shareholders "own" this entity, the corporation, outright. The nexus of contracts theory, on the other hand, abandons the concept of a separate corporate structure and places all its participants, including shareholders, on an equal contractual footing. At a minimum, the two theories pull in opposite directions.

In their foundational work on the economics of corporate law, Frank Easterbrook and Daniel Fischel married these two theories into a simple, intertwined structure. Their 1991 book, *The Economic Structure of Corporate Law*,[18] reaffirmed the shareholder primacy norm by arguing that shareholders were the most economically vulnerable of the firm's participants. This vulnerability, coupled with their shared preference for wealth maximization, meant that shareholders should be accorded the basic governance rights of the corporation.[19] Through their sets of separate contracts, the other participants in the corporation, Easterbrook and Fischel contended, agreed to provide shareholders with residual rights to the corporation's profits and the voting rights that come with them.[20] The shareholder primacy norm gave the corporate form its overriding purpose, while the nexus of contracts theory demonstrated that the parties reached this arrangement through voluntary agreements.

Over the last thirty years, this core law and economics position has diverged into multiple approaches. Some theorists, most prominently Lucian Bebchuk, have sought to support shareholder primacy by providing shareholders with stronger legal powers within the corporation.[21] Such powers include the ability to control corporate political spending, the right to access the company's proxy ballot, and a prohibition on staggered boards.[22] Others have adopted approaches with more indirect and diffused shareholder power, such as Steven Bainbridge's director primacy theory[23] and Margaret Blair and Lynn Stout's team production theory.[24] While these board primacy scholars disagree with each other on the appropriate goals of the corporation, they all believe that a governance system that's less responsive to shareholders will allow the board to make better decisions.[25]

Despite the many differences between these competing approaches, all of these theorists, like Easterbrook and Fischel before them, are committed to corporate governance structures where shareholders alone elect board members and vote on other matters of importance. And this governance feature has long been part and parcel of the broader theory of shareholder primacy, which found its strongest justifications in in the work of the law and economics movement. Indeed, despite playing out in many other areas of legal scholarship, that movement has continued to maintain a hammerlock on corporate governance theory. And its original justifications for the exclusive shareholder franchise, many of which are now more than four decades old, continue to be cited, recited, and relied upon by scholars of corporate governance in countless books, articles, and opinion pieces.

Cracks in the Foundation

It is time to reevaluate the foundational principles of the exclusive share-holder franchise. For too long, the field has rested on faulty assumptions about the preferences of flesh and blood shareholders, has misapplied basic economic and social choice theory, and has failed to question the larger purposes served by the corporate form. Take, for example, the description of a corporation as a nexus of contracts.[26] Although it often hard to tell whether the corporation as contract is intended to be a literal or metaphorical description, there is no doubt that it has done heavy rhetorical work in the service of the law and economics vision of the corporation.[27] If all corporate constituents contractually agree that share-holders alone should have voting rights, then who's to say they've got it wrong? Over time, though, even the most die-hard contractarians have conceded that this description of the corporation is not literally true – there are some key features of modern corporations that cannot be reduced to contract.[28] Indeed, if contracts were sufficient, then there would be no need for corporate law in the first place.

But as corporate governance theorists shifted to using the nexus of contracts more metaphorically, their reliance on contract theory became self-defeating. Easterbrook and Fischel argued that corporate law pro-vides the "ideal" contract that most participants would themselves develop, saving the parties from the transaction costs of developing it on their own.[29] This argument proves too much, though, as the theory then empowers itself with the task of assigning preferences – something that economists are generally loath to do. In fact, the law and economics theory of the corporation turns out to be based on idealized, fictionalized versions of shareholders and other corporate constituents – ones who, coincidentally, happen to agree with normative law and economics principles.[30]

But it's not just the nexus of contracts argument that has collapsed under scrutiny. The principle that all shareholders have a similar interest in the corporate residual – the "leftover" operating profit after all other costs have been paid – has long been central to the idea of shareholder voting.[31] Under the model employed by Easterbrook and Fischel, max-imization of the residual maximizes the return to shareholders while leaving all other constituents (such as employees and suppliers) contrac-tually satisfied. Therefore, shareholder control over a corporation will, of necessity, improve social welfare by increasing its residual profits.[32] Shareholders arguably have a single-minded focus on a corporation's profits because they are only paid through the residual.[33] This connection between the residual and control, as calibrated by the "one share, one vote" rule, appears to set up the proper incentives for shareholders to focus on maximizing the residual – thereby maximizing overall utility.[34]

Over the last couple of decades, however, this assumption that shareholders have homogeneous interests in wealth maximization has fallen apart.[35] Many shareholders – including majority shareholders, shareholders with disproportionate voting rights, members of voting trusts, bribed shareholders, hedged shareholders, sovereign wealth funds, and employee and management shareholders – have interests in the firm that go beyond a simple desire to maximize the residual.[36] In each case, shareholders have interests that may temper or override their shared interest in the residual. And shareholder heterogeneity is not simply a matter of shareholders with discrete competing interests. Shareholders who are otherwise similarly situated may have different definitions of wealth maximization, with different time horizons or risk preferences.[37] And shareholder wealth maximization is not the same thing as shareholder utility maximization. Oliver Hart and Luigi Zingales have suggested that shareholders do in fact value things other than profit maximization, and that corporate governance should be structured to allow them to express their preferences on trade-offs in corporate decision-making.[38] Shareholder interests, however you define them, are quite heterogeneous, which leaves this second argument in favor of the exclusive shareholder franchise on shaky ground.

Shareholder heterogeneity also undercuts another fairly prominent argument for the exclusive shareholder franchise: the argument from Arrow's theorem. Easterbrook and Fischel first raised concerns, based on Kenneth Arrow's impossibility theorem, that corporate constituents with heterogeneous preferences would be more likely to produce intransitive election results, or voting cycles.[39] This, in turn, would lead firms to "self-destruct."[40] This argument has since been repeated by a wide range of law and economics corporate governance scholars.[41] But this argument, like that from the residual, would appear to be diminished by the fact that shareholders have quite heterogeneous preferences with respect to corporate decision-making. The argument actually has much deeper flaws, and falls apart long before we get to the nature of shareholder preferences. It is based on a misguided application of Arrow's theorem from start to finish.[42]

Finally, it is simply untrue that no other participants in the corporation have an interest in the ongoing profitability of the firm. Employee pay and benefits are not static obligations for the corporation to absorb. Wages rise and fall with the fortunes of the business; benefits become more generous as the corporation's revenues increase; bonuses and stock options reflect the overall success of the company. And workers contribute to the overall value of the company in a way that they cannot monetize, without any ownership interests themselves. The corporation controls the ongoing business, owns the company property including the trademark and brand name, and makes the contracts that carry on the business. Employees have no direct representational voice in the organization. So they, too, are vulnerable to opportunism. Because shareholders have operating control over the board, it is not surprising that corporate profits and stock buybacks have skyrocketed, while employee wages have remained stagnant in real terms for decades.[43]

Alternative Approaches

Competing corporate law theories in the law and economics tradition have offered more descriptively realistic stories about corporate law doctrine, but they have failed to cure the ills that beset the basic shareholder primacy model. Stephen Bainbridge's director primacy theory well describes the ambivalence of Delaware corporate law toward the relationship between shareholders and the board of directors.[44] But his theory fails to explain why directors should be given relatively unchecked authority over the operation of the firm. Bainbridge uses Kenneth Arrow's *The Limits of Organization* and its trade-off between authority and accountability to find a "rebuttable presumption in favor of preservation of managerial discretion."[45] However, as Brett McDonnell has explained, this presumption – which Bainbridge rarely finds rebutted – does not find support in Arrow's work.[46] Vesting power in the board of directors may reflect the reality of Delaware corporate law, but it does not explain why society – or even shareholders – are best served by such largely unreviewable power.

Similarly, Margaret Blair and Lynn Stout's team production model accurately takes into account the many participants in the life of the corporation.[47] However, their model also leaves it to the shareholder-elected board to somehow manage these relationships appropriately. Whether they be "Platonic guardians" (Bainbridge)[48] or "mediating hierarchs" (Blair and Stout),[49] there are no governance structures in place to ensure that actual directors live up to the faith that these accounts place in their ability to manage the firm. In both cases, the ultimate check on the board is left in the hands of the shareholders alone. And both simply rely on earlier law and economics arguments to justify the retention of the exclusive shareholder franchise. Board primacy provides no independent arguments for the exclusive shareholder franchise.

In contrast to shareholder primacy, stakeholder theory argues that corporate governance should take all stakeholders in the corporate enterprise into account, rather than focusing on shareholder wealth maximization.[50] Also called the communitarian or multifiduciary model,[51] and sometimes coupled with commitments to corporate social responsibility (or CSR),[52] stakeholder theory argues that corporate governance needs to reflect the interests of all the participants within the life of the corporation. Most academic treatments cast a wide net in defining stakeholders and so include shareholders, management, employees, creditors, suppliers, customers, and even the surrounding community. In terms of concrete governance reforms, supporters of stakeholder theory have advocated for weakening shareholder power within the organizational structure and increasing managerial discretion to take other interests into account. As such, they have generally sided with those voices who support greater managerial discretion and restrictions on shareholder rights.[53]

As an oppositional paradigm, stakeholder theory has served to act as a rhetorical brake on some of the excesses of shareholder primacy.[54] But it is not, at least at present, a real theory of firm governance, as it lacks a model for allocating governance rights and responsibilities among the participants.[55] A stakeholder approach might lend itself to a board elected by a variety of stakeholders, but stakeholder theorists have largely acquiesced to the exclusive shareholder franchise. It makes little sense to attack shareholder primacy but then maintain exclusive shareholder control over all the key features of corporate governance.

A Return to the Basics

With a shadow cast over the basic arguments for the exclusive shareholder franchise, we believe it is time to revisit and critically evaluate the justifications for this central feature of modern corporate governance. That task, however, does not mean abandoning the precepts of standard economic and social choice theory. Indeed, as we make our way through this landscape, we will examine the fissures in corporate governance scholarship using the tools of law and economics itself. That is, this book examines, argument by argument, the fundamental components of conventional corporate law wisdom largely on their own terms. And we start with the one of the most basic units of standard economics: preferences.

The institutions that comprise modern market-based societies – from large governments to small businesses – employ decision-making structures designed to take account of the preferences of their constituents. They sometimes rely upon compacts or contracts, which are thought to ensure that the preferences of all involved are satisfied.[56] Once institutions reach a certain size and complexity, though, contracts alone cannot do the job: they must resort to some type of voting mechanism to aggregate preferences. This is true of almost all institutions, both political and corporate, that claim to serve some sort of constituency. It is certainly true of the modern corporation.

For this reason, public choice theory, with its emphasis on the interests of different groups and its analysis of the effects of different structures on outcomes, would seem to present a natural methodology for studying corporate governance.[57] More generally, political theory concerns the allocation and transfer of power in decision-making and the roles of different institutions in the governance of a polity. The purpose of a system of governance is to manage different interests despite the opportunities for conflict.[58]

Examining how voting works in political institutions may also help illuminate some of the arguments around corporate governance. After all, the disagreements over corporate governance law aren't usually about whether corporations should be structured to maximize the preference satisfaction for their constituents, broadly defined, but how best to do so. The same types of questions animate discussions of both political and corporate voting. One central set of questions, of course, is which constituents count and how we identify them and best capture their preferences. But there are other, related questions as well. Should the voting system be direct, representative, or some mixture of the two? If representative, what is the basis for representation, and how responsive should the system be? Questions like these have been the subject of a lot of thought and experience in the political realm; that work can help us think about the structure of governance within the corporation.

Our analysis of the exclusive shareholder franchise also involves the application of a fair amount of economics and its cousin, social choice theory. Standard economic theory, as deployed by scholars in the law and economics tradition, has been driving corporate governance scholarship for decades. But it also makes sense from a broader point of view – that is, economic theory *should* give us some insights into corporate governance. Economics endeavors to draw out the implications of the view that people act to best get what they want, given what they believe about their circumstances. This basic insight is used to build models that are intended to explain and predict human behavior, and those models, in turn, may be used to structure incentives in order to achieve certain ends.[59] So it should not be surprising that economics is a useful tool when designing the governance features of corporations, which coordinate a wide range of constituencies in the production of goods or services. Indeed, since economic theory has been particularly successful in explaining and predicting behavior in market settings, its application to corporate governance should be especially fruitful.

A subdiscipline of economics focuses particularly on issues of organization and governance – the theory of the firm. The literature on the theory of the firm asks: Why do we have firms, rather than markets?[60] The theory offers a sustained interdisciplinary inquiry into the nature of firms and their legal representations.[61] While much of the current work in other social sciences, such as psychology and sociology, dovetails with economic theory and provides additional insights into the basic economic models, the theory of the firm offers a starting point for these inquiries and a basis upon which to build an alternative academic narrative.

Social choice theory seeks to describe, in some rigorous way, exactly how we move from individual preferences to group choices. More specifically, the theory focuses on the properties and limitations of the social choice functions (usually, some type of voting procedure) employed to make those moves. And one of the main arguments for the exclusive shareholder franchise finds its ground in one of the signature limitations on social choice functions – Arrow's impossibility theorem. For this reason alone, we will delve into social choice theory. That said, given our focus on corporate voting – and, more generally, preference aggregation – social choice theory helps inform the arguments in much of the rest of the book as well.

So while the core of this book involves a critical examination of the main arguments for the exclusive shareholder franchise, we do not question the basic principles of standard economics and social choice theory thought to underlie those arguments. That is, our critiques are not based on questioning economic approaches to corporate governance (or law more generally). There may, in fact, be some good reasons to question some of the fundamental assumptions and aspects of standard economic theory. The theory has been accused of wrongheadedness in using preference fulfillment as the main measure (or very definition) of improved social welfare or, more narrowly, the success of a system of governance.[62] Moreover, some of the assumptions of standard economics have been modified in light of the recent insights and empirical findings of behavioral economics.[63] In this book, we remain agnostic on these kinds of challenges to standard economic theory. We take the principles of standard economics as given. And we take them seriously, perhaps more seriously than some of their most vocal proponents among corporate governance scholars. Thus, in our critiques of the main law and economics arguments, we do not challenge the basic assumptions of standard economics, but instead focus upon their misapplication in corporate governance scholarship.

In a sense, then, this book is a return to the basics. We don't feel the need to go beyond the most fundamental aspects of standard economics and social choice theory to make our arguments – that is something we share with most of the law and economics scholars who write about corporate governance; the democratic, economic, and social choice theory is pretty standard fare. But we will be spending quite a bit of time examining the *application* of those theories to shareholder voting in corporate governance, because corporate law scholars often start with basic economic principles only to discard them when they run into (what they perceive as) problems. We will evaluate their arguments by their own standards; in other words, our critique of current corporate governance theory comes largely from the inside, not the outside, with basic voting rights and preference aggregation theory thrown in for good measure. We hope, in the end, to produce a picture of the corporation that is consistent with these underlying theories and helps inform the evolving theory of the firm.

Plan of the Book

This book makes its case in roughly three sections. In the first section, we look at the purpose and structure of voting in political institutions and corporations. Voting, at its heart, is an effort to aggregate the thoughts and opinions – the preferences – of a group of people around particular candidates or issues. Focusing on preference aggregation as the key aspect of voting, we explain how governments have structured their voting systems to capture (or deflect) the preferences of their constituents, and then apply this understanding to corporations. While the analogy is far from perfect, we believe that in the structure of political systems there are some basic lessons for corporations.

Thus, in Chapter 2, we discuss the basic structure of voting rights in the political arena. Topics include the right to participate and cast a ballot, the right to an equally weighted vote, the right to combine votes with like-minded voters (the issue of qualitative vote dilution), and ballot access laws. The chapter also examines the basic theoretical underpinnings of each of these elements of the right to vote, with a focus on the role of voter interest and the need for institutions to develop accurate and adminis-trable markers of that interest. We then turn, in Chapter 3, to the basic structure of voting in the corporate arena. We begin with some history and background regarding preference aggregation in a range of business organizations, and then focus upon voting within the modern corpora-tion. We sketch out some of the basic aspects of shareholder primacy, and the main theoretical justifications for restricting corporate voting to shareholders alone and the one share, one vote system. The first section of the book lays the foundation for analyzing corporate voting using general notions of preference aggregation.

In the middle section of the book, we critically evaluate the basic arguments for restricting corporate voting to shareholders. We start, in Chapter 4, with the contractarian argument. After a brief discussion of the idea that shareholders are "owners" of the corporation, this chapter concentrates on the view of the corporation as a nexus of contracts. Its proponents argue that virtually all aspects of corporate structure, includ-ing the exclusive shareholder franchise, are the product of an interlocking group of freely bargained-for contracts among all corporate constituents, and this product is therefore, presumptively, the most efficient form of firm structure for those who choose to participate. We believe this view of the corporation is both descriptively wrong and normatively hollow, and thus a deficient theoretical foundation for existing corporate governance law. Indeed, a truly contractarian perspective of business associations may militate in favor of expanding the range of possible arrangements between constituents, including workers, in a way that maximizes con-tractual freedom.

We then consider two other arguments for the exclusive shareholder franchise: the argument from the residual and the argument from Arrow's theorem. As a prelude, we first spend some time in Chapter 5 examining a longstanding assumption about shareholders that underpins both of them: that shareholders are best conceived of as single-minded wealth maximizers focused on increasing corporate profits. Their relatively homogeneous preferences, in other words, are what sets them apart from other corporate constituents. This assumption, however, has been put under quite a bit of pressure over the last couple of decades, so much of the chapter involves cataloging the many (and increasing number of) ways in which shareholders fail to share common interests.

In Chapter 6, we address the argument from the residual – that shareholders, as sole holders of the residual profits, are in the best position to ultimately control the firm through election of corporate board members. Because the link between the right to profits and the incentive to increase those profits is relatively secure, the real questions here are why the residual is thought to belong to shareholders alone. With the original answer – shareholder homogeneity – no longer satisfactory, we need to examine whether there are other reasons to assign shareholders control and, moreover, whether there may be other constituents with similar incentives. Workers with firm-specific skills, for example, also have incomplete contracts and residual interests in a corporation.

The book continues in Chapter 7 with an analysis of the argument from Arrow's theorem. The chapter begins by explaining the basic contours of the argument, surveys its influence, and distinguishes it from a couple of related arguments. The bulk of the chapter is a sustained critique of the argument, which, we contend, misconstrues the import of the theorem and ignores recent work in social choice theory. Indeed, if there were anything to this argument, it would actually counsel in favor of adding another group of constituents to the corporate electorate, so long as they have interests that are in opposition to those held by shareholders.

We wrap up this middle section of the book in Chapter 8, where we discuss the rise and entrenchment of board primacy theories as a reaction, in part, to the newfound awareness that shareholders are not a homogeneous group of wealth maximizers. After discussing some of the shortcomings of the varying approaches to board primacy, the chapter argues that such theorists tend to conflate two very different aspects of group decision processes – the composition of the electorate and the responsiveness of the governance system. This confusion puts them in the curious position of moving away from the public choice emphasis on preference aggregation toward a more civic republican model of more deliberative decision-making. Unfortunately, by clinging to restrictions on the corporate franchise, these theorists have detached the resulting governance structures from the underlying preferences of corporate constituents without substituting anything meaningful in their place. In the end, the breakdown of the distinction between shareholders and other corporate constituents means that we should investigate treating other constituents more like shareholders rather than the other way around.

As we are forced to move away from the existing corporate order, we need to acknowledge the shortcomings (and the strengths) of its intellectual framework and begin to develop new models of firm governance. We begin the process of reconstructing the corporation in the third and final section of the book by developing a new model of the firm that is consistent with both economic and democratic theory. In Chapter 9, we return to the longstanding theory of the firm. This theory, born out of a desire to explain why business firms exist apart from markets in the first place, is not only consistent with but actually militates in favor of greater employee participation in corporate governance. As participants in joint production, those employees should also have voting rights within the firm. And in Chapter 10, we develop a new theory of democratic participation that helps explain which corporate constituents should be accorded the corporate franchise rights (and, just as importantly, which should not). This theory, which is fully consistent with mainstream democratic theory and informed by voting rights jurisprudence, also counsels in favor of extending corporate voting rights to employees.

In Chapter 11, we'll take a fresh look at a long-standing example of employee representation on corporate boards: the German system of codetermination. For over a century, large corporations in Germany have had supervisory boards composed of both shareholder and employee representatives. The system has been almost wholly ignored by American corporate law scholars, despite (or because of) the fact that it represents a real-world counterexample to the theoretical arguments for the exclusive shareholder franchise. But codetermination is beginning to come out of the shadows as a viable alternative to shareholder primacy. Germany rebounded from the 2008–2009 global financial crisis much more quickly than many other countries, and a series of new studies has revealed the benefits of supervisory codetermination for a number of corporate constituents, including shareholders. At a minimum, the stability and recent success of the German system may serve as a kind of proof of concept of the more theoretical arguments for employee representation in earlier chapters. We conclude in Chapter 12 with thoughts on the global challenges of wealth inequality and consider the prospects for change through the transformation of corporate governance.

The overall plan of the book, then, is to introduce the basic features of corporate governance, demonstrate the shortcomings of arguments for exclusive shareholder control, and begin to sketch out why employees should have a more central role in governance. In the end, we believe the economic theory of the firm and the democratic theory of participation can provide the foundation for a new vision of corporate governance, one that includes workers and shareholders, labor and equity, for the benefit of all corporate stakeholders.

2

Preference Aggregation in Political Institutions

Life is full of decisions. It's often difficult for individuals to make decisions, especially important ones. But things get much more complicated when groups need to make decisions. In those cases, we need some systematic way of combining individual opinions, preferences, or interests to reach a collective decision or some version of social welfare.[1] We need, in other words, a social choice function.[2]

There are many kinds of social choice functions. We could delegate the decision to one of the people in the group (the dictator). We could use a random process, like a coin flip, to make the decision. In most cases, though, we seek an approach that better captures the preferences of the members of the group, such as voting. And indeed, most of our major institutions, both political and corporate, have incorporated some form of voting into their systems of governance.

These voting systems, and democracies more generally, come in two basic forms: direct and representative. In the United States, most of our political institutions, state and federal, are representative. Once that matter has been decided, there are still a number of choices to be made, however, about how exactly to structure the democratic process. Those choices come to be embodied in a set of legal entitlements, or voting rights, that collectively sketch the contours of the polity and dictate its rules for decision-making. Far from being one-dimensional, these voting rights have several components, each of which is necessary to ensure full democratic participation.[3]

The most basic component is the ability to cast a ballot. This is voting rights at its most fundamental, and is what people are usually talking about when discussing the "right to vote." But the mere ability to cast a ballot is not sufficient to ensure meaningful participation. One's vote must be accorded sufficient weight and be combined with the votes of other like-minded electors to be able to influence the outcome of an election. Thus, one of the principal aspects of the right involves the weight of a vote – the right to cast a vote that carries an appropriate numerical weight, one that is quantitatively undiluted. For most elections in the United States, this means that the election districts must be drawn in ways consistent with the one person, one vote principle.

Even with equal access and equal weighting, groups of voters may still be denied an equal opportunity to participate and elect candidates of their choice. Thus, decisions about how votes are combined and counted are important. There are hundreds of possible voting systems, and an even greater number of ways to exploit them. In the United States, most political bodies use some version of a plurality system within geographically defined districts, where victory goes to the candidate(s) with the most votes. With these systems, though, comes the worry that those in charge of, say, districting, may be able to qualitatively dilute the voting power of certain groups through practices such as at-large districting and gerrymandering.

A final aspect of the right to vote involves ballot access. Participants must have some meaningful opportunity to get their preferred candidates on the ballot to begin with – otherwise, casting a ballot, even a fully weighted one, is an empty exercise. A robust understanding of the right to vote thus involves several distinct (yet related) components, and full democratic participation depends upon enforcement of all aspects of the right. Only then will people's preferences be accurately reflected in electoral outcomes.

The Many Facets of the Right to Vote

The first aspect of the right to vote – casting a ballot – is the most fundamental.[4] The contours of this right have changed a great deal over time. At the beginning of this country's history, most states extended the franchise only to property-holding white men over the age of twenty-one.[5] That, of course, has changed, and many more groups now have access to the ballot.[6] There are, however, some people who are not allowed to vote – most jurisdictions restrict voting by felons or ex-felons,[7] noncitizens,[8] and nonresidents.[9] Minors and people with certain mental impairments are also prohibited from voting.[10] We do not, therefore, have universal suffrage; nevertheless, a much greater proportion of the population can vote now than when the country was founded.

In a sense, the question of *who* should have a right to vote is relatively straightforward. The debate is essentially over which groups should be considered members of the polity worthy of having their preferences reflected in electoral outcomes. The issue becomes more complicated once we move from *who* votes to *how* they vote. The mechanics of most election procedures – like registration requirements and voting methods – may themselves restrict the right to vote, but in subtle ways that depend upon whether the procedures have a disproportionate effect on some voter-relevant group.[11] For example, if a state requires voters to produce photographic identification in order to vote, and large numbers of poor people lack such identification, then that requirement may skew electoral outcomes. In a sense, then, both *who* has a right to vote and *how* they vote can affect access to the electoral system.

Mere access to the polls, though, guarantees very little, especially in a representative democracy. To begin with, votes may end up carrying different numerical weights.[12] Sometimes, as in weighted voting systems, this is part of the design. The International Monetary Fund, for example, assigns different numbers of votes to each member country based on the size and various other features of its economy.[13] In other cases, votes are weighted differently for less compelling reasons. For example, in the first half of the twentieth century, many state legislatures, for self-interested reasons, simply refused to redraw district lines in the face of tremendous demographic changes.[14] This had the effect of diluting the numerical voting power of those in more populous (largely urban) districts and concentrating it in the less populous (rural) districts[15] – a situation remedied by the Supreme Court in its one person, one vote decisions in the 1960s.[16]

But even the ability to cast an equally weighted vote doesn't guarantee an equal opportunity to participate. There are many other practices designed to keep like-minded voters from electing candidates of their choice.[17] What these are depends, of course, on the election system. Virtually all modern democracies use a plurality-majoritarian system, a proportional system, or some mixture of the two. Under plurality systems, each voter picks one candidate and the candidate with the most votes wins. Some jurisdictions further stipulate that the winner must receive a majority of votes cast, which means there sometimes needs to be a runoff between the top two candidates. Proportional systems involve voting for a party or list of candidates and assigning seats to each party in proportion to the share of votes it receives. This ensures that divisions in the electorate are proportionately reflected in the governing body and helps prevent minority groups from being shut out of the political process.

Within the United States, most elections are plurality systems with, in some cases, a runoff procedure to ensure majority support. These types of systems are not particularly good at protecting minority interests. They are, like all voting systems, vulnerable to manipulations that may take advantage of nascent voting cycles. But, most of the time, you don't need a voting cycle to manipulate the result. The political power of any particular group may be qualitatively diluted by manipulating various features of the elections. For example, at-large elections, anti-single-shot laws, place rules, and gerrymanders have long been used to diminish the voting power of certain groups, especially racial minorities.[18] Gerrymandering district boundaries can take groups that could consti- tute an effective majority in one district and split them into two districts so they are a majority in neither.[19] The legal status of attempts to dilute a group's voting power depends upon the type of group being targeted. Racial groups are currently afforded greater legal protection than, say, members of a political party.[20]

The other way to keep groups from electing their preferred candidates is to interfere with the slating process.[21] This may be done from the top down, such as by prohibiting certain candidates from running for or holding office. In the aftermath of the Civil War, the federal government forced states to allow blacks to vote; Georgia immediately responded by passing a law that prohibited black people from holding office.[22] One may also interfere with group voting power from the bottom up by limiting group members' access to earlier stages of the slating process. In the first half of the twentieth century, Southern states used the white primary as a means of keeping black voters out of the primary elections, eliminating their preferred candidates in those first stages and leaving them to choose between unpalatable alternatives in the general election.[23] In effect, those in control of the slating process can effectively control electoral outcomes.[24] For that reason, the Supreme Court has analyzed ballot access as an integral component of the right to vote, and ballot access laws are supposed to strike an appropriate balance between main- taining electoral stability and preserving meaningful choice. To this day, minor party and independent candidates have a difficult time making it onto the ballots, which diminishes the range of options available to voters and has led some scholars to argue that ballot access laws are the most anticompetitive feature of the American electoral system.[25]

Democratic voting systems, then, should be designed to produce group decisions that accurately reflect the underlying individual preferences. They should begin by identifying people with an interest in the polity and ensuring that they have equal access to the voting system. Those votes are weighted equally unless there's some strong reason to suspect that people's levels of interest are unequal in a way that can be accurately measured (as we will see with special-purpose districts). Once these individual voting rights are secure, care must be taken to ensure that groups of like-minded individuals have an equal opportunity to elect candidates of their choice. In the end, democratic political systems should be designed to translate individual preferences into group choices without skewing the result in any particular direction. In reality, of course, those translations can be manipulated or frustrated in many ways, both obvious and hidden.

Theoretical Underpinnings of the Right to Vote

The political history of the United States is in large part a chronicle of the battles fought over who exactly should receive voting rights. Should African Americans be allowed to cast ballots? Women? Resident aliens? Should urban and rural votes be assigned the same amount of numerical weight? What about full-time residents and part-time residents? Should Hispanics who make up a sufficient proportion of the population be guaranteed a certain number of representatives of their choice? What about Republicans? And how can any group of voters secure a place on the ballot for its preferred candidate?

Even though there has been little agreement over the proper scope of particular aspects of voting rights, some common ground has emerged. There has been a consistent appeal to certain principles by both sides in most of these debates. Sometimes, those principles are too vague to provide much of a basis for debate – references to "fundamental" notions of equality come to mind. But in other cases, these basic principles are a little less slippery and provide a better platform for discussion. We will examine one of them: the relationship between voting rights and one's interest, or stake, in the outcome of an election. We will then discuss the various markers that political democracies rely upon to assess that interest for the purpose of conferring voting rights.

Debates regarding the most fundamental issue in voting rights – who should be allowed to vote – are informed by many things. But chief among these is an assessment of the degree to which a potential voter is affected by the outcome of the election.[26] Those with a strong interest in the outcome, with a sufficient stake, are prime candidates for the franchise. Those with little or nothing riding on the outcome, on the other hand, are rarely granted voting rights. Figuring out which people have a sufficient stake in the outcome of an election, and hence a right to vote,

is contentious. But there is an often an underlying point of agreement –
that we can make that decision based, in large part, on the relative
strength of a person's interest in the election.

This should not come as a great surprise. Voting, after all, is a social
choice mechanism, a way of moving from individual preferences over an
array of alternatives (candidates, propositions, dinner options) to group
choices. And this is done in a way intended to maximize preference
satisfaction.[27] People with a strong interest in the outcome of a vote,
with correspondingly strong preferences, are obviously people who
should be able to vote in such an election. People with weak or nonexistent preferences with respect to the outcome of a vote do not have
much to contribute to this end – their lives, their interests, their happiness are not much affected by the outcome.

There are additional, related reasons for tying the franchise to preference strength. For example, because those with a strong stake in the
outcome have to live with the consequences, they may be more likely to
make better decisions. They may think more deeply about their vote and
be more likely to educate themselves on the specific candidate or issues at
stake. And the outcome of the election may be perceived as more
legitimate when those who are greatly affected had the opportunity to
vote. The rallying cry "No taxation without representation" trades on this
sentiment.

There is, unfortunately, no way to directly test the strength of people's
preferences in order to see who should vote. We could, for example, just
ask people how strong their interests are, but there are problems with that
approach. First, while many individuals may accurately report that they
feel more or less strongly about the outcome of any election, there is no
way for them (or anyone else) to neutrally compare those reports with
those of other individuals.[28] There is no universal scale upon which to
measure everyone's preference strength and, even if there were, there is
no omniscient social scientist to peer directly into everyone's mind and
make a proper assessment.[29] Second, making those kinds of person-by-
person assessments by polling or interviewing people would be prohibi-
tively expensive, especially when you consider the fact that all representative governments would need to assess all potential voters.[30] And,
finally, we would be worried about strategic misrepresentation of the
strength of a person's preferences, especially since something useful
(voting rights) would come with the expression of a strong interest in
the outcome of an election.[31] Relying on first-person reports, then, would
not work, and has not been the way governmental entities have made

such assessments.[32] They have instead relied on various markers to determine people's level of interest in the outcome of an election.

Historical and contemporary examples make this point clear. As mentioned before, many states at the turn of the nineteenth century limited voting to white men who owned a certain amount of real property. These freehold requirements were supported by the idea that those who possessed such property "had a unique 'stake in society' – meaning that they were committed members of (or shareholders in) the community and that they had a personal interest in the policies of the state, especially taxation."[33] The taxpaying requirements that replaced freehold requirements in the early nineteenth century were justified on similar grounds – that only those who shoulder the burdens of government should have a voice in it (and turning the traditional rallying cry on its head: "No representation without taxation").[34] In both instances, economic participation is seen as a marker evidencing an interest in the outcome of an election, and thus a proper prerequisite to the right to vote.

Many modern restrictions on the franchise are justified on similar grounds. Take, for example, residency requirements. These are ubiquitous and such an entrenched part of the democratic landscape that they are rarely analyzed as mechanisms that disenfranchise an awful lot of people. They go largely unquestioned, because we think that residency usually serves as an accurate marker of one's interest in the outcome of an election. Most governmental entities exercise powers that are geographically circumscribed, and the belief is that only those living within the territory under the control of those entities have enough at stake to vote.[35] In those rare situations when academics or courts challenge residency requirements, they challenge this link between residency and interest, arguing that residency, or the lack of it, is not an *accurate* marker of the strength of a person's interest in the outcome of the elections.[36] Instead there may be certain classes of nonresidents – such as people who work in the jurisdiction, who own property in the jurisdiction, or are otherwise affected by the entity's actions – that may be sufficiently affected by the decisions of the governmental entity to be entitled to vote.[37] But the underlying assumption – that only people with a certain degree of interest in the outcome of an election should be allowed to vote – is shared by all.

The Supreme Court has repeatedly endorsed the relationship between the right to vote and the degree of interest in an election. The Court was most explicit about this in *Kramer v. Union Free School District*, a case involving a challenge to a New York statute that limited voting in school board elections to people who either (1) owned or leased taxable real property in the district or (2) had children enrolled in the district's schools.[38] The statute was challenged by a childless man who lived with his parents in the district.[39] The Court struck down the restrictions on the franchise as both overinclusive and underinclusive:

> [A]ppellant resides with his parents in the school district, pays state and federal taxes, and is interested in and affected by school board decisions; however, he has no vote. On the other hand, an uninterested unemployed young man who pays no state or federal taxes, but who rents an apartment in the district, can participate in the election.[40]

The restrictions were problematic to the extent that they didn't correspond well enough to a person's interest in the outcome of the election. The underlying assumption was made explicit by the Court when it explained that a state could indeed limit the franchise to a portion of the electorate that was "primarily affected" by the outcome: it just needed to demonstrate that "all those excluded are in fact substantially less interested or affected than those the [franchise] includes."[41] But the state's goal – to connect the right to vote with the strength of a person's interest in the election – was proper.

The Court even agrees on this basic point in situations where it refuses to extend voting rights to those affected by the powers of the elected body. In *Holt Civic Club v. Tuscaloosa*,[42] for example, the Court held that the Constitution did not require voting rights to be extended to people who lived outside the city limits but within the city's police jurisdiction zone, which subjected them to the city's police and sanitary regulations, among other things. While the Court acknowledged the people's interest in city affairs, and the usual connection this had with voting rights, it felt it had to draw the line somewhere, and that somewhere was the city limits: "The imaginary line defining a city's corporate limits cannot corral the influence of municipal actions. A city's decisions inescapably affect individuals living immediately outside its borders. . . . Yet no one would suggest that nonresidents likely to be affected by this sort of municipal action have a constitutional right to participate in the political processes bringing it about."[43] The connection was too tenuous and, more to the point, too difficult to manage, for many people, near and far, would be able to claim *some* interest in the affairs of any large city. The Court thus reaffirmed the basic connection between interest and the vote, but made the extension of the right to vote dependent on the strength of the interest and the manageability of a rule that extends the right to vote to everyone affected by government action.

With respect to access, then, it is fairly clear, as a descriptive matter at least, that the right to cast a ballot is closely tied to the strength of one's interest in the outcome of the election. Because there is no way to directly assess the level of people's interest, however, we are forced to rely upon various markers of that interest, whether it be property holding, residency, citizenship, or some other characteristic. Many debates over the scope of the franchise are largely debates over how well particular markers match up with voter interest. The underlying agreement, though, is that the markers should reflect the degree of voter interest.

Interest and Weighting Votes

There may be a similar sort of agreement with respect to assigning numerical weights to votes.[44] After all, the strength of people's preferences vary widely. At some point, we may decide that their interests are strong enough that they should have the right to vote. But that simple, binary approach to voting rights (either you have the vote or you don't) doesn't fully capture the range of people's interests. Perhaps the weight of each person's vote should be calibrated to the strength of their interest in the outcome. Every person's vote could be assigned a relative weight that reflects the strength of their preferences – thus providing some optimal level of participation.[45]

If such a value underlay the law of vote weighting, this would mean that, after a decision is made to grant the right to cast a ballot, there would be an additional decision with respect to how much weight to assign to each vote. We should expect to see a wide range of numerical weights assigned to people's votes, reflecting the varying degrees to which they cared about the outcome of the election. Is this something we see when we look at the structure of the second aspect of the right to vote?

At first glance, it appears the answer is no. While it's true that some voting systems assign weight in proportion to the voter's perceived stake in the enterprise,[46] the one person, one vote standard, which assigns about the same weight to everyone's vote, dominates our political landscape. This could mean several things. It might reflect a positive judgment that everyone has roughly the same level of interest in the outcome of most political elections.[47] But that doesn't seem to completely capture what's going on: we know that people have a wide range of levels of interest, at least wider than is captured by a simple decision whether or not to allow them to cast an equally weighted vote. Another possibility is that there may be something else at work here, something that limits our ability to develop a more nuanced vote-weighting system. And given what was discussed above about the difficulties in making interpersonal utility comparisons, this appears to be the case.

In other words, the Supreme Court's one person, one vote standard may actually suggest that we will rarely have the type of information about preference strength to assign more nuanced weight to votes.[48] To some extent, it may be our inability to objectively compare relative preference strengths that drives our reliance on the one person, one vote standard. Of course, a requirement that political institutions assign equal weight to votes, just like a requirement to assign differing weights to votes, is itself a judgment about the relative strengths of preferences that cannot be grounded in neutral principles.[49] But this may just mean that the Supreme Court was fooling itself when it thought it was developing a neutral, judicially manageable standard for quantitative vote dilution (something that the dissenters in the original malapportionment cases argued at the time).[50]

This view is also confirmed, oddly enough, by an exception to the one person, one vote requirement. The equiproportional standard applies to congressional and state legislative districts. And it applies to local governmental units that exercise general governmental powers – those that might be expected to affect everyone within the jurisdiction in a similar manner or to a similar degree.[51] But what about local units that disproportionately affect identifiable groups? The Supreme Court had to confront just that issue in *Salyer Land Co. v. Tulare Lake Basin Water Storage District*.[52]

Salyer involved a sparsely populated water district that covered close to 200,000 acres of farmland.[53] Governed by an elected board of directors, the district was in charge of the acquisition, storage, and distribution of water.[54] Participation in the board elections was limited to landowners, however, and their votes were weighted in proportion to the assessed valuation of the land they owned (a one acre, one vote system).[55] This was challenged as a violation of the one person, one vote requirement, but the Supreme Court rejected the challenge and, in so doing, created the special-purpose district exception to the requirement.[56] The Court found that the exception made sense in situations like this, because the board's powers disproportionately affected landowners (as opposed to mere residents) and did so in proportion to the amount of land they owned.[57]

This exception to the one person, one vote standard may not prove the rule, but it does give us some insight into its foundation. The one person, one vote rule is the default, in large part because we think that voter interest in entities exercising general governmental powers is more or less equal. When we think we have reliable information to the contrary – when, for example, we think we have a good marker for judging the strength of people's preferences regarding the outcome of the election – we allow movement away from the default to a more finely calibrated system of voting weights. So we do, in fact, see a calibrated response to perceived voter strength in our basic political institutions. We just don't see it that frequently in the political arena, because we rarely have markers that we believe are reliable enough to make such subtle distinctions.

Interest, Combining Votes, and Ballot Access

Once we ensure that those with sufficiently strong preferences have the right to vote, and once we've calibrated those votes, if possible, to the degree of preference strength, there's still work to be done. It turns out that there are many ways to prevent groups of voters from successfully aggregating their preferences for candidates of their choice. One way is to qualitatively dilute their votes – that is, develop a way to make it more difficult for people with similar preferences to combine their votes in ways that affect election outcomes. The other is to keep a group's preferred candidates off the ballot to begin with. Voting rights have evolved to deal with these issues – there are now laws that help protect against qualitative vote dilution and that secure ballot access. So do the concerns with voter interest and preference strength also inform these facets of the right to vote?

There are two reasons to think that they do. First, these rights help secure the interest-based justifications for the first two aspects of voting rights. For example, we are worried about placing a large minority of voters with similar views into an at-large districting structure that would result in the election of none of their preferred candidates. We are worried about this because the dilutive device – the at-large voting scheme – tends to increase the likelihood that large numbers of strongly held preferences will be completely neglected in the outcome. So we make sure that qualitatively dilutive devices aren't used to thwart or distort preference aggregation. Thus, laws restraining qualitative vote dilution and securing access to the ballot are not inconsistent with and serve the ends of tailoring votes and voting strength to preference strength.

Second, both the benchmark for claims of qualitative vote dilution and the thresholds for ballot access claims seem to involve some assessment of proportionality. Every election has its winners and losers. The difficulty in assessing claims of qualitative vote dilution is separating out victims from mere losers. For the purposes of section 2 of the Voting Rights Act, for example, how do we tell when a minority group has had less opportunity to participate and elect representatives of its choice? What is the standard for assessing dilution? While there are no simple answers to these questions, almost all solutions depend in part on an assessment of proportionality.[58] Proportionality is not strictly applied in most instances, nor can it be in winner-takes-all systems such as ours. There is even an express prohibition against a guarantee of proportionality in section 2 of the Voting Rights Act.[59] Yet it is difficult to conceive of a qualitative vote dilution standard completely apart from it. Similarly, ballot access laws often demand a showing of a certain level of support – through signatures, or party votes in a prior election – to ensure a place on the ballot.

The structure of voting rights in the political arena, then, involves a series of decisions about how best to aggregate individual preferences into group choices. Generally, we allow those with sufficiently strong interests with respect to the outcome to vote. In cases where we have more nuanced information about the strength of that interest, we allow entities to calibrate the numerical weight assigned to those votes. And in aggregating votes and ensuring ballot access, we worry about various practices that may thwart the collective expression of these preferences. Many of a polity's decisions with respect to voting rights depend, therefore, upon figuring out who has an interest in electoral outcomes and, when possible, assessing the strength of that interest.

Markers of Voter Interest

The relationship between voting rights and preference strength should, on reflection, be fairly obvious – after all, voting is primarily a method used to aggregate individual preferences. Thus, decisions about who has the right to vote and how much weight to assign to that vote are driven in large part by assessments of voter interest in the outcome of the election. Assessing individual voter interest, though, is easier said than done. There is no way to directly observe or compare levels of voter interest, and merely asking people how much they care about an election is unworkable.

For that reason, those who structure and administer democratic institutions rely on various markers for the strength of voter interest. For political entities with general governmental powers, we have tinkered with various markers in the past – owning property, paying taxes – and have now settled on markers such as residency and citizenship that better capture the group of voters who are sufficiently interested in the outcome of elections. The success of the voting structures of both types of institutions depends in large part on how well these markers work.

In order to assess how well a marker works, we generally look to two features: first, whether it accurately reflects the degree of interest and, second, whether it is manageable. The accuracy of a marker for voter eligibility depends on how well it describes the group of people who have sufficient interests in the outcome of the election. There are two basic ways that such a marker may be off target – it may be underinclusive or overinclusive. A marker is underinclusive if it fails to identify people with an interest in the election, and thus disenfranchises them. (Of course, a democratic entity could stitch together several underinclusive markers in order to capture more fully the entire group of interested voters.) A marker is overinclusive if it includes people without an interest in the election and thus dilutes the voting strength of those with a real interest. When it comes to assigning weight to votes, the accuracy of the marker depends upon how well it is calibrated to the strength of voter preferences.

Take, for example, some of the markers that have been used in the United States for voter interest. The early property-holding requirements captured part of what it meant to have a stake in an election, but they were underinclusive, disenfranchising vast numbers of propertyless residents who nonetheless had vital interests in the exercise of governmental powers. Residency requirements, on the other hand, seem to better capture the group of interested people, since most people within the geographic jurisdiction of a governmental entity – and thus subject to its police powers, taxing powers, etc. – have quite a bit at stake in the outcome of an election. Residency, of course, may be underinclusive in that it fails to capture nonresidents who work, own property, or have other interests in the jurisdiction (or overinclusive since it may enfranchise people who are moving out of the jurisdiction the day after the election and thus have little at stake), but not nearly so much as property-holding requirements. And states are often prohibited from using a marker that is too underinclusive, too overinclusive, or both. New York's attempt to use having children in the school system or owning or renting taxable real estate as a marker of interest in the outcome of school district elections, for example, was struck down as both underinclusive and overinclusive.

Of course, democratic institutions, both governmental and corporate, could develop more carefully tailored markers. While there isn't (yet) a machine to peer into people's heads to assess and compare their preference strengths, one could imagine that extensive questionnaires could better determine a person's interest in the outcome of any possible election. The answers on those questionnaires could then be frequently updated and double-checked for accuracy. In the end, we would probably have a better sense of who should be voting in a particular election than we do now. The problem, of course, is that such a system would be unmanageable. For starters, it would be quite costly and fairly easy to manipulate – which brings us to the second characteristic of a useful marker: its manageability.

The manageability of a marker may mean several things,[60] but, for our purposes, we merely mean whether it is realistically workable. There are many reasons why markers might be unmanageable. They may be technologically impossible (using brain scans to compare preference strengths with respect to a particular election). They may be too costly (using extensive, constantly updated surveys). Or they may be too readily manipulated (relying on a potential voter's professed interest in an election). In other words, something – be it cost, fraud, or some other factor – may prevent the marker from accurately reflecting the preference strengths it's designed to test.

Democratic institutions, for good reason, value markers that are easily managed. In the political arena, freehold and taxpaying requirements were easy to administer. There were already lists of people who owned property and paid taxes, usually within possession of the governmental entity holding the election. It would have been difficult for any individual to fraudulently add their name to the list – at least, sufficiently difficult not to be worth the vote that came with it. This doesn't mean, of course, that such requirements, standing alone, accurately picked out the group of people who were interested in the result of a particular political election. But they were quite easily administered.

It is more difficult to come by a manageable standard for the more carefully calibrated markers necessary to assign different weights to votes. Democratic institutions usually look to something that's both readily confirmed and, not to put too fine a point on it, countable. Whether it's the number of people in a general election district or the number of acres owned in a water storage district, the presence of readily ascertained and countable acres or shares allows the institution to administer the voting system. The difficulty in finding manageable markers for more subtle assessments of preference strength may explain why equal weighting is often the default rule in democratic elections. After all, the one person, one vote standard is nothing if not easily manageable: one just needs to be able to count and divide.[61] However, like some of the easily administered markers of basic interest in an election, there may be reasons why the equal weighting of votes doesn't come close to accurately capturing preference strength. As John Hart Ely noted, the one person, one vote standard "is certainly administrable . . . the more troublesome question is what else it has to recommend it."[62]

* * *

There is a great deal of underlying agreement, then, that the right to vote, and the weight assigned to that vote, should correspond to the level of a voter's interest in the outcome of the election. Perfect correspondence between voting rights and interest, though, is unattainable, because we do not have precise methods for assessing the strength of voter preferences with respect to any particular election. We must therefore rely upon various markers that imperfectly capture the degree of voter interest, and strike a balance between the accuracy and manageability of a marker. In this way, a democratic polity is designed to best reflect the interests of those affected by the exercise of its powers.

Preference Aggregation in Corporations

Corporations, like their political counterparts, need some way to aggregate the preferences of their constituents. But who are a corporation's constituents? The founders? The shareholders? The employees? Suppliers and customers? The surrounding community? The corporation is not naturally self-constituting; it is a malleable creation of state statutes. Corporate law dictates the structure of the corporation and defines who matters and who doesn't.

The process of forming a corporation under state law is relatively straightforward. The individuals looking to form a corporation file a corporate charter – a legal document also known as the articles or certificate of incorporation – with the state government.[1] This charter provides the firm's basic structure: the corporation's name, information regarding the incorporators, the total number of shares the corporation may issue, and the nature of the business to be conducted.[2] Other provisions regarding the governance structure, including many of the commonplace voting procedures discussed below, are permitted but are not required.[3]

Once the corporation is up and running, control transitions from the incorporators to the board of directors. The board manages the firm and may bind the corporation through contracts and transfers of property.[4] Shareholders select the directors at the annual shareholders' meeting.[5] Directors are bound to act in the interests of the firm through common law fiduciary duties of care, good faith, and loyalty. However, the directors delegate the actual job of running the business to the officers, primarily through a hierarchical organogram headed by the chief executive officer (CEO). This structure – shareholders elect the directors, who in turn select the officers to run the corporation – represents the foundation of corporate law.

This corporate governance structure is remarkably uniform in its adoption. As we noted in Chapter 1, Delaware corporate law doesn't require corporations to have a board,[6] and yet all of them do. But there are complexities to the corporate governance structure: both in the current iteration of the structure itself and in the many potential changes and reforms that have been considered and, in some cases, adopted. Critical to the governance structure is voting power: who gets to vote, about what, when, and under what circumstances. Despite the many potential permutations to consider, in the last century the corporate form has remained relatively fixed.

In this chapter, we start with a deeper examination of the corporate governance structure, focusing on voting. We then turn to some of the more important corporate governance developments and debates: the concept of one share, one vote; shareholder access to the proxy ballot; and say-on-pay referenda. We end this chapter by introducing a voting rights perspective on corporate governance – one that reveals just how cabined the current debates have become.

The Basics of Corporate Structure

The corporation is not the only form of business organization available under state law. There are also sole proprietorships, partnerships, business trusts, limited partnerships, limited liability partnerships, limited liability companies, and closely held corporations.[7] These other business organizations generally have more flexible governance requirements. In partnership law, the default rule is that each partner has an equal share of the voting power, unless decided otherwise by the partners.[8] The business trust has a similar flexibility in governance: it divides its relevant participants into trustees and beneficiaries (or "beneficial owners").[9] Trustees manage the assets of the trust, and the beneficiaries receive the profits of this management. For the limited partnership, the limited liability partnership, and the limited liability company, we see a move toward the corporate form: there are individuals with stakes in the residual profits who do not participate in management. For example, limited partnerships must make clear who the managerial partners are and who the limited partners are.[10] Limited liability companies have what is known as "chameleon" management: "the firm can choose either direct partnership-type control by the members or centralized control by managers that is closer to, but not as rigid as, the limited partnership format."[11]

What makes the corporation different from other forms of business organization? Scholars have isolated five factors that are considered essential to the corporate form: (1) full legal personality, including the ability to bind the firm to contracts; (2) limited liability for owners and managers; (3) shared ownership by investors of capital; (4) delegated management under a board structure; and (5) transferable shares.[12] Other types of business organizations share some of these characteristics, but none can claim all five. The critical divide between partnerships and corporations used to be the separation of ownership from control. A partnership had been generally owned and controlled by the same people; everyone who had rights to the residual profits also had a say in management. A corporation, on the other hand, has separated ownership from direct control. The shareholders own the rights to the residual and elect the board, but the directors have their own separate fiduciary duties to the corporation and appoint a distinct management group to run the day-to-day operations. This separation of "ownership from control" – the separation of rights to the residual profits from day-to-day managerial control – has been the hallmark of corporate governance.[13] Over time, large partnerships have moved away from the direct participation model and have adopted governance structures that look more like the corporate model.

Even allowing for this separation of ownership from control, shareholders nevertheless have significant governance rights within the corporate structure. Their aforementioned right to elect the board of directors is the chief arrow in their governance quiver. Under existing corporate law, shareholders are the sole "residual claimants" of the corporation: that is, their returns are not payable until the other contractual participants – creditors, employees, customers, suppliers – have been fully satisfied.[14] Shareholder primacy theory argues that maximizing shareholder wealth will generate the highest amount of surplus and thus will result in the greatest overall social utility.[15] Because of their residual interest, shareholders should have the power to control the corporation and make decisions about its ultimate direction. Shareholders do not directly exercise this power, but their appointed agents do. And these agents realize that they will be ousted from the board and from managerial positions if they fail to do their job in maximizing the surplus.

In *The Modern Corporation and Private Property*, Adolf Berle and Gardiner Means argued that the shareholder vote for boards of directors in publicly held companies was not otherwise a particularly effective way to maintain shareholder primacy.[16] Public shareholders holding a small percentage of the overall shares lacked the appropriate incentive to educate themselves about board dynamics and lacked the ability to properly monitor the board. Berle and Means contended that shareholder votes were an empty exercise in rubber-stamping the slate of candidates nominated by the board. But over time, this has proven to be an oversimplification. At the level of closely held corporations, shareholder votes are a much livelier affair. Here, we see shareholder primacy effectuated directly by the shareholders themselves through the vote. Even in publicly held companies, a majority or even a properly situated minority shareholder has the power to appoint its representatives to the board and thus control the corporation's fate.

But in order to be more than a mere description of a typical corporation, this theory of shareholder primacy needs to make clear why, among all the various corporate constituents, shareholders *should* be assigned the sole voting power within the corporation. In *The Economic Structure of Corporate Law*, Judge Frank Easterbrook and Professor Daniel Fischel answer this question in at least three different (though at times related) ways. First, shareholders are best positioned to be assigned the residual because their interests – profit maximization – are more homogeneous than those of other corporate constituents, and thus they are less likely to disagree with each other. Second, this shareholder homogeneity also helps ensure – in light of Arrow's theorem – that corporate voting isn't plagued by intransitivities, or voting cycles. Finally, Easterbrook and Fischel argue that the exclusive shareholder franchise is something that all corporate constituents would have bargained for had they been given the chance. These three basic arguments, along with their many variations, will be critically examined in the following chapters. But at the present time – nearly four decades after they were proposed – they continue to provide the intellectual scaffolding for the exclusive shareholder franchise.

So how is shareholder voting effectuated – what are the mechanics? Board elections are held at shareholder meetings. State corporate statutes require these meetings to be held at least once a year, but additional meetings can be called under special circumstances that vary by state.[17] At the annual shareholder meeting, the board stands for election by the shareholders. The default term for corporate directors is one year, although states allow terms of up to three years under a corporation's charter.[18] And – oddly enough – the shareholder must be present in order to vote directly. The underlying idea is something like that of a colonial New England town hall, where all the electors gather to debate, discuss, and ultimately vote for their leadership.

Of course, the idea of thousands – millions – of corporate shareholders gathering in one place to vote is absurd. In large public companies, the overwhelming majority of shares are voted through proxy votes. The corporate proxy ballot may look like the standard political ballot, with its list of candidates. But the corporate proxy system is different. The proxy ballot is not an actual ballot; instead, it instructs a designated person who will be present at the shareholder meeting to vote on behalf of the designated shares in a certain way. Thus, the proxy is not a ballot but rather an offer from the proxy sender: "If you want me to vote your shares a certain way, return this form to me."

The use of the proxy ballot explains many of the quirky and counter-intuitive features of corporate voting. The board sends out the proxy ballot to the shareholders not as an impartial election body but rather as a partisan within the process. The proxy includes the board's recom-mended candidates and no others. It is as if political voters were expected to either vote in person or give their "proxy" to a partisan who would vote a certain way. The corporation's proxy is akin to government represen-tatives sending you a ballot with their name on it, and then asking you to sign it and send it in to them so that they can vote for themselves on your behalf.

The use of proxies also explains why the incumbent board will never be defeated if shareholders only use the proxy ballots. These ballots do not list all of the available candidates; they list only those recommended by the board. And the choices are "vote" or "withhold vote." A candidate supported by the board will lose only if an opponent gets sufficient votes – either in person or through that opponent's own proxy ballots – to defeat the board candidate. So if 10 shareholders out of 100 vote for the board candidate, and 90 vote to withhold, the candidate will win, as the withhold votes do not matter in the absence of an alternative. However, in the face of a series of embarrassing withhold campaigns, states have adopted certain corporate law mechanisms to give meaning to the with-hold vote.[19] Pursuant to these reforms, corporations have increasingly required that board candidates receive a majority of votes cast to take (or remain in) office.

Each director seat is usually given an up-or-down vote, meaning that even a slim majority of the shareholders would have control over all of the board seats. There was a brief period, around the turn of the twentieth century, when cumulative voting for directors became a tool for protect-ing shareholders with smaller holdings.[20] Under a cumulative voting system, shareholders would receive voting power based on the number of shares as well as the number of director vacancies. So instead of being completely shut out, minority shareholders could allocate their votes in a way that provided at least some representation on the board.[21] Although some states required cumulative voting in the late nineteenth century, it has disappeared from public corporations and now is relegated to closely held corporations.

But shareholder governance is not simply about electing the board of directors. Shareholders have voting rights to amend the corporation's charter as well as its bylaws.[22] The charter, like a state constitution, is meant to be the foundational document of creation and is generally spare in its instructions. Bylaws, on the other hand, tend to handle more common but critical governance issues such as the number of directors, the number and nature of board committees, procedures for calling a board meeting, and special voting procedures or requirements. Shareholders have the right to amend the bylaws, and so too do directors through either an opt-in or an opt-out system.[23] And under federal law, shareholders in publicly held companies can make nonbinding proposals on the board's proxy ballot that are then voted on by the shareholder electorate.[24] These proposals can have an influence on directorial policymaking but can also just be ignored. Transformative corporate decisions – such as mergers, certain acquisitions, and dissolution (the end of the corporation) – also require shareholder approval. The board proposes these matters, which are then voted upon by shareholders.[25]

It is the power of a "controlling" interest[26] that drives the law and economics of shareholder voting. In a traditional publicly held corporation, the individual shareholder has little or no motivation to monitor the company or even vote in the election. But when those votes are amassed into a controlling interest, they can vote out the current board – often immediately.[27] The shareholders' votes can be amassed through the mechanism of a tender offer – an offer by one entity to buy 50 percent or more of the company's shares. The market for corporate control imposes the market discipline necessary to effectuate the shareholder primacy norm. If the shareholders are ignored or unhappy, they can sell their shares to another entity that can agglomerate the shares into a majority holding. This new majority holder then can take complete control and attempt to make the profits that prior management had failed to generate. In this way, the market for corporate control leads to greater efficiency: the shareholders can sell their shares at a premium, and the acquirer can realize the benefits of control. This potential for market discipline keeps the board and management focused on the shareholders' interests.[28]

Shareholders look like the citizens in our corporate republic – holding power over their leaders en masse but removed from actual governing. But there are significant differences. First, corporate citizens – shareholders – are but one of many groups of corporate constituents with a stake in the firm. Employees, suppliers, customers, and others may have quite significant interests in corporate decision-making, yet shareholders, and shareholders alone, vote. While such restrictions are certainly not unknown in the political context – noncitizens and nonresidents, for example, don't vote in most elections – basic principles of democratic theory have, as discussed in Chapter 2, pushed in the direction of expanding the political franchise to include a greater number of groups with a stake in political outcomes. In corporate governance, by contrast, the terms "shareholder franchise" and "corporate franchise" may be used interchangeably. While such usage accurately reflects the current state of affairs in the United States, it also serves to point up how entrenched our views of shareholder primacy have become.

Second, corporate citizenship is much more closely tied, and calibrated, to the particular relationship shareholders have with their corporations. Political citizens are people, and largely vote as such, bringing the full range of their interests to bear in their political decisions. Shareholders are people, too, but they vote not as people but as shares. Their corporate governance power depends on the number of shares they own, relative to other shareholders. While weighted voting schemes are not unknown in the political arena – think of the one acre, one vote systems used in water storage districts – they are a rare exception, employed only when we have a good shot at accurately assessing varying levels of interest. When it comes to the corporate franchise, on the other hand, weighted votes are a core feature of the system of governance.

This emphasis on shareholding and the weighted voting that comes with it lead to important divergences in managing the different electoral systems. People can move their residences or can spend time in multiple places, raising difficult questions about whether a particular person is or should be eligible to vote in a particular locality. Shares, on the other hand, are singular and owned by one person, making their vote easier to manage in some ways.[29] But while people are fairly difficult to create, all things considered, shares can be created quite easily. And so the very idea of being a shareholder immediately raises the question: Who controls the creation of the shares? Corporate law and corporation charters place restrictions on the creation of shares to prevent incumbents from printing enough voters to ensconce themselves in power forever.[30] But shares are much more ephemeral than human beings, and corporate voting rights are therefore more contingent and manipulable than traditional political ones. Indeed, because the corporation is a legal construct, voting rights could be structured however best to suit the needs of the participants.

Below we delve more deeply into three particular voting rights issues that have engaged corporate law judges, attorneys, policymakers and academics: the principle of one share, one vote; proxy access; and say on pay. These controversies illustrate the fierce debates within corporate law over voting structure as well as the creative possibilities permitted by the corporate form.

The Principle of One Share, One Vote

The elections of democratic polities are designed to aggregate the preferences of those with some interest or stake in the polity. Corporate elections are no different. And just as "one person, one vote" became the rallying cry in our democratic polity, so "one share, one vote" became the mantra in corporate law. From a preference aggregation perspective, the two standards share some of the same strengths. Owning shares in a corporation indicates that one has an interest, or stake, in that corporation's decision-making. Further, weighting those votes by shares makes for a symmetrical correspondence between one's interest in the company and the voting power assigned to that interest. In addition, the standard appears to be easily manageable, and it has the ring of fairness – votes are allocated to each according to the number of their shares.

One share, one vote, however, is not the "timeless and natural" voting structure that it appears to be.[31] In neither the United States nor Europe is it a requirement,[32] and in fact the percentage of companies with alternative voting structures is increasing.[33] In the early days of the corporate form, shareholder ownership was not uniformly distributed in the corporate charters. For much of the nineteenth century, the common law of corporations provided for a default rule of one vote per person.[34] This method tracked the default partnership rule, in which each partner has one vote regardless of their financial interest in the partnership. One scholar found that more than a third of a sample of corporate charters from 1825 to 1835 had a one person, one vote system of governance.[35] Other charters provided a "prudent mean" (in the words of Alexander Hamilton) in trying to balance shareholders and shares.[36] Such charter provisions provided that the votes-per-share would decrease as the individual shareholder got more and more shares; a shareholder with 5 shares might get 5 votes, but a shareholder with 100 shares might only get 10 votes.[37] In establishing a "prudent mean" system for the First Bank of the United States, Hamilton rejected a one share, one vote system on the grounds that it would allow a few large shareholders to "monopolize the power and benefits of the bank."[38]

Over the course of the nineteenth century, corporations moved decisively away from these quasi-partnership arrangements. By the end of the century, most states had retreated from mandatory or default rules oriented toward limiting the power of larger shareholders.[39] Then, in the early twentieth century, states and corporations moved toward a one share, one vote structure as a progressive response to the increasing number of no-vote shares being issued.[40] The one share, one vote movement reached its apex in 1988 with the Security and Exchange Commission's adoption of Rule 19c-4,[41] which required companies listed on the major exchanges to refrain from issuing shares with disproportionate voting rights.[42] The rule was subsequently struck down by the D.C. Circuit, however, and was never revived.[43] Exchanges now allow companies to issue dual-class shares and still maintain their listings.[44]

Despite the failure of Rule 19c-4, the one share, one vote norm nonetheless remains a touchstone of corporate governance. Shareholder advocacy groups like Institutional Shareholder Services look unfavorably upon dual-class structures. An unbalanced system of voting rights is likely to hurt a company's corporate governance rating, which may in turn affect how institutional shareholders treat the company.[45] The media has also latched on to the one share, one vote refrain as a litmus test for fair treatment of shareholders.[46] Even with this norm in place, however, many of our youngest and most important companies, such as Google and Facebook, departed from this norm in their initial public offerings and allocated supervoting rights to their founders. Some tech companies have even issued shares without any voting rights at all.[47]

One share, one vote follows logically from the principles used to support shareholder primacy under the law and economics framework. The one share, one vote rule requires all shares to have equal voting weight. In this way, the voting interest is equal to the interest in the residual. Shares with disproportionate voting power would create skewed incentives. As Easterbrook and Fischel argue, "[t]hose with disproportionate voting power will not receive shares of the residual gains or losses from new endeavors and arrangements commensurate with their control; as a result, they will not make optimal decisions."[48] In situations with lopsided voting rights, those with control will have the incentive to seek disproportionate gains that do not directly and proportionally inure to the owners of the residual.[49] The residual will no longer be maximized, discouraging equity investment and leading to a decline in societal efficiency.

A similar concern about incentives lies behind the prohibition on selling a share's voting rights separately from the share itself. State corporate law does not permit a shareholder to disengage the right to vote from the share and sell it permanently.[50] In addition, there are generally restrictions against buying a vote in a particular election or bribing a shareholder to vote a certain way.[51] Such restrictions may seem counter to the general corporate law preference for private ordering through contract. But vote selling is problematic for the same reason as disproportionate voting: it disengages control rights from the rights to the residual.[52] It may make sense for an individual shareholder to sell the vote, given that the value of the vote for any individual share in a public corporation is close to zero.[53] However, the sale gives greater control to a holder who does not have an equivalent interest in the residual.[54] At root, the problem of control without equity interest would remain, and all shares would be less valuable.

Thus, the theory of shareholder primacy rests on the notion that shareholders will improve social welfare by focusing on increasing the corporation's residual profits. Shareholder primacy is enforced through shareholder voting and by the market for corporate control, which uses the shareholder vote to effectuate changes in management. Essential to the theory is the notion of shareholder homogeneity – namely, that shareholders have a common, homogeneous interest in increasing residual profits and that no other set of stakeholders has a similar interest. Thus, the one share, one vote principle remains the gold standard for shareholder primacy and for shareholder-oriented corporate governance. All the more reason, then, that the trend toward dual-class and even nonvoting shares is troubling under traditional theory.

The Rise and Fall of the Federal Proxy Access Rule

As discussed in Chapter 2, the slating process is an integral part of any political election. Because control of the slating process is tantamount to control of electoral outcomes, ballot access laws are structured in such a way as to maintain electoral stability while preserving meaningful choice. The slating process is no less important in corporate elections.

So how do the candidates for corporate boards come to be on the share-holders' ballots?

State law and corporate charters dictate that shareholders must either vote in person at the annual shareholders' meeting or utilize a proxy ballot. The proxy ballot from the company is delivered to shareholders by the incumbent board members and lists only the incumbent board's chosen nominees, who are very often those very board members them-selves. If a shareholder wants to run for director or propose another nominee for the board, they need to provide all other shareholders with a separate proxy ballot.[55] Proxy contests require the distribution of proxy ballots to shareholders, as well as complicated legal disclosure; for a publicly held company, proxy contests can cost millions of dollars.[56] For some time, shareholder rights advocates have sought to enable share-holders to propose their own alternative directors in a way that avoids the extreme costs and efforts required to send out a separate proxy ballot. They want to change the proxy ballot from a one-sided missive into something more akin to a neutral ballot.

In 2010, the Securities and Exchange Commission passed Rule 14a-11, which would have required corporations to put candidates nominated by shareholders on the company's own proxy ballot, as long as certain conditions were met.[57] Allowing shareholders direct access to the board's proxy ballot is, in many ways, an intuitive step. Over time, the proxy ballot has been co-opted by the federal government for various purposes. The proxy is generally accompanied by massive disclosures required by federal law; it includes votes on compensation packages and audit pro-viders; and it provides shareholder access for independent referenda on questions relating to a variety of potential subjects.[58] The ballots are generally sent (via mail or the internet) to an accounting or proxy firm, which collects and counts the proxies, much like an independent election. Because of these accoutrements, the proxy ballot has become more akin to an independent electoral ballot than a request for the board to vote for its own nominees.

Less than a decade after the passage of the Securities Exchange Act of 1934, the SEC first considered proxy access for shareholders.[59] The proposal – debated internally – provided that "stockholders be permitted to use the management's proxy statement to canvass stockholders gen-erally for the election of their own nominees for directorships, as well as for the nominees of the management."[60] Shareholders would have been permitted to add only one additional nominee for each seat; thus, the company could stop adding nominees once they reached twice the number of positions.[61] The Commission did not formally act upon the idea.[62] Proxy access came up for consideration again in 1977 and 1992. In 1977, the SEC deferred on access in favor of supporting the work of board nominating committees; the Commission wanted these committees to consider shareholder candidates as well.[63] And in 1992, the Commission opted to expand Rule 14a-4[64] to allow shareholders to include board nominees on their "short slate" proxy ballots.[65] This reform made it easier for shareholders to seek minority representation on the board by targeting certain board nominees out of management's entire slate.[66]

Starting at the turn of this century, the SEC began to pursue proxy access in earnest. The Commission proposed proxy access rules in 2003 as part of a broader suite of proshareholder reforms. Under the 2003 proposal, proxy access hinged on a "triggering event" – either a vote on a special Rule 14a-8 proposal subjecting the company to proxy access, or a 35 percent or more "withhold" vote for one of the company's directors.[67] Once triggered, shareholders with at least 5 percent of the voting securities, held for at least two years, would be entitled to nominate between one and three director candidates.[68] The proposal received numerous comments but, in the end, was never acted upon.[69]

Three years later, the U.S. Court of Appeals for the Second Circuit in *AFSCME v. AIG* held that a shareholder proposal under Rule 14a-8 to create proxy access for shareholder director candidates was improperly excluded from a company's proxy materials.[70] The SEC had sided with the company, arguing that the proposal related to an election and was therefore excludable under Rule 14a-8(i)(8).[71] However, the court held that the exclusion referred only to proposals concerning a particular election, not those concerning procedural rules that apply to elections in general.[72] The *AFSCME* decision led to a period of some confusion in the corporate governance world, as the court had rejected the SEC's interpretation of its own rule. Thus, the SEC either would be stuck with the Second Circuit's decision or would have to change the rule.

Confronted with this legal fork in the road, the SEC essentially chose to go down both roads at once. In 2007, it released for comment two alternative proposals: a "shareholder access" proposal and a "status quo" proposal. Under the access proposal, the SEC would change Rule 14a-8(i)(8) to allow shareholders to submit proposals amending corporation bylaws that would give proxy access to shareholder nominees.[73] Only shareholders owning more than 5 percent of a company's voting securities would be permitted to make proposals in the proxy materials affecting director nomination and election procedures.[74] The access proposal would allow such shareholders to offer whatever shareholder nomination procedures they desired in the proxy materials.[75] The only substantive limitations on such procedures would be those imposed by state law or the company's charter and bylaws.[76] Thus, like ballot access laws in the political arena, the proposal attempted to enhance meaningful access to the ballot while maintaining the stability of the electoral system (through the 5 percent minimum). The status quo proposal, on the other hand, was a codification of the SEC's pre-*AFSCME* interpretation that would permit corporations to exclude from proxy materials shareholder proposals that affected the director nomination and election procedures.[77] At that time, the SEC adopted the status quo proposal in a divided 3–2 vote.[78]

In 2009, after the financial crisis and the election of President Obama, the SEC released yet another iteration of proxy access. This version created a new rule – Rule14a-11 – that would provide direct access to the ballot for shareholders.[79] The 2009 proposal significantly reduced the requirements for participation. Only 1 percent ownership was necessary for companies with over $700 million in assets, sliding up to 3 percent for those with assets between $75 million and $700 million, and 5 percent for those under $75 million.[80] The period for holding the securities was only one year, and a triggering event was no longer necessary.[81] Most significantly, the proposal would have made this access a mandatory part of the corporate structure, rather than merely allowing shareholders to implement it on their own.

The SEC received comments on the proposal up through 2010, when the Dodd-Frank Act specifically gave the Commission the authority to enact proxy access reforms.[82] Soon thereafter, the Commission adopted Rule 14a-11 on a 3–2 vote.[83] The final rule set a flat ownership requirement of 3 percent but allowed shareholders to pool their holdings to reach that threshold. That 3 percent had to be held for three years prior to the nominations and up through the actual shareholder meeting. Shareholders were limited to nominating candidates for up to 25 percent of the seats on the board, and they could not desire a change in control.[84] In addition, the Commission amended Rule 14a-8 to allow shareholders to propose proxy nomination processes within their individual corporations.[85]

The rule did not last long. Acting on a petition for an injunction from the Business Roundtable and the Chamber of Commerce, the D.C. Circuit struck down the regulation under the Administrative Procedure Act[86] for failing "adequately to consider the new rule's effect upon efficiency, competition, and capital formation."[87] The court found that the SEC failed to calculate the costs and the benefits of the new rule properly, specifically with respect to the incumbent board's costs of opposing a shareholder nominee. According to the court, "the Commission failed to appreciate the intensity with which issuers would oppose nominees and arbitrarily dismissed the probability that directors would conclude their fiduciary duties required them to support their own nominees."[88] The court also held that the SEC neglected the strategic uses of the rule for union and state pension fund shareholders. The court found "there was good reason to believe institutional investors with special interests will be able to use the rule" to advance their "self-interested objectives rather than the goal of maximizing shareholder value."[89] The alleged third failure was the Commission's emphasis on the infrequency of elections when assessing the costs, but not when assessing the benefits. According to the court, "the Commission's discussion of the estimated frequency of nominations under Rule 14a–11 is internally inconsistent and therefore arbitrary."[90]

The D.C. Circuit's decision striking down Rule 14a-11 surprised many observers, including opponents of the rule.[91] Most academic commentators were quite critical of the opinion.[92] Perhaps the strangest thing about the opinion is its rejection of the shareholder franchise as a foundational component of state corporate law.[93] The *Business Roundtable* court viewed the shareholder franchise as a costly nuisance to the incumbent board. It did so based on a bizarre reading of fiduciary duty in which board candidates must always – of necessity – be better selections than rival candidates.[94] Under this reading, if the rival candidates were better, the board would have recognized the error of its ways and endorsed them instead. Its opposition must therefore reflect the reality that these outsiders are not as good. And yet this reading assumes the very thing that voting is supposed to interrogate – namely, that the board truly represents shareholder interests. The court departed dramatically from the standard law and economics of corporate law, which assumes that shareholders and directors will act rationally, that agency costs are a natural byproduct of the separation of ownership and control, and that the shareholder franchise will increase overall efficiency.[95] It is a truly upside-down view of the world: because the board is supposed to act in shareholder interests, it of necessity will do so, and there is no need for something as messy as a contested election.[96]

And yet, the *Business Roundtable* decision is emblematic of a certain antidemocratic strain of corporate law theory based (purportedly) on law and economics. The idea of shareholder wealth maximization is a fictional placeholder developed to replace the actual interests of the shareholders.[97] If shareholders truly expressed their preferences through their votes, there would be no need for the norm of residual maximization.[98] Instead, the board and management would be expected to follow the actual preferences of shareholders, rather than simply a presumed wealth maximization preference.[99] And actual shareholders may not all agree on one homogenized goal. If let loose to express their actual preferences, shareholders might support the pursuit of a variety of interests beyond shareholder wealth maximization.[100] Because shareholder preferences are irrelevant to shareholder primacy, true shareholder democracy is actually a threat to the shareholder wealth maximization norm.

The *Business Roundtable* decision neatly illustrates this hostility. In its review of the SEC's cost-benefit analysis, the court agreed that Rule 14a-11 "will mitigate collective action and free rider concerns, which can discourage a shareholder from exercising his right to nominate a director in a traditional proxy contest, and has the potential of creating the benefit of improved shareholder value."[101] But the opinion never returned to these notions. Instead, it turned to the logistical costs of democracy for the incumbent board – namely, the costs of engaging in a meaningful board election and the potential for "special" shareholders to abuse their right to enter elections.[102]

Some corporate law scholars have argued that democracy should have only a minimal role to play in corporate governance, and that directors should have the authority of Platonic guardians over their shareholder subjects.[103] However, mainstream law and economics has long defended the critical role of shareholder democracy within the overall framework of corporate governance.[104] Shareholders need to hold directors accountable for failing to pursue shareholder interests. Otherwise, the corporation will be riven with agency costs. The split between the ideas of shareholder wealth maximization and shareholder preference aggregation has led to the current split in the law and economics academy. One side maintains its faith that facilitating shareholder democracy will increase corporate efficiency and reduce overall agency costs.[105] The other side now trusts the hypothetical shareholder – a construct of corporate law academics and the Business Roundtable – more than actual shareholders when it comes to pursuing shareholder wealth maximization.

Say-on-Pay and Nonbinding Votes

One surprising aspect of corporate voting, and one that doesn't have a straightforward political equivalent, is the amount of controversy surrounding entirely nonbinding votes. Shareholder proposals, ensconced in federal law since 1942, are the primary example. Under the Security and Exchange Commission's Rule 14a-8, shareholders can place a proposal to other shareholders on the incumbent board's proxy statement.[106] The proposal is then subject to an up-or-down vote from the other shareholders. Only shareholders who own at minimum either 1 percent or $2,000 worth of the company's stock and have held the stock for at least one year prior to the vote are eligible to submit a proposal. Proponents are limited to one proposal per year and must show up to present the proposal at the annual meeting. The company is also allowed to exclude proposals that fall into certain specified categories. Excludable categories include proposals about the ordinary business of the corporation, proposals that are not otherwise significant, and proposals outside the sphere of appropriate shareholder action.[107] The delineation of these categories is meant to provide for meaningful shareholder voice, on the one hand, and appropriate deference and discretion afforded to the board and its appointed management, on the other.

A more recent addition to the precatory-vote category is "say on pay." The underlying idea is to provide shareholders with an up-or-down vote on the compensation provided to the company's top executives. The theory is the most basic of agency costs concerns: when it comes to executive compensation, the interests of executives and shareholders diverge. Directors try to ameliorate this divergence by relying on a board subcommittee of outside and independent directors to set compensation, often with the help of specialized consultants. But the fundamental conflict remains: executives will want more pay, and shareholders will want them to make less. Say on pay provides for an advisory vote, as part of the proxy statement, on the pay for top executives. In 2002, the United Kingdom implemented a say-on-pay policy,[108] and shareholder activists in the United States began to implement such votes at individual companies.[109] In 2010, the Dodd-Frank Wall Street Reform and Consumer Protection Act required publicly traded corporations to have a say-on-pay vote at least once every three years.[110] Many companies have adopted policies requiring such a vote annually.

Critics of say-on-pay voting raise four primary objections. One objection concerns the federally implemented nature of the regulation. Because state law governs the internal workings of the corporation, the argument goes, federal law should not muck around in an area of substantive corporate policy such as executive compensation.[111] Another critique argues that individual companies should have the choice to implement say-on-pay provisions or not, rather than say on pay being imposed on all publicly traded companies.[112] Not all shareholders may feel the need or desire for regular say-on-pay votes, and they should be in a position to make the decision for themselves. Third, commentators have questioned the efficacy of these votes. Pointing to their advisory nature, and the fact that over 98 percent of such votes end up approving the pay packages, critics contend that they are simply a waste of time and resources.[113] Finally, because say on pay challenges the supremacy and authority of the board over managerial issues, it arguably undercuts a board-centric system of corporate governance.[114]

Supporters of say on pay have responses to each of these arguments. Federal law has long played an important regulatory role in shareholder voting and has utilized nonbinding advisory votes as a way of giving shareholders a voice. State governments can be compromised by their interest in staying on good terms with corporate management. In terms of individual company choice, say on pay began at the individual company level, with institutional and activist shareholders pushing for adoption of bylaws that would require say-on-pay votes.[115] However, the say-on-pay reform was passed as part of a broader "shareholders' bill of rights" that provided more governance power to shareholders. These reforms are justified by the basic economics of agency costs and the idea that shareholders can mitigate these costs with certain processes. The low percentage of winning challenges may actually be a good sign, if companies have changed their practices to adopt better compensation policies.[116] And there have been notable defeats for pay packages at companies such as Citigroup, Abercrombie & Fitch, and Oracle.[117] The votes did not mandate any governance changes, but they prompted the boards in question to reconsider the compensation – and even the compensated – because of the vote.[118]

We offer this debate as an example of the panoply of options available to corporations in constructing their internal governance, and as an example of a subject that other stakeholders – such as rank-and-file employees – may view quite differently from shareholders. Excessive executive compensation resurfaced as a concern in the late 1990s, and corporate law academics have wrestled with the problem in earnest.[119] Enacted reforms have included requiring independent directors on the compensation committee, expensing stock options at the time of issue, making it easier to bring lawsuits for corporate waste, and eliminating the corporate tax deduction. Yet voting rights have played an important role in relation not only to say on pay but also to shareholder power more generally. Lucian Bebchuk, a well-known skeptic of corporate pay packages, has focused much of his scholarship and activism on franchise reforms.[120] His reforms include: greater access to the proxy ballot; opposition to three-year director terms; and the use of bylaws to require certain voting procedures, such as a unanimous vote for poison-pill implementation.[121] On the other side, Stephen Bainbridge has argued that boards of directors should have power and authority to make decisions relatively unfettered by shareholder interference.[122] Even though both believe in shareholder primacy, they have radically different ways of implementing it.

A Broader Perspective on Corporate Voting Rights

A president of the Business Roundtable – an advocacy group for corporate executives – once opined, "Corporations were never designed to be democracies."[123] And yet corporations are, indeed, clearly designed as democracies. The corporate governance structure is based on the election of the board of directors by the shareholders. These directors then appoint the executives who run the corporation. This simple structure is repeated in corporation after corporation after corporation. So if we want to think deeply about the problems that lie within the corporate structure, we are going to be thinking – at least in part – about voting.

In the twenty-first century, voting has come to the fore as the instrument of governance through which shareholders can most directly express their preferences. Although some commentators have sought to limit shareholder power,[124] the general trend has been innovation in ways of overcoming the basic costs and design flaws of the shareholder franchise. But as reforms like proxy access and say on pay illustrate, there is room for creativity here. Indeed, we should reexamine the premises of the entire voting structure, starting with the shareholder franchise.

For too long, the basic premises of the shareholder franchise have been taken for granted or assumed away. In *eBay Domestic Holdings, Inc.*

v. Newmark,[125] former Delaware Chancellor William Chandler dismayed many stakeholder theorists and environmental, social, and governance (ESG) investors by reaffirming corporate law's commitment to shareholder primacy.[126] Up until *eBay,* it could plausibly be argued that Delaware law hovered somewhere between shareholder primacy and stakeholder theory.[127] For every *Revlon* case requiring shareholder wealth maximization, there was a *Time Warner v. Paramount* allowing boards to take actions that would favor shareholders only indirectly or over the long term.[128] But the power structure – the shareholder franchise – was already in place. As former Delaware Supreme Court Chief Justice Leo Strine pointed out:

> In current corporate law scholarship, there is a tendency among those who believe that corporations should be more socially responsible to avoid the more difficult and important task of advocating for externality regulation of corporations in a globalizing economy and encouraging institutional investors to exercise their power as stockholders responsibly. . . . Corporate directors, under this rosy view, may consider any or all of the following to be ends as important, or even more important, than the economic well-being of the corporation's stockholders: the employees, the customers of the corporation, the environment, charitable causes, the communities within which the corporation operates, and society generally.
>
>   These well-meaning commentators, of course, ignore certain structural features of corporation law that folks like Madison and Hamilton would have thought important. . . . The contention that [§ 101(b) of the Delaware General Corporation Law ("DGCL")] proves directors are free to promote interests other than those of stockholders ignores the many ways in which the DGCL focuses corporate managers on stockholder welfare by allocating power only to a single constituency, the stockholders. Under the DGCL, only stockholders have the right to vote for directors; approve certificate amendments; amend the bylaws; approve certain other transactions, such as mergers, and certain asset sales and leases; and enforce the DGCL's terms and hold directors accountable for honoring their fiduciary duties. In the corporate republic, no constituency other than stockholders is given any power.[129]

The realpolitik of the modern corporation is that, of all of its many stakeholders, shareholders and shareholders alone control the real levers of governance.

   If we wish to reimagine how corporations work, we have to reimagine their governance structure. The following chapters are an effort to work through the theory behind the existing structure and determine why the shareholder franchise remains the bedrock of corporate law and corporate law theory. In particular, we critically examine the basic arguments for the exclusive shareholder franchise – first offered by Easterbrook and Fischel over forty years ago – that continue to animate the debate. We begin with the argument based on the claim that a corporation is a contract or a nexus of contracts.

4

The Corporation as Contract

The purpose of holding an election is to aggregate the preferences of those who are voting. Elections can be adjusted based on the strengths, divergences, and time-sensitive nature of the preferences at issue. But at root, the purpose of a voting system is to provide a way for a group to sort its preferences with respect to a particular decision.

When we look at corporate voting in this way, we are immediately struck by the fact that it is shareholders, and shareholders alone, who are having their preferences aggregated. The corporation encompasses the daily activities of a variety of different players: directors, officers, executives, management, and frontline employees. Moreover, there are outside stakeholders who have interests in the activities of the corporation akin to those of shareholders: bondholders, suppliers, customers, even the community at large. However, when it comes to aggregating the preferences of the corporate polity in order to determine the leadership of the corporation, only shareholders are invited to participate.

The primary normative justification for shareholder voting is the theory of shareholder primacy. Shareholder primacy is the theoretical driver not only for the vote but also for other governance features such as the fiduciary duties of care and loyalty. Shareholder primacy essentially means that corporations exist to serve the interests of shareholders.[1] Shareholder primacy could simply be viewed as a democratic legitimacy argument: the corporation has to keep shareholder interests at the forefront because shareholders are the voting polity. But this puts the cart before the horse. After all, who made the shareholders the voting polity? The choice of this group as the sole enfranchised citizenry is what needs justifying. A variant of this justification is that shareholders are the corporation's "owners" and thus are entitled to ownership rights over profits and control.[2] However, the ownership justification is also doomed by its circularity. It begs the question: Who made the shareholders the owners?[3] As corporate law commentators have convincingly pointed out, shareholders simply purchase a set of rights from the corporation. The right to vote is made part of the stock ownership bundle, but stocks could be constructed (and have at times been constructed) without the right to elect directors.[4] Even shareholders with the right to vote do not possess many of the rights that traditionally accrue to property owners – the right to exclude, for example, or the right of possession.[5] Labeling shareholders "owners" is no more of a justification for the vote than is labeling them "voters."

These kinds of explanations, therefore, are little more than recapitulations of the way corporate law currently operates. In order to justify the exclusive shareholder franchise, we need to look for something beyond mere labels ("shareholders are owners") or descriptions of the current mechanics of corporate law ("shareholder voting relies on the market for corporate control to effectuate shareholder primacy"). Corporations, after all, are collective enterprises with a range of constituents, all of whom contribute to and benefit from the activities of the firm. Shareholder primacy – and the exclusive shareholder franchise that comes with it – needs to be justified in some noncircular fashion.

There have been a few arguments that go beyond mere labels and investigate these questions. The first of these, and the subject of this chapter, is the contractarian argument. It is grounded in the (surprisingly) persistent idea that the corporation is a contract, or, more specifically, a "nexus" of contracts. This view leads its supporters to maintain that virtually all aspects of corporate structure, including its voting procedures, are the product of an interlocking group of freely bargained-for contracts among all corporate constituents. Indeed, in the strong version of this view, a corporation *is* that set of contracts.

The Nexus of Contracts

As we saw in Chapter 3, most corporations share the same fundamental governance characteristics. The firm is controlled by a board of directors, who in turn select the officers who run the day-to-day business of the operation. This board is elected by shareholders. The shareholders share in the profits of the corporation through dividends and can sell their shares on the open market. This same basic structure – shareholders elect directors who appoint officers – can be found in every public corporation.[6] Why is this tripartite power dynamic so uniform across corporations? Is it because corporate law requires this structure, or because this structure is freely chosen and therefore the most efficient?

For contractarians, the answer is that corporate constituents freely choose the basic features of corporate governance. The nexus of contracts theory, in its purest form, holds that a corporation is merely a central hub for a series of contractual relationships.[7] In other words, a corporation is a legal fiction; it is not a separate individual and has no real independent existence.[8] Instead of thinking of the corporation as an independent entity, the nexus of contracts theory breaks it down into its component parts.[9] These parts are the contractual relationships between the various parties involved with the firm: shareholders, directors, executives, creditors, suppliers, customers, and employees. Under this approach, corporate law is an extension of contract law and should focus on facilitating the interrelationships between contractual participants in the most efficient manner.[10]

While we've noted before that the preferences of corporate constituents are captured through a mix of voting (shareholders) and fixed contracts (everyone else), the contractarian argument goes beyond this description. It grounds this basic division (and other aspects of corporate governance) in the free contractual choices of corporate participants. The exclusive shareholder franchise is, then, part and parcel of this set of contracts. And because it is seen as part of an interlocking set of free choices of all participants, it is therefore the most efficient way to structure the enterprise. To question the corporate governance structure is to dispute the market choices of those who are, presumably, in the best position to make them.

The nexus of contracts theory has been extremely influential in shaping corporate law theory over the past four decades.[11] But despite its dominance, there is still confusion over whether the theory is a descriptive model, a normative prescription, or some combination of the two.[12] Michael Jensen and William Meckling presented it as a positive theory of the corporation and its concomitant relationships.[13] That thread was picked up in the legal literature, with Frank Easterbrook and Daniel Fischel cementing the concept in place.[14] But they, too, have waffled over whether the model should be seen as a positive description or as a normative framework – or both.[15]

The nexus of contracts theory has been sufficiently successful for its branches to have grown in several different directions off the same trunk. We begin with the strong contractarians, who most closely adhere to the idea that a corporation is and should be considered a contract or set of contracts. Second, we talk about the "hypothetical bargain" popularized by Easterbrook and Fischel, as well as by managerialists, who use the theory to support the board-centered status quo of traditional Delaware law. Finally, we explore the influence of the "corporate contract" on recent debates about the power of shareholders within the corporate structure.

Strong Contractarians

In their article *Agency Costs and a Theory of the Firm,* Jensen and Meckling set out the straightforward proposition that "most organizations are simply legal fictions which serve as a nexus for a set of contracting relationships among individuals."[16] Rather than seeing the firm as something different in the economic landscape, Jensen and Meckling sought to remove the fictional conception of organizational identity to expose the network of relationships beneath.[17] They argued that "it makes little or no sense to try to distinguish those things which are 'inside' the firm (or any other organization) from those things that are 'outside' of it. There is in a very real sense only a multitude of complex relationships (i.e., contracts) between the legal fiction (the firm) and the owners of labor, material and capital inputs and the consumers of output."[18]

In a sense, Jensen and Meckling are correct: corporations are fictional legal entities without individual corporeal or spiritual existence. But to claim they are merely an agglomeration of contracts is a legal simplification too far. They are forced to hedge their position when talking specifically about corporations, rather than "most organizations." They state: "The private corporation or firm is simply one form of legal fiction which serves as a nexus for contracting relationships and which is also characterized by the existence of divisible residual claims on the assets and cash flows of the organization which can generally be sold without permission of the other contracting individuals."[19] Notice the framing: there are claims on assets and cash flows "which can generally be sold" without permission. The passive voice elides the exact mechanics, but even Jensen and Meckling admit that these transfers take place without contractual sanction from all parties. Rather, the corporate structure is doing the basic work of managing these flows of claims and cash. And they do not even mention basic aspects of the corporation such as fiduciary duties, the board's managerial power, or limited liability.

In truth, it is unfair to put too much weight on the two pages of Jensen and Meckling's article that gave birth to the nexus of contracts theory. The article itself focuses on the agency costs between shareholders and managers, provides an economic model designed around the different interests of shareholders and managers, and evaluates the use of debt and inside equity to balance these interests.[20] But as subsequent theorists have recognized, the nexus of contracts theory is not a theory of the firm.[21] Rather, it is an illustrative setup for an article that focuses instead on a theory of corporate capital distribution.

Despite the thinness of Jensen and Meckling's claims, their literal take on the nexus of contracts approach has had a profound effect on the legal literature. Advocates of a strong version of contractarianism have argued that the corporation is primarily contractual and, as such, represents terms that the parties have freely chosen among themselves.[22] Since the corporation is merely an intersection of voluntary agreements, corporate law should eschew mandatory rules.[23] Instead, the role of corporate law is to create default terms that line up with the standard terms for which the parties would bargain. And since the terms have been freely chosen, we can presume they are efficient.[24]

This strong descriptive claim is the nexus of contracts theory in its purest form. The corporation is entirely the product of freely bargained-for contracts. These contracts, not corporate law, determine the structure of corporate governance. But this literal version of the "corporation as contract" claim is simply incorrect. Corporations are not creatures of contract. One cannot contract to form a corporation.[25] The individuals involved must apply to a state for permission to create such an entity. The fact that this permission is readily granted (as long as fees and taxes are paid) does not change the fact that permission is required.[26]

Corporate contractarians chafe at the idea of permission, because this permission has been used in the past as a justification for corporate regulation.[27] The idea of concession theory is that corporations only exist thanks to a grant – a concession – by the state, and the state is thereby justified in extracting a quid pro quo for the concession. The history of early business entities, which were in fact specific grants of authority by the crown over industries, territories, infrastructure, or trading routes, lends support for this view.[28] Like the nexus of contracts theory, concession theory is both positive and normative: it provides a descriptive theory of corporations based on state creation and argues that the state should have a freer hand to regulate them because of this creative power.[29] Contractarians have been particularly vicious and dismissive in their rejection of concession theory.[30] But the basic premise of concession theory is sound: corporations are creatures of the state and cannot be formed purely through contract. It is impossible to do so.[31]

When forced to acknowledge the factual reality, contractarians then contend that corporate law statutes are *mostly* default rules, not mandatory rules that might interfere with private bargains struck through contracts. But there is one critical feature of modern corporate law that is not a default rule and could not be reproduced through contract: limited liability. In *The Rise of the Uncorporation*, Larry Ribstein describes corporate limited liability as the result of a grand bargain: "The corporate form represents a quid pro quo: big firms get corporate features, and government gets an opportunity to regulate governance."[32] The corporate tax – characterized as double taxation, since dividends are taxed as well – was "in a sense a fee for incorporating."[33] In return, the corporation's investors were protected by limited liability. As Ribstein makes clear, limited liability is distinctly noncontractarian: "Limited liability is particularly important because, unlike other corporate features discussed above, partnerships could not easily contract for it without lawmakers' cooperation as they have to include the creditors in these contracts."[34] Since it is a feature "that parties cannot replicate by private contract," Ribstein observes, "whether a statutory form provides for limited liability therefore will dominate parties' choice of form."[35] In sum, limited liability is the main reason why the corporation succeeded where the partnership failed.[36]

Nevertheless, the literal interpretation of the nexus of contracts approach does important rhetorical work for strong contractarians. By divorcing the corporation from the state, contractarians render efforts to regulate the corporation as outside interference and illegitimate. In this libertarian approach to corporate law, government can then be cast not as the creator of the corporate form but rather as its opponent.[37] Government should step back and let the private parties create their nexus; any effort to intervene would interrupt and interfere with the market process. This applies to the shareholder vote as well. Contractarians need not come up with an independent justification for the shareholder franchise if that governance structure is simply the outcome of private ordering. Particularly if seen as a *nexus* of contracts, the corporation's exclusive shareholder voting structure can be cast as a joint and consensual arrangement between *all* of the participants in the corporate form. Creditors, suppliers, customers, and employees – all have agreed to the shareholder franchise because none of them included voting rights in *their* contracts.

Of course, the irony is that state corporate law has likely stifled efforts to expand the franchise beyond shareholders. A truly free-flowing contractual approach to governance would open the door to a variety of corporate forms, instead of the directors-shareholders structure that is so ensconced in the law. If corporations were truly just an agglomeration of separate deals, it's unlikely they would all look the same. But corporate law has successfully put its stamp on governance, particularly on the shareholder franchise. It is one of the reasons why a true contractarian like Larry Ribstein seemed to give up on the corporate form in favor of the limited liability company.

The range of choices that do appear within the statutory framework are often illusory. For example, section 141 of Delaware General Corporation Law states: "The business and affairs of every corporation organized under this chapter shall be managed by or under the direction of a board of directors, *except as may be otherwise provided* in this chapter or *in its certificate of incorporation*."[38] This apparent flexibility, however, is belied by the actual structure of corporations and the presence of other mandatory requirements. In practice, for example, corporate charters are extremely homogenous.[39] The diversity that one might expect from a collection of firms with heterogeneous governance needs is nowhere apparent.[40] Moreover, the apparent flexibility of corporate law on paper is undercut by a more complex reality. The textual openness of § 141(a), for example, masks a fairly rigorous defense of managerial power. Shareholders' power to amend the corporation's bylaws under § 109(b) of the Code takes a back seat to the more free-ranging power of § 141 (a).[41] In addition, many aspects of federal securities law, particularly SEC Rule 14a-8[42] and the Sarbanes-Oxley Act,[43] assume the existence of certain governance mechanisms, such as board and shareholder meetings, before adding additional requirements.[44] Centralized management is "[t]he feature that best characterizes the large-firm nature of the corporation," and the board of directors is "one of the most distinctive features of the corporate form."[45] Similarly, shareholder voting, transferable shares, fiduciary duties, and capital lock-in are other essential governance elements of the corporation that are mandated by the form.[46]

There is another, less ambitious form of contractarianism that acknowledges corporate law's imposition of mandatory, noncontractual terms but argues that participants nonetheless exercise a kind of contractual freedom by choosing the corporate form over others. Businesses need not choose the corporation as their organizational form; they can create general and limited partnerships, limited liability companies, benefit corporations, and other variations.[47] But the availability of choice among a set of possible forms does not mean that the choice is contractual. For a variety of reasons, the corporation is the best and/or only choice for certain types of businesses.[48] And although the number of choices has increased, there are still only a handful of options. At best, it might be argued that, of the existing options, the participants who do the choosing seem to prefer the corporate form. This, though, doesn't get you very far when it comes to justifying even the most basic aspects of corporate governance, such as the exclusive shareholder franchise. A similar argument could be made for the many businesses in Germany, with its system of codetermination, that have chosen to locate or remain in Germany and give workers a vote and a seat at the board-room table.[49]

Although sometimes the rhetoric slips,[50] it is hard to find strong contractarians who believe that the nexus of contracts theory is the literal truth.[51] Instead, the theory is used metaphorically, usually to serve a particular narrative about the formation and operation of the firm. In this account, the corporation, while not literally composed of contracts, represents the contracts that parties would have made had they been able to do so. This brings us to what is known as the "hypothetical bargain."

The Hypothetical Bargain

Even if a corporation is not actually a nexus of contracts, perhaps it is a business structure that all firm participants, if given the chance, would have agreed upon. This is the idea behind the hypothetical bargain. Though invoked by many scholars, the hypothetical bargain has been most forcefully articulated by Easterbrook and Fischel. When trying to explain the presence of corporate law in what should – to them – be a world of pure contract, they maintain that "corporate law is a set of terms available off-the-rack so that participants in corporate ventures can save the cost of contracting."[52] They continue:

> There are lots of terms, such as rules for voting, establishing quorums, and so on, that almost everyone will want to adopt. Corporate codes and existing judicial decisions supply these terms "for free" to every corpora-tion .... Corporate law – and in particular the fiduciary principle enforced by courts – fills in the blanks and oversights with the terms that people would have bargained for had they anticipated the problems and been able to transact costlessly in advance.[53]

Thus, in situations where certain features of a corporation cannot be grounded in actual bargaining of any sort, they are justified as the product of an imagined, ex ante bargain among members of the many corporate constituencies.[54]

The hypothetical bargain allows these quasi-contractarians to make three rhetorical moves. First, it allows them to capture much of the power of the more direct nexus of contracts theory without the illogical commitments required by the unalloyed version of the theory. Second, the hypothetical bargain allows supporters to defend current practices by pointing to their roots as bargains (even if only imagined ones).[55] Third, it provides the intellectual support for a corporate law architecture that includes both default and mandatory terms. Judges and legislatures are permitted to impose mandatory terms so long as the narrative supports a hypothetical bargain that would arrive at the same place.

Because the hypothetical bargain is based on a "best guess" as to what the parties really want, the success of the contractarian argument depends on how well this guess matches reality. Contractarians spend at least some time trying to figure out the preferences of corporate constituents. They look to actual bargains on certain subjects. And they make some simplifying assumptions about human motivation and behavior. The problem with these approaches is that the actual bargains are often limited to more minor features of corporate governance negotiated between a few constituents, and the simplifying assumptions are often off the mark. In the end, the hypothetical bargains, and the imagined preferences they are based on, reveal much more about the desires of those doing the guessing than the actual preferences of corporate constituents.

Easterbrook and Fischel, for example, believe that they have a "ready source of guidance" when it comes to making their guesses: "the deals people actually strike when they bargain over the subject."[56] Legislatures and courts, then, should build corporate law by looking at the bargains struck by private actors in similar situations. This seems fine when working out some of the details. For example, there are good reasons to assume that minority shareholders will want protections against opportunism from majority shareholders – majorities that already exist or that assume power in the future. But it's hard to see how this works when it comes to the more fundamental aspects of corporate governance structure, such as who has voting and control rights. There really aren't any guiding bargains over these more basic aspects of governance because there aren't atomistic providers of capital and labor floating around in the aether of free contract to make such deals.[57] The grand hypothetical bargain requires us to visualize all of the corporate constituents sitting around a table negotiating the ideal governance form ex ante. But by the time most of the actual constituents come to the bargaining table, the basic governance procedures have already been selected by the founders – they've approached the state and formed a corporation. There's no real-world analog that allows us to discern much of anything about the form that corporation would take. The "deals people actually strike" are of little use here.

Without the guidance of real-world bargains on the basic aspects of corporate governance, contractarian scholars are forced to take a step back, consider the preferences of all constituent groups, and then argue from those preferences to the hypothetical bargains. Here, the best Easterbrook and Fischel can do is assume that "[i]nvestors and other participants agree on the stakes: money. They therefore would agree unanimously to whatever rule maximizes the total value of the firm."[58] For them, then, every single corporate constituent – shareholders, employees, creditors, or customers – agree on the goal of wealth maximization. Again, most scholars and lawmakers making these guesses have tended to focus more specifically on the preferences of shareholders. But they've largely made the same guess – that shareholders want to maximize wealth.[59] And these guesses, and the hypothetical bargains based on them, are used to justify a broad range of the features of corporate law and governance.

Here, though, we have a guess we can test against reality and see if it makes sense. It doesn't. The guess isn't even accurate when it comes to shareholder preferences. As we shall see in the Chapter 5, there's no reason to think that every shareholder has the same type of preferences – their preferences are much more heterogeneous than previously believed.[60] Indeed, even shareholders who prioritize wealth maximization may still disagree about what, exactly, that means, the proper time-line, and other issues. And when we expand our gaze to other participants, the guess looks even more off the mark. Employees, for example, care about their wages, but they also care about the long-term health of their company and their jobs.[61] Customers care about the cost of their products (and, all things considered, like them lower rather than higher), but they also care about the quality of the goods or services they purchase. The normative force of the hypothetical bargain disappears if the bargain is not based on the actual preferences of corporate constituents.

But even if Easterbrook and Fischel are right about the preferences of corporate constituents – even if every last one of them values money above all else – that alone doesn't lend much insight into the hypothetical bargains they would make. Different corporate constituents may want to strike deals that maximize their own group's wealth, not necessarily the overall wealth of the firm. And even if all constituents could be convinced that the only way to make a deal is to agree to a system that maximizes the value of the firm, that alone doesn't automatically achieve a hypothetical bargain on any particular governance feature. It still must be proven that a particular governance structure is the right one to achieve that shared goal, which brings us back to the very arguments we sought to avoid. Is a structure that gives shareholders alone the right to elect board members the best way to maximize the value of a firm? Maybe, maybe not – but it all depends on the arguments that are made, not upon any actual or hypothetical agreements.

At this point, it should be clear that the hypothetical bargain is an empty concept. It's really just an opening that allows contractarians to try to link various governance features – including the exclusive shareholder franchise – to free choice and all its normative goodness. The bargain doesn't do any work by itself and may be used to justify virtually any corporate feature. As Jonathan Macey explains, "the analytical framework that the contracting paradigm provides for non-contractual law is not much of a constraint on policymakers, since virtually any decision that a judge makes can be justified as being consistent with the hypothetical bargain."[62] As a justification for the shareholder franchise, the hypothetical bargain ends up being a self-fulfilling prophecy.

Of course, the hypothetical bargain serves the same rhetorical purpose as the nexus of contracts theory: it makes the existing arrangements seem like a voluntary agreement among the parties. By conceiving of corporate law as what the parties *would* have bargained for, hypothetical bargainers can achieve a twofer: set corporate law as they desire but then claim that such arrangements represent the will of the participants. Ultimately, the whole enterprise is absurd. But the rhetoric enables these commentators to keep their "private ordering" priors while meddling when the parties do not play the game as expected.

The New Corporate Contract

In the last few years, the contract metaphor has been deployed in a new context: the "corporate contract" that supposedly exists between shareholders and the board. Like the more general nexus of contracts theory, the corporate contract approach views interactions between shareholders and management as primarily contractual in nature. In this instance, the corporate contract analysis has been extended to the specific mechanics of corporate governance: corporate charters and bylaws. Also known as the certificate or articles of incorporation, the corporate charter is the foundation document for the corporation and sets forth the basic structure of its governance, such as the board of directors and the creation and allocation of shares.[63] Bylaws govern interstitial rules of governance that can directly impact specific types of procedural actions or decisions.[64] Both the corporate charter and bylaws provide tools enabling these stakeholders to change the rules through which the corporation is governed. Courts and commentators have come to characterize these instruments of governance as the "corporate contract."[65] As described in one recent Delaware case, "the bylaws of a Delaware corporation constitute part of a binding broader contract among the directors, officers, and stockholders formed within [the state's] statutory framework."[66]

The idea of the "corporate contract" is generally used to justify the parties' use of charter amendments or bylaws as part of the rules of the game. Commentators who favor stronger shareholder participation in governance have argued that shareholders should have broad rights to propose and enact bylaws as part of their "contract" with the corporation.[67] With activist shareholders proposing bylaws concerning proxy access, forum selection, majority voting, advance notice, and litigation expenses,[68] parties have been litigating whether shareholders have the authority to make these changes without board approval. In recent cases, Delaware courts have upheld bylaws concerning forum selection[69] and litigation fee-shifting.[70] In these decisions, the courts have leaned heavily on the notion that these bylaws are part of the corporate contract between the shareholders, the board, and the corporation.[71] However, the Delaware Supreme Court did find that shareholders lacked the authority to propose a bylaw requiring the corporation to reimburse reasonable proxy solicitation expenses.[72] The bylaw, according to the court, improperly conflicted with the board's broad powers to manage the corporation.[73]

Once again, we find the idea of the corporation as contract being used as a metaphor, and not a very useful one at that. First, charters and bylaws are instruments of governance. The whole point of having a system of governance is to create a mechanism beyond simple contract that structures the relationships. As Delaware recognizes, bylaws themselves are supposed to focus on procedural matters rather than substantive business matters.[74] They clearly relate to governance.[75] If the legitimacy of the particular bylaw is in question, it can be justified through the nature of the democratic process through which it was enacted, or it can be struck down as beyond the authority of shareholders to enact. There is no need to layer the additional metaphor of "contract" on top of what are clearly mechanisms for managing relations between the parties.[76]

Second, the rhetoric of corporate contract has been used inconsistently to support a variety of different approaches to governance. Commentators often cite the corporate contract when advocating a hands-off or laissez-faire approach to shareholder-proposed bylaws.[77] Because the corporation allows shareholders to implement procedural rules in their own interests, goes the argument, corporate law should generally presume their enforceability. Delaware courts, however, have used the corporate contract rhetoric to justify board-enacted bylaws that arguably limit shareholder rights. For example, in *Boilermakers Local 154 Retirement Fund v. Chevron Corp.*, the Chevron and FedEx boards of directors adopted forum-selection bylaws naming Delaware courts as the exclusive forums for shareholder litigation. Shareholders then sued to render the bylaws invalid. The Delaware chancery court upheld the bylaws, relying in part on the idea of corporate contract. The then-chancellor Leo Strine explained:

> In an unbroken line of decisions dating back several generations, our Supreme Court has made clear that the bylaws constitute a binding part of the contract between a Delaware corporation and its stockholders. Stockholders are on notice that, as to those subjects that are subject of regulation by bylaw under 8 Del. C. § 109(b), the board itself may act unilaterally to adopt bylaws addressing those subjects. Such a change by the board is not extra-contractual simply because the board acts unilaterally; rather it is the kind of change that the overarching statutory and contractual regime the stockholders buy into explicitly allows the board to make on its own. In other words, the Chevron and FedEx stockholders have assented to a contractual framework established by the DGCL and the certificates of incorporation that explicitly recognizes that stockholders will be bound by bylaws adopted unilaterally by their boards. *Under that clear contractual framework, the stockholders assent to not having to assent to board-adopted bylaws.* The plaintiffs' argument that stockholders must approve a forum selection bylaw for it to be contractually binding is an interpretation that contradicts the plain terms of the contractual framework chosen by stockholders who buy stock in Chevron and FedEx. Therefore, when stockholders have authorized a board to unilaterally adopt bylaws, it follows that the bylaws are not contractually invalid simply because the board-adopted bylaw lacks the contemporaneous assent of the stockholders.[78]

Although acknowledging the argument "that board-adopted bylaws are not like other contracts because they lack the stockholders' assent," the Chancellor dismissed it as "a failure to appreciate the contractual framework established by the DGCL for Delaware corporations and their stockholders."[79]

It is almost a magic trick: take the shareholders' complete lack of power over a forum-selection clause and turn it into a contract.[80] Delaware even seems to allow the board to overturn a bylaw that the shareholders have passed to restrain the board.[81] If this is a contract, it would be an illusory one.[82] There are certainly valid normative reasons for constraining shareholder power and preserving board authority.[83] But cloaking such policy-making under the guise of corporate contract allows the court to make the shareholders responsible for their own disenfranchisement. A cynic might add that Delaware inconsistently deploys the contract metaphor to suit its own purposes. Forum-selection bylaws that choose Delaware, as well as loser-pays bylaws, are justified by the corporate contract; bylaws that require corporations to reimburse reasonable proxy solicitation expenses are not.[84]

Ultimately, the corporate contract between shareholders and the corporation is a system of governance, not a contract. The metaphor of contract blurs, rather than illuminates, the picture. Resolving whether shareholders or boards should have the authority to pass certain kinds of bylaws is a governance issue; framing it as a matter of contract adds nothing to the argument either way. The answers to these and other corporate governance puzzles are not to be found in the realm of offer, acceptance, consideration, and the parol evidence rule.

To return to the issue of corporate voting, the exclusive shareholder franchise, like many other aspects of corporate governance, is not a feature chosen by corporate participants. A corporation is more than a series of individual contracts, and hypothetical bargains fail to bridge the gap. The shareholder vote is not even something that all participants freely choose as part of a package of governance features, because not all participants participate equally in the initial choice of business form and, in any case, there are only a limited number of packages on the table. There are, in other words, all sorts of limitations on the exercise of free choice when it comes to various features of corporate governance. The contractarian view of the corporation is both descriptively wrong and normatively hollow, and is thus a deficient theoretical foundation for the existing features of corporate governance.

The Corporation as Firm

It is strange to see the amount of intellectual energy poured into the flawed nexus of contracts metaphor, especially when the whole idea of a corporation is to differentiate it from the world of contracts. Yes, the individual participants may contract with one another as part of their relationships within the corporation. But we have the corporate form to distinguish the organization and its set of relationships from the market and from general contractual relations. The corporate form – and its family of other business associations – were created by states to allow for a different approach to joint production.

As we discuss further in Chapter 9, corporations are economic firms, not simple contractual agglomerations. The theory of the firm is a branch of economics that is devoted to exploring the differences between firms and market-based transactions. Theorists such as Ronald Coase, Armen Alchian, Oliver Hart, and Oliver Williamson have endeavored to determine why some economic activity is carried out in the marketplace through contracts, while other activity is carried out within firms through direction and command. Firms are creatures of economics – they represent the ongoing businesses – but they are governed through legally created organizational forms such as partnerships, LLCs, and corporations. In order to ascertain why we have these forms in the first place, it makes sense to understand the underlying economic phenomenon of firms and what makes them economically, socially, and legally distinctive.

The nexus of contracts theory is something of an antitheory of the firm. It explains why firms are not necessary, rather than why they exist. Unlike the idea of a firm – which plays a real role in shaping, executing, and enforcing contracts with input providers – the "nexus" at the center of Jensen and Meckling's firm is a mere legal fiction that is *"not an individual"* and has no real independent existence.[85] Jensen and Meckling's model focuses on agency costs created by the upper-level managers who are tasked to do the bidding of principals. Their theory defines agency costs as the costs associated with monitoring by the principal, bonding expenditures by the agent, and the residual loss – in other words, the costs of having someone else manage your resources.[86] Ultimately, they argue that the corporation is a successful vehicle for business enterprises despite the existence of agency costs within the firm, and they explore how financial relationships are constructed to reduce agency costs without excess expense.

As other commentators have pointed out, the nexus of contracts theory is thus not really a theory of the firm at all. Rather, it is a theory of agency costs within a certain type of firm – namely, the corporation.[87] And upon close examination, it falls apart, at least as a theory of the firm, or as a justification for the corporation in the first place. If a corporation is really no more than a nexus of contracts, then there should be no need for corporations or corporate law. For if firms are not necessary as entities separate from the market, there is no need for the law to create and support them.[88] As has been repeatedly recognized, the nexus of contracts approach is not a theory of the firm because it "says nothing about why firms exist or what kind of activity is undertaken by a certain firm."[89]

Stephen Bainbridge, for example, claims to utilize the nexus of contracts theory in developing his director primacy theory of the corporation.[90] Bainbridge's model splits the theory of the firm question into two components: What are the ends for which the corporation exists, and what are the means of achieving those ends?[91] Bainbridge agrees that the goal of the corporation should be shareholder wealth maximization.[92] He believes, however, that control of the corporation rests not with the shareholders but rather with the board of directors that serves as the "Platonic guardian" of the firm.[93]

Bainbridge's theory is thus an amalgam of shareholder primacy and nexus of contracts theory but with important differences. Rather than saying that the firm is itself a nexus of contracts, he argues that the firm has a nexus of its contracts, and that the board is that nexus.[94] According to Bainbridge, the defining characteristic of a firm is "the existence of a central decision-maker vested with the power of fiat."[95] Rather than being participatory democracies, Bainbridge asseverates, firms provide for hierarchies that can direct the allocation of resources through command.[96] Bainbridge bases his theory on Ronald Coase's differentiation between markets and firms, as well as the notion that "firms arise when it is possible to lower these sets of costs inherent to team production by delegating to a team member the power to direct how the various inputs will be utilized by the firm."[97] Drawing upon Kenneth Arrow's *The Limits of Organization*,[98] he contrasts consensus-based decision-making structures with authority-based structures, and argues that the corporation fits Arrow's model of an authority-based system.[99] The board of directors serves as the ultimate seat of authority – the central decision-maker that contracts with all other players and directs them within the firm.

Bainbridge uses the theory of the firm literature to establish the basics of his model (as a combination of contracts and hierarchy) and then to defend its particular configuration of authority and purpose. It is arguably a continuation of Coase's original insight regarding firms, further elaborated with the hypothetical bargain used in law and economics analyses. Ultimately, however, Bainbridge fails to flesh out his theory sufficiently to justify the near absolute control he confers on the board. He repeatedly relies on Arrow's contrast between consensus and authority to resolve any questions of power allocation in favor of stronger authority. This move – characterized by Brett McDonnell as Bainbridge's "Arrowian moment" – is the crux of his model.[100] But, as McDonnell points out, Arrow's description of the trade-off between authority and accountability does not resolve all policy questions in favor of authority.[101] Ultimately, Arrow's dichotomy – and by extension, the director primacy model – is "not able to tell us whether reform in favor of somewhat more accountability at the expense of some, but far from total, loss in authority is a good idea or not."[102]

Moreover, there is nothing in Bainbridge's theory that requires the exclusive shareholder franchise. Shareholder wealth maximization is built into his model, but director primacy itself does not need shareholders to be the only members of the electorate. If we take the nexus of contracts model seriously, then any of the contractual partners should have the right to bargain for participation in the election of directors. Only by relying on the hypothetical bargain can the shareholder franchise be justified. And, as discussed earlier, this fictional agreement fails to justify the shareholder franchise independently.

Lynn Stout and Tamara Belinfanti developed another approach to corporate governance using systems theory.[103] Stout and Belinfanti argue that systems theory – a design and performance assessment methodology used in engineering, biology, computer science, and management science – better models the operation and function of business entities. Rather than limiting the firm to one undifferentiated whole, systems theory recognizes that independent subparts interlock together to create the larger unit. These subparts are distinct yet interconnected, and they operate together as a unit over time to serve a given function or purpose.[104] Studying a system thus involves acknowledging the many subsystems (and subsystems of subsystems) that make up the larger whole. A subsystem may have a specific subpurpose but still be committed overall to the organization's ultimate goals. Systems theorists would be wary of a single metric that purported to demonstrate the success of the entire organization – say, for example, share price.

Systems theory sounds a bit like a nexus of contracts; both involve interwoven and overlapping layers of relationships between various parties. Systems theory, however, recognizes that the firm is not just a set of independent relationships; it is rather a set of independent parts or groups that work together to serve a larger whole. These parts may not "naturally" come together, as does an agglomeration of contracts: there must be an overall structure that works to harmonize the subsystems. Rather than trusting that individual contracts will create a private order of maximal efficiency, systems theory looks to understand how successful organizations structure themselves to achieve that success.

In Chapter 9, we will delve more deeply into the concept of the corporation as a firm and play out the ramifications of looking at the corporation as an ongoing economic entity engaged in the process of joint production. Although the nexus of contracts theory masquerades as a theory of the firm, it is in fact an antitheory. It is an example of legal scholarship taking a concept from a brief passage in the finance literature and running with its ramifications. It is not an idea that has gotten serious exploration in the theory of the firm literature.

* * *

The exclusive shareholder franchise, like many other features of the modern corporation, is not the product of real or hypothetical bargaining among all corporate constituents. Nor is the result of those constituents freely shopping among various state law regimes for that, or any other, particular feature. The exclusive shareholder franchise will need to find its justification elsewhere.

Shareholder Homogeneity

One way to justify the exclusive shareholder franchise would be to point to some feature that makes shareholders different from other corporate constituents, different in a way that supports their special position in the corporation. Such a difference would obviously need to go beyond empty rhetorical claims – think of shareholders as "owners" – and describe some unique characteristic of shareholder interests or preferences that puts them in a position such that they, and they alone, should be accorded corporate voting rights. Such a difference would also help salvage the contractarian claim that all parties to a hypothetical bargain would choose to assign corporate voting power to shareholders. So how are shareholders different from other constituents? And do those differences support the grant of exclusive voting rights to them?

The most obvious difference between shareholders and other constituents follows the nature of their interests, which, of course, turns on their role in the corporation. Shareholders contribute capital, workers contribute labor, customers buy products, and creditors lend funds. These different roles result in different beliefs and desires about the firm and firm decision-making. But this alone doesn't get us very far, and few scholars have relied on this type of difference to make their arguments. Merely asserting that particular interests are more important and thus more deserving of governance powers is a little like calling shareholders owners and thus assigning them voting rights. It does not shed much light on basic questions of firm governance. The whole point of a system of a preference aggregation system is that we don't prejudge which kinds of preferences are more or less important, or who's more likely to be "right."

We can (and do) make some basic judgments about the relative strength of people's interests with respect to certain institutional decisions. We can make an educated guess that an average worker probably has a much stronger interest in corporate decision-making than an average shareholder, and that both probably have a stronger interest than an average customer. But whether all workers, taken together, have a stronger interest than all shareholders is a more dubious proposition. As we saw in earlier chapters, anyone designing a system of preference aggregation needs to make some basic decisions about whose preferences need aggregating, and those with a greater stake in the enterprise lead the list. When it comes to corporations, there are certainly people that we can say have a greater interest in firm decisions – shareholders and workers typically have a significant stake in the firm, but other groups, depending on the type of corporation, are somewhere behind them. Scholars, however, have not made extensive use of these distinctions between constituents in developing or justifying their theories of firm governance.

Instead, many scholars looking to support the exclusive shareholder franchise have pointed to what they view as a unique feature of shareholder preferences – their uniformity. The claim is that, unlike other corporate constituents, shareholders have homogeneous preferences with respect to the corporation. More specifically, they are thought to have a uniform interest in wealth maximization. Frank Easterbrook and Daniel Fischel rely to a great degree on the claim that shareholders are likely to have "similar if not identical" interests because "the shareholders of a given firm at a given time are a reasonably homogenous group."[1] Robert Thompson and Paul Edelman, in their "error correction" theory of corporate voting, also rely upon this characteristic to some degree, explaining, "Shareholders are the unique homogeneous constituency who are sensitive to the stock price, which is a decent proxy for the interests of the corporation."[2] In Chapters 6 and 7, we'll see exactly how this claim of shareholder homogeneity grounds these and some of the other prominent arguments for the exclusive shareholder franchise.

The problem with these arguments, though, is that the claim of shareholder homogeneity has come under quite a bit of pressure over the last two decades. Shareholders, it turns out, are not single-minded wealth maximizers. Shaun Martin and Frank Partnoy flatly pointed out in 2004 that "[i]t is simply not true that the 'preferences of [shareholders] are likely to be similar if not identical.'"[3] Martin and Partnoy were focusing on the problems caused by equity derivatives, which carve up various shareholder rights into discrete financial securities. But there are many ways in which shareholders fail to share common interests – many opportunities for conflict along what have been called "horizontal power relations."[4] Shareholders preferences are not homogeneous in new ways as well as old. The remainder of this chapter catalogs the many axes along which the commonality of shareholder interests may splinter.

The Problem of the Control Group: Majority Rule and Minority Oppression

The notion of shareholder homogeneity assumes that all shareholders are similarly situated and share similar preferences. However, shareholders may have very different economic interests depending on a variety of factors. Perhaps the most fundamental difference is the difference between a shareholder who is in a control group and a shareholder who is not in a control group. A control group is a grouping of shares, held by one person or a small consortium of cooperating individuals, that have a sufficient percentage to exercise practical control over corporate governance. A corporation does not necessarily have a control group – for example, if shares are distributed widely among public shareholders with no one holding over 5 percent. But if a corporation – public or closely held – has a control entity or control group, then the interests of the majority are likely to differ from those of the minority.

The primary benefit of control is the right to apportion the benefits of control entirely to oneself while sharing the costs of such control with the minority shareholders. For example, Corporation X has A as a 52 percent shareholder, while the remaining shareholders, B, C, and D, each own 16 percent. If A appoints herself as the chief executive officer, she will get 100 percent of the benefits of her salary. However, since the corporation as a whole pays the salary, A will only incur (by extension) 52 percent of the costs. Similarly, if A sells a valuable asset of Corporation X to another company that she owns by herself, she will have a strong incentive to underprice the asset. In her management of the corporation, A will have a clear incentive to use her control to drain away corporate assets for her own personal benefit.

The structure of the corporation's control mechanisms is ill-equipped to deal with this basic problem. Most corporations are arranged under a "majority rules" system, in which each director is elected by a majority vote of all of the shareholders. Some states allow corporations to opt for cumulative voting, in which each shareholder has a set of votes to distribute among the entire slate of directors.[5] Cumulative voting allows for minority shareholders to have representation on the board. But cumulative voting is relatively rare, especially in Delaware corporations,[6] and even under cumulative voting the majority shareholder still controls the corporation. This system of majority control sets up the fundamental problem of minority shareholders not having any control or even input.[7]

This structural problem has led to supplemental doctrines intended to ameliorate or eliminate the effects of majority rule. The fiduciary duty of loyalty, for example, is an implied, mandatory duty for all corporate directors and officers. It requires them to act in the interests of the corporation as a whole, rather than in their own personal interests. Because the duty applies to directors, it applies by extension to majority shareholders, as their board representatives will be subject to this duty. However, controlling shareholders also have a duty of loyalty to the corporation's minority shareholders.[8] The duty of loyalty has a structural governance element, in that conflict transactions can find a safe harbor through approval by a majority of shareholders or independent directors.[9] However, in Delaware such transactions can also survive the conflict through an after-the-fact "entire fairness" test.[10] Thus, there is some flexibility and discretion in the administration of the duty.

Another mechanism for constraining the majority is the duty of care, which requires directors and officers to act with the level of ordinary care expected of a reasonably prudent person.[11] This rule is designed more to counteract agency costs, but it does prevent the majority from running the company in a way that may seem irrational to others. However, the strength of the rule is severely limited by the business judgment rule, which provides that directors and officers are free to use their own business judgment in making managerial decisions.[12] As a result, the duty of care has largely become a mechanism for requiring directors and officers to be appropriately informed about the corporation's operations and financial health.[13] In the past, the doctrine of ultra vires was also used to cabin the majority's discretion on business matters. The doctrine held that corporate directors and officers were not permitted to act on behalf of the corporation outside the scope of the corporation's purpose. This limitation could, for example, be interpreted as preventing a corporate board from giving a large charitable donation to the majority shareholder's pet charity. However, given the expansive and nonspecific nature of most corporations' "purposes," as designated in the corporate charter, the ultra vires doctrine no longer has much effect.

Finally, the doctrine of minority oppression is designed as a backstop in cases involving matters in which the majority generally has discretion to operate. The doctrine is applied to closely held corporations in which shareholders participate in the company as both shareholders and employees. Because there is no outside market for shares in a closely held corporation, shareholders cannot sell their shares and exit if they disagree with the majority's direction. The difficulty of exit has led some courts to rule that shareholders in closely held corporations must treat each other as more akin to partners and with "utmost good faith and loyalty."[14] This duty is defined ambiguously in order to capture a range of discretionary activities that would not breach other fiduciary duties on their face.[15] These discretionary activities would in theory be seen as opportunities to be enjoyed by all participants in the corporation, rather than being reserved for the exclusive benefit of the control group. As one court put it:

> A shareholder who reasonably expected that ownership in the corporation would entitle him or her to a job, a share of corporate earnings, a place in corporate management, or some other form of security, would be oppressed in a very real sense when others in the corporation seek to defeat those expectations and there exists no effective means of salvaging the investment.[16]

In his article on the history of the shareholder primacy norm, Gordon Smith argued that in the nineteenth century the norm served as the foundation for the doctrine of minority oppression.[17] According to Smith, notions of shareholder primacy were actually generated to resolve horizontal conflicts between different groups of shareholders. As he points out, the seminal "shareholder primacy" case – *Dodge v. Ford Motor Co.*[18] – actually involved a dispute between two groups of shareholders about the direction of the company.[19] In *Dodge*, the court required Ford Motor to issue dividends to its stockholders. The court used the language of shareholder primacy to compel the controlling shareholder (Ford) to distribute profits to minority shareholders (the Dodge brothers). Refusal to issue dividends is a classic example of minority oppression. Smith pointed out that this development of the shareholder primacy doctrine has much more to do with horizontal relations between shareholders and much less to do with the vertical relations between directors, shareholders, and other corporate constituents.[20]

Thus, there are a number of "softer" doctrines designed to deal with the structural differences between the interests of majority and minority shareholders. However, as has been noted, finding a balance between these interests can be difficult, since the majority has legitimate interests in exercising its right of control.[21] These interests will conflict with those of minority shareholders, particularly over issues such as control of the corporation, employment opportunities, dividends, and other means of sharing the surplus.

The Problem of Differential Voting Powers Among Shares

As discussed in Chapter 3, the efficiency of the one share, one vote hypothesis assumes that each share has the right to an equal portion of the residual interest. Otherwise, voting shareholders will have different incentives depending on the ratio of voting power to residual interests. A shareholder with strong voting power but a reduced interest in the residual will have different incentives than a shareholder with less voting power and a greater stake in the profits. Easterbrook and Fischel noted that the "most basic statutory rule" of shareholder voting was the default rule of one share, one vote, and that this was "the same in every state."[22] They also claimed that agreements to alter this default rule were rare.[23] However, there is evidence that they may have been writing at the high water mark of such a norm, and that differential voting powers among shares may have become more common than in the past.[24]

Easterbrook and Fischel were writing in the wake of the Securities and Exchange Commission's adoption of Rule 19c-4.[25] The rule required self-regulatory organizations, such as the New York Stock Exchange or NASDAQ, to prohibit listed companies from issuing securities that reduced the rights of existing shareholders. The purpose of the rule was to reinforce the one share, one vote standard by prohibiting the issuance of shares with disproportionate voting rights.[26] However, the rule was struck down by the D.C. Circuit and was never revived.[27] The exchanges allow companies with multiple-class shares, including nonvoting stock, to be listed; however, certain safeguards are required before such shares can be listed.[28]

Although scholars still call for the abolition of dual-class voting structures,[29] they appear to be here to stay. Several recent shareholder controversies have involved corporations with dual-class shares. Many of the biggest and hottest tech companies – Google, Facebook, Snap, and (formerly hot) WeWork – have dual-class or even nonvoting shares.[30] The New York Times and the Wall Street Journal were long controlled by families with shares that have voting power disproportionate to their economic stake.[31] Critics have claimed that the individual entrepreneurs or controlling families do not have the proper incentives because they do not have the same economic risk as the other shareholders.[32] However, such criticisms are subject to the rebuttal that shareholders knew what they were getting when they purchased the stock. Indeed, that is the general justification for multiple-vote or no-vote shares: corporate law should facilitate private ordering, which includes the possibility that certain shareholders will accept less control as part of the bargain. Less control probably means a cheaper price, and shareholders should be permitted to make this bargain if they wish to do so.[33] However, from the perspective of shareholder wealth maximization, shareholders with more control and less risk will have skewed incentives in maximizing shareholder wealth.

In addition to dual-class shareholders, there are certain groups of shareholders – primarily holders of preferred shares – who have voting rights that change depending on the circumstances. The primary purpose of a preferred share is to give the holder the right to a regular dividend of a specific amount, with priority over common-stock shareholders. Holders of preferred shares do not generally have straightforward voting rights within the corporation on matters such as the election of directors.[34] However, many preferred shares have clauses that give each preferred share the right to vote under certain circumstances, such as the failure to pay the regular dividend.[35] Often, preferred shares are given some multiple of common-share votes for each share – for example, ten votes in the election for each share of preferred stock. Thus, once certain circumstances trigger these rights, preferred shareholders go from non-voters to supervoters. Bondholders may have similar clauses of protection when, for example, the corporation misses a payment.

Thus, the notion of a uniform shareholder polity is often factually incorrect. Dual-class shares, as well as convertible shares, provide control rights to groups that are not aligned with those groups' interests in the residual. In fact, preferred shares often hold voting rights in order to give the holders of such shares, in certain circumstances, the right to trump the concerns of the common shareholders.[36]

The Problem of Shareholder Vote Buying and Voting Trusts

Corporate law generally prohibits shareholders from selling their right to vote without simultaneously transferring the underlying interest in the residual.[37] The converse is also true, although courts have allowed for the theoretical possibility that the seller of stock could retain the vote in order to protect a legal interest.[38] With regard to bribery – paying a shareholder to vote a particular way – there has been a shift in the law. In the past, vote bribery was not permitted – it was seen as a violation of a shareholder's duty to other shareholders.[39] Over time, however, the rule has become more permissive.

In *Schreiber v. Carney*,[40] the company was seeking shareholder approval of a corporate restructuring in the wake of a merger. The company, Texas International Airlines, needed shareholder approval, and it needed majority approval from each class of stock, which included not only common stock but also three series of convertible preferred stock. Jet Capital held a majority of shares in one of the preferred stock series as well as warrants for a large number of common shares. Jet determined that if the restructuring went through, it would incur a large tax liability unless it had already exercised the warrants. However, it did not have enough cash on hand to exercise the warrants. Thus, it decided that it would have to vote against the merger. In order to resolve this difficulty, Texas International decided to lend money to Jet so that it could exercise the warrants.

The Delaware Chancery Court upheld the loan against a challenge of vote buying. The court recognized two principles behind the general prohibition against vote buying: (1) protecting shareholders against fraud and deceit, and (2) requiring shareholders to exercise their own independent judgment.[41] The court found no hint of fraud or deceit in the instant case, as it was in the other shareholders' interests to bribe Jet into voting for the restructuring. Indeed, Texas International had already secured approval for the loan from other shareholders.[42] The court recognized that shareholders had different interests and that it may be in the interests of certain shareholders to work with other shareholders in developing a negotiated solution. As for the independent judgment principle, its traditional justification was that "by requiring each stockholder to exercise his individual judgment as to all matters presented, the security of the small stockholders is found in the natural disposition of each stockholder to promote the best interests of all, in order to promote his individual interests."[43] However, the court found that this rationale was "obsolete because it is both impracticable and impossible of application to modern corporations with many widely scattered stockholders."[44] Instead, the court held the loan transaction to a standard of entire fairness.[45]

Voting trusts are somewhat analogous to vote buying in that two voters agree to bind their votes to each other, rather than to their independent self-interest. The Delaware corporation statute, for example, allows parties to contract with each other to vote the same way.[46] The statute allows for a great deal of flexibility – one party may agree to vote as directed by another party in exchange for consideration. In addition, parties may put their shares into a voting trust that is subsequently voted by a trustee.[47] What these arrangements demonstrate is that corporations are not simply a mass of like-minded individuals who are all voting based upon the same self-interest. Instead, conflicts between shareholders may arise, and corporate law allows for mechanisms to resolve them contractually. Given the emphasis on private ordering in corporation law generally, it would make sense to allow for these private arrangements. However, these arrangements contradict the notion of shareholders as a mass of undifferentiated profit seekers.

The Problem of Hedging the Residual Interest

As discussed above, selling the vote separately from the stock is generally prohibited, and vote "bribes" are subjected to the fairly rigorous "entire fairness" scrutiny. However, new financial derivative products are making it easier to vote in shareholder elections while at the same time having interests divergent from traditional shareholder interests. In effect, shareholders are able to engage in "empty voting," in which they vote their shares without having the same financial stake in the game as other shareholders.

How does this work? The simplest way is to purchase shares in the company while simultaneously shorting the stock. The stock can be shorted through equity derivatives that increase in value as the share price falls.[48] Thus, a party will have countervailing interests – the stock will still have its residual attached, but the "short" position will reward a drop in the price of the stock. If the short position is strong enough, the shareholder will actually be encouraged to act against the interests of the corporation in order to trigger a decrease in the share price. There are also less extreme possibilities that would nevertheless allow shareholders to vote despite a complex set of interests that do not overlap with other shareholders. For example, in 2004, Perry Corporation bought 9.9 percent of the shares in Mylan Labs and voted in favor of a merger between Mylan and King Pharmaceuticals.[49] Perry acquired the stake because it owned King, and it wanted Mylan to agree to the merger. However, Perry also hedged its voting stake in Mylan through a series of equity swaps and other undisclosed transactions. Thus, Perry acquired voting power in Mylan while simultaneously hedging the residual interest in Mylan. Perry was sued by another Mylan shareholder for voting without true economic ownership; the case, however, was rendered moot when Mylan called off the merger with King.

Another potential for vote buying is through the borrowing of shares specifically around the record date – the date on which shareholders are locked in as the voting polity for purposes of the election at hand.[50] The object of this transaction is to borrow the share specifically for the vote, and then return it to the original owner after the vote. Lending shares for a short period of time is a fairly common practice; it is designed to facilitate short selling by making the shares available for sale when the short comes due. But if the borrowing is done not to facilitate a short sale, but rather to allow a borrower to vote without economic risk, the practice looks fairly close to vote selling.

Why would shareholders lend their votes to someone else – someone whose interests might be counter to theirs? The main reason is money, coupled with ignorance. Financial institutions can lend out the shares for a fee and make money while at the same time keeping the share and the residual. Given the lack of importance or drama in most share-holder votes, these institutions have not really focused on the possibi-lity that borrowers could be targeting shares not to facilitate a short, but rather for the vote. In fact, fund managers have been caught unawares by borrowers who use the vote contrary to the managers' interests.[51] If the practice becomes more widespread, shareholders will likely take more steps to prevent vote borrowing. But the complexity of many of these transactions may make monitoring them more and more difficult.

The Problem of Management, Employee, and Pension Fund Shareholders

When considering the kaleidoscope of potential financial interests among shareholders, there is one financial interest that perhaps is more important than all of the others: employment. For most people, their job is the single most important financial interest that they have. In a diversified portfolio, shares in one particular company are close to irrelevant – it is the overall health of the portfolio that matters. However, one cannot diversify one's employment portfolio to any sig-nificant degree. Thus, if one holds a job at as well as shares in a particular company, the effect of the vote on one's employment is likely to deter-mine how one would choose to vote the shares.

Certainly, there are similarities between the interests of a shareholder and the interests of an employee. Both wish the company to perform well. But within the organization, shareholders and employees have different interests when it comes to issues like the level of risk the company should bear, how employees are to be compensated, and how the surplus is to be split. Particularly when it comes to mergers and acquisitions, employees might have very different interests from shareholders if the transaction will bring downsizing or worker replacement.[52] Conversely, employees with shares as well as stock options might choose to vote their shares so as to increase the potential for upside risk.[53] Stock options may have led employees to favor a strategy of short-term stock appreciation without due regard for the potential for downside risk.[54] In the late 1990s, employees may have been more concerned about their stock and stock option holdings than their job; even so, they had different interests than those shareholders who did not also hold options.[55]

Pension fund shareholders have received significant attention lately for their increasingly visible activities in the realm of corporate governance.[56] Teaming with other institutional investors, pension funds have taken the lead in promoting greater shareholder involvement in corporate issues such as shareholder nominations for directors and approval of executive compensation. Some commentators who are otherwise committed to shareholder primacy draw a distinction between these activist pension fund shareholders and other shareholders.[57] Since pension funds are often run by unions, commentators accuse pension fund leaders of pursuing their own proworker agenda when it comes to shareholder proposals, director votes, and other shareholder matters.[58] Fund-manager discretion is limited, as the Employee Retirement Income Security Act requires pension fund managers to run the fund in the sole financial interests of the fund participants. But there is room within this discretion to pursue various agendas that have ramifications beyond corporate governance and share price.

Specifically singled out for concern are pension funds for government employees. For years, the biggest player in the corporate governance arena has been CalPERS, the pension fund for approximately 1.5 million California state and local employees. The CalPERS board is made up of directors elected by the fund participants, directors appointed by the governor along with other state officials, and ex officio directors who are state officials or agency appointees.[59] CalPERS has long been active in corporate governance and has its own "Focus List" of companies that had questionable corporate governance practices.[60] However, CalPERS has been criticized for pursuing its governance agendas overzealously and for caring more about workers' rights than profits. Most notoriously, the CalPERS 2004 corporate governance campaign against

Safeway was characterized as a "jihad"; critics maintained it was a response to Safeway's harsh stance in labor negotiations, rather than to real concerns about underperformance.[61] Ever since, the Safeway incident has served as a rallying cry for the divergent interests between pension funds and "regular" shareholders when it comes to labor.[62]

Despite the potential conflicts between employee-affiliated shareholders and the other shareholders, commentators have not called for such shareholders to be deprived of the franchise. And for the most part, the law has encouraged management and employee ownership of equity interests in their corporation. In fact, the notion of "pay for performance" led to the exponential growth of stock options as a compensation device throughout the 1990s.[63] Agency costs would be reduced and investors would feel more secure, it was argued, if investors knew that the managers and executives also had their income riding on the success of the stock. But such shareholders clearly have different interests than their nonemployee counterparts.

The Problem of Sovereign Wealth Funds

Yet another category of shareholder has caused consternation among corporate law theorists. These shareholders are not individuals, companies, or private funds but, in effect, countries – political states. Known as sovereign wealth funds, these governmental financial entities have attracted a fair amount of attention from the media and scholars. And there is no real consensus on how they should be handled.

Sovereign wealth funds (SWFs) are not a new phenomenon. The oldest such funds have been around for more than fifty years and have operated with little attention.[64] Essentially, an SWF is a fund owned and operated by a country. Unlike state-owned banks or enterprises, however, SWFs are investment funds that have national funding and pay their dividends to a state government. Pension funds can be characterized as SWFs, but they are generally not included unless they are financed through state commodity exports.[65] These funds also vary in their investment strategies. Some invest primarily in government bonds (such as U.S. T-bills), while others invest more aggressively in private companies. A few funds have actually sought to take significant stakes in corporations, while many others have pursued a quieter strategy of private investment.[66] Most recent estimates place the collective wealth of SWFs at around $10–$15 trillion on a global basis, far more than the amount invested in hedge funds.[67]

The notion of foreign countries investing in private corporations is troubling to many. The most obvious concern would be a foreign government taking over an otherwise private corporation, particularly one with links to national security. The United States has erected a system of oversight for all foreign acquisitions of U.S. companies: such transactions are reviewed by the Committee on Foreign Investment in the United States (CFIUS).[68] There is an automatic forty-five-day review process whenever a foreign government seeks a controlling interest in a U.S. corporation.[69] The 2019 U.S. ban on the Chinese company Huawei illustrates the potential for conflicting loyalties.[70]

Control of private corporations by foreign powers is not the only worry surrounding SWF share ownership. Since SWFs are controlled by foreign governments, they may have interests divergent from those of the traditional private shareholder. In fact, many see a sinister side to the investments from countries such as Abu Dhabi, Russia, and China. These countries' funds have taken significant stakes in Citibank,[71] the Blackstone Group,[72] and Advanced Micro Devices, a chipmaker with Department of Defense contracts.[73] These holdings trigger concerns not only about security issues, but also financial and internal governance issues.[74] SWFs could use their voting power as shareholders to effectuate their governmental agenda, rather than the agenda of shareholder wealth maximization.[75] As one set of commentators puts it, the threat is that the SWFs will engage in "strategic behavior – behavior that benefits the SWF or its sovereign owner in ways that do not proportionately benefit other shareholders."[76]

For some, these potential motives are so threatening that they counsel for the suspension of SWF voting rights in the corporation. National security and welfare concerns may justify restrictions on SWF takeovers and tender offers. The voting power of an SWF's shares could also be suspended for as long as the SWF holds the stock.[77] Alternatively, SWFs may either voluntarily agree not to vote their shares or to disclose how they voted.[78]

SWFs are yet another example of a shareholder with potential "ulterior" motives.[79] It is hard to see, however, why these potentially ulterior motives should disqualify them from voting. The most distressing potential example is the SWF using its voting power to secure favor for its own domestic industries or companies.[80] However, without a controlling interest, it seems unlikely that the SWF would succeed in effectuating its policy, especially if it was a blatant rent-seeking endeavor. Assuming the SWF has a significant but noncontrolling stake, the SWF would need to rally the support of a majority of shareholders in order to effectuate its scheme. The tension would thus resolve itself – either a majority would fail to sign on, rendering the strategic behavior moot, or a majority would agree with the SWF that the plan was in their best interests. Neither event seems to warrant taking away the SWF's ability to vote. A more realistic concern, perhaps, is that SWFs would join with other "nontraditional" shareholders (such as union pension funds and socially responsible investment vehicles) to promote policies based on political concerns rather than wealth maximization.[81] Or SWFs may potentially be more acquiescent to management in an effort to appear as "passive investors." In such cases, SWFs may stifle the efforts of more active shareholders to hold management accountable.[82] Further restrictions on the franchise, however, seem based less on actual security concerns and more on the notion of what a true shareholder should believe. The limitation of SWF voting rights would be yet another deviation from the standard of one share, one vote that is deemed necessary to protect the underlying principle.

The Problem of Defining "Wealth Maximization"

The assumption behind the one share, one vote norm is that shareholders have a uniform interest in wealth maximization. Since all shareholders are entitled to part of the residual, they all have an interest in maximizing the size of that residual. The notion that shareholder wealth maximization is not only a goal for the corporation but in fact the only legitimate goal has become the dominant normative theory of the corporation. Indeed, Hansmann and Kraakman have proclaimed the dominance of this view: "there is no longer any serious competitor to the view that corporate law should principally strive to increase long-term shareholder value."[83]

Even assuming a mass of shareholders with no other complications or interests, there are still difficulties in implementing the notion of shareholder wealth maximization. The main problem is *when*. What is the time horizon for wealth maximization? Hansmann and Kraakman specify "long-term shareholder value" but do not define it. And in fact, shareholders have radically different time horizons for the maximization of their shareholder wealth.[84] Some shareholders may buy the stock at the time of the initial public offering and hold it until it passes to their heirs and assignees. But other shareholders hold the stock for a day, a week, a month. There are some shareholders who also have options, and they would want to max out on the stock at the option exercise date.[85] Participants in passive index funds no longer hold the share once it drops out of a particular index.[86] There are some shareholders who have yearly or quarterly profit margins to meet, and they need the stock to rise to meet those horizons. There are some shareholders who buy the stock with their sights set on a takeover, and then either buy all of the stock or walk away; other shareholders buy the stock on a bet that the takeover attempt will succeed.

Ultimately, there are very different notions of what "wealth maximization" means. Let us take, for example, a corporation whose shares have been trading at $35. A takeover firm offers shareholders $45 for the stock. The board believes that if they fight off this tender offer for a period of time but ultimately agree to the takeover, shareholders will eventually get $50 for their shares within two months. But the board also believes that technology in development will eventually lead the stock to be worth $100 two years from now, if the current management remains in place. However, if the technology fails, the shares will be worth only $20. What is the best path toward wealth maximization? Believers in a strong efficient capital markets hypothesis will argue that the $45 is the best choice, as will short-term shareholders. But shareholders with a medium-term horizon may want the board to resist and shoot for $50 per share. Those with even longer-term horizons may hope the board fights off the offer entirely and remains in place, aiming for the $100 share price down the road.

Because uncertainties multiply as the timescale lengthens, shareholder primacy becomes more and more meaningless as it stretches from short to long term. Paying high wages to employees or corporate management can be justified based on retention of key talent or reduction in turnover, leading to longer-term value. Customer goodwill justifies slashed prices or expensive research and development. As one commentator has argued, "the mantra of [shareholder wealth] maximization has no distinctive meaning and policy implications if it is not interpreted to mean maximization of short-term value."[87] However, maximization of short-term shareholder value leads to short-time horizons that can cripple business planning and stability. Moreover, a short-term focus encourages corporate fraud and misreporting designed to bolster the stock price now (with the possibly bad consequences to come later).[88]

In addition, shareholders with a diversified portfolio have different interests than shareholders with most of their wealth tied up in one company.[89] Fully diversified shareholders, who have been referred to as "universal owners,"[90] have a stake in corporate success as a whole. Their notion of wealth maximization will be quite different from a shareholder who has invested entirely in a particular company. Scholars have argued that portfolio shareholders prefer a policy of portfolio value maximization, rather than individual firm value maximization.[91] In contrast, undiversified shareholders have an incentive to oppose transactions that maximize wealth for all shareholders by increasing the value of one firm by more than the decrease in value at the shareholders' firm.[92] Commentators have argued that a hands-off approach to vote selling and buying is appropriate, as vote buying may be necessary to allow diversified shareholders to pull off transactions that actually hurt shareholders at the company. The portfolio shareholders would buy the votes necessary to carry off the transaction as long as the transaction creates overall positive value for the portfolio.[93]

The notion of maximization of portfolio value strikes at the heart of the shareholder primacy norm. Under this theory, social wealth will not be maximized if each firm seeks to maximize returns for its own shareholders. Instead, social wealth depends not on the actions of individual companies, but on the actions of all companies in the economy. What this means is that, in some instances, it would be more efficient (on a societal level) for a company to do something that decreased its own shareholders' wealth. Yet directors would be violating their fiduciary duties if they went forward with the transaction, since it would harm the company's shareholders. This example demonstrates yet another axis on which shareholders split into different groups based on different interests.

The Problem of Utility Maximization

Finally, we must consider the possibility that shareholders will, in fact, choose something very different from wealth maximization as their goal for the corporation. Descriptively, shareholders are assumed to be rational actors, and thus are assumed to desire the maximization of their utility. Although scholars recognize that utility can come in many forms, the role of "shareholder" is seen as easily translatable into a wealth-based utility model. In other words, since shareholders invest money in stock in order to make more money (through dividends and appreciation of stock price), the utility of holding the stock seems to be derived solely from the financial appreciation of the stock. Conveniently for law and economics theory, this assumed reality is also normatively the optimal outcome, since (as economic theory provides) self-interested shareholders will push to maximize the corporation's residual profits, which in turn will maximize the social wealth generated by the corporation.

Despite the importance of wealth, however, not all shareholders maximize their utility through a program of shareholder wealth maximization.[94] Instead, some shareholders may gain utility through lower profits but higher levels of some other good. A number of Disney shareholders hold the stock because of their fondness for Disney animation,[95] and many of these shareholders attend annual meetings in order to celebrate their association with the company.[96] These shareholders played an important role in the no-confidence vote against Michael Eisner in 2004, in which 43 percent of shareholders voted to withhold their votes from him.[97]

Beyond these individual instances, the success of ESG (environmental, social, and governance) investment funds is testament to interests that are outside the simple profits model. As individuals, most shareholders do not generally have sufficient power to justify the time and energy required to vote their shares according to their overall social utility, as opposed to just their wealth. Increasingly, however, investors are putting their money into socially responsible funds – funds that invest in companies that meet certain social responsibilities targets or thresholds.[98] At the start of 2018, there were about $12 trillion in assets under management in the broad category of sustainable and responsible investing, a number that had grown 38 percent over the previous two years.[99] Such funds often underperform the market as a whole.[100] However, their popularity attests to the desires of some investors to promote companies that adhere to certain principles beyond wealth maximization. As the number of socially responsible funds increases, investment houses are diversifying the types of such funds to appeal to a broader variety of investors. Alongside funds favoring companies based on labor or environmental policies, there are funds that invest based on Catholic social teaching, as well as funds that invest in companies that donate to Democratic candidates.[101]

Furthermore, the notion that shareholders have a shared interest in wealth maximization is a simplifying assumption. Shareholders are heterogeneous with respect to their utility preferences in that these preferences do not match up directly with wealth. A recent article by Oliver Hart and Luigi Zingales affirms the economics of this basic point.[102] Taking on the wealth maximization perspective of Milton

Friedman, Hart and Zingales argue that it is "too narrow" to simply associate wealth maximization with actual shareholder preferences. Their model shows that in the face of trade-offs, "Friedman's conclusions do not hold: shareholder welfare is not equivalent to market value."[103] Instead, shareholders should have the right to vote not only for representatives but also on the broad outlines of corporate policy. This expression of preferences, they argue, would do a better job in steering the corporation toward economic activities that match the actual choices that shareholders would make between competing values.

It may be that the overwhelming desire of most shareholders is simple wealth maximization. But it may also be that the new era of socially responsible consumerism and investing, when coupled with the shareholder democracy movement, will lead shareholders to support policies that do not directly correlate with wealth maximization. In the end, a system based on and legitimated by shareholder control must admit the possibility that shareholders may choose not to maximize profits.[104] If shareholders choose this route more frequently, a normative theory that justifies the shareholder vote based on the efficiency of shareholder wealth maximization may in fact find that the shareholder vote is no longer the best tool for achieving it.

The Problem of Market Hegemony

The norm of shareholder wealth maximization may actually reveal a shortcoming in the application of the economic theory of shareholder voting (and many other aspects of commercial behavior).[105] Most economic models, for example, treat profit maximization as the sole objective of corporations; nonmarket values are to be (appropriately) ignored.[106] And indeed, there is plenty of evidence that most corporations really do make decisions based on these profit-maximizing considerations.[107] Shareholders tend to vote on those considerations.[108] Consumers, too, tend to focus on bottom-line considerations when making their marketplace decisions.[109] Everyone, it seems, focuses on the bottom line when acting in market contexts. This is in marked contrast, by the way, to how people behave in political elections – indeed, it has been suggested that people's votes in political elections are driven by generalized "values," while their votes in the marketplace are driven by individual "tastes."[110]

Markets, then, are hegemonic: people act for personal gain, and other values are only reflected in what they do with that gain.[111] Both proponents and critics of markets agree on this point – their disagreement turns on whether this is a good or a bad thing.[112] Either way, however, economic theory should account for the fact of market hegemony. The traditional explanation is that acting on nonmarket values (social values, prejudices) is costly and market competition drives out high-cost competitors.[113] But this is just bad economics. Standard economic theory tells us that markets should reflect consumer values, not shape them. And those preferences, taken as given, show that people care about a large variety of things, many of which are not self-focused.[114] While economic theory does a good job explaining what happens when people act solely on bottom-line considerations, this just shows that the theory presupposes market hegemony, not that it explains it.

Standard economic theory may not give a good account of market hegemony, because it posits that people are consulting all of their desires and beliefs when making decisions. In other words, their utility functions are univocal and fixed (or, to the extent that they change, they change slowly).[115] For that reason, economic theory lacks the resources to explain why, for example, people appear to consult their "other-regarding" values in some (nonmarket) situations and not in other (market) situations. The "on-again, off again" nature of people's preferences is also unlikely to be adequately captured by some of the basic extensions of economics, like the various versions of the multiple-selves model.[116] A more convincing extension of economics is one that posits that people do not consult their entire set of preferences when making decisions, but instead rely on a proper subset of their interests.[117] This would account for the highly contextual nature of action generally and further explain why people seem to be attending to only bottom-line considerations when making decisions in market contexts.

Perhaps this just confirms what was discussed above: that restricting voting rights to shareholders drives the wealth maximization norm rather than the other way around. When people are voting as shareholders, they are acting in one of those market contexts that activate all of their bottom-line desires and not their other values. Just as looking at a glass of cold water may focus one's attention on one's thirst, staring at a prospectus may make one focus on a corporation's profitability. A shareholder's interaction with a corporation, in other words, is structured in such a way as to lead naturally to a focus on profit maximization. It does not, however, tell us that shareholders or others do not have nonpecuniary interests in the corporation – those interests are just not always being adequately reflected in the corporate voting scheme.

* * *

Over the past two decades, it has become increasingly clear that shareholders do not have homogeneous preferences with respect to their corporations. Majority and minority shareholders have different interests, as do shareholders with different types of stock. Many groups of shareholders may have distinct interests that lead them to favor employees, pensioners, particular social causes, or other sovereign nations. Some may have interests directly contrary to the financial well-being of their corporation. And even shareholders who agree on the goal of wealth maximization may have very different ideas about what, exactly, is meant by that term. Shareholders, it turns out, are just like us – they have a wide variety of interests that may give rise to very different preferences with respect to corporate decision-making.

While each newly discovered set of shareholder differences suggests its own tweaks to the mechanisms of corporate governance, those changes are nothing compared to the broader implications of shareholder heterogeneity. The diversity of shareholder interests suggests that shareholders are not unique among corporate constituents, at least when it comes to the similarity or dissimilarity of their preferences. This heterogeneity undercuts some of the most prominent justifications of the exclusive shareholder franchise. Two of those justifications – the argument from the residual and the argument from Arrow's theorem – are the subject of Chapters 6 and 7. While both of these arguments have plenty of shortcomings of their own, they also crucially depend, in one way or another, upon the mistaken assumption of shareholder homogeneity.

6

The Argument from the Residual

Shareholder homogeneity is important to the shareholder franchise because it supports the conception of shareholders as single-minded protectors of corporate value. As we have seen, this homogeneity is greatly overstated. Nevertheless, shareholders do share a common interest in receiving dividend payments from the corporation out of its profits. This interest in profits binds shareholders together with a mutual cause. And it is perhaps the strongest argument for why shareholders should be given the right to control the corporation.

In *The Economic Structure of Corporate Law*, Frank Easterbrook and Daniel Fischel endeavored to ground shareholder primacy in standard economic theory, arguing that it would create the highest level of efficiency.[1] Maximizing shareholder wealth would, they believe, generate the highest amount of surplus and thus would result in the greatest overall social utility.[2] How? Through the idea of the residual. They argue that shareholders are the sole residual claimants within the corporation: that is, their returns are not payable until the other contractual participants – creditors, employees, customers, suppliers – have been fully satisfied.[3] Because shareholders are not paid until these set contractual payments have been made, all other claimants receive their contractual entitlements and the shareholders benefit from the maximization of the residual. As Easterbrook and Fischel write:

> As residual claimants, shareholders have the appropriate incentives . . . to make discretionary decisions. . . . Those with fixed claims on the income stream may receive only a tiny benefit (in increased security) from the undertakings of a new project. The shareholders receive most of the marginal gains and incur most of the marginal costs. They therefore have the right incentives to exercise discretion.[4]

Although shareholders do not directly exercise this discretion, their appointed agents do. And these agents realize that they will be ousted from the board and from managerial positions if they fail to do their job of maximizing the surplus.

Thus, the theory of shareholder primacy rests on the notion that shareholders will improve social welfare by focusing on increasing the corporation's residual profits. Shareholder primacy is enforced through shareholder voting and by the market for corporate control. This connection between the residual and control, as calibrated by the one share, one vote rule, appears to set up the proper incentives for maximizing the residual.

While it's true that, under modern corporate law, shareholders have contractual entitlement to the residual, the corporate structure could be arranged to give it to a different set of claimants. One could imagine assigning the residual to any one of the corporate constituents, and then giving them the voting rights as well, in order to maximize the residual and generate the greatest amount of social utility. Capital contributors could all be contractually assigned a fixed rate of return, as other constituents are under the current structure. (Bondholders and preferred shareholders already get something like this.) Easterbrook and Fischel believe that shareholders are best suited for this because their preferences are so alike, much more alike than those of other constituent groups, and certainly more than any combination of groups. They think shareholders are likely to have "similar if not identical" interests because "the shareholders of a given firm at a given time are a reasonably homogenous group."[5]

Easterbrook and Fischel believe this homogeneity has several beneficial effects. First, it gives all shareholders an equal incentive to monitor agency costs so as to reduce such costs for all shareholders.[6] If shareholders have different interests, they will have different incentives to reduce agency costs incurred by the corporate form. Second, shareholders with the same interests will have the same objectives for the firm. This consistency of purpose will prevent the firm from becoming a war zone of competing preferences. Easterbrook and Fischel, along with others, have argued that this consistency among voter preferences is the key to the stability and prosperity of the corporate form.[7]

Moreover, shareholder homogeneity would solve the interpersonal utility problem discussed in Chapter 2. In a democratic state, voting systems based on one person, one vote assume that each person has an equal interest and set of preferences to be expressed in the election. This assumption is almost certainly incorrect.[8] With shares, however, we can better define each person's interests and preferences in a corporate election as the number of shares that they hold. Like landowners in a "one acre, one vote" water district, shareholders have an interest in the company that is clearly defined: it is the percentage of the residual they are entitled to based on the number of shares they hold. If we define utility for shareholders as their interest in the residual, shareholders' voting power is perfectly correlated with that interest.

The argument from the residual, then, turns largely on this unitary shareholder interest. It is what turns this discussion of the shareholder residual into normative support for the shareholder franchise, rather than a simple restatement of positive corporate law. By making sure that all other stakeholders are taken care of first, shareholders can then maximize their gains with a clear conscience. And this approach maximizes overall social utility, since it maximizes the returns to all of the corporations' stakeholders.

But there are problems with this simple, even elegant theory. First, shareholders do not have a unitary interest – they have diverse preferences that affect their voting interests. Second, shareholders are not well positioned to act on their preferences, as they lack the information necessary to make choices based on those preferences. Finally, and most importantly, shareholders are not the only stakeholder with an interest in the ongoing success of the business. The residual matters to other stakeholders – most importantly, to employees. These three problems are taken now in turn.

Heterogeneity of Preferences

The first problem with the argument from the residual is that shareholder preferences are not, in fact, homogeneous. As we just discussed in Chapter 5, majority shareholders, shareholders with disproportionate voting rights, members of voting trusts, bribed shareholders, hedged shareholders, sovereign wealth funds, and employee and management shareholders are just some examples of the mixed motives that individual shareholders may have when holding shares. In each case, the shareholders have other interests that threaten to override their shared interest in the residual. Shareholders are also heterogenous with respect to their definition of wealth maximization. Shareholders have differences on the time horizon of maximization, the maximization of a diversified portfolio versus a single company, and differences as to risk preferences.[9] Shareholders might also disagree about strategic choices in the course of maximizing business revenue and profits.[10]

Wealth maximization itself is a simplifying assumption. Shareholders are heterogeneous with respect to their utility preferences in that these preferences do not match up directly with wealth.[11] If it seems far-fetched that most shareholders have value heterogeneity in the context of shareholding, it is only because shareholders in publicly held companies have no avenues for displaying it. By contrast, the panoply of shareholder concerns and interests are on constant display in closely held corporations: there are conflicts over dividend schedules, management staffing, environmental damage, charitable contributions, corporate culture, and product development.[12] When shareholders have real power to change corporate policy, they exercise this power in a variety of ways.

The notion of a monolithic shareholder interest comes not from shareholder democracy but from rational shareholder apathy. Shareholders in a public company have long been divorced from real control of the firm.[13] Most shareholders in public companies are rationally uninterested in exercising their voting in an informed manner. The time and costs associated with researching how best to exercise their preferences would greatly outweigh the utility they would gain from voting in a largely meaningless election. As such, most shareholders will not become properly informed and thus will not use the vote to further their disparate interests. Instead, share voters generally tend to follow the directions of the board and management, when they bother to vote at all.[14]

Shareholders' inability to exercise their control rights results in a power vacuum at the center of the firm. The incumbent board and management are well placed to occupy that vacuum. The shareholder primacy norm acts as a counterweight on behalf of the shareholders – a norm that the board and management are expected to follow. But it is important to remember that the norm of shareholder wealth maximization is a fictional placeholder developed to replace the actual interests of the shareholders.[15] If shareholders truly expressed their preferences through their votes, there would be no need for the norm of residual maximization. Instead, the board and management would be expected to follow the actual preferences of shareholders, rather than simply a presumed wealth maximization preference.

Easterbrook and Fischel, among others, have used this strange cycle to justify shareholders as the sole participants in the franchise. Shareholders, we are told, will single-mindedly focus on increasing the residual as their sole preference for corporate policy. Because it is in the interests of all corporate stakeholders that the residual be maximized, we should give power to those who have a single-minded focus on such an outcome.[16] However, this single-minded focus is simply an assumption. And in reality, the varying interests of shareholders do not comport with the notion of a shareholder electorate with one goal. Thus, neither the ends nor the means hold up: shareholders will not all have the same preferences, and they will not all seek to effectuate those preferences (even when similar) in lockstep voting patterns.

It is for this reason that the shareholder primacy norm has been described as a tool for constraining horizontal conflict among shareholders rather than for maintaining shareholder power over other corporate stakeholders. As Gordon Smith has described, the shareholder primacy norm developed as a response to minority oppression.[17] The oppression doctrine prevents the controlling shareholder from pursuing their own individual interests; they instead must seek to maximize the value of the shares of the corporation as a whole and benefit all shareholders equally.[18] The shareholder primacy norm, accompanied by the equitable antioppression doctrine, is necessary because the power of the franchise will not mitigate the tyranny of the shareholder majority; in fact, it is the cause of the problem. The shareholder primacy norm forces a norm of interest homogeneity onto a very diverse set of shareholder interests.

Viewed this way, the shareholder franchise is not justified on the grounds of actual shareholder preferences for wealth maximization. Instead, the franchise is simply one tool in the corporate law arsenal for enforcing the norm of shareholder wealth maximization.[19] However, the shareholder primacy norm is about more than just the vote. The norm is indifferent or even hostile to the preferences of actual shareholders. Instead, the norm assumes that shareholders all prefer wealth maximization and then requires corporations to be run accordingly.[20] In the end, Easterbrook and Fischel's argument from the residual does not escape the circularity of earlier arguments for the exclusive shareholder franchise. It, too, assumes the very thing it sets out to prove.

Because shareholder preferences are irrelevant to shareholder primacy, true shareholder democracy is actually a threat to the shareholder wealth maximization norm. If let loose to express their actual preferences, shareholders might express preferences for a variety of interests beyond maximizing their own wealth.[21] Perhaps this explains the move of board primacy theorists such as Stephen Bainbridge, who support the goal of shareholder wealth maximization but argue against greater shareholder input.[22] Bainbridge bases his argument primarily on the need for centralized and largely unreviewable discretion in order to maximize efficient business operations.[23] According to Bainbridge, shareholders should have only limited voting rights: "shareholder voting is properly understood not as a primary component of the corporate decision-making structure, but rather as an accountability device of last resort, to be used sparingly, at most."[24] Instead, the corporation requires "the centralization of essentially nonreviewable decision-making authority in the board of directors."[25] As long as the directors operate within shareholder wealth maximization norms, their decisions in leading the company will be left alone. In the interest of shareholder protection, director primacy takes the power away from actual shareholders and hands it to "Platonic guardians."[26]

Shareholders have a diverse set of competing interests. The right to vote provides a mechanism for shareholders to express those interests vis-à-vis the actual control of the company. In reality, however, only shareholders in closely held companies have the power and incentive to vote their preferences. In the absence of actual expressions of preferences, the shareholder wealth maximization norm serves as a theoretical stand-in for shareholder preferences. But this norm is just that – a stand-in. If corporate law theory justifies the shareholder franchise based on a homogenous, uniform interest in increasing the residual, it is based on a fiction. In reality, shareholders have a heterogeneous set of interests that are muted only because of the weakness of the shareholder franchise. A stronger form of shareholder democracy would, in all likelihood, exacerbate these divisions by providing more expression for actual preferences. A true shareholder democracy, then, would not reflect the vision of a single-minded electorate pursuing the goal of residual maximization. It would instead reflect what it really is: control of the corporation by one group of stakeholders.

Heterogeneity of Information

In their classic exegesis of the firm, *Production, Information Costs, and Economic Organization*, Armen Alchian and Harold Demsetz provided an economic model of joint production based on the theory of the firm.[27] They, too, argued that the control rights in the firm should be given to the individual – the entrepreneur-coordinator – who owned rights to the residual in the firm.[28] In a remarkable footnote, however, they argued against the power of shareholders to control the corporation through voting rights:

> In sum, is it the case that the stockholder-investor relationship is one
> emanating from the *division of ownership* among several people, or is it
> that the collection of investment funds from people of varying anticipa-
> tions is the underlying factor? If the latter, why should any of them be
> thought of as the owners in whom voting rights, whatever they may
> signify or however exercisable, should reside in order to enhance effi-
> ciency? Why voting rights in any of the outside, participating investors?
> . . . [I]t is hard to understand why an investor who wishes to back and
> "share" in the consequences of some new business should necessarily have
> to acquire voting power (i.e., power to change the manager-operator) in
> order to invest in the venture. In fact, we invest in some ventures in the
> hope that no other stockholders will be so "foolish" as to try to toss out the
> incumbent management.[29]

In the same footnote, Alchian and Demsetz also observe with interest the
existence of nonvoting shares in an earlier era before the practice was
prohibited. Why were such shares generally of equal value with voting
shares, they wonder, if those shareholders were getting such a bad deal?[30]

The nonvoting shares distributed in the recent Snap, Inc. initial public
offering have raised anew the wisdom of deviating from the traditional
one share, one vote paradigm.[31] The traditional approach has seen nonvoting shares as unfair impositions on shareholders – an expectation that
they should pay to play but then not get involved in the game.[32] However,
as Alchian and Demsetz suggested, voting rights are not much use for
outside investors who have (rationally) decided to remain uninformed
about the variety of their investments. Nonvoting shares may actually be
a better deal if shareholders do not have the information sufficient to
translate their preferences into voting choices.[33]

This relationship between information and control is, of course,
a crucial part of the argument from the residual. The holders of the
residual are thought to have the proper incentives to maximize the
fortunes of the corporation because they have a clear stake in the
outcome. This stake should motivate them to gather information
about the firm that would allow them to cast informed votes. This,
remember, is one of the reasons for limiting voting to interested
parties. Shareholders do not usually have ready access to low-cost
information about the interior workings of a firm – that's one of the
reasons for the existence of securities disclosure laws for public corporations. But if shareholders, for one reason or another, do not have
a sufficient stake in firm decision-making to seek out relevant information, the connection between shareholding and exercising appropriate
control is severed.

With the rise of index fund shareholders,[34] investors are getting even more rationally apathetic than ever. Index funds exist solely to own shares to a set of financially successful companies while charging management fees that are as low as possible. Any effort to investigate the issues at play in any particular election, or – in extreme circumstances – to run and fund a proxy challenge to incumbent directors, will be at the cost of the fund's participants while providing benefits to participants in the other index funds, who spend nothing. Such activity will redound to the detriment of the particular fund, as all funds get the benefit but only the particular fund incurs the cost.[35] Index funds have been shaving expenses in an effort to charge the lowest possible fees. In this world, every extra analyst may be an unnecessary luxury. So these funds will not have the information to know when to challenge corporate insiders, let alone the interest in taking on those insiders in an election.[36]

Shareholders are also likely to lack critical information when voting to approve a corporate combination, such as a merger or sale of substantially all assets. The M&A process generally follows a prescribed pattern. After a set of each side's top corporate officers agree to a deal, the companies must secretly and expeditiously conduct due diligence using high-level management and outside consultants. If this hastily conducted due diligence uncovers no problems, the boards approve the combination and announce the deal to the public and shareholders. The shareholders generally have a couple months to digest the proxy materials and media reports before they vote to approve or quash the merger. If the combination receives shareholder and regulatory approval, it ultimately goes into effect.[37]

There are strategic reasons for the structure of this process: secrecy prevents poaching and keeps failed negotiations under the rug.[38] While this secrecy serves a purpose, it also narrowly restricts both the information and the perspectives that can be brought to bear on the decision. As a result, corporate combinations are extremely top-down affairs. The critical decision to combine is made at the very top, often by the CEO alone, and the board and the shareholders are often handed something of a fait accompli. Although shareholders are given time to make their decision, the process is designed not to give shareholders an active role in the combination, but rather to secure their yes vote with as little controversy as possible. While state law and federal securities regulations require substantial disclosure when public companies solicit proxies,[39] the disclosure tends to be a static, lump-sum document written primarily to advance the proposal while meeting legal requirements. From start to finish, shareholder voting on the typical corporate combination is hampered by the absence of critical information.

There was a time, relatively early in the latest shareholder primacy age, when savvy and empowered institutional shareholders were seen as the key participants in making corporate governance work.[40] In league with independent directors,[41] shareholders would monitor management, reduce agency costs, and hew to shareholder wealth maximization. Much of the 1990s and early 2000s was spent developing mechanisms to empower shareholder participation. Although this approach worked in theory, it has not been matched in reality. Instead, small hedge fund "wolfpacks" search for idiosyncratic short-term gains, while large index funds pay even less attention to governance.[42] The concern of Alchian and Demsetz, and before them of Berle and Means, about disengaged and uninformed shareholders has not yet been solved.

Employee Stake in the Residual

The Easterbrook and Fischel model posits that shareholders invest their money in the firm in order to get the rights to residual profits from the firm in the form of dividends.[43] These dividends are truly discretionary; shareholders have no contractual right to demand dividends from the company, even if it has a large surplus.[44] Because dividends are provided at the discretion of management, shareholders need some way to hold management accountable for its creation and distribution of the surplus. The right to elect directors is that mechanism. As Easterbrook and Fischel have stated, "As the residual claimants, shareholders have the appropriate incentives (collective choice problems notwithstanding) to make discretionary decisions."[45]

There are two ways of characterizing the meaning of the residual in this context. In one sense, dividends are residual payments made only after all other stakeholders in the business have gotten their payments.[46] It is the amount left over after other expenses have been paid. But this characterization only blurs the underlying issue, since shareholders could agree to another contractual system of repayment. Shareholders could get a designated payment – a minimum capital "wage," so to speak – as part of their bargain with the company. The structure of the payment in return for capital is what separates shareholders from creditors. Both have given the corporation a specific amount of capital, but they have agreed to very different repayment structures. Loan payments are required under contract, while dividends are contingent.[47] Under current laws and commercial customs, shareholders receive payment from the business in a significantly more contingent way than the other stakeholders. But wages too could also be completely contingent, with employees only getting paid after all other participants – including capital contributors – had been paid. In fact, many employees have aspects of their pay that are contingent and depend on firm performance: commissions, bonus pools, stock options, and even shares. However, federal and state laws require not only that employees get a minimum wage, but also that the wages be paid regularly, and most employees expect to be paid regular amounts at regular times for their time worked.[48] There are no such rules for shareholders.

The critical point is that the residual is not a natural part of running a business; it does not exist as a matter of economic fact. Instead, the residual is a contractual creation borne of the relationships between the various parties. There is, in fact, no such thing as a residual, as the corporation always has other uses for the funds: it can put them in savings, invest them in securities, pay a bonus to workers, make charitable contributions, or put them into research and development.[49] Dividends are simply what the board decides to pay shareholders out of the funds on hand.

So, in fact, the whole idea of a residual is misleading. Rights to the residual essentially means rights to completely discretionary payments, paired with control of the company – the firm, the ongoing business, the set of relationships that can be characterized by one brand name. Easterbrook and Fischel acknowledged that voting rights are not given to shareholders simply to force the corporation to make dividend payments. Instead, Easterbrook and Fischel believe that because shareholders have a claim on the firm's residuals, they are in the best position to run the entire enterprise:

> The firm should invest in new products, plants, and so forth, until the gains and costs are identical at the margin. Yet all of the actors, except the shareholders, lack the appropriate incentives. Those with fixed claims on the income stream may receive only a tiny benefit (in increased security) from the undertaking of a new project. The shareholders receive most of the marginal gains and incur most of the marginal costs. They therefore have the right incentives to exercise discretion.[50]

As depicted by Easterbrook and Fischel, the firm is a game in which all other players take their allocated spoils until the shareholders mop up what is left at the end. So let the shareholders run the company and they will make sure that not only does everyone else get paid their due but they themselves make the most of the leftovers. This result is a priori efficient, as it maximizes the value of the surplus and thus the overall value of the firm.

But this story is incomplete and overstated. Over time, employees are much more akin to shareholders than to the other fixed claimants. Employees may agree to a specific wage at a particular time, but only fixed-term employees are entitled to that wage for any ongoing length of time. The overwhelming majority of employees in the United States are at-will employees who can be fired for any reason.[51] They have no continuing expectation of payment beyond the time they have already worked, and their wages can be adjusted at any time. And as mentioned earlier, a significant chunk of many employees' pay is expressly contingent, even after performance, in the form of bonuses, stock options, and other forms of profit sharing. So employees' pay is not fixed over time; it too is contingent and dependent on the ongoing success of the firm.

Easterbrook and Fischel's model of control over the residual may make sense as a way to differentiate between providers of capital. Creditors have provided their capital with a fixed repayment scheme; they are "selling" their capital for a fixed price, and their return is not affected by firm performance. Shareholders, on the other hand, contribute capital with no expectation of repayment and no entitlement to specific payments. In terms of fixed costs, shareholders are comparable to employees, and creditors are comparable to outside contractors with term contracts. Both shareholders and employees depend on the success of the firm over time for their earnings. However, like creditors, outside contractors generally agree to provide labor and the necessary materials for a specific project for a specific cost. If the firm decides to stop the project prematurely, the contractor will still have a contractual right for payment for the work that would have been done under the terms of the contract (minus any cost savings). The contractor has no ongoing interest in the success of the firm – only in being paid for the work contracted to the firm on the specific project.

The notion of shareholder vulnerability is often bolstered by the idea of capital lock-in – the fact that shareholders, unlike creditors or even general partners, cannot exchange their shares for their capital contribution or for a pro-rata percentage of firm value.[52] Under the shareholder contract, these equity contributors have no right to withdraw their contributions to the firm.[53] Of course, shareholders in public companies can sell their shares to another buyer and generally recoup at least some percentage of their investment.[54] But there is no guarantee that there will always be a buyer at the other end. In the case of dissolution or bankruptcy, shareholders also have rights in the firm's assets, but they have the lowest priority of the potential claimants and generally can expect only a small percentage of their investment, if anything.

Singling out shareholders for their vulnerability, however, understates the extent to which employees are also locked into their particular firms. Employees cannot diversify like shareholders can. Most employees work for one company, spend their working time there, and earn their salary and benefits there.[55] Shareholders, on the other hand, are generally diversified among hundreds or even thousands of economic investments in companies, real estate, or government bonds. Mutual funds, which hold more than a third of the shares in publicly held companies,[56] generally have shares in hundreds of companies. In terms of the effect on personal wealth, people invariably are more financially dependent on employment than they are on their shares in any one particular company.[57]

The ability of employees – even at-will employees – to leave their jobs free and clear is also overstated. Yes, employees can quit and take a new position elsewhere. But they often lose significant economic value. If a covenant not to compete is in place, the employee cannot work in their chosen field for some period of time – six months, a year, even two years. Such covenants are subject to reasonableness standards, but they are common and have been applied across a variety of fields and incomes.[58] In addition, employees invest in their positions and often must leave those investments behind. When considering the ongoing "human capital" of workers,[59] academics have differentiated between employee-specific human capital and firm-specific human capital. Employee-specific capital is held by the individual person and comes with the employee when they take another job. Examples include education, certifications, or general knowledge of an industry. Firm-specific human capital, on the other hand, is the value that an employee brings to a particular firm by dint of their knowledge, experience, and relationships. Margaret Blair described firm-specific human capital as "[k]nowledge and skills that are specialized to a given enterprise, as well as effort that has been put forth toward the goals of the enterprise."[60] This capital is valuable to the firm, as it makes the employee's contribution to productivity greater than the contribution of a replacement employee.

The ongoing investment in firm-specific capital means that employees are residual claimants as well.[61] They have a financial stake in the ongoing enterprise – one that workers cannot sell or carry away. In fact, an employee's residual claim is even harder to withdraw, because it represents a blend of skills, knowledge, and relationships; unlike shares, human capital is not an investment that can be monetized according to a variety of metrics.[62] Employees are thereby subject to the holdup threats and opportunism that are used to justify the governance rights provided to shareholders. The corporation can pay employees less than their marginal value to the corporation because the employees cannot credibly threaten to make that amount elsewhere.

A focus just on an individual employee's firm-specific capital understates the amount of investment that the employee has in the firm. Firm-specific capital is tied to the employee; if the employee leaves, both the employee and the firm suffer from the loss of this capital. However, employees can also contribute to the overall value of the firm in a way that is no longer tied to the particular employee. Instead, this contribution improves the firm's brand, trademark, goodwill, reputation, and ongoing value. And the employee has no right to any ongoing claim on that value.

As an example, imagine a drugstore-chain cashier that is so warm and friendly with customers that a nationally syndicated talk show singles him out for praise.[63] That worker has firm-specific capital; customers know him and like him, and they may visit that particular store just to see him. Due to his television appearance, he may even have some employee-specific capital that can be transferred to another company. But he has contributed a significant amount of value to his employer, who received local and national attention from having one of its employees praised for his excellent service. The vast majority of national drugstore consumers will have no opportunity to visit this particular store, but they will see and remember that the employee worked there, and the chain's national reputation will benefit from his exposure.

Most employees will not be singled out on national television for their great work. But particularly in service-oriented businesses, employees are the key to building the value of the brand. Popular business titles are replete with advice for executives and managers on how to cultivate terrific employees who will provide customers with excellent service.[64] With reputation scores available on dozens of websites, and with social media holding a vast mélange of observations and complaints about commercial interactions, individual employees are more important than ever to brand reputation and business value.[65] Every day of work well done adds to the store of the employer's reputational value. And yet employees cannot participate in that created value unless they also have ownership interests. Employees cannot take the employer's trademark with them when they leave the company. Unlike the standard rule for business partners, employees do not get a share of the company upon leaving.[66]

It is this control over the firm's ongoing value that gives "owners" of the firm the decisive bargaining advantage over labor. Owners control the name, the trademark, the reputation, the ongoing value – the business itself. Owners can fire all employees and replace them and still keep the brand name – even in a primarily service-based industry. On the other hand, those same fired employees could open up a business and provide the same set of services, but they would have to call themselves by a different name. Owners have the ultimate control over the value of the business that employees have built up over days, months, years, sometimes decades.

So both employees and shareholders have handed over value to the company – value that cannot be taken back – and must trust the company to use that value well and compensate them appropriately. But only shareholders have governance rights. As a result, shareholders have complete control over the management of the business, and their representatives can threaten lower wages and termination without threatening the brand value. Since about the time when shareholder primacy started to take hold, workers' wages have remained stagnant in real terms, even while productivity growth has soared.[67] During the same period of time, the share of corporate profits as part of the economy has been growing.[68] The balance of power between capital and labor has decisively shifted in favor of capital, even as we have transitioned to a more service-based economy.

Shareholder primacy has done its job of protecting shareholders against the vulnerability endemic to their contractual status. By providing governance rights, the shareholder franchise empowers shareholders to select boards of directors and board-appointed managers who favor their interests. As a result, corporations are incentivized to maximize the share of corporate wealth going to dividends and share value. In the absence of any countervailing weight such as union representation or worker board seats, management has put the squeeze on employees, reducing their share of the corporation's economic gains.[69] The idea that employees have fixed payouts, leaving the residual for shareholders, is a dangerous oversimplification of the way in which corporations operate over time. Workers too are open to opportunistic actions by management, and they too thus have reason to participate in governance.

* * *

The primary law and economics argument for shareholder voting is on shaky ground indeed. While few question the basic concept of giving control to those with an interest in an enterprise, the subsequent contention that shareholders alone should be anointed voters has fallen apart. Shareholders are not a homogeneous group of wealth maximizers, and, even when they do have overlapping preferences, there's no evidence that they alone meet some measure of preference homogeneity necessary to hold corporate voting rights. Moreover, their relationship with the firm does not give them ready access to the information necessary to cast informed votes, and many shareholders – such as index fund shareholders – lack the incentive to seek out that information. And, finally, this vision of shareholders as the sole owners of the residual is just descriptively wrong. Employees are at least as invested in the long-term success of the firm, cannot easily diversify that interest, and often possess firm-specific skills and make contributions to the ongoing value of the business. The argument from the residual does not justify exclusive governance rights for shareholders.

The Argument from Arrow's Theorem

Along with the argument from the residual, corporate law scholars have relied upon a second argument to justify the existing corporate regime. They have focused on the dictates of Arrow's theorem, the crown jewel of social choice theory, to raise concerns about expanding the corporate electorate. Arrow's theorem posits that no social choice function, including any voting procedure, can simultaneously fulfill four conditions of democratic fairness and guarantee a transitive outcome.[1] Citing the theorem, corporate law commentators have argued that lumping different groups of stakeholders together into the electorate would result in a lack of consensus and, ultimately, the lack of coherence that attends intransitive social choices.[2] Plagued by these voting pathologies, such a corporation could even be led to "self-destruct," a dreadful result that, presumably, may be avoided only by restricting corporate voting to shareholders alone.[3]

We begin this chapter by describing the basic contours of the argument, surveying its influence, and distinguishing it from a couple of related arguments. The bulk of the chapter, though, is a critical assessment of the argument, examining everything from its factual premises to its theoretical conclusions. To begin with, the argument relies heavily on the claim that shareholders possess homogenous preferences with respect to wealth maximization, which, as we saw in Chapter 6, is an increasingly flawed premise. Moreover, the argument applies the theorem at the wrong level of the decision process, misconstrues its import, and ignores a great deal of recent work in social choice theory. Indeed, if anything, Arrow's theorem actually points us in the direction of expanding the corporate electorate to include other stakeholders. In the end, the argument from Arrow's theorem will be revealed as a bit of a law and economics sleight of hand, one that's fooled a generation of corporate law scholars eager to embrace any argument that supports their position.

The Basic Argument

Like the argument from the residual, the argument from Arrow's theorem was first made by Frank Easterbrook and Daniel Fischel in their article on corporate voting[4] and later recounted in their book on the economic structure of corporate law.[5] After presenting the residual claim argument, Easterbrook and Fischel provide a second reason why shareholders alone have voting rights. Citing Kenneth Arrow's groundbreaking work, they explain:

> The voters, and the directors they elect, must determine both the objectives of the firm and the general methods of achieving them. It is well known, however, that when voters hold dissimilar preferences it is not possible to aggregate their preferences into a consistent system of choices. If a firm makes inconsistent choices, it is likely to self-destruct. Consistency is possible, however, when voters commonly hold the same ranking of choices (or when the rankings are at least single-peaked).[6]

Shareholders, as a class, have relatively homogeneous preferences with respect to profit maximization.[7] The corporate franchise, therefore, is correctly limited to this particular class of like-minded participants.[8]

So what is Arrow's theorem? The theorem is the centerpiece of a broader enterprise known as social choice theory.[9] Social choice theory attempts to rigorously explain how individual desires are aggregated into social choices. More specifically, it focuses upon the mechanisms, known as social choice functions, used to move from individual preference orders to social preference orders. Most democratic institutions have used some type of voting procedure to aggregate preferences (as opposed to, say, flipping a coin or asking a dictator).[10] The trustworthiness of all social choice functions was cast into doubt, however, with the publication of Arrow's theorem.[11]

Arrow's theorem holds that no social choice function can simultaneously satisfy four relatively undemanding conditions of democratic fairness and guarantee a transitive outcome.[12] The first fairness condition, nondictatorship, requires that no single person's preference order should determine the social preference order, regardless of what others prefer.[13] The second condition, Pareto efficiency, holds that if everyone prefers one alternative to another, then the social choice procedure must reproduce that ordering.[14] The third condition, universal domain, requires that the social choice procedure works with any possible set of individual preference orders.[15] The final fairness condition, independence from irrelevant alternatives, ensures that the introduction of a new "irrelevant" alternative into the preference profile does not affect the orderings of the other alternatives relative to each other.[16] The logical condition of transitivity guarantees that the social choice function will produce a complete and transitive social preference order: if A is preferred to B, and B to C, then A must be preferred to C.[17] The contrary – an intransitive preference order where A is preferred to B, B to C, and C to A – is referred to as a voting cycle and indicates that the social choice function is unable to declare a winner, at least one that is meaningful.[18]

As applied to corporate voting, then, the argument from Arrow's theorem may be described as follows: The theorem tells us there is no corporate voting procedure that meets the four fairness conditions and, at the same time, guarantees a consistent (i.e., acyclical) outcome. Something – either one of the fairness conditions or a guaranteed transitive outcome – must yield. For example, adhering to the condition of universal domain by allowing those with dissimilar (or, at a minimum, multipeaked) preferences to vote in corporate elections could result in inconsistent corporate decision-making, which in turn would cause a corporation to, in Easterbrook and Fischel's terms, "self-destruct."[19] Relaxing the condition of universal domain by restricting the vote to a class of participants with similar individual preference profiles would avoid such an outcome.[20] Given their homogeneous interest in profit maximization, shareholders are just such a class.[21]

Influence of the Argument from Arrow's Theorem

This argument has been quite influential in the decades since its initial formulation. Henry Hansmann used it to argue against allowing every group of stakeholders to have representation on a corporate board of directors. "[B]ecause the participants are likely to have radically diverging interests, making everybody an owner threatens to increase the costs of collective decision making enormously."[22] Among these costs is the possibility of a voting cycle, which "increases as preferences among the electorate become more heterogeneous."[23] Such cycles, Hansmann explained, would lead to repeated alteration of the firm's policies and a grant of "extraordinary power" to those in control of the voting agenda.[24]

The argument appears to give particularly powerful ammunition to those arguing against codetermination or employee board representation. It led Gregory Dow, for example, to worry that employee representatives might introduce the possibility of "voting … pathologies."[25] He explained that "under most proposals for employee representation, the board would need to reconcile a far wider range of conflicting interests [than when the board merely represents shareholders]."[26] Merely expanding the franchise to include this one additional class of constituents, then, is thought to be enough to trigger the damaging intransitive outcomes.[27]

This argument for the exclusive shareholder franchise has even been cited by scholars whose vision of corporate governance does not otherwise demand it. Margaret Blair and Lynn Stout, for example, advocate a "team production model" of corporate law,[28] where the corporate boards "exist not to protect shareholders *per se*, but to protect the enterprise-specific investments of *all* the members of the corporate 'team,' including shareholders, managers, rank and file employees, and possibly other groups, such as creditors."[29] When it comes to determining the proper board electorate, however, Blair and Stout take a more traditional line, proposing that the franchise should probably be limited to shareholders alone.[30] Their first argument for this proposition? "[P]lurality voting by shareholders who have a relatively homogeneous interest in maximizing share value may exhibit fewer pathologies and be less conducive to rent-seeking than a vote taken among many competing constituencies with conflicting interests."[31] The perceived power of the argument from Arrow's theorem, then, is such that a fairly wide variety of corporate scholars have made use of it.

The influence and durability of the argument from Arrow's theorem appear to come from the strength of the theorem itself, which, at this point, has withstood scrutiny for over half a century.[32] Indeed, the strength and power of the theorem may be the reason why this argument for exclusive shareholder voting is frequently raised but rarely examined, as if invocation of the theorem is all that is required. Before turning to the task of critically examining the argument, however, we must distinguish it from two related arguments.

As Distinguished from the Argument from Politics

First, the argument from Arrow's theorem is different (and more powerful) than the argument for the exclusive shareholder franchise based on mere disagreements among constituents or the board members they elect. The latter, which we will call the argument from politics, is that a board representing more diverse constituents will come to agreement on corporate decisions less readily than a board representing a single class of constituents. A board may represent more diverse interests when an election has been opened up to more than one corporate constituency or when certain constituencies are allowed to elect their own board representatives (as with the German codetermination model). Either way, the resulting process, the argument goes, would be prone to disagreements, internal bickering, information asymmetries, and the like, which would make for less efficient corporate decision-making. The argument from politics, then, draws on a range of difficulties (other than lurking Arrovian intransitivities) in collective decision-making introduced by voters with more heterogeneous interests.

Many corporate law theorists have advanced the argument from politics. Henry Hansmann and Reinier Kraakman, for example, argue for the exclusive shareholder franchise because stakeholder representation would lead to more cumbersome decision processes.[33] Stephen Bainbridge makes a similar point, largely on the basis of Arrow's models of consensus and authority decision-making,[34] explaining that differing interests and levels of information would bog down corporate decision-making.[35] In a related vein, Blair and Stout ask us to "[i]magine the chaos and politicking likely to attend an election in which a firm's creditors, executives, rank-and-file employees, and other stakeholders with unique and often conflicting interests could vote on their favored candidates."[36] It is, at times, difficult to discern which argument for the exclusive shareholder franchise is being advanced.[37] Bainbridge, for example, concentrates on the argument from politics, but at times refers to more generalized worries about collective decision-making that may include the possibility of Arrovian intransitivities.[38]

We take care to separate the two arguments, not only because they are analytically distinct, but also because the argument from politics is far less theoretically powerful than the one from Arrow's theorem. The argument from politics postulates that a more diverse board electorate may have difficulty choosing board members, or that a board composed of members representing more diverse constituencies may not reach consensus as easily as a board representing those with more homogeneous interests. Even if consensus comes more slowly, the difficulties that animate the argument from politics may, at least theoretically, be reduced or eliminated by tinkering with institutional design features. For example, boards traditionally follow internal procedures requiring majority votes, with the chair having tie-breaking authority.[39] In the end, one can always design a procedure for forcing a vote and thus reaching a decision on any particular issue – there may be winners and losers, but a decision will be made that is based on voter preferences.

The argument from Arrow's theorem, if correct, involves a more fundamental objection to heterogeneous board electorates. Unlike the argument from politics, the theorem applies to *all* social choice procedures. This means, among other things, that there is no independent mechanism to check the reliability of an election outcome in any particular case. Any such checking mechanism would need to explicitly or implicitly equate voter preferences with social choices, and thus would be vulnerable to violations of the same set of the theorem's conditions that it is designed to test.[40] This is part of the reason why the theorem is so devastating, and explains why some commentators argue that the theorem makes the very notion of a popular will, at some level, meaningless.[41] The argument from Arrow's theorem cannot be overcome by simply tinkering with the decision procedures.

Further, the consequences of the theorem itself are, if anything, understated by Easterbrook and Fischel. In their version of the argument, expanding the corporate board electorate would result in "inconsistent" firm choices.[42] But the true impact of the theorem goes beyond choices that are merely inconsistent. One famous corollary of Arrow's theorem – the Gibbard-Satterthwaite theorem – tells us that all nondictatorial voting schemes are subject to strategic manipulation.[43] In the presence of intransitive social preference orders, the social choice may depend upon the order in which alternatives are presented to the electorate – control of the agenda is tantamount to control of the outcomes. This is, in part, what worries Hansmann about the possibility of intransitive results.[44] There is a possibility not only of inconsistent firm decisions but also of decisions that may be manipulated by whoever sets the agenda (which, in this setting, would most likely be the board itself). The argument from Arrow's theorem, then, is distinct from and more powerful than the argument from politics.

As Distinguished from the Argument for Absolute Delegation

The argument from Arrow's theorem for the exclusive shareholder franchise may also be distinguished from a similar argument for the absolute delegation rule in corporate law. The absolute delegation rule refers to the fact that shareholders typically lack the power to directly participate in a firm's business decision-making; that power is instead delegated to corporate managers.[45] One argument advanced in favor of this particular institutional arrangement is based on Arrow's theorem. Jeffrey Gordon argues that direct shareholder control over day-to-day business decision-making through, say, an initiative process, would greatly increase the risk of cyclical outcomes because the risk of intransitivities grows with increasing numbers of voters and alternatives.[46] According to Arrow's theorem and its corollaries, this would lead either to inconsistent corporate decisions or the manipulation of the corporate decisions by shareholders interested in private gain.[47] In either case, shareholder initiative of this sort would make the corporation less productive, hence the need to delegate such authority to management.[48]

The argument from Arrow's theorem with respect to the exclusive shareholder franchise has much in common with this argument for absolute delegation. Both trade on the possibility that Arrovian intransitivities will result in inconsistent or manipulable corporate decisions. There are, however, some differences, the principal one being that the alternatives are candidates for board membership in one case and specific business decisions in the other. The specter of cycling may not loom as large with respect to board elections because there are typically fewer candidates standing for any particular seat on the board than there are possible directions in which to take a business. Board elections may be held much less frequently than a system of direct shareholder initiatives on day-to-day business decisions, further reducing the opportunities for cycling.[49] And, more generally, the argument for the exclusive shareholder franchise depends upon a more complicated (and more tenuously connected) series of events to get from inconsistent board membership choices to inconsistent corporate decisions – a connection that is more direct in the argument for absolute delegation.

Thus, some of the arguments that follow – for example, those that make use of the distinction between voting on board members and voting on firm decisions – would not apply with any force to this related argument for absolute delegation.[50] Other arguments, however, may have some application to both. For example, the arguments below that involve balancing the likelihood of intransitivities in the corporate setting against the costs associated with limiting the franchise may also apply, with some variation, to the argument for absolute delegation.

Shareholder Heterogeneity Redux

The argument from Arrow's theorem for exclusive shareholder voting is not compelling. This stems not from a vulnerability in the theorem itself, but instead from its application to the social choice function in question – corporate board voting. That application has been undertheorized by those who make the argument and taken as an article of faith by those who rely upon it.

Initially, we note that the argument from Arrow's theorem shares a central premise with the argument from the residual – that shareholders have homogeneous preferences with respect to wealth maximization. But, as discussed in Chapter 5, shareholders have interests that diverge along a number of dimensions. The presence of heterogeneous shareholder preferences undercuts a crucial assumption of the argument from Arrow's theorem. But even if shareholder preferences are not identical, proponents of the argument may be able to salvage their position by showing that the preferences are sufficiently similar to make the argument work. If, for example, shareholder preferences are more homogeneous than the preferences of those of other corporate constituencies or, at a minimum, than the preference profile of a combined corporate electorate, then there may be some support for a weakened version of the argument from Arrow's theorem. As we discuss below, this will, in part, depend upon the exact nature of the asserted homogeneity. But, in any case, there may be enough of the premise of shareholder homogeneity left to examine the strength of the argument itself.

Shareholder Preferences over Candidates

Even assuming shareholder homogeneity, there are several reasons why Arrow's theorem fails to provide a suitable foundation for restricting corporate voting to shareholders alone. Shareholder agreement on the goal of wealth maximization, even if true, does not indicate agreement on how best to achieve that goal.[51] Shareholders may, and often do, wildly disagree over the proper course of action for their corporation.

Indeed, it is not at all clear that shareholder preferences with respect to methods are more likely, as Easterbrook and Fischel argue, to be single-peaked or otherwise value restricted. Take, for example, three groups of shareholders (S_1, S_2, and S_3), each of which owns a third of the voting shares of the tech company Pied Piper. Let us also suppose that Pied Piper has three sets of strategic opportunities in front of it: it could merge with Microsoft; it could set up a strategic alliance with Microsoft; or it could set up a strategic alliance with Google. Different shareholders are likely to have different preferences for each of these options. These preferences could be described as: merge with Microsoft (mm), set up an alliance with

Microsoft (am), or set up an alliance with Google (ag). The first two groups, S_1 and S_2, believe that Pied Piper is floundering and needs to set up a relationship with either Microsoft or Google in order to thrive. The first group, S_1, thinks a great deal of Microsoft, and believes a merger or, to a lesser extent, a contractual relationship with Microsoft will generate the most profitable synergies. Thus, S_1 prefers mm, followed by am, then ag.[52] Group S_2 believes the profit potential is greater with Google, and hence prefers ag, followed by mm, then am. The third group of shareholders, S_3, slightly prefers Microsoft over Google, but greatly values Pied Piper's unique corporate culture, and believes that the resulting culture clash with either of the potential partners would overwhelm any productive synergies from an alliance or, worse, a merger. This group also believes Google would be more aggressive than Microsoft in a partnership. Thus, S_3 prefers am, followed by ag, then mm. The resulting preference profile is:

S_1	mm	am	ag
S_2	ag	mm	am
S_3	am	ag	mm

This profile is not single-peaked or otherwise value restricted. Rather, it is an instantiation of the Condorcet paradox and yields the voting cycle mmPamPagPmm.

With respect to general methods of achieving corporate goals of wealth maximization, then, there is no reason to believe that shareholders are uniquely situated to have preference profiles that are single-peaked or otherwise domain restricted. In the Pied Piper example, given a plausible two-dimensional division in the preferences of shareholders – their relative feelings about the two potential partners and their views on the importance of Pied Piper's corporate culture – it was quite simple to generate a preference profile that returned an intransitive outcome.[53] This was true despite the fact that all three groups of shareholders wanted to maximize profits. Given the multiple dimensions of most significant business decisions, shareholder preferences are not particularly likely to fall into patterns that ensure transitive outcomes.

More specifically, even if shareholders were to agree on the direction for their corporation, they may well have very different ideas about which director candidate(s) would best effectuate it. This additional degree of detachment is less likely to play a role with respect to significant corporate decisions, where slates of board candidates are elected precisely to effectuate a particular decision. But it would add a layer of complexity when translating agreement on more mundane aspects of a corporation's direction into preferences over board candidates. The proponents of the argument from Arrow's theorem never make clear why underlying agreement on profit maximization, or even upon the method of achieving that goal, generally makes it more likely that shareholder preferences are single-peaked with respect to director candidates. Because Arrow's theorem operates on the level of individual preference orders over an array of alternatives (here, director candidates), agreement on the general goals or methods of the corporation does little to ensure that a particular voting system for board membership will be free of Arrovian intransitivities.

Making Choices Among Arrow's Conditions

Even if shareholder homogeneity with respect to profit maximization reduced the incidence of cycles in corporate director elections, that is not necessarily a powerful argument in favor of allowing only shareholders to vote. Arrow's theorem demonstrates that no social choice function can simultaneously fulfill the four conditions of democratic fairness and one condition of logicality, but it says nothing about which condition should be sacrificed when designing a voting structure. That decision depends on an assessment of the costs associated with sacrificing one of the conditions of democratic fairness and, on the other side, the practical likelihood and costs of intransitive outcomes. And those who use Arrow's theorem to argue in favor of restricting voting rights to shareholders have not made the case for their choice of conditions to sacrifice.

Because Arrow's theorem applies to all social choice functions, including all corporate voting systems, we know that a voting system where shareholders alone may cast votes must violate one of the conditions of democratic fairness or transitivity.[54] And, as mentioned above, it does: restricting voting rights to shareholders because of their purported agreement with each other is a straightforward violation of the condition of universal domain. That condition, remember, demands that a voting procedure work with every permutation of voter preferences over a set of alternatives. And like the other fundamental requirements of democratic fairness, universal domain is relatively uncontroversial. Giving up this condition – by restricting individual preference orders – runs counter to a fundamental democratic principle: people should not be declared ineligible to vote because of their preferences. It also runs counter to a fundamental principle of standard economics that we take people's preferences as they come.

And, to be clear, this is not one of those situations where people with an interest in an election, to whom we would otherwise extend the right to vote, just naturally happen to have preferences that, collectively, do not produce intransitivities.[55] In those situations, the condition of universal domain is not sacrificed by denying anyone the right to vote from the outset. Because the voters encounter no prior restraint on their preference orders, the principal justification for universal domain – the immorality of denying the ballot to people with certain preference orders – is not implicated. Sacrificing universal domain in such situations sacrifices very little. Here, however, the argument is that people other than shareholders, even if they have an interest in an election, should be denied the right to vote from the outset *because* they have preference orders that, when combined with those of the shareholders, may produce a voting cycle. The argument, then, implicates the full weight of the justification for the condition of universal domain.

Given the obvious democratic cost of disenfranchising interested voters because of their opinions, the argument that Arrow's theorem inevitably leads us to restrict voting rights to shareholders is not compelling. If one is willing to sacrifice universal domain, why not further restrict voting rights to those who agree on the precise direction in which the corporation should go, or, better still, on the slate of directors to take it there? (After all, that kind of agreement, unlike a shared goal of profit maximization, may actually guarantee a transitive outcome.) Or why not sacrifice one of the other conditions of democratic fairness? Restricting the vote to shareholders is certainly not the only choice procedure that may eliminate the possibility of cyclical results – one could also have a system where the person reading this book chooses the directors (which, despite the obvious upside, violates nondictatorship) or a system where the directors are randomly chosen (which violates Pareto efficiency). There is something weird about "solving" the problem of preference aggregation by deciding not to listen to certain people. But, more broadly, the point here is that the case for sacrificing universal domain in this instance has not been made, and we're really just left with the question we started with: Should voting rights be restricted to shareholders?

Likelihood of Intransitive Results

The argument from Arrow's theorem is all the more surprising given that the law and economics version does not analyze the likelihood or cost of intransitive results. As it turns out, the likelihood of cyclical outcomes, even when voting is not limited to shareholders, is probably quite small, and the cost of such outcomes, when they do occur, is probably negligible (and certainly not likely to cause corporations to "self-destruct"). This is true for several reasons.

Initially, we note that empirical observations across a broad range of voting mechanisms have failed to discover the large number of intransitivities initially predicted by social choice theory.[56] This is probably because those early predictions were based on the assumption that all individual preference orders were equally likely to occur in a preference profile – that individual preference orders were somehow randomly distributed.[57] In such cases, for example, almost one-third of the possible preference profiles in a large election with as few as six alternatives produce intransitive outcomes.[58] Without this assumption of an impartial culture, however, the predicted frequency of cycles varies tremendously, and there are several aspects of real-world preference profiles that greatly increase the likelihood of transitive outcomes.

One feature of a preference profile that ensures transitive outcomes is something loosely referred to as spectrum agreement, which is a domain restriction that occurs when all voters array their preferences upon a common spectrum. It should not be confused with agreement on the order of those alternatives. To make this point clear, take the extreme example of a case where all the individuals rank candidates for corporation director based on whether the candidates promise to maximize profits (one end of the spectrum) or to minimize profits (the other end of the spectrum).[59] There are three candidates running for office – a profit maximizer (p), a wastrel (w), and some evenhanded chap in the middle (m). Voters who want to maximize profits will prefer candidate p over candidate w, with m somewhere in between. Conversely, voters who want to throw money away will most prefer w, followed by m, with p last. Moderate voters will have preference orders of m-p-w or m-w-p, depending on whether they are closer to the profit-maximizing or wastrel side of the spectrum. Although these voters rank the candidates in different orders, their preferences can all be aligned along the same spectrum. And no voter would rank the moderate candidate last, as agreement on the spectrum precludes such an ordering.

This type of spectrum agreement is important because it is a sufficient condition for transitivity.[60] When all voters align the alternatives on a common spectrum, a simple majoritarian voting procedure will produce a transitive social ordering.[61] This is true despite the fact that the voters vehemently disagree on the relative merits of the candidates;[62] indeed, the example included voters who wanted profits maximized and those who wanted profits minimized. But so long as there is agreement on the spectrum, an acyclic result is guaranteed.

Spectrum agreement of this sort may be described in a variety of ways, all of which constitute a sufficient condition for transitive outcomes. For example, a group of individual preference profiles may be single-peaked if there is a single horizontal ordering (a spectrum) where every one of the individual orders may be arranged such that each has a most desired alternative and desires other alternatives less as they are further from his ideal point.[63] The outcome of a simple majority vote is guaranteed to be transitive, and the winner will be the alternative closest to the ideal point of the median voter.[64] The same sort of outcome is true of profiles that are, analogously, single-caved or polarized.[65]

More broadly, domain restrictions where a preference profile is "value restricted" are a sufficient condition for transitive outcomes.[66] A triple of alternatives is value restricted if at least one alternative is never first, middle, or last in every individual's preference order.[67] The example mentioned earlier – with the profit maximizer, wastrel, and moderate – involved a preference profile that was both single-peaked (on the array of profit maximizing or minimizing) and value restricted (candidate m was never ranked last).

One potential drawback to these various indicia of spectrum agreement is that they must be complete in order to guarantee transitive outcomes.[68] If, for example, even one voter in an otherwise value-restricted preference profile ranks an alternative where they shouldn't (the rank order that made the profile value-restricted to begin with), the guarantee of a transitive outcome disappears.[69] For this reason, one early commentator explained that "the various equilibrium conditions for majority rule are incompatible with even a very modest degree of heterogeneity of tastes, and for most purposes are probably not significantly less restrictive than the extreme condition of complete unanimity of individual preferences."[70] Perhaps, then, we should still be wary of the possibility of cyclical outcomes in our voting procedures.

Fortunately, subsequent work in social choice theory has shown that the likelihood of transitive outcomes does not wholly depend upon the assurance of complete spectrum agreement. Instead, much lesser degrees of voter homogeneity may be sufficient. Richard Niemi, for example, proved that a larger proportion of single-peaked or otherwise value restricted preference orders increased the probability of an acyclic result.[71] This is especially true, counterintuitively, as the number of voters increases.[72] His result was confirmed by later studies using other measures of social homogeneity.[73] And it was supported by other work that looked at preference profiles as a whole, which concluded that society often acts in a way that is more ideological than the individuals that compose it.[74] Overall, then, it turns out that "[t]he [voting] paradox can be very satisfactorily avoided if common frames of reference are widespread but far less than unanimous."[75]

There is a range of political, economic, and sociological reasons why members of societies will exhibit a large degree of spectrum agreement. Most democracies, for example, require a degree of consensus at their formation, and common socialization may further shape individual frames of reference,[76] which may explain why so few cycles have been observed in the political arena. Those reasons would apply with particular force in corporate ventures, which, after all, involve participation in an organization designed to facilitate certain kinds of economic activity. The various categories of people interested in the organization may disagree about many aspects of its governance, but very likely share the common frames of reference that lead to transitive election results. There is reason to believe, in other words, that the number of intransitivities in corporate director elections, even when the electorate is expanded, is likely to be quite low. In any case, the proponents of this argument have not made the positive case for the proposition that expanding the corporate electorate will, in fact, significantly increase the risk of intransitive outcomes when compared with an election restricted to shareholders alone.

Indeed, it may well be that expanding the corporate electorate to include at least one other group of stakeholders may further reduce the expected number of intransitivities in board elections. Take, for example, a governance system where both shareholders and employees have the right to vote on a single slate of candidates for board membership in the same election.[77] That electorate may very well view candidates for board membership through the common lens of whether the candidates are friendlier to the interests of capital or labor. There would, in other words, be the sort of spectrum agreement that increased the likelihood of a transitive outcome in any given board election. There would not, of course, be agreement on the candidates themselves, as members of each group would likely favor candidates more friendly to their interests. And there would not be any guarantee that the resultant board would necessarily make better decisions (though at least the board would represent a greater number of stakeholders in the enterprise). But if, as here, the entire concern is the destructive possibilities of voting cycles, introducing a second set of voters may polarize voter preferences over the array of candidates in a way that greatly *increases* the chance of a transitive outcome. Thus, in this sense, Easterbrook and Fischel are not merely wrong to pronounce it "well known … that when voters hold dissimilar preferences it is not possible to aggregate their preferences into a consistent system of choices";[78] they have it exactly backwards. Expanding the corporate electorate to include constituencies whose interests are clearly oppositional reduces the chances of a multipeaked social preference profile. The argument from Arrow's theorem, then, may actually be turned on its head as an argument in favor of expanding the electorate to include at least one other significant group of stakeholders in a shared election.[79]

The prospect of a corporate board election with multiple voting constituencies brings to light another flaw in the argument from Arrow's theorem – the assumption that the entire expanded electorate would necessarily be voting in a single election. It is much more likely that, were the electorate expanded, each group would be allocated a certain number of board representatives. In other words, there would be a prior decision about how many representatives each group had a right to elect, and then each would hold its own elections. This, roughly speaking, is how the German codetermination system is set up. And the argument from Arrow's theorem would then come down to showing that other constituencies are more likely than shareholders to have suitably domain-restricted preference profiles (a dubious prospect, especially given recent work on the diversity of shareholder preferences) or claiming that the argument really is about cycling at the level of board decision-making, not candidate elections.

The Consequences of Intransitive Results

Finally, the case has not been made that the occasional intransitivity in corporate board elections would harm an organization, and certainly not that it would cause a firm to make "inconsistent choices" that would lead it to "self-destruct."[80] Initially, a large proportion of intransitive results are middle or bottom cycles that still allow us to pick clear winners despite producing cycles involving lower-ranked alternatives.[81] Thus, the estimates of the number of social preference profiles that result in intransitive social preference orders include many that would be incon-sequential in a board election.

Once we're past such general observations about the possibility of cycles, though, it is somewhat difficult to assess the nature of the incon-sistency that gives rise to Easterbrook and Fischel's worries about expanding the corporate electorate. The inconsistency would ostensibly involve the choice of board candidates, which would need to be incom-patible with some other outcome. But it is unclear what that other out-come is thought to be. It cannot be that we are worried about the actual choice of board members being inconsistent with the "correct" choice, because, of course, there is no such choice in this situation. Indeed, the main problem with a preference profile that produces a top cycle is that there is no single "best" social choice.

Like many aspects of the argument from Arrow's theorem, it is difficult to understand what, exactly, its proponents are worried about. Because we are talking about preference consistency, it may be useful to divide the discussion into concerns about synchronic and diachronic consistency. Simply put, synchronic consistency involves having a preference order-ing that fits together at a particular time, while diachronic consistency has to do with coherence over time. They are related (synchronic inconsis-tency may result in diachronic inconsistency), and fear of one, the other, or both may be implicated here.

Although worries about Arrovian intransitivities usually involve con-cerns about synchronic consistency (indeed, cycling is a form of syn-chronic inconsistency), it is difficult to see how those concerns alone could be behind this argument. The synchronic inconsistency in this situation would be that, at one time, a board electorate has preferences with respect to board candidates that give rise to an intransitive ordering. But a nascent intransitivity does not automatically translate into an unstable outcome, since many aspects of corporate (and political) elec-tions operate to produce stability. Initially, most corporate board voting procedures are structured to produce a winner regardless of the presence of lurking intransitivities. Board elections generally require only a plurality vote; indeed, if a candidate runs unopposed and receives one vote, that candidate will win.[82] Some boards have staggered seats, in which directors have three-year terms, and only one-third of the direc-tors are elected in any given year.[83] In cases where there actually are top cycles, the candidate selected by the voting procedure may indeed be the contingent product of that process. But the voting procedures themselves, and the "structure-induced" equilibria they produce,[84] would ensure that the firm would not suffer for lack of directors. And the other director candidates within the cycle have no greater claim to the position than the chosen member.

The more plausible argument here is that a synchronic inconsistency could easily lead to diachronic inconsistency if the choice that resulted from a preference cycle were determined at random. This would mean that, in certain situations, we may have successive board elections with somewhat similar sets of candidates and end up with different board members. These board members would, presumably, have different ideas about the best strategies for the firm, implement them, and thus cause the firm to lurch from one strategy to another. This type of diachronic inconsistency would also fit with the standard inconsistency complaint about firms: that they change courses too often.

But, even assuming the presence of a top cycle, this sort of diachronic inconsistency in the choice of board members is extremely unlikely to occur. The decision processes themselves may operate to produce stability across time.[85] Once a decision is made, there are new actors and new interests involved; the same alternatives are rarely confronted twice. Indeed, in corporate elections, it is quite plausible that both voters and candidates would change from election to election. For example, voters for the "losing" candidate in the first election – especially the shareholder voters, given their low exit costs – may not be around for the next election. The same can be said for the losing candidates themselves, further reducing the possibility of successive elections that produce intransitive outcomes. And if the first board makes certain decisions, the result is a fait accompli at the next election – even the opposition cannot undo it in a costless way.

The ultimate worry here, though, appears to be that expanding the electorate will result in inconsistent *firm* decisions. But even in the rare case where successive board elections produce "inconsistent" board members, they are not likely to result in inconsistent board decisions, much less ones that would cause a firm to self-destruct. For instance, the board member would be only one of, say, eleven directors. In addition, even assuming a complete board turnover, the subsequent board members would presumably know the recent history of the firm's decisions, its current situation, and whether it is now in the firm's interest to change course. In other words, the board members would be able to exercise independent judgment as to whether their original plans for the firm still make sense in the current situation. (Indeed, Gordon claims that cycling at the board level is, for this and several other reasons, very unlikely.)[86] Those who make the argument from Arrow's theorem never explain this move from inconsistent board elections to inconsistent corporate decisions, and it seems anything but obvious.

The intransitivity concerns are even more out of place in the typical corporate election. Our discussion thus far has assumed a robust democracy in which many candidates compete for the right to represent the voting populace. In most corporate elections, the board puts forth its proposed slate of candidates (who may all be incumbents), and the shareholders ratify those choices. This separation of ownership and control, in which shareholders "own" and managers "control," has long been a foundation of corporate law in both theory and practice.[87] Consistency in corporate policy comes not from the uniformity and stability of voter preferences, but rather from a lack of responsiveness and (economically rational) voter apathy. Indeed, efforts to reinvigorate the shareholder franchise have met with only limited success. For this reason, a preference for a hypothetical shareholder franchise (as opposed to a more inclusive voting polity) seems out of touch with the modern reality of the impotence of the corporate franchise.

The related worry that intransitivities in board elections would mean the election results could be manipulated is also not that compelling. If we were in one of those relatively rare situations where voter preferences may produce a cyclical outcome, we know that the election process can be strategically manipulated to achieve a desired outcome. But for this to be possible, potential manipulators must have a pretty good read on the set of voter preferences far enough in advance of the election to actually carry out their plans (by tinkering with the election process or the slate of candidates). In corporate board elections, the set of preferences is typically enormous, and the processes and candidates are usually set far enough in advance of the actual election to make such manipulation quite difficult. More to the point, current board members, who would presumably be in the best position to manipulate the agenda, would manipulate outcomes in a way that *consistently* favored their interests (which should allay the fear of inconsistent firm decisions).[88] Manipulation removes synchronic inconsistency, and consistent manipulation removes diachronic inconsistency. And to the extent that the fear of manipulation is independent of the fear of inconsistency, it is worth pointing out that a manipulated outcome would just be a fallback tiebreaker between top cycle alternatives – which would not result in damaging corporate behavior. Of course, all of this should not be of much concern to those who favor some version of board primacy anyway, for this would just allow the board to further solidify its own power. Thus, the potential for the manipulation of board member elections, like the possibility of inconsistent members over time, does not seem that worrisome.

Proponents of the argument from Arrow's theorem have not connected the long series of points between a board election cycle and a self-destructive firm. There are many aspects of the voting process itself that produce stability in individual elections and across time. Inconsistent board member elections, if and when they do occur, would not normally be expected to produce inconsistent firm decisions, much less ones that would translate into the "destruction" of the firm. In other words, it would take a fantastic story to move from a nascent intransitivity in a board election to a firm that makes self-destructive choices, a story so fantastic as to be completely implausible.

* * *

The argument that relies on Arrow's theorem to explain the present state of the corporate franchise is flawed at many levels. Shareholders do not have a homogeneous interest in profit maximization. Even if they did, it would not directly translate into the kind of agreement on candidates necessary to avoid intransitive results in corporate elections. Further, even if shareholder homogeneity did translate into the requisite agreement on candidates, restricting voting rights to shareholders involves sacrificing a fundamental condition of democracy in a situation where the likelihood and impact of intransitive results is already negligible. This argument for restricting corporate voting rights to shareholders, then, is far from compelling.

The Shareholder Franchise and Board Primacy

Throughout the reign of shareholder primacy as the dominant theoretical narrative of corporate law, there have always been dissenting voices. At various points, some of these voices have coalesced into groups of like-minded theorists.[1] As it now stands, there is no unified school of thought standing in opposition; there are, however, several academic commentators who have individually rallied around various versions of "board primacy." All of these commentators agree that the board of directors should be accorded more power and deference within the corporate structure. They stand opposed to greater shareholder democracy and believe that the corporation is best served by a board that can make decisions largely free of shareholder influence. These commentators come from a variety of backgrounds – law professors, economists, and corporate attorneys – as well as a variety of political viewpoints, ranging from conservative to progressive. While they disagree on the appropriate purpose and goals of the corporation and of corporate law, they all support a version of board primacy in which the board can operate in a more independent manner than shareholder primacists currently advocate.

In this chapter, we situate and critically evaluate these board primacy theories in the broader context of public choice and civic republican approaches to democratic decision-making. We believe that the arguments underlying many of the positions of board primacists conflate two very different aspects of group decision-making processes: the responsiveness of the governance system and the composition of the electorate. This confusion ends up putting the board primacy theorists in the curious position of moving away from a public choice emphasis on preference aggregation toward a more civic republican model of less responsive, more deliberative decision-making. But by restricting the franchise to shareholders, they have needlessly detached their governance structures from the underlying preferences of their constituents without substituting anything in their place. In other words, these theorists are civic republicans with conflicting and contradictory notions of the public (or, in this case, corporate) good.

Public Choice and Civic Republican Approaches to Decision-Making

In political theory, there are two basic ways of conceptualizing democratic decision processes: a public choice approach and a civic republican approach.[2] The public choice version views group decision processes mainly as an exercise in preference aggregation. Individual preferences are taken as given, and individual and social welfare is measured in terms of preference satisfaction. The best group decision processes, then, are those that best aggregate individual preferences into social choices.[3] A civic republican approach, by contrast, posits a substantive concept of the public good that goes beyond mere preference aggregation.[4] This notion of the public good is capable of being perceived and refined through deliberation and, in fact, may lead to a decision that does not maximize the satisfaction of existing preferences. The public good is not unrelated to preference satisfaction but is not beholden to it.[5]

While these two theories of group decision processes are rarely seen in their pure forms, they provide a useful way of illustrating some of the features of actual decision processes and, more to the point, examining the scholarship in support of them. When focusing on the aggregative function of decision-making, for example, it makes little sense to describe outcomes as good or bad; however, one may decide that some flaw in the process led to an outcome that was "not really what most people wanted."[6] From the point of view of a civic republican, on the other hand, decisions are good or bad depending upon whether they advance or retard a particular version of the public good.[7] Most democratic decision procedures are designed to take advantage of the benefits of both approaches and thus are composed of a mix of public choice and civic republican features.

These two views may also help sharpen our assessment of some of the scholarly claims about governance structures. For example, scholarship that tends to emphasize aggregation sometimes overlooks the value of deliberation in decision-making, and scholarship that focuses on deliberation and the public good may overlook the useful corrective force and empirical grounding of actual preferences in the decision process.[8] This simple dichotomy – between aggregative and deliberative processes, preferences and judgments – may help us critically evaluate various versions of board primacy by allowing us to assess and compare features of group decision-making structures and the scholarly arguments in support of them.

We will focus our attention on four prominent board primacy theories: Stephen Bainbridge's director primacy theory, Margaret Blair and Lynn Stout's team production theory, Lawrence Mitchell's self-perpetuating board, and Martin Lipton and Steven Rosenblum's quinquennial election model. Based on similarities in their approaches, we categorize Bainbridge as well as Blair and Stout as "wise ruler" theorists, while we characterize Mitchell as well as Lipton and Rosenblum as "long-term interest" theorists.[9] Though they disagree on many aspects of corporate governance, all four reject the notion that voters should have more power to choose their representatives, and argue for a more insulated board. They all believe that facilitating shareholder democracy, and thereby shareholder power, would create costs that would outweigh the purported benefits.

The Wise Ruler Theorists

Shareholder democracy advocates generally bemoan directors' independence from their electorate. They view the disconnect between shareholders and directors as the primary source of intrafirm agency costs – namely, the costs shareholders must bear for delegating control of the corporation to someone else. They posit that if shareholders can find ways of exerting more power over the board, the corporation will focus more on shareholder interests (and less on the interests of board members or managers).[10] This change will cut down on agency costs and lead to both greater firm and societal efficiency. However, certain corporate law scholars disagree with this analysis. They have argued instead that the board must be free to make its own decisions without undue pressure from shareholders. Freed to operate more independently, directors will make better choices about how the firm should proceed.

We call these commentators the "wise ruler" theorists because they invest the board with a great deal of acumen, as well as power. Bainbridge has described the board as the "Platonic guardian" of the firm.[11] He argues that the board sits at the center of a nexus of contracts between various constituents of the firm and the fictional firm itself.[12] Similarly, Blair and Stout describe the board as "mediating hierarchs" who manage the relationships of various corporate constituencies.[13] Under both scenarios, the board is envisioned as a body that exists above all the other participants, with authority apart from them. Indeed, independence and insulation are critical to the performance of its role.

Bainbridge's "director primacy" theory has a significant descriptive component in that he believes it offers the best account of why boards are structured to have the independence that they are generally afforded.[14] However, Bainbridge also defends the status quo, arguing that shareholder democracy reforms would be harmful to corporate welfare.[15] He largely relies on the work of Kenneth Arrow with regard to the tension between authority and accountability.[16] Although greater board accountability to shareholders might reduce agency costs, Bainbridge argues that such reforms would create much inefficiency within the corporation. As he describes it:

> Active investor involvement in corporate decisionmaking seems likely to disrupt the very mechanism that makes the widely held public corporation practicable: namely, the centralization of essentially nonreviewable decisionmaking authority in the board of directors. The chief economic virtue of the public corporation is . . . that it provides a hierarchical decisionmaking structure well-suited to the problem of operating a large business enterprise with numerous employees, managers, shareholders, creditors, and other constituencies.[17]

Bainbridge does not quarrel with shareholder primacy as the goal of the corporation; in fact, he believes that the board should direct itself toward shareholder wealth maximization.[18] However, he believes that the proper means to achieve this end is through director primacy.

Blair and Stout see a comparable role for the board within their model of the corporation. Like Bainbridge and other contractarian theorists, Blair and Stout see the firm as a series of relationships between the various constituencies that make up the business.[19] These relationships result in the joint production of goods or services that in turn create wealth. The directors serve as the ultimate authority when it comes to assigning responsibilities, mediating disputes, and divvying up the profits.[20] Board insulation and independence are therefore critical to their role. The board must be independent from all constituencies in order to be trusted with such a crucial and uncertain responsibility. If the board were to favor one constituency over others, the unfavored groups would be less willing to make the proper investments of capital and labor to make the firm function.

Unlike Bainbridge, Blair and Stout do not argue that shareholder wealth maximization should be the goal of the corporation.[21] Instead, they argue that directors owe a duty to the corporation and that the corporation consists of all of the stakeholders who are responsible for the business of the enterprise.[22] Blair and Stout focus on shareholders and employees, but they also include creditors and the local community as potential stakeholders.[23] According to their model, these stakeholders contribute their resources to the enterprise under an implicit bargain that the enterprise itself will fairly apportion the responsibilities and rewards.[24] The board is hired by these stakeholders to serve as the apportioning body. Thus, although the board is in some sense an agent for the stakeholders, it must have authority above them in order to carry out its function. The role is thus less one of an agent and more that of a trustee.[25]

Neither Bainbridge nor Blair and Stout offer extensive policy reforms. Instead, their theories are best characterized as descriptions of the status quo that explain, as well as justify, the current regime. Both Bainbridge and Stout have extensively criticized efforts to expand shareholder democracy.[26] However, they have not argued (unlike the commentators below) for efforts to further insulate or protect directors' discretion. Instead, they largely believe the status quo offers the proper balance.[27]

The Long-Term Interest Theorists

Another set of theorists also argues for board primacy in the form of board insulation and independence from shareholder pressure. However, they base their analyses not on a model of corporate structure, but rather on concerns about the influence of short-term interests. In their view, shareholders have developed an extremely short time horizon for judging the success of the corporation and its leadership. As boards and officers have come under more pressure to follow the desires of these shareholders, they have adopted the goal of short-term share price maximization. This focus, these theorists argue, has skewed the perspectives of shareholders and, as a result, has hurt the long-term efficiency of corporations.

Although a number of commentators share this concern about short-termism, Lawrence Mitchell and Martin Lipton stand out for their long-standing critiques of shareholder primacy on the grounds that it inexorably leads to short-term share price primacy. And both have proposed somewhat dramatic solutions to this problem.

In an article and a subsequent book, Mitchell has argued that the boards of large public companies should be self-perpetuating.[28] As Mitchell describes his proposal: "[O]nce the members of the board

[are] put in place, either by a one-time stockholder vote or public appointment or something like it, the board itself [is] to fill the periodic vacancies resulting from death, resignation, and increases in board size by selecting the people to fill those vacancies."[29] Mitchell acknowledges that this is a "pretty radical idea,"[30] but he believes such a radical approach would best free managers to manage the firm. Because any control by shareholders would focus directors on share price, Mitchell believes that complete freedom from shareholder oversight would "enable them to manage responsibly and for the long term."[31]

In a somewhat less dramatic departure from current law, Mitchell also endorses the quinquennial election proposal of Lipton and Rosenblum.[32] In the article outlining their approach, Lipton and Rosenblum also deplore the short-term focus that shareholder primacy brings to the corporation.[33] In a complex set of reforms, they establish a new framework for corporate governance, the centerpiece of which is the lengthening of directors' terms to five years. During these five years, directors could not be ousted save for illegal conduct or "willful malfeasance."[34] Directors would also be entitled to approve all mergers, acquisitions, buyouts, or takeovers, except that such changes could be accomplished only at the time of the directors' election.[35] As part of the election, the directors would be required to propose an in-depth five-year plan, and their compensation would be tied to achieving the goals set forth in the plan.[36] The board would also be responsible for hiring independent advisors prior to the election to provide a critique of their plan.[37]

Both the self-perpetuating board and the quinquennially elected board are significantly more insulated from shareholders than current law provides. Neither set of commentators seems too concerned about the downgrade in shareholder power, as they view that power as the problem in the first place. Under the quinquennial election plan, Lipton and Rosenblum believe that shareholders would in fact have a limited but revitalized role, as they conceive of the election as a time for shareholders to make a meaningful vote on the corporation's future. They provide that shareholders holding at least 5 percent of the corporation's equity would have access to the proxy ballot.[38] In the original description of Mitchell's self-perpetuating plan, the board becomes self-perpetuating once when the corporation goes public. Therefore, the board of a privately held company – elected by the private shareholders – would essentially become the board ad infinitum. Mitchell recommends, however, that this board "replace itself with a group of directors who are neither managers nor stockholders"; instead, the board would be made up of independent directors.[39] Mitchell believes that this change would render the board "far less likely to feel allegiance to management."[40] In his later discussion of the policy, Mitchell is more oblique about the composition, stating that "the members of the board [would be] put in place, either by a one-time stockholder vote or public appointment or something like it."[41] And when he endorses Lipton and Rosenblum's proposal, he also tepidly endorses an expansion of the electorate to include employees and creditors. Mitchell argues that "there's no reason to think, unless you view stock price maximization as the corporation's only legitimate goal, that allowing employees and creditors to vote too would damage the corporation."[42] In later work, Mitchell has gone even further, arguing that "ideally (although most likely improbably), the right of public shareholders to vote should be eliminated."[43]

From these brief sketches, it is clear that all board primacists believe the board should not become more responsive to shareholder concerns. The wise ruler theorists largely believe the system is balanced properly, while the long-term interest theorists would reorient the board toward a longer-term outlook by extending the tenure of board members. Only Mitchell suggests any changes to the electorate, and he does so in a somewhat offhanded way. Instead, these theorists largely believe that tinkering with the board itself, rather than those who choose the board, would be the best course of reform. We now turn to a deeper examination of the theories and, in particular, the issue of the electorate.

Shareholder Diversity and the Rise of Board Primacy

Shareholders are a diverse group. As we saw in Chapter 5, they are not the homogeneous wealth maximizers they were once thought to be; instead, they have interests that diverge along a number of dimensions.[44] Some commentators have focused attention upon the problems caused by equity derivatives, which carve up various shareholder rights into discrete financial securities.[45] But there are many other ways in which shareholders fail to share common interests.[46] And even when the interests of shareholders line up and they agree on a definition of wealth maximization, they may differ as to how best to achieve that goal.[47] Ultimately, the notion that shareholders have homogeneous preferences of any sort is a simplifying assumption that is increasingly under strain.[48]

One possible response to shareholder heterogeneity is to move away from shareholder primacy toward a system of governance that is less responsive, in the direction of board primacy. The argument is that because the preferences of the shareholder electorate are as diverse (read: scary) as those of other constituents, many of the reasons for restricting the voting rights of those constituents (the procedural and substantive inefficiencies) now apply to shareholders as well. For those reasons, then, corporate boards should be less responsive to shareholder interests, and more power and discretion should be accorded to these boards.

Shareholder diversity has pushed many scholars, touting both board and shareholder primacy, in this direction. One sees this new pressure throughout the corporate law literature when a question arises as to the appropriate level of responsiveness of a system of corporate governance. Hedge funds, for example, may have shorter time horizons than other investors, and critics have cited this potential for a short-term focus as a reason for dampening their influence.[49] Others have argued that sovereign wealth funds – investment funds run by nations rather than capitalists – have skewed incentives that differ from those of other shareholders. In fact, one set of commentators has even suggested that sovereign wealth funds should forego the right to vote in shareholder elections.[50] Divergent interests among shareholders may point in a variety of different governance directions. That is, although shareholder heterogeneity provides general support for board primacy, it is relevant to almost any feature of corporate governance that makes the system more or less responsive to the shareholders, and it generally exerts pressure in the direction of making the system less responsive.

Thus, it is important to disentangle the two kinds of arguments that are generally made in response to the diversity of preferences exhibited by shareholders and other corporate constituents. One set of arguments, which go to the level of responsiveness in the governance system, make some sense. The other set, however, goes beyond responsiveness and continues to argue for a particular and exclusive electorate – shareholders. These claims are often made together and are sometimes conflated. But they are very different aspects of a governance system, corporate or otherwise.

System Responsiveness to the Electorate

The worries about an overresponsive system of corporate governance drive most board primacy theories.[51] The corporation, board primacy proponents argue, should be structured in a way that allows the board to be relatively insulated against the whims of the shareholder electorate.[52] The arguments here echo debates from political science about the relative strengths and weaknesses of direct and representative democracies.[53] Direct democracies have a great deal of responsiveness to the electorate's preferences, and, as a result, may be viewed as more legitimate. The downsides to such responsiveness, however, are that decision-making on such a massive scale is relatively costly and that direct democracies are more susceptible to "tyranny of the majority" types of issues. Representative decision-making procedures, by contrast, are less responsive (and thus less susceptible to a tyrannical majority) and more conducive to deliberation by the elected representatives. The shortcoming of such a system, though, is that as its representatives become less responsive to the electorate, they may fail to advance the interests of their constituents.

It should come as no surprise that this distinction between direct and representative decision structures maps, somewhat roughly, onto our earlier discussion of the difference between public choice and civic republican theories of democracy. Public choice theories, with their emphasis on preference aggregation, tend to favor more direct decision procedures, such as initiatives that allow the immediate aggregation of preferences into policy or, in some cases, markets driven by individual choices. Civic republican theories favor the detached deliberation afforded by more insulated groups of representatives. The overlap isn't perfect, and most theories of governance fall somewhere in between the extremes, but it may help sharpen some of the different approaches.

The fear of an overresponsive system of governance is the primary force motivating a shift in power away from shareholders to the board. As mentioned above, it resolves into two kinds of concerns. First, a system that is too responsive to shareholders may give rise to various procedural inefficiencies. Put simply, being more responsive costs time and money. A system of shareholder initiative, for example, is viewed as problematic because it slows down corporate decision-making and because of the potential cost of running the electoral machinery.[54]

The main proponent of board primacy, Stephen Bainbridge, makes this point largely on the basis of Kenneth Arrow's models of consensus and authority decision-making.[55] According to Bainbridge, shareholders with differing interests and levels of information would bog down corporate decision-making.[56] Bainbridge, citing Arrow, argues that decision-making by consensus works best when the participants have similar – if not identical – preferences and information. There are, initially, "mechanical difficulties" in achieving consensus among thousands of shareholders.[57] But even if such difficulties could be overcome, "active shareholder participation in corporate decision making would still be precluded by the shareholders' widely divergent interests and distinctly different levels of information."[58] Thus, Bainbridge concludes, corporate governance systems are – and should be – structured to enhance authority-based decision-making, with the board being the ultimate authority.[59]

Along these lines, a system responsive to shareholder preferences may also be prone to voting pathologies, or cycles, which further diminish the ability of firms to move decisively in some consistent direction. The voting cycles argument was originally made in defense of the exclusive shareholder franchise. Its premise, though, was that there is a direct relationship between the diversity of an electorate and the likelihood of damaging voting cycles. With mounting evidence that shareholder preferences are actually quite a bit more diverse than previously thought, such an argument would also militate against expanded voting powers for shareholders as well. Indeed, Jeffrey Gordon, for one, argued in favor of the absolute delegation rule (and against shareholder initiatives) on precisely those grounds years ago,[60] and Bainbridge has made a similar point.[61] The possibility of voting cycles has been seen as problematic enough for these scholars to distance the board from its shareholder electorate and, as noted earlier, keep other constituents out of that electorate altogether.

The second and greater drawback to more responsive corporate governance systems is that they give rise to a tyranny of the majority. They are, in other words, *too* efficient at translating the will of a majority of the electorate into corporate action. This criticism comes in various guises. For some, the worry is that certain "special interest" shareholders will exploit other shareholders rather than act for the good of all shareholders.[62] Others worry that shareholders generally will exploit other corporate constituents.[63] Either way, a more responsive system of corporate governance will enable these self-interested, sometimes transient majorities to manipulate corporations toward their own selfish ends.

Several of the board primacy theorists refer to this fear of "tyranny of the shareholder majority." Blair and Stout establish their model of "mediating hierarchs" on the notion that shareholder dominance will lead the other team members to disinvest or invest less than optimally. As they explain: "[T]eam members [including shareholders] understand they would be far less likely to elicit the full cooperation and firm-specific investment of other members if they did not give up control rights."[64]

Thus, it is the directors' job to "balance team members' competing interests in a fashion that keeps everyone happy enough that the productive coalition stays together."[65] Accordingly, it only makes sense to Blair and Stout that "American law in fact grants directors tremendous discretion to sacrifice shareholders' interests in favor of management, employees, and creditors."[66] This need to "sacrifice" shareholder interests explains the desire to insulate the board from shareholder importuning.

Similarly, the long-term theorists want to insulate the board against shareholder pressure to maximize short-term gain. Lipton and Rosenblum argue that institutional shareholders – the shareholder group with the greatest voice and power – are biased toward short-term results, and as a consequence such shareholders have pushed companies to favor quick results over long-term growth.[67] Insulating the board with five-year terms allows the directors to pursue a longer-term strategy without the risk of shareholder wrath.[68] In turn, this will "benefit the corporation's other constituencies, which prosper if the enterprise's business operations prosper over the long term."[69] Similarly, Mitchell argues that his self-perpetuating board would best free directors "to do what it is they do best, and that is manage (or provide for the management of) corporations for the long term."[70] In order to accomplish this, "[c]orporate management should be entirely separated from stockholder pressure."[71]

These arguments all point to a disconnection between the will of the electoral majority and the good of the corporation. In order to properly pursue the social good, the board has to be insulated from the shareholders. Thus, these reformers all seek to dampen the responsiveness of the corporate structure to shareholder concerns. As a result, the board is (or would be) freed up to use its own discretion to make decisions, even if they conflict with the clear preferences of a majority of the electorate.

Board Primacy and Shareholder Homogeneity

It is clear that shareholders have less homogeneous preferences than previously believed. This, in all likelihood, provides some additional support for less responsive systems of corporate governance. It does not, however, counsel in favor of a corporate electorate restricted to shareholders. Indeed, as discussed in the Chapters 5, 6, and 7, the recent recognition that shareholders are more diverse than once thought actually undercuts many of the arguments for their favored position among corporate constituents. Board primacists, however, have generally eschewed such analysis and simply kept the shareholder electorate unchanged.[72] But there is nothing in the typical arguments in favor of a less responsive system that entails this result. The exclusive shareholder franchise just gets dragged along for the ride into board primacy positions. And the failure of board primacists to reconsider the proper composition of the electorate leaves them in an increasingly untenable position. Some, like Blair and Stout, operate under the assumption that shareholder preferences are quite homogeneous and argue accordingly when it comes to the proper composition of the electorate.[73] Others, like Bainbridge, concede that shareholder preferences are less homogeneous than once thought and instead argue that they are still more homogeneous than those of other constituents, or of a combined electorate.[74] Either way, the arguments from (relative) shareholder homogeneity to their exclusive entitlement to the franchise are similar.

Coming from advocates of board primacy, with its civic republican emphasis on detached deliberation, these arguments for the exclusive shareholder franchise are surprising. Take the first set of concerns about procedural inefficiencies. These concerns include the argument that expanding the board electorate to include other constituents will lead to the kind of bickering that will frustrate corporate decision-making. Blair and Stout, for example, ask us to "[i]magine the chaos and politicking likely to attend an election in which a firm's creditors, executives, rank-and-file employees, and other stakeholders with unique and often conflicting interests could vote on their favored candidates."[75] The electorate's diverse interests, it is argued, would bog down the decision-making process, either at the point of the election or in the boardroom.

Of course a more diverse electorate would, at some level, result in less harmonious decision-making. But this is not a compelling argument for restricting the franchise to shareholders alone, especially coming from advocates of board primacy. Any group choice procedure is intended to work with diverse preferences. The entire point of most voting systems or other social choice procedures is to take a set of individual preference profiles and aggregate them into a group choice.[76] A diverse board electorate could vote in a single election (as shareholders now do) or in separate elections for stakeholder representatives (like the German code-termination model).[77]

The worry should be no greater at the board level – one can always force a decision. Corporate boards, for example, traditionally follow internal procedures requiring majority votes, with the chair having tie-breaking authority.[78] If the particular decision procedures don't seem to be working smoothly, one can usually identify the problem and reduce or eliminate the difficulty by tinkering with institutional design features. In the end, one can always design a procedure for forcing a vote and thus reach a decision on any particular issue – there may be winners and losers, but a decision will be made that is based on voter preferences.

More to the point, though, advocates of board primacy appear to be overvaluing consensus in the boardroom.[79] One of the primary benefits of more deliberative governance processes is that representatives, in addition to expressing their own views on the interests of their constituents, may also persuade others to change their minds. And they may be persuaded to change their own minds. Indeed, a wide range of studies demonstrate that a greater diversity of views mediated through the deliberative process may well lead to better decision-making.[80] A governance system in which a diverse body of voters elects a relatively insulated group of representatives should be especially appealing to civic republicans with no fixed sense of the good. Through the deliberative process and, if it comes to it, a vote, board members can come to a shared notion of the common good. Consensus among the voters or the board members, in other words, is overrated, especially when that consensus is bought at the price of excluding from the process those with differing views. And claims about the efficiency of the decision-making process all depend upon what is being maximized, which is sometimes at the heart of the disagreement.

Bainbridge frames his argument for board homogeneity in terms of Kenneth Arrow's scheme of consensus and authority decision-making.[81] Bainbridge argues that an electorate expanded to include other constituents, like employees, would be even more diverse in its views than a simple shareholder electorate.[82] The vote should accordingly be limited to shareholders alone, according to him, to stave off conflict between directors and allow a hierarchical system to have its full effect.

Bainbridge's version of this argument does not work that well as a general matter or as applied to this issue of the proper scope of the corporate electorate. Initially, his position – that, according to Arrow, constituents with differing interests and levels of information call for an authority-based structure – is incomplete. Arrow does postulate a tension between authoritarian and consensus-based governance.[83] But, as Brett McDonnell pointed out, "Bainbridge moves very, very quickly from recognizing the tension between authority and accountability to arguing that we should presume a legal structure that favors authority over accountability."[84] These moves, which McDonnell dubs "Arrowian moments," occur throughout Bainbridge's work, and are noteworthy for their lack of substantive argument showing that the more authoritarian, board-centric solution is the correct one.[85] In other words, recognizing the tension does not tell us where on the continuum we should be with respect to each institutional design feature and certainly doesn't tell us that we should always tilt toward the more authoritarian solution.

Bainbridge's argument becomes even more tenuous when it is applied to other constituencies and their voting power. First, it conflates the responsiveness of the governance system with those to whom it is responsive. Arrow's conceptual scheme argues for more authoritarian (that is, less responsive) systems in certain situations, not a restriction on the scope of the (however distant) electorate. Second, once Bainbridge concedes shareholder diversity, his point on the exclusive shareholder franchise hangs on the difference in preference homogeneity between a shareholder electorate and either an electorate composed of another constituency or an electorate expanded to include shareholders and other constituents. There is little argument demonstrating that a material difference even exists.[86] And, as with the general version of his argument, there is nothing here to suggest that the difference justifies this move to the extreme end of the authority-consensus spectrum. In this situation, Bainbridge needs an even stronger argument than when he makes his general arguments from shareholder diversity to board primacy, for here he is deploying Arrow's concepts of consensus and authority decision-making with a view to cutting other constituents out of the governance process completely, not merely making the process less responsive to them.

A second, related argument made for the exclusive shareholder franchise trades on the looming specter of voting cycles related to Arrow's impossibility theorem. Its basic premise, as discussed in Chapter 7, is that there is a direct relationship between the diversity of an electorate and the likelihood of damaging voting cycles. But even assuming that there is something to this argument, what's left of it in the face of the recent assaults on the concept of shareholder homogeneity? Not much – but that hasn't prevented board primacy theorists from continuing to rely on it. Bainbridge, for example, appears to think that preference homogeneity is a one-dimensional concept and that more is better when it comes to reducing the incidence of cycling.[87] There are, however, various conditions that reduce or eliminate the incidence of cycling, and, short of complete agreement, most have less to do with shared preferences over outcomes than they do with shared dimensions upon which those preferences may be arrayed.[88] Indeed, it turns out that placing two constituencies with oppositional interests within the same electorate (say, shareholders and employees) may be the best way of reducing the incidence of cyclical outcomes, because preferences would polarize across a shared dimension of capital and labor.[89]

A third procedural argument for the exclusive shareholder franchise is also undercut by the revelation of shareholder diversity. The argument, remember, is that shareholders alone have a very good marker of the degree of their interest in the firm, which allows us to perfectly calibrate their voting power – namely, the number of shares owned. The precision of this calibration is thrown off by the presence of heterogenous shareholder preferences, as discussed in Chapter 5. But an even bigger problem is that the concept of one share, one vote tells us little about whether or how voting power should be distributed among stakeholders. The number of shares owned by particular shareholders may be a good indication of their interest in comparison to other shareholders; it tells us nothing, however, about their interest in comparison to, say, an employee, a creditor, or a customer. More specifically, it is not an independent reason for concluding that the present arrangement, which gives shareholders alone the right to vote, is any better at capturing the preferences of interested parties than, say, giving employees alone the right to vote and capturing everyone else's interests through contract. The difficulty in assessing how much to weight the aggregate shareholder interest against the aggregate interests of any other group of stakeholders runs both ways and does not demand resolution in any particular direction.

Perhaps a simpler way to think about this point is in terms of a board with members who represent different constituencies.[90] On an eleven-member corporate board that represents the interests of many different stakeholders, the fact that one group of stakeholders has a particularly nuanced way of apportioning voting power among its own members tells us nothing about how many board representatives that group should be assigned as a whole. The one share, one vote rule may be a good way of divvying up voting power among common-stock shareholders, but it tells us nothing about how voting power should be distributed among different stakeholders.

This is not to say that the presence of an effective measure of stakeholder interest is irrelevant to determining whether any particular group of stakeholders receives the right to vote. Distribution of a corporate franchise operates, at one level, like that of a political franchise. As discussed in Chapter 2, voting is a collective decision-making process designed to reflect preferences of those interested in the outcome of an election. For that reason, we usually tie the right to vote to the strength of one's preferences in the election.[91] Because we have no direct method of observing people's preferences, we are forced to rely on various markers of the strength of their interest.[92] In the political arena, we historically relied upon property-holding and taxpaying requirements as markers of voter interest; we now use residency and citizenship requirements for much the same purpose.[93] Because the presence of a good marker of voter interest is central to the issue of the scope of the franchise, the fact that shareholders have a pretty good marker is an appropriate factor to consider when doling out corporate voting rights.

But, again, the fact that we have a good marker of shareholder interest does not mean that we lack good markers for other corporate constituents, or that shareholders, therefore, should receive all of the voting power. Remember, when assessing markers of voter interest, we are usually looking for two things: Does the marker accurately capture voter interest, and is the marker manageable?[94] As we'll examine in more detail in Chapter 10, shares are a relatively accurate and manageable marker of shareholder interest, and therefore shareholders are a group whose interests can be reasonably captured through voting (rather than through some other device, like contract).[95] Employment status is also a good marker: it is a good indication of interest in corporate decision-making, and employees are pretty easy to identify. But there may not be good markers for all corporate constituents. It may be difficult, for example, to devise an accurate and manageable marker for customer interest in a typical retail firm. Any individual customer's interest in the firm may be irregular, and it may be hard to identify the customers before they become interested parties (and make, or decide not to make, a purchase). For that reason, individual contracts may be the best way to capture their interests.[96] The presence of a good voting marker for one group of constituents has little bearing on the decision to extend the franchise to any other group; those decisions can, and should, be made independently.

The second argument for the exclusive shareholder franchise was that more diverse constituents, if granted the vote, would pursue their own special interests to the detriment of others in their group or, more generally, other stakeholders. This is the tyranny of the majority issue. Once again, before examining how this argument fares without the assumption of shareholder homogeneity, we should examine it on its own terms. The premise – that democratic processes may allow a majority to exploit minority interests – is well known.[97] The conclusion, though, is a bit perverse. The presence of a tyrannical majority is usually offered in support of structures designed to protect the exploited minority; here, though, it is offered as a reason for pushing the majority group out of the decision process altogether!

Tyranny of the majority can still be an issue. It is an issue in corporate governance as it is in any democratic decision procedure. Most political democracies attempt to blunt the effects of what the Founders called "factions" by making a system of government less responsive to the electorate and providing substantive protections for minorities.[98] The same approach is taken in corporate law, where there are many layers between shareholders and corporate decision-making as well as various protections for minority shareholders.[99] Minority shareholders in closely held corporations, for example, enjoy wide-ranging equitable protections through the doctrine of minority oppression.[100] Minority shareholders in publicly held corporations are protected by the fiduciary duty of loyalty, which prevents the majority shareholder from pushing through lopsided, self-interested transactions that harm the corporation as whole.[101] Such protections are a rational response to the possibility of an exploitive majority faction; eliminating minority (or majority) interests from the corporate electorate just adds insult to injury.

Once shareholder diversity enters the picture, this argument, like the others, makes even less sense. The claim again comes down to one of relative diversity and the assumption that any marginal increase in the diversity of the electorate militates in favor of a less responsive system and restrictions on the scope of the electorate. In corporate governance, as in politics, there are many reasons for embracing more deliberative systems of governance. Some of those reasons have to do with the cost of more responsive systems – putting every single corporate decision to a vote of an electorate, however defined, is a waste of time and money. Some of those reasons have to do with the heterogeneity of the electorate and the worry that permanent or even temporary majorities may pursue their own interests to the detriment of a minority.[102]

But, in such cases, it takes only a slight departure from complete homogeneity to push in favor of a less responsive system of governance. For example, even shareholders who are completely unanimous in their support of maximizing shareholder value may still disagree on, say, the time frame for that, and thus may want to pursue very different strategies. In an overly responsive system, a tyrannical majority may be able to exploit a minority given this, or really any, differentiation in preference profiles. The recognition that shareholder interests are actually more diverse than once theorized doesn't really add that much weight to arguments for less responsive systems. Most of the arguments in favor of a less responsive system, such as the costs and potential for exploitation, apply regardless of the exact level of diversity within the electorate.

So, in sum, what does increased shareholder diversity mean for the scope of the electorate or, more to the point, the exclusive shareholder franchise? To the extent that shareholders now have diverse interests, they are more prone to inefficient squabbling, more likely to produce damaging voting cycles, in a better position to exploit their differences, and the one share, one vote system is less well calibrated to their interests. Scholars attempt to salvage the arguments for the shareholder franchise by hanging them on the *relative* homogeneity of shareholder interests, but their arguments are not fine-tuned enough to turn on these supposed differences in the preference profiles of different constituents. Instead, shareholder diversity just makes these bad arguments worse.

So we are left with slightly stronger arguments for a less responsive governance structure and increasingly poorer arguments for the exclusive shareholder franchise (arguments that, for the most part, came out of shareholder primacy positions to begin with). To a large degree, this occurs because preference homogeneity, or the lack thereof, is viewed as having an equivalent effect on both the ideal level of board responsiveness and the composition of the board electorate. It does not.

Board Primacy and the Corporate Good

As shareholder preferences have been revealed to be not quite as homogenous as envisioned, board primacists have continued to distance the decision-making processes from the shareholder electorate. This push is consistent with the civic republican impulse of board primacy theorists to insulate decision-makers from the whims of the electorate. An insulated board is in a better position to deliberate and reach decisions that advance the interest of the firm. But what exactly is their sense of the corporate good? It is here that we see a strange feature of this move in the direction of board primacy. It is civic republicanism without any sense of what counts as the public good. Where does the sense of the corporate, or public, good come from? And how does the system of governance keep the corporate board honest in its duty to pursue those ends?

Those are questions that board primacy theorists have trouble answering. Shareholder primacy dictates that both the corporate and public good are best pursued by maximizing shareholder wealth. Within that framework, there may be debates about the best means of achieving that maximization, but the ends are agreed upon. Bainbridge fits within this category. Even though he has set up his "director primacy" theory in opposition to shareholder primacy, he still believes that shareholder wealth maximization is the proper corporate purpose.[103] His debates with shareholder primacists such as Lucian Bebchuk revolve around the best means for pursuing these agreed-upon ends.

However, other board primacists have difficulty in establishing the corporate good and the board's connection to it. Blair and Stout give a perfectly respectable answer as to corporate purpose: the board is supposed to be advancing the interests of all corporate constituents and needs to be somewhat insulated in order to do that (so as not to be dominated by shareholder interests).[104] The directors are viewed as the "independent hierarchs" serving the interests of the corporation, which "can be understood as a joint welfare function of all the individuals who make firm-specific investments and agree to participate in the extracontractual, internal mediation process within the firm."[105] The list of possible individuals may include executives, employees, and shareholders, as well as creditors and even a local community.[106] But when it comes to the composition of the electorate that will, ultimately, make the board accountable to all parties, they oddly fall back upon some of the arguments that turn on shareholder homogeneity – like the argument from politics and the argument from Arrow's theorem – to justify the exclusive shareholder electorate.[107]

This is a strange turn for several reasons. Initially, it seems to run against the rest of their theory, which views the board as acting on behalf of all corporate constituents. On this front, the best they can do is argue that the exclusive shareholder franchise is not inconsistent with the rest of their theory, which is true, but it is certainly not dictated by it.[108] Moreover, we are left with the question of why a board elected by shareholders alone would feel any pressure to act on behalf of all corporate constituents. It is one thing to say that the board should act on behalf of all corporate stakeholders, but it is unclear why they actually would.

The history of corporate constituency statutes should be instructive here. Thirty-one states have provisions that permit directors to take the needs of all corporate constituencies into account when making certain decisions.[109] Some constituency statutes apply only to change-in-control transactions, while others apply more broadly to all board decisions.[110] The purpose of these statutes is to give directors the freedom to consider the impact of a board decision on stakeholders other than shareholders.[111] However, most commentators generally recognize that constituency statutes fail to provide any meaningful incentive for the board to actually consider all constituencies.[112] The statutes merely authorize boards to consider these broader sets of needs; they provide no sanction for failing to do so.[113] Directors are not legally accountable to any of the stakeholders for failure to consider the decision's impact on their group.[114] Instead, directors can use constituency statutes as a "fig leaf" for decisions that are in their own interest.[115] Even those who have supported constituency statutes have deep concerns about this lack of accountability.[116]

Blair and Stout's model suffers from a similar flaw in its incentive structure. Directing a board to consider the interests of various members of the team does not mean that they will do so. Blair and Stout argue that corporate law provides for such discretion, and much of their argument is descriptive.[117] However, to the extent they are making a normative case for the team production model, it is difficult to see where team members other than shareholders would have any leverage over the board or input into its composition. Although they acknowledge that exclusive shareholder voting rights "pose[] something of a problem for the mediating hierarch approach,"[118] they make two arguments attempting to resolve this anomaly. First, they argue that shareholders may have the best preferences for serving the corporation as a whole.[119] As discussed above, they argue that shareholder homogeneity provides for a cleaner electorate with "fewer pathologies."[120] Because of this, shareholders serve as the best possible electorate for serving the interests of the corporation as a whole.[121] Second, they argue that shareholder voting rights may be "partial compensation for shareholders' unique vulnerabilities."[122] These arguments are contradictory, of course; in one, the shareholders are acting as representatives for all stakeholders, while in the other they are using the vote to protect themselves against other stakeholders. Blair and Stout ultimately dismiss such concerns, however, by hearkening back to the relative impotence of the shareholder franchise.[123] One wonders why they did not further consider the possibility of expanding the electorate to include other team members.[124]

The long-term interest theorists have not laid out their model as clearly as Blair and Stout, and thus it is more difficult to pinpoint where exactly they fit on the spectrum. Their chief problem with shareholder primacy seems to be its endemic short-term focus.[125] Lipton and Rosenblum want corporations to focus on long-term success, and they emphasize that corporations need to "realign[] . . . the interests of stockholders and corporations around the long-term health of the business enterprise."[126] However, they do not differentiate between the communal stakeholder success emphasized by Blair and Stout and the long-term shareholder wealth maximization that others such as Bainbridge would endorse. Instead, they seem to imply (at least under our reading) that long-term success would benefit both shareholders and other stake-holders equally.[127] While their quinquennial board would still be elected solely by shareholders,[128] Lipton and Rosenblum seem to advocate the "we're all in this together" model, rather than a long-term, but otherwise traditional, shareholder primacy norm.

Mitchell presents a more complicated case. Like Lipton and Rosenblum, Mitchell is most aggrieved by the short-term focus induced by shareholder control, and thus his main concern is separating the board from short-term shareholder influence.[129] But Mitchell also seems con-cerned about the cost in externalities generated by a share-price max-imization norm, whether it be short- or long-term.[130] Mitchell opens his book *Corporate Irresponsibility* with tales of massive layoffs, forced labor, product defects, and a corporate restructuring that harmed debt holders.[131] He criticizes the singular corporate focus on share price so strongly that he ultimately compares this focus to that of genetically engineered man-eating sharks.[132]

Given his concern about share-price maximization and corporate externalities, Mitchell seems less interested than Lipton and Rosenblum in ever getting shareholder input. In fact, as he puts it, "[m]aking directors accountable to constituencies with specific interests will lead them to favor those interests unless the incentive structures to do so are broken."[133] Thus, his initial and preferred proposal is for a self-perpetuating board.[134] When it comes to the quinquennial election proposal, Mitchell is open to the possibility of including other stake-holders in the electorate.[135] However, Mitchell only briefly entertains this idea before noting that he does not want to "thoroughly develop" the proposal.[136] Like the others, Mitchell does not follow the logic of his concerns out to the composition of the corporate electorate.

Bainbridge is at least more consistent here, wholeheartedly importing the idea that corporate actions should be directed at increasing share-holder wealth, and thus making the board answer, albeit weakly, to a shareholder electorate.[137] But Bainbridge is making the familiar mis-take of assuming he knows what it is that shareholders want. He does not seem to care what shareholders actually want in particular circumstances;

instead, he is content to make "shareholder wealth maximization" the constant and easily implemented goal of the board.[138] He avoids the messiness of actual elections by assuming that boards will act in what he considers to be the best interests of the electorate.[139]

Of course, as we have discussed in Chapter 5, it is unclear what, exactly, it means to maximize the utility of a shareholder electorate with a very diverse set of preferences. Some shareholders may desire short-term share-price maximization, while others prefer long-term dividend maximization. Some may want to maximize their overall utility by advocating for corporate activity that promotes social welfare goals. Elections can be useful devices for sorting out these various preferences into results that best map onto the preferences of the electorate.

Thus, directing a relatively unresponsive board to maximize shareholder wealth gives them, at best, incomplete guidance. The only way to make it more complete is by building a system of governance that responds in some way to the actual preferences of shareholders. The problem with Bainbridge's argument is that just as the governance system should be getting more responsive to shareholder interests, he argues that it should be less responsive.[140] What we are left with is a vision of shareholder "wealth" that bears less and less of a relationship to the well-being of actual shareholders.

So why should we expect a less responsive board to better manage this diverse set of interests? For Bainbridge, as for Blair and Stout, the answer is that corporate boards can be trusted to pursue proper ends.[141] But Bainbridge goes a step further than Blair and Stout's notion of the board as a group of "meditating hierarchs"[142] constrained by norms of trust: for Bainbridge, "the corporation's board of directors in fact is a Platonic Guardian."[143]

Such a claim would ordinarily be laughable, or accepted as a reductio ad absurdum of the whole board primacy project, if it weren't delivered with such seriousness (and so often). Describing directors as Platonic guardians is a complete surrender of any workable notion of what directors should be doing or why they would be expected to do it. We can't rely on philosopher-kings to act as directors of our corporations, for the same reason that we can't rely on them to run our governments: Platonic guardians do not exist. For that reason, we tend to favor more democratic decision structures with a little more accountability to the electorate.

Board primacy theorists never viewed any constituents other than shareholders as the proper board electorate, in large part because those other constituents had such heterogeneous preferences. And now that shareholders are known to be similarly diverse, they, too, are to be further distanced from the board (though at least they retain the ability to vote). All this leaves the board in a curious position – it must pursue the corporate good, but is not accountable to many of its constituents and is only weakly accountable to shareholders. The resultant corporate board, as Adolf Bearle and Gardiner Means pointed out over seventy-five years ago, ends up resembling a communist committee of commissars:

> The communist thinks of the community in terms of a state; the corporation director thinks of it in terms of an enterprise; and though this difference between the two may well lead to a radical divergence in results, it still remains true that the corporation director who would subordinate the interests of the individual stockholder to those of the group more nearly resembles the communist in mode of thought than he does the protagonist of private property.[144]

The commissars, at least, had something that corporate directors lack: a well-defined notion of the public good.

9

A Firm-Based Approach
to Corporate Voting Rights

The traditional arguments for the exclusive shareholder franchise are not compelling. The privileged position of shareholders is not simply the result of freely bargained-for contracts among all of the corporate constituents. It cannot be justified, in any noncircular fashion, by describing shareholders as "owners" or pointing to their contractual entitlement to the residual when employees also have claims to residual value. And arguments that hinge on shareholder homogeneity, some of which are misguided to begin with, are undercut by a growing body of evidence that real shareholder preferences are quite diverse in a variety of different ways.

Many scholars of corporate governance – even those writing about shareholder voting rights – have ignored the breakdown of these traditional arguments or have bracketed them as side issues in ongoing debates about the nuts and bolts of shareholder rights. Other scholars, worried that some of the distinctions between shareholders and other corporate constituents appear to be disintegrating, have gotten more creative, relying on "hypothetical" shareholders (ones that, invariably, happen to share the scholars' views of the corporate good), or conceiving of the corporate board as a group of superheroes of one sort (Platonic guardians) or another (mediating hierarchs), able to rise above their own self-interests and those of their voting constituencies and make decisions that respond to the interests of all corporate constituents. These responses largely trade on fanciful conceptions of shareholders or board members and, as a result, are ultimately unsatisfying.

To say that arguments for the exclusive shareholder franchise are flawed is not to say that shareholders should not vote in board elections. Rather, their privileged place in corporate governance may not be warranted. They are instead just one set of many constituents with an interest in firm decision-making. All corporate constituents – from the single-minded, short-term-profit-maximizing shareholder to the longtime employee to the supplier of some component of the corporation's product – should have their preferences reflected, to some degree, in corporate actions. So which constituents should express their preferences through the most powerful feature of corporate control – voting – and which through contractual agreement or governmental regulation? If we are to move beyond the current shareholder primacy model of corporate governance, we need a theory of governance to answer this question and more broadly ground our conception of the corporation.

Over the next two chapters, we develop a new model of the corporation. We begin that project in this chapter by reconsidering the long-standing economic theory of the firm as it applies to corporate governance. This theory, born out of a desire to explain why business firms exist apart from markets in the first place, is not only consistent with but actually counsels in favor of greater employee participation in corporate governance. Then, in Chapter 10, we develop a new theory of democratic participation to help resolve the question of which corporate constituents should or should not be accorded corporate franchise rights. In the end, the economic theory of the firm and the political theory of democratic participation provide the foundation for a new vision of corporate governance.

Applying the Theory of the Firm to Corporate Governance

The "theory of the firm" is a subdiscipline of economics that focuses particularly on issues of organization and governance. Research on the theory of the firm asks: Why do we have firms rather than markets?[1] The theory of the firm offers a sustained interdisciplinary inquiry into the nature of firms and their legal representations.[2] Markets allocate resources based on the best information available at the time.[3] Firms, however, operate outside this market structure, standing like "lumps of butter coagulating in a pail of buttermilk."[4] The law reflects this differentiation, as market transactions are generally governed by contract, while firms are created as specific legal entities with their own identity – partnership, corporation, or LLC, among others. Firms are meant to operate outside the market. But why?

In early neoclassical economics, the theory of the firm was quite rudimentary; it saw the firm simply as a black box that took in inputs and produced outputs.[5] No further dissection was undertaken. However, the black box did differentiate between what was inside the firm and what was outside: employees and capital assets were within it, while customers and suppliers were not.[6] Despite its crude form, this conception of the firm was useful in early economic modeling and retains that purpose even today.

An exploration of the internal workings and purpose of the firm begins with the work of Ronald Coase.[7] In an oft-quoted passage from his concise masterpiece *The Nature of the Firm*, Coase considered the firm/market distinction:

> Outside the firm, price movements direct production, which is coordinated through a series of exchange transactions on the market. Within a firm these market transactions are eliminated, and in place of the complicated market structure with exchange transactions is substituted the entrepreneur-coordinator, who directs production. It is clear that these are alternative methods of coordinating production. Yet, having regard to the fact that, if production is regulated by price movements, production could be carried on without any organization at all, well we might ask, why is there any organization?[8]

In answering this question, Coase turned to a theory of transaction costs. Contracting through markets and using the price mechanism can be costly. For certain transactions, Coase posited, it is cheaper to simply direct the production to occur rather than contracting for it each time. The hierarchy of the firm allows such transactions to be carried out by fiat, rather than through pricing, negotiating, and drafting a contract for each transaction.[9] In other words, hierarchical governance within the firm is thought to be more efficient than market transactions.

Coase's theory of the firm relies heavily on the idea of the employment relationship. The structural difference between firm and market lies in the relationship between individual employees and the firm's ownership or management. The employment relationship is not based on individual transactions but is rather an ongoing organizational relationship. As Coase famously noted: "If a workman moves from department Y to department X, he does not go because of a change in relative prices, but because he was ordered to do so."[10] The relationship between the firm and the employee is the primary distinction between the firm and the market. It is the reason for the firm's existence.

This conclusion was cemented when Coase considered "whether the concept of a firm which has been developed fits in with that existing in the real world."[11] His answer? "We can best approach the question of what constitutes a firm in practice by considering the legal relationship normally called that of 'master and servant' or 'employer and employee.'"[12] He then quoted at length from a treatise concerning the common law "control" test, which provides that "[t]he master must have the right to control the servant's work, either personally or by another servant or agent."[13] He concluded, "We thus see that it is the fact of direction which is the essence of the legal concept of 'employer and employee,' just as it was in the economic concept which was developed above."[14] For Coase, the employer-employee relationship defined the firm.[15]

Coase envisioned firms as having a hierarchical nature, in which managers controlled the efforts of employees. But the relationship between firm and employee need not be hierarchical. In an important response to Coase's work, Armen Alchian and Harold Demsetz likewise considered the relationship between employees with other participants within the structure of the firm.[16] However, they argued that Coase's focus on control, authority, and direction was misleading.[17] They memorably put it this way: "Telling an employee to type this letter rather than to file that document is like my telling a grocer to sell me this brand of tuna rather than that brand of bread."[18] Because employees are generally hired and fired at will, neither the employer nor the employee is bound to continue the relationship by any contractual obligation.[19]

Alchian and Demsetz instead took a more holistic approach, focusing on the firm's role in coordinating production in the midst of a variety of inputs. Team production is what separated firms from markets. Alchian and Demsetz defined team production as "production in which 1) several types of resources are used and 2) the product is not a sum of separable outputs of each cooperating resource."[20] As a result, team production is used when the coordinated effort increases productivity, after factoring out the costs associated with monitoring and disciplining the team.[21]

In Alchian & Demsetz's "joint production" theory of the firm, the lack of separable outputs is the key problem that the firm is designed to manage. When capital providers and workers join together to carry on a business, it is difficult to assess the relative importance or value of the individual contributions to that business according to a continuing and consistently measurable formula. Firms allow these contributors to work together, sell their joint product, and then use the firm to manage both responsibilities and spoils. Alchian and Demsetz argue that a specialized, independent monitor is likely the best way to manage these issues.[22] Rather than an individual, the central component of team production is the firm itself: a legal "person" that contracts for all other team inputs.[23] The legal entity – such as the corporation – serves the role of coordinator. And the purpose of the Alchian-Demsetz firm remains the management of employees and capital through the coordination of team production.[24]

As the theory of the firm literature continued to develop, team production and the identification of transaction and monitoring costs remained central concepts. Using the transaction costs model, Oliver Williamson and affiliated scholars have identified the types of contractual difficulties that lend themselves to firm governance rather than market solutions.[25] In situations where contributions and compensation can be complicated to define, the parties will be left with incomplete contracts that require a governance structure to prevent opportunism.[26] This opportunism will be particularly problematic where one or both of the parties must invest significant resources in assets specific to the particular firm, project, or transaction.[27] This asset specificity makes the parties susceptible to hold-ups at the hands of their contractual partners in the absence of a system of governance. Firms can be useful in providing the structures that deter opportunism.[28]

The property rights theory of the firm, developed in a series of articles by Sanford Grossman, Oliver Hart, and John Moore, posits that firms are necessary as a repository of property rights for assets used in joint production.[29] By owning the property outright, the firm prevents the problem of the commons (in which no one holds property rights over valuable assets) as well as the problem of the anticommons (in which property rights are divvied up among too many disparate actors). The Grossman-Hart-Moore model dictates that those who contribute the most valuable and most asset-specific property to the joint enterprise should control the firm.[30] They are not only most necessary to the firm's success; they are also the most vulnerable to holdup problems as the joint enterprise moves forward in time.

Under a property rights model, employees' contributions must be recognized as assets of both the firm and the employee – often described as "human capital." Some types of human capital are transferable, such as education or general skills, but others are specific to the firm and generally worthless outside it. Employees who have invested in firm-specific skills are subject to opportunistic behavior, since they have little leverage to secure the full value of those skills. Thus, the most valuable contributors to the joint enterprise are also the most vulnerable to opportunistic behavior.[31]

The access model defines a firm "both in terms of unique assets (which may be physical or human) and in terms of the people who have access to these assets."[32] Access to the unique assets is what defines the power of the individuals within and without the firm. Raghuram Rajan and Luigi Zingales define access as "the ability to use, or work with, a critical resource."[33] Examples of critical resources include machines, ideas, and people. As Rajan and Zingales make clear, "[t]he agent who is given privileged access to the resource gets no new residual rights of control. All she gets is the opportunity to specialize her human capital to the resource and make herself valuable."[34] Combined with her right to leave the firm, access gives the employee the ability to "create a critical resource that she controls: her specialized human capital." Control over this critical resource is a source of power. Gordon Smith has further developed this critical resource theory of the firm in outlining a theory of fiduciary duties that are responsive to vulnerabilities created by critical resources.[35]

One particular subcategory of human capital – knowledge – serves as the basis for a set of knowledge-based approaches to the firm.[36] Knowledge is defined as both retained information and the ability to apply a repository of unspecified information in developing an answer or approach to a particular problem.[37] Rather than emphasize the ownership of physical assets, which can be fungible and nonspecific, the knowledge-based theory focuses on the need to produce, distribute, and ultimately retain valuable knowledge-based assets within the firm.[38] Choices between centralized and multidivisional organizational structures,[39] or between covenants not to compete and employee stock options,[40] are made to manage the control of knowledge within the firm. Along the same lines, a capability-based theory of the firm focuses on firm-specific knowledge and learning that can be translated into joint production.[41] Under this theory, employees are repositories of the firm's capabilities.

Knowledge-based theories of the firm serve as something of a bridge between economic, organizational, and sociological theories on the nature of the firm.[42] Management historians such as Alfred Chandler have long considered the actual roles of employees within the firm to be the centerpiece of firm dynamics.[43] Organizational theory has built upon these insights and carried them over to today's firms, which generally offer flatter hierarchical structures and more work in teams. In fact, one set of scholars examined the role of the firm as a "collaborative community" in which employees work together toward common goals.[44] Such a firm must have a shared ethos of contribution to a collective purpose and the success of others; it must be structured so as to allow for flexible organizational boundaries but highly specialized knowledge; it must base status on knowledge and expertise, rather than hierarchy; and it must create an identity of independence and personal consistency.[45] Such collaborative-community firms are contrasted with hierarchical firms, which manage employees with a traditional command-and-control structure, and with market-based firms, which break down traditional firm barriers through outsourcing and contingent workers.[46]

Looking over the trajectory of the theory of the firm, we see that the primary concern has been over the shape and internal organization of these entities that sit outside standard market relationships. And the theories of the firm all seem to acknowledge the important role of workers within the firm. Going back to Coase, the firm was designed to manage the relationship between those who started or managed the business and those who worked for the business. The work of the business was best managed internally, rather than through external markets. And the firm itself was made up of those who worked for the firm, along with a nebulous collection of those who "managed" the firm – also workers – and those who "owned" the firm through financial assets.

The Legal Construction of Firm Governance

Because the firm is the primary organizational engine of economic activity and growth, the internal governance of the firm takes on supreme importance. Of course, the story of modern corporate law is the systematic exclusion of employees from governance. But this model is not endemic to economic organization. Partnerships, for example, were the original legal structure for organizing a group of people into a firm. Unlike corporations, partnerships have never required an explicit grant of authority from the government to operate.[47] Instead, individuals take it upon themselves to form a partnership under the basic guidelines set forth in the law. In addition, courts can determine that a group of people has been operating as a partnership even if they had never declared themselves to be partners or considered themselves to be within a partnership.[48] Instead, the test is whether the parties had formed "an association of two or more persons to carry on as co-owners a business for profit."[49] There are numerous examples of situations where people working together on the assumption that one of them was an employee turned out to be partners according to the law.[50]

Under the default rules of a partnership, all participants have equal voting rights and equal rights to vote on partnership matters.[51] The control rights in a partnership extend even to ordinary, everyday matters of the business.[52] Of course, "one partner, one vote" is only the default rule. Partners who contemplate varying levels of input and interest will generally construct a partnership agreement that allocates votes as well as shares of the residual profits according to mutual agreement.[53] Partners are free to divvy up voting power according to differences in monetary or labor contributions, seniority, experience, and other factors relevant to governance. The default rules are a bit more structured for the limited partnership, the limited liability partnership, and the limited liability company. These organizations envision participants with stakes in the residual who do not participate in management. For example, limited partnerships must make clear who the managerial partners and who the limited partners are.[54] Limited liability companies have what is known as "chameleon" management: "the firm can choose either direct partnership-type control by the members or centralized control by managers that is closer to, but not as rigid as, the limited partnership format."[55] Participants in these enterprises have substantial flexibility in arranging the division of ownership and control rights.

The corporation, by contrast, requires a specific charter from a state government to exist and has a fairly uniform governance structure across the United States. The corporation's shareholders elect the board of directors, and the board appoints the officers who run the corporation. Because the legal corporate form controls the governance of the economic firm, the two have come to seem coterminous. But the corporation represents a shareholder-oriented governance structure – one that leaves out other participants. In smaller, so-called closely held corporations, the same basic corporate structure is used.[56] Because the corporate form's rigidity does not fit the economic reality of these kinds of businesses, they must adapt the corporate form for their purposes. Many closely held companies have different classes of shares as a method of allocating control among different groups of shareholders.[57] In addition, shareholders may agree to certain voting arrangements, such as the pooling of votes into a voting trust or agreeing to vote along certain lines.[58] These voting arrangements are often executed to consolidate a group of disparate shareholders into a majority or to provide protection for minority shareholders in regard to certain critical matters.[59] Corporate law generally protects minority shareholders against undue oppression through specifically tailored equitable relief. Such oppression often relates to the ability of minority shareholders to partake in other aspects of the corporate pie, particularly employment.[60] Even if shareholders are all sharing equally in the profits, the minority oppression doctrine may still order the majority shareholders to approve a dividend or to provide employment opportunities within the company for minority shareholders.[61]

This divergence between the cookie-cutter structure of corporation governance and the more tailored approaches of other organizational forms, including closely held corporations, suggests that corporations could reconsider their lockstep approach. Indeed, recent developments in shareholding structures illustrate a breakdown in the monolithic one share, one vote model. Companies such as Facebook, Google, and the New York Times have stock structures that grant the company founders special control rights beyond the number of common stock shares they hold.[62] Preferred stock is also used to provide control rights in certain circumstances, such as the failure to make a payment or the approach of the company's dissolution.[63] Companies are getting creative in order to accommodate the special circumstances of their particular businesses.[64]

Corporate law needs to embrace these departures from the traditional governance structure and go even further. It needs to reexamine the premise that corporate governance is only about shareholders, directors, and officers. In particular, corporate law policymakers and theorists need to reexamine the status of all of the corporation's stakeholders and determine if governance rights are appropriate as a way of managing their preferences. Prior to recent proposed legislation,[65] the corporate law community had not seriously entertained any significant changes to the corporate franchise. Even those commentators who have suggested a team-production model of corporate governance have only asked the board of directors merely to consider the interests of stakeholders. With the power structures already in place, it makes little sense to imagine a stakeholder-rights theory without any positive governance power for stakeholders. As Delaware Supreme Court Chief Justice Leo Strine has emphasized:

> Under the DGCL [Delaware General Corporate Law] only stockholders have the right to vote for directors; approve certificate amendments; amend the bylaws; approve certain other transactions, such as mergers, and certain asset sales and leases; and enforce the DGCL's terms and hold directors accountable for honoring their fiduciary duties. In the corporate republic, no constituency other than stockholders is given any power.[66]

Voting rights are the only way of providing a real voice within the corporation's governance structure.[67]

Participation in Joint Production

Corporations exist to facilitate economic production.[68] The corporate form is not the same thing as a business; an actual business consists of ideas, relationships, economic activity, and legal rights. The corporate form is part of this mix.[69] The corporation is a legal fiction that creates rights and duties; the economic firm is the ongoing social phenomenon that we think of when we consider companies such as Apple, Facebook, and Ford. The legal part of the business equation is meant to facilitate the social and economic phenomenon.

The distribution of the responsibilities for production, as well as the distribution of the fruits of production, will ultimately rest in the hands of those with organizational power. Much of the debate in corporate law over the last forty years – perhaps even the last century – has concerned the distribution of corporate power between the board, the officers, and the shareholders.[70] On one side, shareholder advocates have pushed for corporate law reforms that provide more direct power for stockholders.[71] On the other side, management and stakeholder advocates have argued that boards need more insulation from shareholders and more unreviewable discretion, even if their ultimate aim remains shareholder wealth maximization.[72] In this second group, there is a subset of advocates who argue that stakeholders such as employees, creditors, consumers, and communities deserve some protection within the process.[73] But stakeholder supporters generally provide directors with the freedom to merely consider all stakeholder interests rather than granting voting power to these stakeholders.[74]

If the firm is designed to help manage a system of joint production, then the governance of the firm should include those who participate in the joint production. The distinction between markets and firms corresponds to this distinction between the use of straightforward contracts to manage relationships and the need for governance mechanisms to manage relationships.[75] Firms enable the complexity of joint production between participants who cannot reduce their interactions simply to contractual performance metrics. Instead, the participants create another entity – the firm – to serve as the locus of their production and to structure the inputs required by the participants and divvy up the outputs among them.

Shareholders and employees are invested in the firm in such a way that they need firm governance to protect against opportunism. When it comes to their contractual vulnerability, shareholders are in fact situated differently from other capital providers such as creditors.[76] Shareholders put their money into the firm with no ability to withdraw it and subject to uncertain payoffs, largely at the discretion of management.[77] Employees are also firm investors. They pour their labor, reputations, and firm-specific individual capital into the firm and cannot pull these investments out.[78] Under the law, they are compensated on a more regular basis, and with less discretion, than shareholders.[79] However, they still operate within the firm, as opposed to suppliers and outside contractors that provide their services through markets.[80]

	CAPITAL	LABOR
INSIDE THE FIRM	Shareholders	Employees & Management
OUTSIDE THE FIRM	Creditors & Bondholders	Independent Contractors & Suppliers

The theory of the firm supports a governance model that includes employees. Theory of the firm scholars have long appreciated the importance of the employee to our conception of the firm.[81] In fact, Coase looked to the relationship between employer and employee to demonstrate empirical support for his theory of the firm.[82] Alchian and Demsetz argued that the importance of the firm (as separate from the market) stems from the need to coordinate production from a variety of inputs.[83] Team production is used – and firms replace markets – when the coordinated effort increases productivity, after factoring out the costs associated with monitoring and disciplining the team.[84] Margaret Blair and Lynn Stout relied on this notion of team production in developing their stakeholder-based theory.[85] But the nonseparable inputs within team production really only belong to employees and shareholders.[86] Shareholders provide the capital that is taken up within the firm and turned into discretionary funds.[87] Employees work together under the aegis of the firm to produce goods or services in a manner that makes it difficult to assign separate, specific values.[88] They need firm governance to allocate the responsibilities and benefits of production.

Other participants are not integrated into the team production process and therefore do not need to work within the firm.[89] Creditors provide money on fixed terms.[90] Suppliers and independent contractors provide specific services outside of the firm's scope.[91] Consumers purchase the firm's goods or services after the production process is complete.[92] And the surrounding community regulates the firm as it does all other individuals and organizations within its jurisdiction. If we say that all of these participants are engaged in the production process, it proves too much. It is only when we have a team production process – when the parties cannot effectively use the market – that we need to create a firm and facilitate the process of team production.[93] Employees and shareholders are part of that team production process in a way that stakeholders outside the firm are not.[94]

Concern for the fates of other stakeholders is understandable and may, in some circumstances, warrant a species of governance protection.[95] Creditors, for example, may receive specific protections when the company is close to bankruptcy as a way of mitigating their particular vulnerabilities in such situations.[96] Certain consumers may have long-term invested interests such that some governance rights may make sense.[97] In the main, however, government regulation will be the most straightforward way of managing issues that arise and are not amenable to contractual resolution. Creditors have statutory rights within bankruptcy.[98] Consumer protection laws can place mandatory terms or disclosure requirements on firms.[99] Environmental protections address externalities by imposing costs on firms (and individuals) for creating those externalities.[100] But corporate governance, like all firm governance, should be directed at solving problems that arise within the firm structure, problems related to team production.[101] Employees and shareholders are the stakeholders who are engaged in the process of team production within the firm.[102]

Information Within the Firm

In addition to capturing the team production process at the heart of a firm, a shared governance system better reflects the flow of information within the firm. Information has always been the paradox at the heart of corporate law theory. Shareholders delegate governance power to management because they do not have the information – nor the time and resources to get the information – necessary to make independent and informed governance decisions. And yet shareholder primacy assumes that shareholders vote with sufficient knowledge and understanding to curb agency costs and efficiently direct the corporation. This paradox has come into fuller view of late, as theorists raise powerful concerns about the "competence costs" of principal governance[103] and the voting rights of passive fund participants.[104]

Employees have information about the firm that they obtain through their everyday working experience without additional cost. Yet they have no formal governance mechanisms enabling them to use this information to help guide the company. The overwhelming majority of private-sector employees are not represented by a union.[105] Even if employees are represented by a union, that union does not have the right to bargain with the company over issues of managerial prerogative, such as new product lines, marketing, acquisitions, or the composition of the board.[106] At many workplaces, the proverbial suggestion box may be the sole institutional mechanism for employee input.

In the 1980s and 1990s, both academic and popular business literature explored ways in which firms could better utilize information held by employees.[107] The success of Japanese businesses led many to investigate ways in which Japanese firms better integrated employee decision-making.[108] Internal systems involving quality circles and quality improvement teams were heralded as a way of drawing employee know-how into daily operations.[109] Such methods stood in opposition to hierarchical management structures and the Taylorist method of production, which held that managers generated the information and disseminated it down the ladder.[110] Although many of these structures are in use today,[111] they mainly concern issues taking place at the shop floor, rather than the higher echelons of power.

This gap between employee knowledge and shareholder power is inefficient. Shareholders and employees could work together to pool their information and their power to police decisions of management. As discussed in Chapter 6, the process of carrying out a corporate combination, such as a merger or sale of substantially all assets, would offer the opportunity for employees to play an informational role. Merger and acquisition negotiations are conducted in secret, in order to prevent poaching and keep failed negotiations under the rug.[112] While this secrecy serves a purpose, it also narrowly restricts both the information and the perspectives that can be brought to bear. With their independent sources of information about the company, workers are a natural fit to help overcome this information deficit. They have information that complements the financial disclosures provided by the investment banks managing the process.[113]

Employees also have information about the agency costs associated with managerial opportunism – information that shareholders are not likely to have when voting on the merger. A merger or significant acquisition triggers an informal network of chatter about what is happening with jobs and why management agreed to the deal. Workers will be especially sensitive to news that executives are making out like bandits while layoffs are on the horizon for everyone else. While directors may be expected to police such opportunism, there are a variety of reasons to doubt their effectiveness. First, the directors themselves may be in on the deal; the firm may decide to award transaction bonuses to directors as well as managers.[114] Second, directors may already feel beholden to managers. Top-level executives have significant power over the board nomination and reelection process as well as the directorial compensation process.[115] Personal ties help cement the feelings of loyalty and friendship.[116] Third, directors are part-timers; they themselves do not have the same quantity and depth of information as employees. Boards may end up trusting that investment bankers, compensation consultants, and other advisors have dealt with the compensation issue sufficiently, when in fact these advisors have their own set of conflicts.[117]

Employees are ideally situated to ally with shareholders in an effort to police management. Indeed, this already appears to be taking place. Over the last thirty years, labor unions have become much more involved in traditional corporate governance activism.[118] In the 1980s, unions were generally antagonistic to shareholder concerns and supported antitakeover tactics such as constituency statutes.[119] However, unions and union-associated pension funds have joined the side of shareholders in pushing through shareholder-friendly corporate governance measures.[120] Pension fund managers have been at the forefront in governance efforts to strengthen shareholder voting rights, rein in the power of the CEO, and fight fraud and abuse by insiders.[121] These measures suggest an ongoing role for union activism: an alliance with shareholders in an effort to maximize long-term growth for shareholders and other stakeholders as well as to prevent executives from taking advantage of the company.

Outside the Firm: Stakeholder Theory

Stakeholders who are outside the firm generally do not have a claim to participate in governance. They participate in the process of joint production through markets, and their interests can be captured through contract. Like shareholders, creditors provide capital to the corporation, but they do so under very different terms. While shareholders provide funds with no expectation of repayment, creditors have a contractual right to repayment, generally with specified rates of interest, and may also have secured rights to property interests if the loan is not repaid in accordance with the terms. Suppliers and independent contractors may provide goods or services that are used within the process of joint production, but their contributions are discrete and can be completed on the market. Moreover, these goods or services are often provided in the context of a separate firm – one that exists apart from the firm at issue. For example, a painting contractor could not operate without buying the paint from a supplier, but that supplier is itself a separate firm that makes paint and sells it to a variety of customers. That does not make the supplier a part of the painting contractor's firm.[122] An economy consists of interwoven relationships, but we still can draw a distinction between firms and markets. This simple dichotomy between firm and market may obscure greater complexity in relationships, as recent examinations of joint ventures and "braided" contracts have revealed,[123] but complications in categorization do not mean that the separate categories do not exist.

This dichotomy between firms and markets, largely delineated within economic theory, has been complicated in corporate law by stakeholder theory, which has been burbling in the background as an alternative to shareholder primacy for years. Sometimes referred to as the communitarian or multifiduciary model,[124] stakeholder theory argues that corporate governance should take all stakeholders in the corporate enterprise into account.[125] In a sense, it draws upon the nexus of contract theory in identifying the many participants that have a role in conducting the business of the corporation. However, unlike the law and economics contractarians, who limit organizational protections to shareholders, stakeholder advocates argue that all participants deserve consideration.[126] Stakeholder reforms have sought to insulate the board from political pressures by fencing off shareholder power and giving the board and management discretion to take other interests into account.[127]

As discussed in Chapter 8 with reference to board primacy, stakeholder theory lacks a model for allocating governance rights and responsibilities among the participants.[128] Stakeholder theory does not, for example, argue that corporations are simply contractual nexuses and, thus, should not exist as legal entities.[129] Nor, more surprisingly, have stakeholder theorists sketched out a system whereby all stakeholders can participate in firm governance. Instead, stakeholder theorists have largely glommed on to the existing structure of corporate law, whereby shareholders elect directors who appoint officers. The only real difference is that under stakeholder theory, directors have more discretion to act in the interests of all stakeholders.

Stakeholder theory could develop a new system of corporate governance giving all stakeholders direct ways of participating in firm governance. But the theory would have to do the difficult work of assigning rights to all participants in a meaningful way beyond the contractual protections they already hold. Yet stakeholder theory seems content with the current power structure, as long as directors do not get too beholden to their shareholding electorate. This approach is not internally coherent. It makes little sense to attack shareholder primacy but then maintain the exclusive shareholder franchise.[130] Stakeholder theory has failed to present a viable alternative to the shareholder primacy model; at best, it advocates for a watered-down version of the status quo.

Some stakeholder theorists argue that a stakeholder approach is the best way to incorporate community or societal interests within firm governance. However, the community has a more powerful tool than firm governance for influencing the firm: regulation. Governments can subject firms to restrictions that manage their behavior regardless of their internal governance structures. Communities have interests that transcend firm boundaries; firm governance, on the other hand, concerns the allocation of the responsibilities and benefits of joint production within a particular firm. There may be certain circumstances in which a particular stakeholder is sufficiently enmeshed in the workings of the firm, or particularly vulnerable to opportunism, such that firm governance rights would better manage the relationship between the firm and the stakeholder. And, as detailed above, the theory of the firm gives us some pretty good tools for deciding when those circumstances occur – that is, when a group of constituents should be considered insiders instead of outsiders. As a matter of course, though, only shareholders and employees participate within the firm in a way that should entitle them to governance rights.

* * *

With the central arguments for the exclusive shareholder franchise on the ropes, it makes sense to revisit some of the basic economic theory informing the creation and governance of corporations. The theory of the firm, in confronting the question of why firms even exist, separates corporate insiders from outsiders in a way that allows firms to carry out joint production most efficiently. Those inside the corporation should have their preferences captured through governance mechanisms such as voting, those outside the firm through processes like contract or regulation. Under this understanding of the firm, employees are, of course, the classic insiders, a conclusion that's only reinforced by more recent work on the generation and flow of information within firms. The economic theory of the firm, then, provides a powerful argument for extending the corporate franchise to employees.

10

Democratic Participation
and Shared Governance

When it comes to the corporate franchise, the theory of the firm provides a solid economic foundation for separating the interests of shareholders and employees from those of other corporate constituents. It is not, however, the only theoretical justification for that separation. In this chapter, we explore the lessons that democratic theory has to offer to corporate governance. In particular, we look at governance from the broad perspective of preference aggregation and revisit and further explore the theory of democratic participation developed earlier in the book. That theory, which allows us to determine whose preferences are best captured through voting rather than contract or regulation, is then applied to corporate governance. Like the economic theory of the firm, the theory of democratic participation also counsels in favor of a shared governance model in most business situations.

Revisiting Interest and Participation Rights

As discussed more fully in Chapter 2, preference aggregation mechanisms typically limit input to people who have a stake or interest in the enterprise.[1] If possible, the degree of input should be calibrated to the weight of that interest or the strength of those preferences. We aggregate those preferences to ensure more thoughtful decision-making and to lend a measure of legitimacy to electoral outcomes. Most discussions of the governance systems – corporate or political – take it for granted that input should be limited to those with an interest in the enterprise. After that, though, the difficulties start almost immediately. First, who has interests that are sufficiently substantial to merit some kind of input into the future of the enterprise? Second, how are those interests best captured: through mutual agreement, voting, or external regulation?[2]

The modern corporate structure dictates that shareholders have their preferences captured through voting – primarily by voting on boards of directors, but also more directly for decisions such as mergers or dissolutions – while all other constituents, from employees to suppliers to customers, have their preferences captured largely through individual agreements. As an institutional entity, a corporation needs a process whereby it can make decisions, effectuate actions, and carry on business. From the perspective of preference aggregation, voting is the basic process used to capture an ongoing set of preferences that are then translated into firm decisions. The shareholders have been designated as the body politic whose preferences are collated through various voting procedures.

The principal corporate stakeholders – those with an interest in firm decision-making – are well known. Employees, shareholders, suppliers, customers, contractors, and even the community at large all have interests in the operation of a typical corporation. The nature of their interests, of course, may vary tremendously between groups and, as we've seen before, even within groups. This is true with respect to both the content of their preferences (what they care about) and the strength of the preferences (how much they care). With few exceptions, democratic and economic theorists take the contents of preferences as they come. In politics, for example, we don't prevent people from voting because of whom they support or what they believe.[3] Standard economics treats preferences in much the same way or, if anything, elevates them to an even more exalted position. Revealed preference theory holds that the best way to tell what consumers want is to observe their purchasing decisions.[4] Economists do not typically claim that consumers didn't (or shouldn't) really want something – they just register existing preferences and build their theories accordingly.[5]

The strength of constituent interests is a different matter. While we don't tell citizens or consumers what to care about, we do make basic decisions about the structure of governance based on how much we think they care, how much they have at stake in the outcome of government or firm decision-making. Ideally, in both polities and corporations, we figure out who has strong interests in the enterprise and assign them the right to vote – a voice in the governance process. Those with a sufficient level of interest vote; those with even more interest may get some type of additional weight added to their vote.

Though, as an initial matter, it makes sense to tie voting to preference strength, we immediately run into a problem: we do not have a foolproof way of measuring the strength of anybody's preferences.[6] We could, of course, just ask people how strongly they feel about an election outcome. But with voting or, more generally, governance tied to interest, people would have an incentive to strategically misrepresent the strength of their preferences. And even if we have accurate reports from people about how strong their interests are in an election, we lack a method of neutrally comparing those reports with those of others who report having an interest. There is no universal scale upon which to measure people's preference strengths. This is the problem of making interpersonal utility comparisons that we confronted in Chapter 2.[7]

For these and other reasons, our political system has not generally relied upon first-person reports to assess preference strength and, thus, the right to participate. Instead, it has relied upon other proxies or markers of a person's interest in the outcome of an election. Throughout our history, states have relied on a wide variety of such markers, including property holding, taxpaying, and residency.[8] Ultimately, the decision is this: whether the person, based on certain factors relating to their interests, should have the right to participate in governance.

The search for a good marker of voter interest, remember, boils down to coming up with an indication of voter interest that is 1) accurate and 2) manageable.[9] The accuracy of a marker is a measure of how well it picks out the group of people who have a sufficient interest in the outcome of an election. A marker could be off by either including too many people who lack a sufficient interest or excluding people who have a strong interest; in other words, it could be overinclusive or underinclusive. With an overinclusive marker, we risk extending the franchise to those with a weak or nonexistent interest in the election, thus diluting the votes of those with a stronger interest. An underinclusive marker is even worse: it leads to outright disenfranchisement of those with a real stake in the outcome.[10] When it comes to assigning weight to votes, the accuracy of the marker depends on whether and how well it can be calibrated to the strength of voter preferences.[11]

Because there is no direct way of assessing the accuracy of any marker, we have to make educated guesses about how much various people are affected by the decision-making of a particular elected body and to make an assumption that the people more strongly affected will be those with stronger electoral preferences. These judgments about the strength of people's interest may be contested, but they are essential to get any governance system up and running. As discussed in depth in Chapter 2, we make these kinds of judgments all the time in the political arena. The early freehold requirements, for example, were an attempt to capture one's stake in an election, and those with a large amount of property did indeed have a strong interest in governance. But the requirements were underinclusive, disenfranchising large numbers of propertyless people who were also greatly affected by the exercise of governmental powers. More contemporary requirements, such as residency and citizenship, are better markers of voter interest. Those who are residents within the jurisdiction of a particular government, for example, are subject to its police powers and taxation and dependent on its services, and thus have quite a bit at stake in an election. Residency isn't perfect, of course. It's a little underinclusive, in that it fails to capture those who work or own property in one place and reside in another. At times, it can also be overinclusive, as when it allows voting by people who plan to move out of town right after election day. But despite debates around the margins, residency is a more accurate marker of voter interest than, say, owning property. And when governments try to use markers that a court deems too overinclusive or underinclusive, they are often disallowed from doing so for that very reason.[12]

Of course, we could always come up with some more extensive survey of voter interest to get a better fix on whether any particular person has a strong interest in the outcome of an election. For example, perhaps a survey reveals that while both Luke and Ben are residents of a certain town, Ben plans to move away in just a few weeks. A third potential voter, Milo, lives nearby but works and owns property in the town, including the house where his elderly, dependent mother lives. With such information, we might conclude that while residency is a good starting point, our additional information reveals that, really, Luke and Milo have a sufficient interest in the jurisdiction to vote, and Ben, despite his current residency, does not. But this kind of individualized preference information would be incredibly costly to obtain, not to mention keep up to date. And, of course, if we obtain this information by asking everyone about their interests, we'd worry about strategic misrepresentation. An ongoing process of surveying everyone about their potential interests in every jurisdiction is simply unworkable, which brings us to the second feature of any good marker: its manageability.

Democratic institutions have long valued markers of voter interest that are easily managed. The property-holding and taxpaying requirements of old were not only useful because they ensured that voters had a financial stake in election outcomes, they did so with information that was readily available to the state. In fact, the state and local governments that ran the elections usually had lists of both property holders and taxpayers, which made it very easy to administer the voter rolls. Residency has been a little harder to pin down – state and local governments do not, usually, have ready lists of all of their residents – so residency is often confirmed by requesting some sort of identification with a name and address on it (a utility bill, for example). Manageability, then, is a key feature of any marker used to pick out a potential voter's interest in the outcome of an election.

Developing a method of aggregating individual preferences demands that we first figure out who has preferences to aggregate. This typically involves finding some way of measuring the level of interest that a potential voter has in the outcome of an election. Because we do not have direct, reliable access to that kind of information, we usually depend upon some sort of marker of that interest. But not all preferences are expressed through markers. We generally divide the electorate into those whose preferences can be expressed through voting, and those who preferences cannot. Until now, corporate governance has allowed only shareholders to express their preferences through votes. It is time to reexamine this reality.

As detailed in Chapter 9, the economic theory of the firm counsels that two groups of constituents – shareholders and employees – have a special relationship to the corporation that militates in favor of assigning voting rights to them. In this chapter, we argue that core features of democratic theory – namely, the tie between voting and interest and the accompanying need for markers of that interest – point in the same direction. Here, too, there are features of shareholders and employees that allow us to distinguish them from other stakeholders: their relationship with the firm gives them the accurate and manageable markers of interest that other corporate constituents, in ordinary business situations, lack. We start our examination of democratic participation theory with an evaluation of shareholders, move on to employees, and finish with "outside" constituents such as customers and suppliers.

Shareholders

For shareholders, the value of the capital contribution and the percentage of the dividend interest provide fairly quantifiable measures of the shareholder's interest in the corporation. Putting aside any outside interests of the shareholder, the allocation of one vote for each share accurately correlates with the shareholder's financial interest in the corporation.[13] The system of one share, one vote calibrates the level of interest to the level of input. Shareholding, in other words, initially appears to be both an accurate and a manageable marker of interest in a corporation, and thus shareholders should be accorded voting rights.

The familiarity of this conclusion, however, belies the factors complicating this democratic argument for shareholder voting. Although shares are originally sold for the same price during the initial public offering, publicly traded shares soon enter the marketplace, where their values may change drastically over time. One shareholder may have purchased Facebook shares for $30 in 2012, while recent shareholders may have paid more than $200.[14] Although everyone's shares may have the same value at any given moment in time, individual shareholders have likely invested different amounts per share to obtain those shares (and votes).

Shareholders also have differing interests outside the firm. Those interests may swamp the shareholder's interest in the corporation's residual. Shareholders may tailor their financial holdings to match shareholder voting power to countervailing interests in derivatives or short positions.[15] They may have personal interests, such as family ties[16] or religious and political values,[17] that conflict with the principle of shareholder wealth maximization. The shareholders themselves may be social investing funds[18] or sovereign wealth funds[19] or an algorithm.[20] Pension funds may want to promote worker power, while hedge funds may want to make a quick sale after juicing up the price. Shareholders do not have "pure" interests as shareholders, no more than citizens have "pure" interests in the republic.

There is also an accuracy issue when it comes to measuring shareholder preferences, in that it may not be worth the shareholder's time and investment to correlate the vote in question accurately with the shareholder's preferences. We want to identify interested parties and give them the vote not only because it makes the decision-making process more legitimate but because we want to ensure they have enough at stake to gather information and cast an informed vote. That is, we do this to facilitate better decision-making. But the shareholder interest for those holding only a few shares is rather weak. And the move to passive index funds further removes the shareholder's interests from any effort to express those interests through a vote.[21] Fully diversified shareholders may be close to indifferent to the fortunes of any particular corporation.

There are also underappreciated difficulties in the manageability of shareholder voting. Shareholder governance is still centered around the idea of the annual shareholders' meeting, which shareholders in theory are expected to attend.[22] If unable to attend, shareholders assign their voting power to proxies, who then act on their behalf. Shareholders receive proxy ballots from the incumbent board, which makes the process much easier while subverting its democratic nature. Further complicating matters, modern shareholding is generally managed through intermediaries who hold the shares on behalf of the actual owner.[23] As a result, confusion over voting rights can abound in the context of custodial ownership, short sales, lending shares, and changes in ownership after the record date.[24] Trading shares is also accomplished through lightning-fast technology, and the allocation of particular shares to particular holders has not caught up with this technology.[25] Although certain reforms may address specific uncertainties over voting rights for particular shares, there remain difficulties in matching up particular shareholders with voting rights in any given election.

Despite these concerns, we think that shareholders have interests that are sufficiently defined to constitute accurate and manageable markers for their voting rights. They have a clear stake in the outcome of decision-making. They have a straightforward way to calibrate the strength of their interest. And because shareholders provide unencumbered capital to the corporation in exchange for certain rights to the residual profits, they cannot register their preferences meaningfully through agreement alone; they need a governance mechanism. Shareholder voting rights are designed to manage those preferences.

Employees

Employment is also an accurate and manageable marker of interest in the success of a firm. Employees have a clear stake in the ongoing success of a corporation as expressed through their continued employment. Workers contribute to the process of joint production through their labor and create both specific value (creation of particular goods or services) and longer-term indefinite value (the value of the ongoing business as expressed through goodwill, trademark, and share price). Employees receive wages and benefits and may, in some cases, participate as shareholders through a 401(k) plan or individual purchases. But they also have an interest in the ongoing business of the company simply by virtue of having a job. This job renders them participants in the ongoing production and entitles them to have a voice in the joint production process through the governance of the firm.

Compared to shareholders, it is both easier and more difficult to correlate employment interests with a schema of voting rights within the firm. Employees are smaller in number, easier to keep track of, and have an attachment to the firm that makes the logistics of election participation easier to manage. Employees cannot "short sell" their employment or "flash trade" their jobs before the election. At the same time, there are some factors that could complicate the assignment of particular voting interests to employees. First, the category of employment is less clearly defined than the category of shareholder. The test for employment has traditionally been the common law control test, which asks whether the employer has the right to control the actions of the employee within the scope of employment.[26] The test has vague boundaries and can result in uncertainty over whether a particular worker is an employee or an independent contractor.[27] At the same time, however, corporations officially designate their employees for tax purposes and withhold employee income taxes.[28] This tax designation would be a fairly straightforward way of delineating employees, and workers could contest that designation if they felt improperly excluded from the employment rolls.

Corporations may also struggle over the specific voting rights to be granted to each employee. The easiest system to administer would allocate one set of voting rights to each employee. But employees might object to this allocation along a variety of lines, arguing instead that employees with more seniority, higher wages, more hours, or greater stature within the company deserve increased voting rights. Unlike a unit of shares, a "unit" of employment is not the same for each employee in terms of interest in the firm. The conflict over the allocation of employee voting rights is one argument against them.[29]

But this disparity between shareholders and employees can also be overstated. As already mentioned, shareholder voting rights are not always allocated along the lines of one share, one vote. Many of the largest and most prominent companies – e.g., Google, Facebook, Viacom – have allocated voting rights disproportionately among shareholder groups to give a group of founders, family members, or insiders more power than their fellow stockholders. These companies made this choice to take account of competing interests by providing more governance to a select group because of that group's role within the firm.[30] Similar analyses could apply in the employee voting rights context: the company could design a system of voting rights based on the relative importance of employee voice to the company.[31] As a starting point, corporations could choose between a straightforward allocation of employee voting rights on the basis of one employee, one vote, or the distribution of voting rights according to more individualized metrics of employee interests, such as seniority or position.

One other structural concern with adding employee voting rights to the corporate governance mix is their potential incommensurability with shareholder voting rights. If we have one share, one vote on one side, and one employee, one vote on the other, how will we match up these two systems? How many shares' worth of votes will one employee have? We imagine that most corporations would want to take one of two approaches. The first would provide for separate systems of voting rights, in which there would be no need to measure commensurability. So, for example, shareholders would vote for a set of shareholder directors, and employees would vote for a set of employee directors. The voting rights would not need to be commensurable as they would be participating in different elections. Both the German system of codetermination[32] and bills recently introduced in the U.S. Senate track this approach.[33]

The second possible system would combine shareholders and employees into a single electorate. The corporation would then have to make a judgment about how to weight the votes of individual shareholders and employees. Corporations following this approach would probably start with a judgment about the general allocation of voting power between shareholders and employees, and then translate that into individual voting weights. So, for example, a corporation could decide that employees should have roughly 40 percent[34] of the voting rights within the corporation, and then allocate votes between the two groups based on this rough proportion.

At this stage, it's enough to say that the logistical challenges are not insurmountable. More importantly, they do not justify the exclusion of a set of corporate participants from participation in governance. Employees are participants in the firm and contribute their efforts to the process of joint production. They should not be excluded from governance simply because we currently have systems in place that find it easier to exclude them.

Other Corporate Constituents

The theory of the firm and democratic participation theory both counsel in favor of extending the corporate franchise to shareholders and employees. Those two groups deserve voting rights because they are within the economic firm – they participate in a process of joint production as carried on by the firm. They also have the accurate and manageable markers of interest that allow for the creation of a workable system of corporate governance. The same cannot be said of other corporate constituents.

Along with the theory of the firm, democratic participation theory provides a second means of separating the insiders – shareholders and employees – from other constituents outside the corporation. With most firms, it doesn't make sense to capture the preferences of customers, suppliers, and other constituencies through the franchise. This is both because their interests in the success of the firm are not as significant as those of the insiders and because their status and relationship with the firm do not provide particularly accurate or manageable markers of that interest. For those reasons, participation theory generally counsels against extending the franchise to these outside stakeholders.

Take, for example, the customers of a large corporation. Customers certainly have some relationship with a firm such that they have a stake in, and preferences regarding, its success. But their interest in the continued success of the company is more tenuous, and their ongoing contacts with the company, even assuming planned obsolescence, are likely to be relatively sporadic. Their status as customers is not a particularly strong marker of interest in the future success of the firm. Nor is it a particularly manageable marker, given that the company's interaction with the person may be limited to the point of sale, if that; after that, tracking the customers becomes more difficult. The same may be said of a corporation's suppliers. Suppliers provide anything ranging from a few office supplies up through the core raw materials of a business. Some are long-standing, others are one-timers. But the key interaction is the transaction, and that is best managed legally through contract. For those stakeholders who have no contractual relationships with the corporation, the markers are even more attenuated. Members of the same industry, community, or nation best express their preferences through participation in industry trade groups, local municipalities, or the federal government.

Of course, there may be certain sets of stakeholders who enjoy a continuous and significant relationship with a corporation such that they have a more significant interest, making their identification for the purpose of extending the franchise more manageable. Some utility customers, for example, have that kind of relationship with their providers.[35] In those situations, democratic participation theory may counsel in favor of according them voting rights. Similarly, some suppliers enjoy such a close relationship with their customers that mechanisms of shared governance may make sense.[36] The theory is flexible enough to deal with unique situations and the attendant possibility of accurate and manageable markers of constituent interest, and to assign voting rights accordingly. In the regular course of corporate governance, however, the theory of democratic participation counsels in favor of extending voting rights to shareholders and employees and leaving the interests of other constituents to contract or government regulation.

* * *

Democratic participation theory provides a unique argument for extending governance rights to both shareholders and employees. The theory is derived from the uncontroversial propositions that governance rights should be tied to interest and that we must be able to assess that interest in a way that is both accurate and manageable. These propositions largely spring from political theory, but are also consistent with economic and social choice theory and their focus on preference fulfillment and the construction of incentive structures designed to promote good decision-making. Like the theory of the firm, democratic participation theory generally counsels in favor of adding employees to the corporate electorate, but also tells us when we might be in one of those rare situations where governance rights should be extended to other stakeholders. That is, both the theory of the firm and the theory of democratic participation have a flexibility that the arguments for the exclusive shareholder franchise always seemed to lack. They also have some empirical support, as we'll see now in Chapter 11.

The German Codetermination Experience

Shareholder primacy is so deeply entrenched in American corporate law and scholarship that it's sometimes difficult to imagine any other way of thinking about the corporation. This lack of imagination may help explain why arguments for the shareholder franchise – despite their shortcomings – continue to plod along in the background of an awful lot of scholarship. Rather than seriously considering alternative models, scholars have spent a lot of time dickering over how responsive the corporation should be to various shareholder interests. And this scholarly torpor has carried over into the popular imagination, where the stale idea that shareholders "own" a corporation ends up framing most public discussions.

This focus on shareholders is surprisingly narrow-minded. And what initially appear to be radical proposals look more like tempests in teapots. The majority of states, for example, have passed stakeholder statutes that allow, but do not require, companies to consider the interests of other constituents, particularly in the context of mergers and acquisitions.[1] The Business Roundtable issued a letter from CEOs declaring their commitment to other stakeholders.[2] But these states and CEOs are not grappling with an underlying governance structure whereby shareholders alone elect boards of directors who then appoint officers to run the company. Given this governance structure, is it any wonder that corporations tend to prioritize shareholder interests, and that everybody comes to believe that's what they *should* be doing?

The lack of interest in alternative models is even more surprising in light of the theoretical nature of the arguments for the exclusive shareholder franchise. Just think of some of the arguments discussed in earlier chapters. All corporate constituents prefer and would have, hypothetically, bargained for shareholder control (Chapter 4). Nonshareholder participants do not want to bargain for control; they would rather leave the entirety of the residual profits to shareholders (Chapter 6). Expanding the electorate to include other corporate participants will lead to voting cycles that destroy firms (Chapter 7). These arguments aren't particularly good on their own terms. But they also make testable predictions about the impact of expanding the corporate electorate beyond shareholders, which means they are subject to empirical rebuttal as well.

The same, of course, may be said of our shared governance model. We argue that adding some form of employee board representation is consistent with both the economic theory of the firm and the theory of democratic participation. This conclusion, too, may be measured against real-world outcomes. So we'd like to know whether firms with shared representation are possible and how they might perform compared to their shareholder-driven counterparts. Fortunately, there are good examples of shared governance, some of which have been around for more than a century, in countries such as Denmark, Germany, Norway, Slovenia, and Sweden. We will focus our attention on the most prominent (and best studied) example: Germany's program of supervisory codetermination.[3]

German Codetermination

While the United States has some history of employee involvement in corporate governance, it's pretty thin gruel.[4] The oldest codetermination law still in force is a 1919 Massachusetts statute that expressly allows a corporation to have employee representatives on its board.[5] That law, however, is permissive, and there's not much evidence that corporations in that state have made use of the option. Union members actually served on the boards of several large corporations in the 1980s and 1990s, including United Airlines, Pan Am, Avis, and Chrysler.[6] And, more recently, several bills proposed in Congress would require employee representation on corporate boards.[7] But the American experience with employee board representation has been isolated, sporadic, and often aspirational.

Europe, though, is another story. A majority of EU and OECD countries give employees some degree of access to corporate boards.[8] But the German system of codetermination offers the most robust protection of employee representation. German codetermination has also been in place for decades as part of a large, modern economy, making it the obvious exemplar of such a system.[9]

Codetermination actually describes two very different features of German corporations.[10] "Social codetermination" involves employee representation on shop-level works councils at all companies with at least five employees.[11] The works councils have a broad range of rights in the workplace, including the right to receive economic and financial information, the right of consultation on matters relating to the organization and structure of jobs, and the power to negotiate work agreements.[12] "Supervisory codetermination," on the other hand, describes employee representation at the level of the corporate board,[13] and is of greater interest here.

Supervisory codetermination laws dictate the composition of the boards of directors for large German companies.[14] Unlike the United States, Germany uses a two-tiered corporate board structure.[15] The supervisory board provides more general oversight of the company and appoints the members of the management board.[16] The management board runs the company, directing resources and making the day-to-day business decisions.[17] Management boards of larger companies also have a personnel director responsible for all matters relating to labor relations.[18] The supervisory board is thus more analogous to the American board of directors, while the officers in U.S. corporations share many of the responsibilities of the management board.[19]

The degree of supervisory codetermination on German corporate boards depends on the type of industry, the number of employees, and a few other factors.[20] Corporations with fewer than 500 employees have supervisory board members elected by shareholders; corporations with 500 to 2,000 employees must have one-third of their board members elected by employees (called, unsurprisingly, one-third board parity); and those with more than 2,000 employees have one-half of their supervisory board members elected by employees.[21] In most of these large companies with one-half codetermination, employees enjoy "quasi parity" because shareholders elect the chair (and potential tiebreaker vote). In the coal, iron, and steel industries, however, there is a neutral chair (and tiebreaker), giving the employees "full parity," or a truly shared system of governance.[22] Thus, in Germany, we have a long-standing example of shared corporate governance, with shareholder and employee representatives working side by side on the supervisory boards of major companies.

Codetermination in American Corporate Governance Scholarship

So what have American corporate law scholars done with this alternative version of corporate governance, one that actually exists in the form of flesh-and-blood German supervisory boards? For decades, codetermina-tion has received little more than passing attention from corporate governance scholars.[23] It is rarely given the kind of in-depth treatment that a fully functioning, alternative model of corporate governance would seem to demand.[24]

Codetermination shows up most often in a variant of the contractarian argument for the exclusive shareholder franchise. This version of the argument is as follows: If codetermination is so great, then firms should (and would) voluntarily adopt it. But American firms have not done so. Codetermination, therefore, is not that great and, in fact, is less efficient than the method of governance chosen in the United States, with corpo-rate boards elected by shareholders alone. In fact, the argument goes, the only way a firm would end up with employee representation on its board is if you force it to do so, as Germany does by law. Nobody freely chooses codetermination; it is therefore less efficient than having shareholders run the show.

A number of legal scholars – including Stephen Bainbridge,[25] George Dent,[26] Henry Hansmann and Reinier Kraakman,[27] and Roberta Romano[28] – have argued that codetermination must be inefficient because it has not been voluntarily adopted by firms.[29] But the argument may have been first (and in any case, most forcefully) made by Michael Jensen and William Meckling in the late 1970s.[30] "Without fiat," they claimed, "codetermination would be virtually nonexistent."[31] They then backed up this argument with a prediction: German codetermination would soon devolve into a system in which either shareholders or employees had complete control.[32] If the former, then codetermination would just go away and be replaced by the shareholder control that dominates the landscape in the United States.[33] If, however, employees succeed in controlling firms, then the German economy would grind to a halt like Tito's Yugoslavia, with "fairly complete, if not total, state ownership of the productive assets in the economy."[34]

Some forty years later, Jensen and Meckling's prediction looks laugh-able. German codetermination remains in place and, as we shall soon see, is an important aspect of its robust economy. More broadly, though, the key assumption underlying the argument – that codetermination can arise only through fiat, not voluntary agreement – has itself been revealed to be false.

Ewan McGaughey, a legal historian and economist, recently showed that German codetermination first arose through collective agreements and only later was enacted into law.[35] Codetermination arrived at the end of World War I, "not as a law, not as a regulation, but as an agreement."[36] Only afterward did supervisory codetermination get codified into legislation.[37] Codetermination was then abolished by the Nazi regime with a 1934 statute,[38] only to be recreated – again through agreement – at the conclusion of World War II.[39] The basic sequence was that codetermination arose through consensual agreement, developed into social consensus, and later became embodied in the law.[40] This history shows that the law and economics scholars are not just wrong on this point but may have the picture completely upside down: codetermination was created by agreement not once but twice, while the law was sometimes used to quash it.[41]

So if codetermination arose through voluntary agreement in Germany, why didn't the same bargain get struck everywhere else? What was so special about Germany? McGaughey identifies two, relatively rare "Goldilocks" conditions that existed in postwar Germany: (1) employers and employees had relatively equal bargaining power, and (2) the labor movement was unified around a common objective of securing meaningful representation at work.[42] These two conditions made the codetermination bargain possible.

Now, it might be argued that the historical rarity of these Goldilocks conditions makes the German example unique, ingermane to the more typical bargains struck by labor and capital. But a closer look at those conditions shows that, if anything, the opposite is true. Remember, the contractarian argument draws its normative force from the assumption that freely bargained-for agreements better reflect the preferences of the parties.[43] All things being equal, they reflect the most efficient outcome. But in order for this to work, the parties must actually be free to bargain. That freedom may be limited if the parties are in unequal bargaining positions (making it less likely that the weaker party is really getting what it wants), one group of constituents has coordination problems (again, reducing their bargaining power), or there are legal or logistical roadblocks to certain kinds of agreements. The contractarian argument for the exclusive shareholder franchise fails to account for all three of these issues: employees have never had equal bargaining power; labor unions have never represented more than one-third of private-sector employees, and currently represent less than 7 percent; and both legal and logistical roadblocks make it difficult for unions to participate in corporate governance.[44]

The Goldilocks conditions, in other words, do not reflect the conditions that surround the formation of U.S. corporations, but they *do* reflect the kind of rare situation that gets the contractarian arguments up and running and gives them their normative force. But, in the presence of those conditions, corporate constituents do not, as predicted by contractarians, hand over all governance authority to shareholders. They instead put both shareholder and employee representatives on the board. Like the argument from Arrow's theorem – where we learned that the presence of an oppositional electorate actually *decreases* the chance of a voting cycle – the contractarian argument, if anything, ends up militating in favor of employee representation.

There is an additional reason to think that the bargain for employee representation may not be struck by individual corporations – namely, the path-dependency and network effects of the widespread adoption of a particular system of governance. David Levine and Laura Tyson have argued that codetermination needs to be adopted on a broad scale because individual firms find themselves in a prisoner's dilemma with regard to their existing entitlements and constituents.[45] Unilateral adoption of codetermination may lead to wage compression (resulting in the loss of managerial and executive employees) and dismissal protections (resulting in the retention of poorly performing employees), disadvantaging the adopting firm in relation to its competitors in terms of capital and sales.[46] Without some kind of industrywide (or economywide) agreement, the boards of individual firms – which are at that point still governed solely by shareholders – will rationally fail to adopt the approach that would have the greater utility overall because of the effect on shareholder value.[47] The industrywide bargaining that took place in postwar Germany involved exactly the kind of cooperation needed to lift corporate players out of this dilemma.

There have also been a growing group of studies evaluating the effect of codetermination on a range of economic outcomes. Those, too, have gone largely ignored by American scholars of corporate governance.

Evaluating German Codetermination

So how well has codetermination worked in Germany? Much of the scholarship evaluating the system has centered on its role in promoting broader goals such as social cohesion and fairness.[48] The bottom-line, economic effects of codetermination (which we'll turn to shortly) are either seen as secondary or as necessarily following from the achievement of these societal goals.[49] That is, codetermination is viewed less in terms of an economic system than as one designed to promote a well-functioning democracy and help prevent social division – in particular, the division between labor and capital. And, on this broad level, it is thought to be quite successful.

The success of codetermination on the social level has carried over to the boardroom, where the relationship between labor and capital is relatively harmonious.[50] Shareholder and employee representatives typically meet separately with the managing board before coming together at the supervisory board meetings.[51] These premeetings allow representatives to focus on the interests of their constituents and raise concerns with the management boards.[52] Recent studies have revealed that the supervisory meetings themselves are marked by a great deal of cooperation between shareholder and employee representatives.[53] This cooperation may be fostered in part by the legal requirement that shareholder and employee representatives must, at that point, put the interests of the corporation over those of their respective constituents.[54] While the relationships at the supervisory board level are not perfect, they are a far cry from the law and economics predictions of firm-destroying voting cycles and other visions of interboard squabbling and dysfunction.

There are a limited number of studies that evaluate the actual effects of codetermination on firm behavior and economic success. And most of those studies focus on a relatively narrow set of outcomes associated with shareholder interests. Robert Scholz and Sigurt Vitols recently cataloged the thirty-seven extant studies on the relationship between codetermination and firm performance and found that fourteen of them focused on stock market performance and thirteen on profitability.[55] Seven studies analyzed codetermination's impact on productivity, which would be of interest to both shareholders and employees (and, more broadly, society).[56] Very few studies analyzed issues that would seem to be most important to employees, such as wages, employment levels, and job security.[57]

This evaluative approach is odd and continues to infect most discussions of codetermination. One would expect that, all things being equal, a shift from full shareholder control to partial shareholder control would decrease the gains allocated to shareholders. Employees can, in various ways, allocate a greater proportion of the returns from joint production to themselves if they have governance power. These distributional shifts would leave shareholders with less of the pie, even if overall the firm had the same or greater gains.

In any case, we should not be misled into thinking that the effect of codetermination on shareholders alone tells us its effect on the firm – if appropriately construed to include all corporate constituents.

Shareholder interests do not equate to firm interests, and we are left to wonder why so many studies appear to assume they are one and the same thing. Prominent academics have critiqued this focus on shareholder wealth maximization as the sole metric of success, even in the context of U.S. companies.[58] A comprehensive assessment of codetermination must include its impact on all corporate constituents.

What this means is that many studies we're about to discuss necessarily render an incomplete picture of codetermination, one that largely focuses on the success of the firm as measured by stock price or profits. This puts us in a curious position when trying to make a broader assessment. If these studies show that shareholders come out behind, we still need to ask whether their losses are counterbalanced or even outweighed by gains for other constituents. If, on the other hand, shareholders' fortunes are unaffected by codetermination, or they even come out ahead, then we can be pretty confident that the German system of shared governance delivers across the board.[59]

A number of studies have assessed the economic effects of codetermination, with a consensus that has shifted back and forth over the last four decades.[60] Some early studies from the 1980s found that codetermination had very little impact on corporate performance.[61] Those studies, however, were criticized on a number of methodological grounds,[62] and several more sophisticated evaluations in the 1990s and early 2000s gave a more pessimistic account, finding that codetermination was associated with, among other things, lower productivity and lower profits.[63] That consensus, though, soon gave way to a third phase in the literature, one that both reversed the principal findings of the second-phase studies (considering them to be artifacts of a particular method of assessment)[64] and found that codetermination was also modestly associated with greater innovation.[65] These more optimistic assessments were bolstered by a couple of modern financial studies on the market value of the firm, which found that "prudent" levels of employee representation led to better board decision-making by improving monitoring and thus reducing agency costs.[66] Uwe Jirjahn, summing up the studies in early 2010, reported that codetermination was connected to higher productivity and that more recent studies (unlike earlier ones) had found that codetermination also had a positive effect on profitability and capital market valuation.[67] This third, rather optimistic phase of assessment brought us right up to one of the most profound tests of all systems of corporate governance: the global financial crisis.

The financial crisis did not spare any of the world's major economies, but some recovered more quickly than others. Germany, in particular, recovered more quickly and more thoroughly than many other countries and did so, at least in part, because of its corporate governance model.[68] Economic downturns are always difficult for companies and their employees. But in many cases codetermination will allow the management of a company "to more easily seek the consent of its workforce for carrying out more or less drastic measures."[69] These measures include a system that temporarily reduces the working hours (and salaries) of many of the employees (*Kurzarbeit*).[70] It helped to avoid painful layoffs and allowed companies to retain their core workforces, thereby enabling the economy as a whole to weather the worst of the economic slump.[71] This led one group of scholars to conclude: "Particular to Germany was the social partners' willingness to work together during this specific economic hardship. . . . [I]t cannot be denied that the *quality* of industrial relations was a factor in overcoming the crisis."[72]

There are, of course, some caveats to this story. The labor stockpiling that smoothed over the effects of the recession was tailor-made for the particular economic woes that hit Germany: a short-term demand shock that primarily affected the manufacturing sector.[73] More typically, German employment follows GDP, sometimes with a slight delay.[74] But the system worked surprisingly well this time around, and the resulting difference between Germany and the United States was apparent in the early part of the recovery period.[75]

A number of new studies came out during the period of recovery that were consistent with the third phase of the literature, showing that codetermination generally had positive economic effects. One of the stronger results came from a 2020 study by Simon Jäger, Benjamin Schoefer, and Jörg Heining, which showed that shared governance "resulted in positive rather than negative effects on capital formation."[76] This shift toward more capital-intensive production may be the result of worker involvement in investment decisions, the fact that worker representatives may have longer-term views than shareholders or executives, or because shared governance generally facilitates cooperation between firms and their employees.[77] Shareholders, it turns out, may be better off investing in firms where employees have a stronger governance role.

What about employees? One would think that employees would lead the pack of corporate constituents expected to gain from more direct board representation. And, in fact, employees do appear to be better off under codetermination, at least by their own measures. But, as foretold by the story of German employment during the global financial crisis, those employees may measure success in ways that aren't limited to the size of their paychecks.

As described above, Germany's bounceback from the financial crisis was largely a result of the ability of firms to keep employment levels relatively stable. Those employment levels didn't come without a cost, however: they were maintained at the price of the number of hours worked, bonuses (or the lack of them), and resulting lower wages and salaries. But this is exactly the kind of deal that employees bargained for under the *Kurzarbeit* system.

A recent study by E. Han Kim, Ernst Maug, and Christoph Schneider confirmed that employees at full-parity-codetermined firms are better protected against layoffs during industry downturns.[78] This job security, however, comes at the price of significantly lower wages. Employees at codetermined firms pay a premium equal to 3.3 percent of their wages for this employment insurance.[79] Importantly, this swap of wages for job security has no effect on shareholders one way or the other.[80] This is similar to the finding by Jäger, Schoefer, and Heining, who found "no increases in wages or rent sharing in shared governance firms . . . ."[81] This suggests, then, that this feature of employment insurance at codetermined firms was not a result of employee entrenchment in the form of employee-manager collusion, and it did not come at the expense of other corporate constituents.[82]

That's not to say, however, that codetermination does not affect other corporate constituents. Employee representation, for example, turns out to be good for creditors. Employees have interests that align with those of creditors along a couple of dimensions. As Chen Lin, Thomas Schmid, and Yuhai Xuan explained in a 2018 study, "Employee representatives who aim to protect the interests of the firm's employees can (unintentionally) also help to protect the interests of banks as both stakeholders are interested in the long-term survival and stability of the firm."[83] For that reason, employee representation and bank ownership can act as "substitutes" for one another.[84]

The result of this interest alignment redounds to the benefit of both the firm and the banks. The study found that codetermination was associated with favorable financing conditions, lower costs of debt, longer debt maturities, and fewer covenants.[85] Codetermined firms were also found to have entered into fewer and better merger and acquisition deals, had more stable cash flows, and were exposed to less idiosyncratic risk.[86] The authors of the study concluded that "a direct voice of employees in firms' governance structure can be a powerful mechanism to reduce agency conflicts between debt providers and firms and to improve their financing opportunities and conditions."[87]

Creditors aren't the only constituents who might benefit from employee representation. Scholz and Vitols recently evaluated the impact of codetermination on a firm's commitment to substantive corporate social responsibility (CSR) measures.[88] The study was novel in several respects. Unlike earlier work, which assumed that worker influence was the same at all codetermined firms, the authors developed a measure of the strength of codetermination based on a number of factors, including obvious ones such as the level of codetermination (one-third, quasi, or full) and less obvious ones such as the extent of worker representation on board committees and the importance of the supervisory board in firm governance.[89] The study was also the first to look at the effect of codetermination on CSR outcomes.[90]

The authors found that the strength of codetermination was positively related to substantive CSR policies, including setting concrete goals on emission reductions, the publication of a separate CSR report (or section in its annual report), and the presence of a job security (no-layoff) policy.[91] These were deemed "substantive" CSR measures because they required an expenditure or investment in company resources.[92] There was no corresponding relationship to merely symbolic measures, indicating that employee representatives have little interest in measures that do not result in direct improvements for workers.[93]

The recent performance of the German economy has begun to change the way people view codetermination. By 2016, its popularity among the German people rose to an all-time high.[94] The German business community looks at it in a more positive light,[95] and foreign businesspeople – long baffled by the complex codetermination laws – have come to see some of its advantages.[96]

* * *

So what does all this mean? To start with, the success of the German system serves as an empirical rejoinder to the hypothetical arguments used by law and economics scholars to justify the exclusive shareholder franchise. Codetermination was born of consensual agreement at a time when labor and capital had roughly equal bargaining power, and only later became enshrined in law. German firms have not been paralyzed by more heterogeneous board electorates. And they have not been destroyed by voting cycles. The arguments against employee representation were already in trouble on their own theoretical terms; the presence of a significant, well-functioning counterexample should be decisive. Those committed to the proposition that economic and social choice theory somehow dictate the exclusive shareholder franchise need to overhaul their old arguments or come up with some new ones.

Does this mean that German-style codetermination is without faults? Of course not.[97] The system has been criticized for its large, two-tiered board structures.[98] It makes use of an unnecessarily baroque version of an electoral college to elect employee representatives.[99] And the recent success of the German system also doesn't mean that it would directly translate to corporations in the United States. Perhaps supervisory codetermination can flourish only in conjunction with the strong union presence and works councils found in Germany. (Or perhaps it's the other way around.) But, at this point, German codetermination is working well enough to help confirm many of the arguments made in this book.

Codetermination ultimately serves as a kind of proof of concept when it comes to our model of shared corporate governance. The arguments we make in favor of adding employee representatives to corporate boards, just like the arguments against, are largely theoretical. They necessarily sweep quite broadly and don't attend to many of the mechanical details of how best to structure a shared governance system, much less how to get from here to there. Germany provides an example of how such a system might work. And recent research suggests that it's working quite well for a variety of corporate constituents, including shareholders.

12

Conclusion

In 2019, the United States Census Bureau reported that income inequality had hit its highest levels since the Bureau began tracking these disparities in 1967.[1] This shift in economic fortunes is accounted for almost entirely by rising gains in the top tiers of income distribution. While wages for the bottom half of income earners have stagnated, crawling up by only $200, the top 1 percent has seen its average income rise from $428,000 in 1980 to $1.3 million (in inflation-adjusted dollars).[2] The higher income echelons have seen even more staggering gains, with the very top 0.001 percent now receiving seven times their 1980 income – an average of $122 million.[3] In terms of wealth inequality, the global top 1 percent controls 44 percent of the world's wealth, while the bottom 64 percent (owning $10,000 or less) holds a mere 2 percent.[4] The International Monetary Fund recently highlighted the growing disparity in wealth within different regions of otherwise prosperous countries, a trend that started in the 1980s and continues to deepen the divide.[5]

Politicians, commentators, and academics have pointed the finger at a number of possible culprits for these trends: globalized trade, automation, immigration, technology, the increasing importance of education and skills. But not enough blame has been directed at the corporation and corporate governance. The legal mechanisms of corporate law and shareholder primacy direct wealth away from labor and toward capital. Corporations are the initial point of distribution, and they are designed to be inequality machines.

Certainly, the key players in corporate governance and finance – officers and directors, investment banks, hedge funds, private equity, and Wall Street more generally – have come under heavy fire for their outsize salaries and insider deals. The 2010 Dodd-Frank Act required large public companies to report the ratio between the CEO's pay and that of the median worker, and the results have been staggering, if not surprising. In 2018, CEOs in S&P 500 companies earned an average 287 times more than their median employee, with an average compensation of \$14.5 million compared to \$39,888.[6] The outrage stoked at this massive disparity has largely provoked calls for higher taxes on income and wealth. But this lopsided allocation of income demonstrates a problem with its distribution – not just its redistribution. Corporate governance has thrown the allocation of the gains of production out of whack.

Moreover, the misallocation of corporate profits is further exacerbated by the political system. As representatives of worker interests, unions have been among the biggest institutional spenders in politics; in 2016, they donated \$35 million to individual federal candidates and \$132 million to superpolitical action committees.[7] But their spending is dwarfed by individual spending from millionaires and billionaires who made their money through corporations and corporate finance. A mere five people contributed more than \$210 million during the 2016 campaign, and \$757 million was given in donations of more than \$500,000 apiece.[8] Wealth obtained through stock, stock options, or other instruments of corporate finance absolutely swamps whatever funds workers can provide to influence the political system.

The United States political and academic ecosystems have underappreciated the importance of corporate governance to many of the issues facing our society. Control of corporations by capital leads to unequal distribution of corporate funds, which then allows capital to funnel its wealth back to capital-friendly politicians, reinforcing the divide. As a result, working people are squeezed out of the political and economic dialogue across the board and feel more powerless and alienated.[9]

This book centers on the complex of statutes, cases, and institutions that form our system of corporate governance. We contend that corporate governance has stopped working for the women and men who work at these corporations – who drive trucks, serve meals, manufacture equipment, and provide care for the sick. Their actions are what enable firms to succeed, but their voices are not heard in boardrooms. It is time to reconsider the foundational principles of corporate law in light of the effects of corporate governance on our economy, our workforce, and our society.

The Demise of Shareholder Primacy

For the last half century, shareholder primacy has been the dominant ideology in corporate governance theory. That vision of the firm has driven the theoretical literature and provided a clear narrative about the corporation's nature and purpose. Corporate governance theorists, working largely in the law and economics tradition, developed an intellectual framework to support the whole enterprise. That framework is anchored in the arguments for the corporation's central governance feature – the exclusive shareholder franchise – whereby shareholders, and shareholders alone, elect the board of directors and vote on other significant corporate transactions.

The arguments for shareholder voting, though, no longer can support the tremendous doctrinal and societal weight that has been placed upon them. In some cases, they were based on a mistaken assumption of shareholder homogeneity. In others, like the contractarian and Arrow's theorem arguments, they were fundamentally flawed from the very beginning. And these arguments aren't merely defective, but defective when measured by the theoretical framework that their authors hold so dear – that of standard economics and social choice theory. These shortcomings have been cataloged in a variety of different places; by collecting and analyzing them in one place, we hope to put a stop to the ever-shifting justifications and lazy hand-waving that have come to pass for argument.

Perhaps the most surprising thing about the collapse of these arguments is that there's been so little in the way of rehabilitation or reformation. Instead, most corporate law scholars are content to assume that the theoretical foundations of shareholder primacy are intact, and go from there. Most of the time, that assumption isn't even acknowledged. But once in a while it will be made explicit, as when Paul Edelman, Randall Thomas, and Robert Thompson noted as follows in their article on institutional investors:

> A few caveats before we begin. First, we are not making normative claims about the merits of shareholder voting. We are agnostic on the question of whether shareholder voting leads either to social or corporate efficiency. We offer a positive theory that explains what we observe in the world about the role of the shareholder franchise.[10]

This approach may be understandable, since shareholder voting is, in fact, the current regime. And the caveat is refreshingly honest. But at some point we must confront the fact that the intellectual foundation of the shareholder franchise is broken, and nobody is making much of an attempt to fix it or offer a replacement.

The collapse of the intellectual foundations of shareholder primacy has, with some delay, been accompanied by at least some recognition in the business community that times are changing. In August 2019, the

Business Roundtable pivoted away from its longtime commitment to shareholder primacy, issuing a new statement signed by nearly 200 CEOs on the purpose of the corporation, which declared a "fundamental commitment to *all* of our stakeholders."[11] A couple of months later, Leo Strine, Chief Justice of the Delaware Supreme Court, opined that "workers must be given more voice within the corporate boardroom, and top managers and directors must give great thought to how they treat their employees."[12] These sentiments represent a significant change in the way major actors are thinking about the corporation. But they are unaccompanied by any suggestion of structural changes that could effectuate them. At best, Strine proposes the creation of board-level committees devoted to employees, ones that "ensure quality wages and fair worker treatment."[13] But they are all still firmly committed to shareholder control; they just want shareholders and managers to act in a more kindly way toward other constituents.

Politicians have also begun to see the wisdom of moving away from shareholder primacy. Senators Tammy Baldwin and Elizabeth Warren have introduced legislation that would provide employees with representation on the boards of directors of corporations of a certain size.[14] Warren further promoted the issue as part of her presidential candidacy,[15] as did Senator Bernie Sanders.[16] While these proposals may not make it through Congress in the immediate future, they open up the debate and help send a message that shareholder primacy is not the only game in town. And the concept of employee representation on corporate boards has been brought into the public consciousness. In fact, one of the demands of the employee leaders behind the Google walkout was a worker director on the board.[17] The question now is: Where do we go from here?

A New Start

There are no simple answers to complicated issues like inequality, global warming, and the distortion of democratic politics. But those problems do share at least one common root: the modern corporation. Corporations account for most of the economic activity in the country and are the initial point of the distribution of the gains of production. Those corporations are currently structured in such a way as to maximize returns to shareholders, using a governance system buttressed by the arguments from law and economics scholars reassuring us that what's good for shareholders is good for society. And while we cannot devise simple answers to the substantial issues of public policy born out of this viewpoint, we can catalog the theoretical failures of shareholder primacy and begin to reorient the corporation in a way that diminishes, rather than exacerbates, those issues. For the reasons laid out in this book, we believe that means a decisive move in the direction of employee representation on corporate boards.

Such a move, at first glance, might seem radical, or even reckless. But staying the course – and sticking with a governance system coasting on inertia and a handful of discredited theoretical arguments – carries risks of its own. There is a solid theoretical basis for a system of shared representation based on the long-standing theory of the firm. Moreover, such a system is supported by a theory of democratic participation that operates at the fundamental level of preference aggregation consistent with standard economic theory. The German system of codetermination serves as an example of how one such system might work in a way that delivers for employees, creditors, the environment, *and* shareholders.

The shareholder primacy paradigm, rooted in the law and economics movement, has had a long, sustained, and amazingly influential run. Its teachings are now mainstream dogma in company boardrooms, business law classrooms, and Delaware courtrooms.[18] Its proponents have declared the "end of history" in corporate law[19] and have concluded that the theory has been pretty much worked out in its entirety.[20] They have mocked efforts to rein in the excesses of their model – excesses that led to a flood of corporate scandals and the worst financial crisis since the Great Depression – as "quack" corporate governance.[21] But like the traditional corporate law doctrinalists before them, they have failed to notice that their theory has become stagnant and ossified.[22] And the basic principles of their theory have led our economy, and the world, into significant peril.

But a new revolution is in the works. We are on our way to a new approach to joint production – new models of corporate governance that incorporate worker participation, create fairer distributions, and systematize a more democratic process. The exact contours of this new theory and these new models are just beginning to be worked out. But the time is well past to recognize the limitations and failures of the shareholder primacy model and to develop a better way. We look forward to participating in this progression.

NOTES

Preface

1. *See* Henry Hansmann & Reinier Kraakman, *The End of History for Corporate Law*, 89 Geo. L.J. 439, 439 (2001) ("There is no longer any serious competitor to the view that corporate law should principally strive to increase long-term shareholder value.").

2. *See, e.g.*, Zohar Goshen & Richard Squire, *Principal Costs: A New Theory for Corporate Law and Governance*, 117 Colum. L. Rev. 767 (2017); Dorothy S. Lund, *Nonvoting Shares and Efficient Corporate Governance*, 71 Stan. L. Rev. 687 (2019).

3. Oliver Hart & Luigi Zingales, *Companies Should Maximize Shareholder Welfare Not Market Value*, 2 J.L. Fin. & Acct. 247, 248 (2017); Michael C. Jensen, *Value Maximization, Stakeholder Theory, and the Corporate Objective Function*, J. Applied Corp. Fin., Winter 2010, at 32, 33 (arguing that corporations should pursue "maximization of the long-run value of the firm" rather than shareholder wealth maximization); Leo E. Strine Jr., Toward Fair and Sustainable Capitalism: A Comprehensive Proposal to Help American Workers, Restore Fair Gainsharing Between Employees and Shareholders, and Increase American Competitiveness by Reorienting Our Corporate Governance System Toward Sustainable Long-Term Growth and Encouraging Investments in America's Future (John M. Olin Ctr. for Law, Econ. & Bus., Discussion Paper No. 1018, 2019), https://papers.ssrn.com/sol3/papers.cfm?abstract_id=3461924 (opining that "[t]he incentive system for the governance of American corporations has failed in recent decades to adequately encourage long-term investment, sustainable business practices, and most importantly, fair gainsharing between shareholders and workers").

4. *Business Roundtable Redefines the Purpose of a Corporation to Promote "An Economy That Serves All Americans"* (Aug. 19, 2019), https://www.businessroundtable.org/business-roundtable-redefines-the-purpose-of-a-corporation-to-promote-an-econ omy-that-serves-all-americans.

5. Ben Popken, *What Did Corporate America Do with That Tax Break? Buy Record Amounts of Its Own Stock*, NBCnews.com (June 26, 2018), https://www.nbcnews .com/business/economy/what-did-corporate-america-do-tax-break-buy-record-amounts-n886621; Vanessa Fuhrmans, *Tax Cuts Provide Limited Boost to Workers' Wages*, Wall St. J. (Oct. 2, 2018), https://www.wsj.com/articles/tax-cuts-provide-limited-boost-to-workers-wages-1538472600 ("U.S. companies are putting savings from the corporate tax cut to use, but only a fraction of it is flowing to employees' wallets, new data show.").

6. Edmund L. Andrews, *Greenspan Concedes Error on Regulation*, N.Y. Times, Oct. 23, 2008, at B1.

1. Introduction

1. Andrew Lundeen & Kyle Pomerleau, *Corporations Make up 5 Percent of Businesses but Earn 62 Percent of Revenues, Tax Foundation* (Nov. 25, 2014), http://taxfoundation.org /blog/corporations-make-5-percent-businesses-earn-62-percent-revenues (noting that only 5 percent of the organizational entities in the United States are corporations, but 62 percent of organizational tax revenues come from corporations).

2. JOHN MICKLETHWAIT & ADRIAN WOOLDRIDGE, THE COMPANY: A SHORT HISTORY OF A REVOLUTIONARY IDEA xv (2005). *See also* LARRY E. RIBSTEIN, THE RISE OF THE UNCORPORATION 4 (2010) ("The corporation undeniably has driven business growth in the United States since the Industrial Revolution.").

3. *Corporate Profits After Tax (without IVA and CCAdj)/Gross Domestic Product,* FEDERAL RESERVE BANK OF ST. LOUIS, https://fred.stlouisfed.org/graph/?g=1Pik (last visited Nov. 5, 2019). *See also* Tim Worstall, *Why Have Corporate Profits Been Rising as a Percentage of GDP? Globalisation,* FORBES (May 7, 2013), https://www .forbes.com/sites/timworstall/2013/05/07/why-have-corporate-profits-been-rising -as-a-percentage-of-gdp-globalisation/#6a27a3fb2a6e.

4. An Act to Provide for Reconciliation Pursuant to Titles II and V of the Concurrent Resolution on the Budget for the Fiscal Year 2018, Pub. L. No. 115-97, 131 Stat. 2054 (codified as amended in scattered sections of 26 U.S.C) (known as the "Tax Cuts and Jobs Act of 2017") (cutting the corporate tax rate from 35 percent to 20 percent).

5. Citizens United v. FEC, 558 U.S. 310 (2010).

6. Burwell v. Hobby Lobby Stores, Inc., 134 S. Ct. 2751 (2014).

7. *See, e.g.,* DEL. CODE ANN. tit. 8, § 101(a) (2015).

8. Matthew T. Bodie, *Employees and the Boundaries of the Corporation, in* RESEARCH HANDBOOK ON THE ECONOMICS OF CORPORATE LAW 86 (Claire Hill & Brett McDonnell eds., 2012).

9. DEL. CODE ANN. tit. 8, § 141(c)(1)–(2).

10. *Id.* § 211(b).

11. Bodie, *supra* note 8, at 86.

12. *See, e.g.,* DEL. CODE ANN. tit. 8, § 142(a) ("Every corporation organized under this chapter shall have such officers with such titles and duties as shall be stated in the bylaws or in a resolution of the board of directors which is not inconsistent with the bylaws . . . .").

13. *Id.* § 141.

14. Matthew T. Bodie, *AOL Time Warner and the False God of Shareholder Primacy,* 31 J. CORP. L. 975, 977 (2006) ("This [shareholder primacy] norm is much more than a descriptive account of shareholders' rights; it is instead a normative judgment on the most socially efficient way of organizing the economy.").

15. We originally discussed these issues in Grant M. Hayden & Matthew T. Bodie, *The Uncorporation and the Unraveling of "Nexus of Contracts" Theory,* 109 MICH. L. REV. 1127 (2011) [hereinafter *The Uncorporation*], and Grant M. Hayden & Matthew T. Bodie, *Shareholder Voting and the Symbolic Politics of Corporation as Contract,* 53 WAKE FOREST L. REV. 511 (2018) [hereinafter *Symbolic Politics*].

16. *Cf.* Bernard S. Black, *Is Corporate Law Trivial?: A Political and Economic Analysis,* 84 NW. U. L. REV. 542, 544 (1990) (developing the "triviality hypothesis" – namely, that "appearances notwithstanding, state corporate law is trivial: it does

not prevent companies – managers and investors together – from establishing any set of governance rules they want").

17. *See* KENT GREENFIELD, THE FAILURE OF CORPORATE LAW: FUNDAMENTAL FLAWS AND PROGRESSIVE POSSIBILITIES 252 (2006) (proposing that a board of directors selected by a variety of stakeholders would be "a genuine realization of the 'nexus of contracts' view of the firm").

18. FRANK H. EASTERBROOK & DANIEL R. FISCHEL, THE ECONOMIC STRUCTURE OF CORPORATE LAW (1991).

19. *Id.* at 67–68.

20. *Id.* at 17, 37.

21. *See, e.g.*, Lucian Bebchuk, *The Case for Increasing Shareholder Power*, 118 HARV. L. REV. 883 (2005).

22. *See* Lucian A. Bebchuk & Robert J. Jackson, Jr., *Corporate Political Speech: Who Decides?*, 124 HARV. L. REV. 83 (2010); Lucian Arye Bebchuk, *The Case for Shareholder Access: A Response to the Business Roundtable*, 55 CASE W. RES. L. REV. 557 (2005); Lucian Arye Bebchuk, John C. Coates IV & Guhan Subramanian, *The Powerful Antitakeover Force of Staggered Boards: Further Findings and a Reply to Symposium Participants*, 55 STAN. L. REV. 885 (2002).

23. Stephen M. Bainbridge, *Director Primacy: The Means and Ends of Corporate Governance*, 97 NW. U. L. REV. 547 (2003).

24. Margaret M. Blair & Lynn A. Stout, *A Team Production Theory of Corporate Law*, 85 VA. L. REV. 247 (1999).

25. *See* Grant Hayden & Matthew T. Bodie, *Shareholder Democracy and the Curious Turn Toward Board Primacy*, 51 WM. & MARY L. REV. 2071, 2089–92 (2010).

26. *See* Michael C. Jensen & William H. Meckling, *Theory of the Firm: Managerial Behavior, Agency Costs and Ownership Structure*, 3 J. FIN. ECON. 305, 309 (1976) (providing the original description of the theory); *see also* EASTERBROOK & FISCHEL, *supra* note 18, at 1–39 (providing one of the most prominent iterations of the theory).

27. Michael Klausner, *The Contractarian Theory of Corporate Law: A Generation Later*, 31 J. CORP. L. 779 (2006); Melvin A. Eisenberg, *The Conception That the Corporation is a Nexus of Contracts, and the Dual Nature of the Firm*, 24 J. CORP. L. 301 (1999); Lewis A. Kornhauser, *The Nexus of Contracts Approach to Corporations: A Comment on Easterbrook and Fischel*, 89 COLUM. L. REV. 1449 (1989); William W. Bratton, Jr., *The "Nexus of Contracts" Corporation: A Critical Appraisal*, 74 CORNELL L. REV. 407 (1989).

28. RIBSTEIN, *supra* note 2, at 67–75 (describing the mandatory elements of the corporate structure); Fred S. McChesney, *Economics, Law, and Science in the Corporate Field: A Critique of Eisenberg*, 89 COLUM. L. REV. 1530, 1537 (1989) ("Admittedly, as a descriptive matter state corporation codes and other sources of law contain many mandatory terms that parties cannot contract around .... [T]o claim that contractarians would deny the existence of coercive legal rules is to accuse them of blindness or stupidity.").

29. *See* Frank H. Easterbrook & Daniel R. Fischel, *The Corporate Contract*, 89 COLUM. L. REV. 1416, 1418 (1989) (discussing how "much of corporate law is designed to reduce the costs of aligning the interests of managers and investors").

30. *See* Hayden & Bodie, *Symbolic Politics*, *supra* note 15, at 539–42.

31. *See* EASTERBROOK & FISCHEL, *supra* note 18, at 67–69.

32. *See id.* at 35–39, 67–69.

33. *See id.* at 69–70.

34. *See id.* at 73; Bernard Black & Reinier Kraakman, *A Self-Enforcing Model of Corporate Law*, 109 HARV. L. REV. 1911, 1945–46 (1996).

35. *See* Zohar Goshen & Richard Squire, *Principal Costs: A New Theory for Corporate Law and Governance*, 117 COLUM. L. REV. 767, 791 (2017); Grant M. Hayden & Matthew T. Bodie, *One Share, One Vote and the False Promise of Shareholder Homogeneity*, 30 CARDOZO L. REV. 445, 505 (2008).

36. *See* Iman Anabtawi, *Some Skepticism About Increasing Shareholder Power*, 53 UCLA L. REV. 561, 574–92 (2006); Hayden & Bodie, *supra* note 35, at 477–98.

37. *See* Anabtawi, *supra* note 36, at 579–83; Hayden & Bodie, *supra* note 35, at 492–94. For a thoughtful review of the short-termism debate, see Michal Barzuza & Eric Talley, *Short-Termism and Long-Termism* 12–21 (Va. Law & Econ. Research Paper No. 2, 2016).

38. Oliver Hart & Luigi Zingales, *Companies Should Maximize Shareholder Welfare Not Market Value*, 2 J.L. FIN. & ACCT. 247 (2017).

39. *See* EASTERBROOK & FISCHEL, *supra* note 18, at 69–70.

40. *Id.* at 70.

41. *See, e.g.,* HENRY HANSMANN, THE OWNERSHIP OF ENTERPRISE 41–42 (1996); Blair & Stout, *supra* note 24, at 257; Gregory K. Dow, *The New Institutional Economics and Employment Regulation, in* GOVERNMENT REGULATION OF THE EMPLOYMENT RELATIONSHIP 57, 69 (Bruce E. Kaufman ed., 1997).

42. For a critical evaluation of this argument, see Grant Hayden & Matthew Bodie, *Arrow's Theorem and the Exclusive Shareholder Franchise*, 62 VAND. L. REV. 1219 (2009). For a condensed version, see Hayden & Bodie, *Symbolic Politics, supra* note 15, at 524–30.

43. *See* Niv Elis, *Falling Investment Revives Attacks Against Trump's Tax Cuts*, THE HILL (Nov. 10, 2019), https://thehill.com/policy/finance/469708-falling-investment-revives-attacks-against-trumps-tax-cuts.

44. *See generally* STEPHEN M. BAINBRIDGE, THE NEW CORPORATE GOVERNANCE IN THEORY AND PRACTICE (2008).

45. *Id.* at 13.

46. Brett H. McDonnell, *Professor Bainbridge and the Arrowian Moment: A Review of the New Corporate Governance in Theory and Practice*, 34 DEL. J. CORP. L. 139, 168 (2009) ("In sum, the Arrowian moment on its own does not succeed as a critique of existing proposals for greater accountability through expanded shareholder power. . . . Indeed, if anything, Arrow's argument, properly understood, calls Bainbridge's own positions into doubt.").

47. *See generally* Blair & Stout, *supra* note 24.

48. Bainbridge, *supra* note 23, at 560.

49. Blair & Stout, *supra* note 24, at 280.

50. *See* David Millon, *Communitarianism in Corporate Law: Foundations and Law Reform Strategies, in* PROGRESSIVE CORPORATE LAW 1, 11–12 (Lawrence E. Mitchell ed., 1995) (discussing efforts to provide protections to nonshareholder constituencies); Blair & Stout, *supra* note 24, at 293–94 (arguing that directors owe a duty to the corporation and that the corporation consists of all of the stakeholders who are responsible for the business of the enterprise).

51. *See* Simone M. Sepe, *Directors' Duty to Creditors and the Debt Contract*, 1 J. Bus. & Tech. L. 553 (2007) (noting that "communitarians . . . advocate a multifiduciary model where all corporate stakeholders benefit from the attribution of directors' fiduciary duties"). *See also* Millon, *supra* note 50, at 11–12 (discussing the use of the multifiduciary model by communitarian corporate law scholars).

52. *See* Susan N. Gary, *Best Interests in the Long Term: Fiduciary Duties and ESG Integration*, 90 U. Colo. L. Rev. 731, 757-58 (2019) ("The terms 'corporate sustainability' and 'corporate social responsibility' (CSR) describe a company's voluntary actions to manage its environmental and social impact, and to consider stakeholders as well as shareholders.").

53. *See, e.g.*, Martin Lipton & Steven A. Rosenblum, *A New System of Corporate Governance: The Quinquennial Election of Directors*, 58 U. Chi. L. Rev. 187, 190 (1991).

54. For a discussion of those excesses, see William W. Bratton, *Enron and the Dark Side of Shareholder Value*, 76 Tul. L. Rev. 1275 (2002).

55. *See* Eric W. Orts & Alan Strudler, *Putting a Stake in Stakeholder Theory*, 88 J. Bus. Ethics 605, 611 (2009) (arguing that stakeholder theory fails to provide a system of mechanisms for governance, other than "balancing" stakeholder concerns); Joseph Heath, *Business Ethics Without Stakeholders*, 16 Bus. Ethics Q. 533, 543 (2006) (arguing that stakeholder theory creates "extraordinary agency risks" because of the potential for conflicts).

56. *See, e.g.*, Stephen E. Ellis & Grant M. Hayden, *The Cult of Efficiency in Corporate Law*, 5 Va. L. & Bus. Rev. 239, 248-49 (2010).

57. *See generally* Daniel A. Farber & Philip P. Frickey, Law and Public Choice (1991).

58. The Federalist No. 10, at 43 (Alexander Hamilton, James Madison & John Jay) (Gary Wills ed., 1982) (defining faction as "a number of citizens amounting to a majority or a minority of the whole, who are united and actuated by some common impulse of passion, or of interest, adverse to the rights of other citizens, or to the permanent and aggregate interests of the community").

59. *See* Grant M. Hayden & Stephen E. Ellis, *Law and Economics After Behavioral Economics*, 55 Kan. L. Rev. 629, 629 (2007).

60. Oliver Hart, *An Economist's Perspective on the Theory of the Firm*, 89 Colum. L. Rev. 1757, 1757-65 (1989) (discussing various theories of the firm).

61. Eric W. Orts, Business Persons: A Legal Theory of the Firm (2013); Scott E. Masten, *A Legal Basis for the Firm*, 4 J.L. Econ. & Org. 181 (1988).

62. *See, e.g.*, Ellis & Hayden, *supra* note 56.

63. *See generally* Behavioral Law and Economics (Cass R. Sunstein ed., 2000); Hayden & Ellis, *supra* note 59.

2.   Preference Aggregation in Political Institutions

1. The study of how we make such moves comes under the heading of social choice theory, which has entered the legal literature largely under the guise of public choice theory. *See, e.g.*, Maxwell L. Stearns, Public Choice and Public Law: Readings and Commentary (1997); Daniel A. Farber & Philip P. Frickey, Law and Public Choice: A Critical Introduction (1991).

2. Some of the terminology here, as in subsequent chapters, follows WILLIAM H. RIKER, LIBERALISM AGAINST POPULISM: A CONFRONTATION BETWEEN THE THEORY OF DEMOCRACY AND THE THEORY OF SOCIAL CHOICE (1982). A social choice function is just any rule that translates a preference profile (a set of individual preference orders, one for each member of society) into a social preference order (a complete arrangement of alternatives in order of their attractiveness to society as a whole). *Id.* at 18, 296–97.

3. Parts of this taxonomy is borrowed from Pamela S. Karlan, *Maps and Misreadings: The Role of Geographic Compactness in Racial Vote Dilution Litigation*, 24 HARV. C.R.-C. L. L. REV. 173, 176 (1989); *see also* Grant M. Hayden, *Resolving the Dilemma of Minority Representation*, 92 CALIF. L. REV. 1589, 1594–602 (2004) (giving a brief account of the history of each aspect of the right). Other ways of parsing out the right to vote – *see, e.g.*, Richard H. Pildes, *What Kind of Right is "The Right to Vote"?*, 93 VA. L. REV. IN BRIEF 45 (2007); Pamela S. Karlan, *The Rights to Vote: Some Pessimism About Formalism*, 71 TEX. L. REV. 1705, 1709–20 (1993) – are not inconsistent with this conception.

4. For a relatively recent history of the right to vote, see generally ALEXANDER KEYSSAR, THE RIGHT TO VOTE: THE CONTESTED HISTORY OF DEMOCRACY IN THE UNITED STATES (rev. ed. 2000). For information about voting in the early years of the republic, see generally MARCHETTE CHUTE, THE FIRST LIBERTY: A HISTORY OF THE RIGHT TO VOTE IN AMERICA, 1619–1850 (1969); CHILTON WILLIAMSON, AMERICAN SUFFRAGE: FROM PROPERTY TO DEMOCRACY, 1760–1860 (1960). For information about voting rights in more recent years, with an emphasis on the quest for minority representation, see generally BERNARD GROFMAN ET AL., MINORITY REPRESENTATION AND THE QUEST FOR VOTING EQUALITY (1992); J. MORGAN KOUSSER, THE SHAPING OF SOUTHERN POLITICS: SUFFRAGE RESTRICTION AND THE ESTABLISHMENT OF THE ONE-PARTY SOUTH, 1880–1910 (1974); STEVEN F. LAWSON, BLACK BALLOTS: VOTING RIGHTS IN THE SOUTH, 1944–1969 (William E. Levchtenburg ed., 1976); QUIET REVOLUTION IN THE SOUTH: THE IMPACT OF THE VOTING RIGHTS ACT, 1965–1990 (Chandler Davidson & Bernard Grofman eds., 1994).

5. *See* KEYSSAR, *supra* note 4, at 306–15 (listing property and taxpaying requirements in the colonies and states between 1776 and 1855).

6. African Americans and other racial minorities initially secured voting rights through a series of constitutional amendments. *See* U.S. CONST. amend. XIII (abolishing slavery); U.S. CONST. amend. XIV (granting national citizenship, rights of due process, and equal protection); U.S. CONST. amend. XV (prohibiting voting rights discrimination on the basis of race). For a discussion of the passage of the Fifteenth Amendment, see generally WILLIAM GILLETTE, THE RIGHT TO VOTE: POLITICS AND THE PASSAGE OF THE FIFTEENTH AMENDMENT (1965); KEYSSAR, *supra* note 4, at 74–83. Those protections were lost as a result of Southern resistance and Northern indifference, see GROFMAN ET AL., *supra* note 4, at 5–10; Hayden, *supra* note 3, at 1595, but largely restored with the passage of the Voting Rights Act of 1965, 42 U.S.C. §§ 1971, 1973 to 1973bb-1 (2000). KEYSSAR, *supra* note 4, at 107, 111–16; KOUSSER, *supra* note 4, at 31–39; *see* GROFMAN ET AL., *supra* note 4, at 12–21; LAWSON, *supra* note 4, at 329–52. For more information on the passage of the Voting Rights Act, see LAWSON, *supra* note 4, at 288–328; KEYSSAR, *supra* note 4, at 211–15. Women secured access to the polls in 1920 through the Nineteenth Amendment, U.S. CONST. amend. XIX, and eighteen-to-twenty-one-year-olds through the Twenty-Sixth Amendment, U.S. CONST. amend. XXVI.

7. *See* Pamela S. Karlan, *Convictions and Doubts: Retribution, Representation, and the Debate over Felon Disenfranchisement*, 56 STAN. L. REV. 1147, 1147–48 (2004).

8. *See* Jamin B. Raskin, *Legal Aliens, Local Citizens: The Historical, Constitutional and Theoretical Meanings of Alien Suffrage*, 141 U. PA. L. REV. 1391, 1397–418, 1460–67 (1993).

9. *See* Glenn P. Smith, Note, *Interest Exceptions to One-Resident, One-Vote: Better Results from the Voting Rights Act?*, 74 TEX. L. REV. 1153, 1159 (1996).

10. *See* KEYSSAR, *supra* note 4, at 287–88.

11. *See* Anderson v. Celebrezze, 460 U.S. 780, 788 (1983) (noting that "[e]ach provision of these [state election codes], whether it governs the registration and qualifications of voters, the selection and eligibility of candidates, or the voting process itself, inevitably affects – at least to some degree – the individual's right to vote and his right to associate with others for political ends"); Christopher S. Elmendorf, *Structuring Judicial Review of Electoral Mechanics: Explanations and Opportunities*, 156 U. PA. L. REV. 313, 314–36 (2007) (explaining the sliding scale of scrutiny applied to election codes).

12. For background on this aspect of the right to vote, see generally STEPHEN ANSOLABEHERE & JAMES M. SNYDER, JR., THE END OF INEQUALITY: ONE PERSON, ONE VOTE AND THE TRANSFORMATION OF AMERICAN POLITICS (2008); ROBERT G. DIXON, JR., DEMOCRATIC REPRESENTATION: REAPPORTIONMENT IN LAW AND POLITICS (1968); REPRESENTATION AND MISREPRESENTATION: LEGISLATIVE REAPPORTIONMENT IN THEORY AND PRACTICE (Robert A. Goldwin ed., 1968); GORDON E. BAKER, THE REAPPORTIONMENT REVOLUTION: REPRESENTATION, POLITICAL POWER, AND THE SUPREME COURT (1966); ROBERT B. MCKAY, REAPPORTIONMENT: THE LAW AND POLITICS OF EQUAL REPRESENTATION (1965); Grant M. Hayden, *The False Promise of One Person, One Vote*, 102 MICH. L. REV. 213 (2003).

13. *IMF Members' Quotas and Voting Power, and IMF Board of Governors*, INTL MONETARY FUND, http://www.imf.org/external/np/sec/memdir/members.htm (last visited Aug. 29, 2019).

14. *See* Hayden, *supra* note 12, at 219.

15. *See id.*

16. *See generally* Reynolds v. Sims, 377 U.S. 533 (1964); Wesberry v. Sanders, 376 U.S. 1 (1964); Gray v. Sanders, 372 U.S. 368 (1963); Baker v. Carr, 369 U.S. 186 (1962).

17. *See* Hayden, *supra* note 3, at 1600–02 (detailing minority vote dilution); Samuel Issacharoff, *Gerrymandering and Political Cartels*, 116 HARV. L. REV. 593 (2002) (discussing political gerrymandering).

18. *See* GROFMAN ET AL., *supra* note 4, at 23–24.

19. *See* Frank R. Parker, *Racial Gerrymandering and Legislative Reapportionment, in* MINORITY VOTE DILUTION 85, 86–99 (Chandler Davidson ed., 1984) (discussing techniques used in racial gerrymandering). These strategies of "cracking" and "packing" voters are discussed in several Supreme Court opinions as well. *See, e.g.*, Thornburg, Att'y Gen. of N.C. v. Gingles, 478 U.S. 30, 46 n.11 (1986).

20. *Compare* Miller v. Johnson, 515 U.S. 900, 916 (1995) (applying strict scrutiny when race is the predominant factor in districting), *with* Rucho v. Common Cause, 139 S. Ct. 2484 (2019) (finding partisan gerrymandering to be a nonjusticiable political question).

21. For a good general discussion of the jurisprudence of primary ballot access laws, see Nathaniel Persily, *Candidates v. Parties: The Constitutional Constraints on Primary Ballot Access Laws*, 88 GEO. L.J. 2181 (2001). For a more recent rundown of state ballot access laws, see Richard Winger's website BALLOT ACCESS NEWS, http://ballot-access.org/ (last visited Aug. 30, 2019).

22. *See* KEYSSAR, *supra* note 4, at 86.

23. *See generally* DARLENE CLARK HINE, BLACK VICTORY: THE RISE AND FALL OF THE WHITE PRIMARY IN TEXAS (2003).

24. This is also true for the less obvious reason that a group with agenda control can take advantage of potential voting cycles and manipulate an agenda in a way that favors its desired outcome. *See* Grant M. Hayden, *Some Implications of Arrow's Theorem for Voting Rights*, 47 STAN. L. REV. 295, 312–13 (1995).

25. *E.g.* Oliver Hall, *Death by a Thousand Signatures: The Rise of Restrictive Ballot Access Laws and the Decline of Electoral Competition in the United States*, 29 SEATTLE U. L. REV. 407, 414–15 (2005).

26. *See* Hayden, *supra* note 12, at 251–61 (discussing the relationship between preference strength and various manifestations of the right to vote); Melvyn R. Durchslag, Salyer, Ball, *and* Holt: *Reappraising the Right to Vote in Terms of Political "Interest" and Vote Dilution*, 33 CASE W. RES. L. REV. 1, 38–39 (1982) (discussing the fact that "'interest,' implicitly or explicitly, must be the touchstone of the [Supreme] Court's analysis" of several types of voting rights cases). We do not claim that this reason motivates all decisions to enfranchise or disenfranchise people. There are obviously people with strong interests in the outcomes of elections (e.g., people with mental disabilities, children) who are nonetheless prohibited from voting for other reasons, mostly having to do with their competency.

27. Hayden, *supra* note 12, at 248–49.

28. This is generally discussed as the difficulty in making interpersonal comparisons of utility. For a summary of the problem, see Hayden, *supra* note 12, at 236–47. *See also* INTERPERSONAL COMPARISONS OF WELL-BEING (Jon Elster & John E. Roemer eds., 1991); JAMES GRIFFIN, WELL-BEING: ITS MEANING, MEASUREMENT, AND MORAL IMPORTANCE 113–20 (1986); Peter Hammond, *Interpersonal Comparisons of Utility: Why and How They Are and Should Be Made, in* INTERPERSONAL COMPARISONS OF WELL-BEING 200, 238–254 (Jon Elster & John E. Roemer eds., 1991).

29. *See* Hayden, *supra* note 12, at 245.

30. You could not rely on some other marker for strength of voter interest, such as residency, for that would beg the question.

31. *See* Hayden, *supra* note 12, at 240.

32. Except to the extent that voting is not compulsory in the United States. Qualified voters could always just signal their lack of interest by staying home on election day. *See* Hayden, *supra* note 12, at 258–59.

33. KEYSSAR, *supra* note 4, at 5.

34. *See id.* at 50, 131.

35. *See* Hayden, *supra* note 12, at 256–57; Smith, *supra* note 9, at 1159.

36. *See* Holt Civic Club v. City of Tuscaloosa, 439 U.S. 60, 69 (1978) (explaining that "the imaginary line defining a city's corporate limits cannot corral the influence of municipal actions. A city's decisions inescapably affect individuals living immediately outside its borders."); Richard Briffault, *The Local Government Boundary Problem in Metropolitan*

Areas, 48 STAN L. REV. 1115, 1132 (1996) ("Boundaries exclude people who may be interested in or affected by the decisions made within the boundaries.").

37. *See* Hayden, *supra* note 12, at 257. For this reason and others, some scholars have suggested decoupling voting from residency. *See* Richard Thompson Ford, *Beyond Borders: A Partial Response to Richard Briffault*, 48 STAN. L. REV. 1173, 1187–89 (1996); Richard Thompson Ford, *The Boundaries of Race: Political Geography in Legal Analysis*, 107 HARV. L. REV. 1841, 1909 (1994); Jerry Frug, *Decentering Decentralization*, 60 U. CHI. L. REV. 253, 324–25 (1993). For a critique, see Briffault, *supra* note 36, at 1158–62.

38. 395 U.S. 621, 622 (1969).

39. *Id.*

40. *Id.* at 632 n.15.

41. *Id.* at 632.

42. 439 U.S. 60 (1978).

43. *Id.* at 69.

44. One would expect these two aspects of voting rights to be closely related since numerically diluting a vote may have the same effect as prohibiting voting. *See* Hayden, *supra* note 12, at 255.

45. *See id.* at 248.

46. The IMF, for example, largely determines a member's voting power by the resources that member contributes to the fund. *See IMF Members' Quotas and Voting Power, and IMF Board of Governors, supra* note 13.

47. *See* Hayden, *supra* note 12, at 251.

48. *See id.* at 251–52.

49. *See id.* at 249–50.

50. *See id.* at 250; Baker v. Carr, 369 U.S. 186, 300 (1962) (Frankfurter, J., dissenting) (arguing that an equiproportional standard is just one among many "competing bases of representation").

51. *See* Morris v. Bd. of Estimate, 489 U.S. 688, 694–96 (1989); Hadley v. Junior Coll. Dist., 397 U.S. 50, 54 (1970); Avery v. Midland Cty., 390 U.S. 474, 484–85 (1968); Hayden, *supra* note 12, at 252–53.

52. 410 U.S. 719 (1973).

53. *See id.* at 723.

54. *See id.*

55. *See id.* at 724–25.

56. *See id.* at 730.

57. *See id.* at 729 & 734; *see also* Ball v. James, 451 U.S. 355 (1981).

58. *See* Sanford Levinson, *Gerrymandering and the Brooding Omnipresence of Proportional Representation: Why Won't It Go Away?*, 33 UCLA L. REV. 257 (1985).

59. *See* 42 U.S.C. § 1973 (2006) ("[N]othing in this section establishes a right to have members of a protected class elected in numbers equal to their proportion in the population.").

60. In voting rights, the manageability of a particular voting rights requirement might mean, for example, that courts will be able to administer the standard in a neutral manner, without injecting its own biases into the case.

61. Avery v. Midland Cty., 390 U.S. 474, 510 (1968) (Stewart, J., dissenting) (maintaining that apportionment is "far too subtle and complicated

a business to be resolved as a matter of constitutional law in terms of sixth-grade arithmetic").

62. JOHN HART ELY, DEMOCRACY AND DISTRUST 121 (1980).

3.   Preference Aggregation in Corporations

1. DEL. CODE ANN. tit. 8, § 101(a) (2019).
2. *Id.* § 102.
3. Such structures may include a limitation on the liability of directors for breaches of the duty of care (*id.* § 102(b)(7)) or provide for a staggered board of directors (*id.* § 141(d)).
4. *Id.* § 141.
5. *Id.* § 211.
6. *Id.* § 141.
7. JAMES D. COX & THOMAS LEE HAZEN, CORPORATIONS 2 (2d ed. 2003) (including the joint stock company and the partnership association in some states). Within the corporation category, closely held corporations are sometimes separated from publicly held corporations, although they are formed through the same state incorporation statutes.
8. UNIF. P'SHIP ACT § 18(e), 6 U.L.A. 526 (1995); REV. UNIF. P'SHIP ACT § 401(f) (amended 1997). The control rights in a partnership extend even to ordinary, everyday matters of the business. *See* UNIF. P'SHIP ACT § 18(h), 6 U.L.A. 526 (1995); REV. UNIF. P'SHIP ACT § 401(j) (amended 1997).
9. *See, e.g.,* DEL. CODE ANN. tit. 12, § 3801 (2018) (defining "statutory trust" as "an unincorporated association which [i]s created by a governing instrument under which . . . business or professional activities for profit are carried on or will be carried on, by a trustee or trustees or as otherwise provided in the governing instrument for the benefit of such person or persons as are or may become beneficial owners or as otherwise provided in the governing instrument . . . .").
10. *See* UNIF. LTD. P'SHIP ACT § 7 (1916), 6A U.L.A. 336 (1995); REV. UNIF. LTD. P'SHIP ACT § 303 (amended 1985), 6A U.L.A. 144–45 (1995). However, under the original Uniform Limited Partnership Act, limited partners could be subject to liability as managing partners if they participated in the governance. UNIF. LTD. P'SHIP ACT § 7 (1916), 6A U.L.A. 336 (1995) ("A limited partner shall not become liable as a general partner unless . . . he takes part in the control of the business.").
11. Larry E. Ribstein, *The Evolving Partnership,* 26 J. CORP. L. 819, 843 (2001).
12. Henry Hansmann & Reinier Kraakman, *The End of History for Corporate Law,* 89 GEO. L.J. 439, 439–40 (2001). *Cf.* ROBERT CHARLES CLARK, CORPORATE LAW 2 (1986) (listing four characteristics of the corporation: (1) limited liability, (2) free transferability of investor interests, (3) legal personality, and (4) centralized management).
13. Closely held corporations have the same basic corporate structure as publicly held corporations: the shareholders elect the board of directors, and the board appoints the officers who run the corporation. In closely held companies, however, these roles often overlap, leading to a governance structure more akin to a partnership than a large corporation. *See* Donahue v. Rodd Electrotype Co. of New England, Inc., 328 N.E.2d 505, 511 (Mass. 1975) (defining closely held corporations as having

"(1) a small number of stockholders; (2) no ready market for the corporate stock; and (3) substantial majority stockholder participation in the management, direction and operations of the corporation").

14. FRANK H. EASTERBROOK & DANIEL R. FISCHEL, THE ECONOMIC STRUCTURE OF CORPORATE LAW 35–39 (1991).

15. *Id.* at 36–37.

16. ADOLF A. BERLE, JR. & GARDINER C. MEANS, THE MODERN CORPORATION AND PRIVATE PROPERTY 6 (1932).

17. STEPHEN M. BAINBRIDGE, CORPORATE LAW 233 (2d ed. 2009). In Delaware, only the board can call a special meeting, while other states allow a specified percentage of shareholders to call a meeting without board consent. *Id.*

18. *Id.* at 238.

19. Delaware statutory law enables corporations to change their bylaws to require that a candidate receive a majority of votes cast. DEL. CODE ANN. tit. 8, § 141(b) (2019) (allowing for required director resignation in the face of a successful "withhold" campaign), *id.* § 216 (protecting bylaws requiring a majority vote to be elected against board interference).

20. Colleen A. Dunlavy, *Social Conceptions of the Corporation: Insights from the History of Shareholder Voting Rights*, 63 WASH. & LEE L. REV. 1347, 1362 (2006).

21. For example, assume that out of ninety shares, A has sixty and B has thirty. There are nine seats on the board. Under a traditional majority-rule voting system, A would elect all nine directors. However, under a proportional system, A would elect six directors and B would elect three.

22. Generally, the board of directors must first propose an amendment to the charter, and then the shareholders must approve the amendment. *See, e.g.*, MODEL BUS. CORP. ACT § 10.03 (Am. Bar Ass'n 2016). In Delaware, the amendment must be approved by a majority of all shares outstanding, rather than just a majority of shares voting. DEL. CODE ANN. tit. 8, § 242(b)(1) (2019).

23. Delaware has an opt-in system: the corporation's charter must give directors the power to amend the bylaws. DEL. CODE ANN. tit. 8, § 109(a) (2019). However, the Model Business Corporation Act allows directors to amend the bylaws, unless specifically prohibited by the charter. MODEL BUS. CORP. ACT § 10.20(b) (Am. Bar Ass'n 2016).

24. 17 C.F.R. § 240.14a-8 (2017).

25. WILLIAM A. KLEIN, ET AL., BUSINESS ORGANIZATION AND FINANCE 222–25 (11th ed. 2010) (describing different types of mergers and acquisitions).

26. A majority will have de jure control, but a minority interest may also have de facto control over the corporation. *See, e.g.*, Kahn v. Lynch Commc'n Sys., Inc., 638 A.2d 1110 (Del. 1994) (finding ownership of 44 percent of shares to be a controlling interest).

27. DEL. CODE ANN. tit. 8, § 228 (2019) (allowing a majority of shareholders to execute any action that may be taken at a shareholders' meeting (including removal of directors) through the written concurrence of those shareholders).

28. *See* Paul H. Edelman & Randall S. Thomas, *Corporate Voting and the Takeover Debate*, 58 VAND. L. REV. 453, 454 (2005) (discussing the importance of shareholder votes in the takeover setting).

29. Perhaps surprisingly, there can be a real issue about the particular owner of a particular share. *See* George S. Geis, *Traceable Shares and Corporate Law*, 113 NW. U. L. REV. 227 (2018).

30. *See* DEL. CODE ANN. tit. 8, § 153(a) (2019). For a discussion of watered stock, see BAINBRIDGE, *supra* note 17, at 420–22.
31. Dunlavy, *supra* note 20, at 1356 (discussing this perception).
32. *Id.* at 1349.
33. Marco Becht & J. Bradford DeLong, *Why Has There Been So Little Block Holding in America?*, *in* A HISTORY OF CORPORATE GOVERNANCE AROUND THE WORLD: FAMILY BUSINESS GROUPS TO PROFESSIONAL MANAGERS 613, 653–57 (Randall K. Morck ed., 2005) (noting that the number of dual or multiclass share corporations listed on the New York Stock Exchange more than doubled from 1994 to 2001); Dorothy S. Lund, *Nonvoting Shares and Efficient Corporate Governance*, 71 STAN. L. REV. 687, 706–07 (2019) (noting that tech companies such as Google, Zillow, and Snap have issued nonvoting shares).
34. Dunlavy, *supra* note 20, at 1354.
35. *Id.* at 1354–55.
36. *Id.* at 1356.
37. *Id.* at 1357.
38. Alexander Hamilton, 1ST CONG., REPORT ON A NATIONAL BANK, H.R. (1790), *reprinted in* 2 THE DEBATES AND PROCEEDINGS OF THE CONGRESS OF THE UNITED STATES, app. 2032, 2049 (Washington, Gales & Seaton 1834).
39. Dunlavy, *supra* note 20, at 1358–59.
40. Stephen M. Bainbridge, *The Short Life and Resurrection of SEC Rule 19c-4*, 69 WASH. U. L.Q. 565, 569 (1991).
41. 17 C.F.R. § 240.19c-4 (1988), *invalidated by* Bus. Roundtable v. SEC, 905 F.2d 406 (D.C. Cir. 1990).
42. At the time, some companies had issued a new class of stock, as a dividend to current shareholders, that provided an abnormally large number of votes per share. However, these new shares were not transferable and could be sold only if they were converted to regular one-vote shares of common stock. The effect of such an issuance was to provide "lock in" power for long-term shareholders and/or managers. *See* Bainbridge, *supra* note 40, at 566.
43. *Bus. Roundtable*, 905 F.2d at 406.
44. *See, e.g.*, NYSE, Listed Company Manual § 313(B) (2005).
45. *See, e.g.*, Kathleen Pender, *Google's Weak Governance Rating*, S.F. CHRON., Aug. 24, 2004, at C1 (noting that "Google's low mark was largely a result of its dual-share -class structure, which gives founders and other insiders 10 times as many votes per share as outside stockholders.").
46. *See, e.g.*, Gretchen Morgenson, *One Share, One Vote: One Big Test*, N.Y. TIMES, Apr. 2, 2006, at 31.
47. Lund, *supra* note 33, at 706–07.
48. EASTERBROOK & FISCHEL, *supra* note 14, at 73. *See also* Bernard Black & Reinier Kraakman, *A Self-Enforcing Model of Corporate Law*, 109 HARV. L. REV. 1911, 1945–46 (1996) ("The case for the one share, one vote rule turns primarily on its ability to match economic incentives with voting power and to preserve the market for corporate control as a check on bad management.").
49. *See* Henry T.C. Hu & Bernard Black, *The New Vote Buying: Empty Voting and Hidden (Morphable) Ownership*, 79 S. CAL. L. REV. 811, 851 (2006) (discussing concerns that controlling shareholders without a commensurate economic stake in

the corporation are more likely to "tunnel" away a disproportionate share of firm value).

50. *See, e.g.,* Hall v. Isaacs, 146 A.2d 602 (Del. Ch. 1958).

51. *See* Schreiber v. Carney, 447 A.2d 17, 26 (Del. Ch. 1982) (noting that individual instances of vote buying are "easily susceptible of abuse" and thus "subject to a test for intrinsic fairness").

52. EASTERBROOK & FISCHEL, *supra* note 14, at 74 ("Separation of shares from votes introduces a disproportion between expenditure and reward.").

53. This is based on the notion that any individual vote has an extremely low probability of affecting the outcome. *See* Yair J. Listokin, *Management Always Wins the Close Ones*, 10 AM. L. & ECON. REV. 159, 171 (2008) (noting that "management sponsored proposals typically pass easily," with a mean approval rate of 85 percent).

54. Larry E. Ribstein & Bruce Kobayashi, *Outside Trading as an Incentive Device*, 40 U. C. DAVIS L. REV. 21, 39 (2006) ("Vote buying and selling can, however, be inefficient in some situations because it enables the buyer and the seller to realize gains while losses are incurred by other shareholders.").

55. *See, e.g.,* DEL. CODE ANN. tit. 8, § 215 (2010); MODEL BUS. CORP. ACT § 7.22 (2007).

56. RANDALL S. THOMAS & CATHERINE T. DIXON, ARANOW & EINHORN ON PROXY CONTESTS FOR CORPORATE CONTROL § 21.01 (3d ed. 1990) (reviewing proxy contests in the late 1980s and finding that insurgents spent an average of $1.8 million and incumbents an average of $4.4 million); Lucian A. Bebchuk, *The Myth of the Shareholder Franchise*, 93 VA. L. REV. 675, 688–90 (2007) (explaining how proxy costs entail not only distribution and disclosure costs but also the services of proxy advisors and other outreach efforts to persuade voters).

57. Facilitating Shareholder Director Nominations, Securities Act Release No. 9136, Exchange Act Release No. 62,764, Investment Company Act Release No. 29,384, 75 Fed. Reg. 56,668 (Sept. 16, 2010). The regulation was formerly codified as Rule 14a-11. *See* 17 C.F.R. § 240.14a-11 (2010), *vacated by* Bus. Roundtable v. SEC, 647 F.3d 1144, 1146 (D.C. Cir. 2011). The Commission recognized the vacation of the rule in Facilitating Shareholder Director Nominations, 76 Fed. Reg. 58100 (Sept. 20, 2011).

58. For a list of the excluded subject areas for proxy proposals, see Rule 14a-8(i), 17 C.F. R. § 240.14a-18(j) (2011).

59. SEC Securities Exchange Act of 1934 Release No. 3347 (Dec. 18, 1942) [hereinafter 1942 SEC Release].

60. *See Hearings on H.R. 1493, H.R. 1821, and H.R. 2019 Before the House Comm. on Interstate and Foreign Commerce*, 78th Cong., 1st Sess. 17–19 (1943) (testimony of Chairman Ganson Purcell), *cited in* DIV. OF CORP. FIN., U.S. SEC. & EXCH. COMM'N, STAFF REPORT: REVIEW OF THE PROXY PROCESS REGARDING THE NOMINATION AND ELECTION OF DIRECTORS 3 (2003), http://www.sec.gov/news/studies/proxyreport.pdf [hereinafter 2003 SEC PROXY REPORT].

61. *Id.*

62. *See* 1942 SEC Release, *supra* note 59.

63. 2003 SEC PROXY REPORT, *supra* note 60, at 3. However, there were no formal requirements that the committees actually place dissident candidates on the ballot.

64. Rule 14a-4, 17 C.F.R. § 240.14a-4 (2011).

65. 2003 SEC Proxy Report, *supra* note 60, at 4. A "short slate" is a group of dissident directors that falls short of the number of open seats. *Id.* The change in Rule 14a-4 allowed shareholders to single out a certain number of board nominees for inclusion on the shareholders' proxy ballots, even if the nominees did not want to be included. As an example, directors B1, B2, B3, B4, and B5 are running for reelection. If shareholders want to nominate S1 and S2 to run against B1 and B2, the shareholders can submit a proxy with S1, S2, B3, B4, and B5, in order to isolate B1 and B2, even if B3, B4, and B5 do not want to be on the shareholders' proxies.

66. *Id.*

67. Security Holder Director Nominations, Exchange Act Release No. 48,626, Investment Company Act Release No. 26,206, 68 Fed. Reg. 60,784, 60,789–90 (Oct. 23, 2003). The Rule 14a-8 proposal would need to have been submitted by a shareholder with at least 1 percent beneficial ownership for at least one year. *Id.* at 60,790.

68. *Id.* at 60,794–98. The formula for the number of nominees was as follows:

> As proposed, a company would be required to include one security holder nominee if the total number of members of the board of directors is eight or fewer, two security holder nominees if the number of members of the board of directors is greater than eight and less than 20 and three security holder nominees if the number of members of the board of directors is 20 or more. The proposal would have a separate standard for companies with classified or "staggered" boards of directors. Where a company has a director (or directors) currently serving on its board of directors who was elected as a security holder nominee, and the term of that director extends past the date of the meeting of security holders for which the company is soliciting proxies, the company would not be required to include on its proxy card more security holder nominees than could result in the total number of directors serving on the board that were elected as security holder nominees being greater than one if the total number of members of the board of directors is eight or fewer, two if the number of members of the board of directors is greater than eight and less than 20 and three if the number of members of the board of directors is 20 or more.

> *Id.* at 60,797–98.

69. Marcel Kahan & Edward B. Rock, *The Insignificance of Proxy Access*, 97 Va. L. Rev. 1347, 1354 (2011).

70. Am. Fed'n of State, Cty. & Mun. Emps. v. Am. Int'l Grp., Inc., 462 F.3d 121 (2d Cir. 2006).

71. *See id.* at 123 (discussing the previous version of Rule 14a-8(i)(8), which allowed companies to exclude a shareholder proposal under 14a-8 that "relates to an election").

72. *Id.* at 130.

73. Shareholder Proposals, Exchange Act Release No. 56,160, Investment Company Act Release No. 27,913, 72 Fed. Reg. 43,466 (Aug. 3, 2007).

74. *Id.* at 43,472. In addition, to be eligible, shareholders could not have acquired or held their securities for the purpose of or with the effect of changing or influencing the control of the company and also had to meet the requirements of Schedule 13G.

Any shareholder wishing to circumvent the rule would have to follow the SEC's other disclosure requirements for hostile takeovers and similar actions. *Id.*

75. *Id.*

76. *Id.* The actual form and substance of the bylaw amendments proposed by the shareholders would still be governed by the corporation or state law, and the SEC would intervene only with respect to the procedures for proposing such a bylaw and the disclosure requirements.

77. Shareholder Proposals Relating to the Election of Directors, Exchange Act Release No. 56,161, Investment Company Act Release No. 27,914, 72 Fed. Reg. 43,488, 43,493 (Aug. 3, 2007).

78. Kahan & Rock, *supra* note 69, at 1355.

79. Facilitating Shareholder Director Nominations, Securities Act Release No. 9,046, Exchange Act Release No. 60,089, Investment Company Act Release No. 28,765, 74 Fed. Reg. 29,024 (June 18, 2009).

80. *Id.* at 29,035.

81. *Id.* at 29,032, 29,035.

82. Dodd-Frank Wall Street Reform and Consumer Protection Act of 2010, Pub. L. No. 111–203, § 971(b), 124 Stat. 1376, 1915 (2010) (codified as amended in scattered sections of 12 U.S.C.) [hereinafter Dodd-Frank Act] ("The Commission may issue rules permitting the use by a shareholder of proxy solicitation materials supplied by an issuer of securities for the purpose of nominating individuals to membership on the board of directors of the issuer, under such terms and conditions as the Commission determines are in the interests of shareholders and for the protection of investors.").

83. Facilitating Shareholder Director Nominations, Securities Act Release No. 9,136, Exchange Act Release No. 62,764, Investment Company Act Release No. 29,384, 75 Fed. Reg. 56,668 (Sept. 16, 2010).

84. *Id.*

85. 17 C.F.R. § 240.14a-8(i)(8) (2012). The revised Rule 14a-8 excludes only proposals that "(i) Would disqualify a nominee who is standing for election; (ii) Would remove a director from office before his or her term expired; (iii) Questions the competence, business judgment, or character of one or more nominees or directors; (iv) Seeks to include a specific individual in the company's proxy materials for election to the board of directors; or (v) Otherwise could affect the outcome of the upcoming election of directors." *Id.*

86. 5 U.S.C. § 551 *et seq.* (2006).

87. Bus. Roundtable v. SEC, 647 F.3d 1144, 1146 (D.C. Cir. 2011). *See also id.* at 1148 ("The petitioners argue the Commission acted arbitrarily and capriciously here because it neglected its statutory responsibility to determine the likely economic consequences of Rule 14a-11 and to connect those consequences to efficiency, competition, and capital formation. . . . We agree with the petitioners and hold the Commission acted arbitrarily and capriciously for having failed once again . . . adequately to assess the economic effects of a new rule.").

88. *Id.* at 1149.

89. *Id.* at 1152.

90. *Id.* at 1153.

91. Stephen M. Bainbridge, *Proxy Access Invalidated on APA Grounds*, PROFESSORBAINBRIDGE.COM (July 22, 2011), http://www. professorbainbridge.com/professor bainbridgecom/2011/07/proxy-access-invalidated-on-apa-grounds.html ("Candidly, while I'm pleased, I'm also

surprised. I had thought – and said publicly – that this suit was a long shot.").

92. Recent Case, *Administrative Law – Corporate Governance Regulation – D.C. Circuit Finds SEC Proxy Access Rule Arbitrary and Capricious for Inadequate Economic Analysis:* Business Roundtable v. SEC, *647 F.3d 1144 (D.C. Cir. 2011)*, 125 HARV. L. REV. 1088 (2012) (saying that the opinion "made missteps similar to those for which [it] scolded the SEC," and calling it "troubling"); Steven M. Davidoff, *Proxy Access in Limbo After Court Rules Against It,* N.Y. TIMES DEALBOOK (July 27, 2011), https:// dealbook.nytimes.com/2011/07/27/proxy-access-in-limbo-after-court-rules-against-it/ (noting that "the opinion appears to create an almost insurmountable barrier for the S.E.C. by requiring that it provide empirical support amounting to proof that its rules would be effective"); Brett McDonnell, *Dodd-Frank @ 1: An Overall Assessment,* THE CONGLOMERATE BLOG (July 22, 2011), http://www.theconglomerate.org/2011/07/ dodd-frank-1-an-overall-assessment.html ("This opinion is little more than the judges ignoring the proper judicial rule of deference to an agency involved in notice-and-comment rulemaking and asserting their own naked political preferences. Talk about judicial activism."); Gordon Smith, *Comment to* Business Roundtable v. SEC, THE CONGLOMERATE BLOG (July 22, 2011), http://www .theconglomerate.org/2011/07/ business-roundtable-v-sec.html#comment-261374058 ("I had told my students that I thought the lawsuit was not well-founded, so I was surprised by the opinion. I understand why people would oppose proxy access, but 'arbitrary and capricious'? The process hardly seems to qualify for that characterization. . . . I am not enamored with the result here.").

93. The Delaware Chancery has characterized the right to vote more in terms of legitimacy than economic efficiency: "The shareholder franchise is the ideological underpinning upon which the legitimacy of directorial power rests. . . . It has, for a long time, been conventional to dismiss the stockholder vote as a vestige or ritual of little practical importance. . . . [W]hether the vote is seen functionally as an unimportant formalism, or as an important tool of discipline, it is clear that it is critical to the theory that legitimated the exercise of power by some (directors and officers) over vast aggregations of property that they do not own." Blasius Indus., Inc. v. Atlas Corp., 564 A.2d 651, 659 (Del. Ch. 1988).

94. *Bus. Roundtable*, 647 F.3d at 1150.

95. EASTERBROOK & FISCHEL, *supra* note 14, at 66–72 (defending the shareholder franchise); Hansmann & Kraakman, *supra* note 12, at 441 (finding that "as a consequence of both logic and experience, there is convergence on a consensus that the best means to this end (that is, the pursuit of aggregate social welfare) is to make corporate managers strongly accountable to shareholder interests and, at least in direct terms, only to those interests").

96. For a further critique of the *Business Roundtable* decision along these lines, see Grant M. Hayden & Matthew T. Bodie, *The Bizarre Law & Economics of* Business Roundtable v. SEC, 38 J. CORP. L. 101, 128 (2012) ("Focusing on the costs of the election for the incumbents is like focusing on the costs of political campaigns to incumbents in assessing whether we want to facilitate challenges to the incumbents.").

97. Daniel J.H. Greenwood, *Fictional Shareholders: For Whom Are Corporate Managers Trustees, Revisited*, 69 S. CAL. L. REV. 1021, 1052 (1996) ("For fictional shareholders, whatever else the people behind them may want, all want to maximize the value of their shares.").

98. Oliver Hart & Luigi Zingales, *Companies Should Maximize Shareholder Welfare Not Market Value*, 2 J.L. Fin. & Acct. 247 (2017).

99. *Id.*

100. Greenwood, *supra* note 97, at 1052–53 ("If the corporation were run by and for real people, it would be a hotbed of political controversy. . . . If the real people disagree with the fictional representation, the real people may simply be disregarded as not real shareholders.").

101. Bus. Roundtable v. SEC, 647 F.3d 1144, 1149 (D.C. Cir. 2011).

102. *Id.* at 1149–52.

103. Stephen M. Bainbridge, *Director Primacy: The Means and Ends of Corporate Governance*, 97 Nw. U. L. Rev. 547, 560 (2003) [hereinafter *Director Primacy*] Bainbridge supports the goal of shareholder wealth maximization but argues against greater shareholder input. *See id.*; Stephen M. Bainbridge, *Director Primacy and Shareholder Disempowerment*, 119 Harv. L. Rev. 1735 (2006) [hereinafter *Director Primacy II*]. He bases his argument primarily on the need for centralized and largely unreviewable discretion in order to maximize efficient business operations. *Id.* at 1749 ("Active investor involvement in corporate decisionmaking seems likely to disrupt the very mechanism that makes the widely held public corporation practicable: namely, the centralization of essentially nonreviewable decisionmaking authority in the board of directors. The chief economic virtue of the public corporation is . . . that it provides a hierarchical decisionmaking structure well-suited to the problem of operating a large business enterprise with numerous employees, managers, shareholders, creditors, and other constituencies."). *See also* Margaret M. Blair & Lynn A. Stout, *A Team Production Theory of Corporate Law*, 85 Va. L. Rev. 247, 280 (1999) (discussing their "mediating hierarchs" approach to board leadership).

104. Easterbrook & Fischel, *supra* note 14, at 63 (arguing that "the *structure* of voting – who votes, using what institutions – is contractual, and efficient, too").

105. *See, e.g.*, Bebchuk, *supra* note 56.

106. 17 C.F.R. § 240.14a-8 (2017).

107. Stephen Bainbridge, The New Corporate Governance in Theory and Practice 266–69 (2008).

108. Directors' Remuneration Report Regulations 2002, SI 2002/1986 (UK).

109. Prior to 2010, there was ambiguity over the legality of a say-on-pay referendum, as it was seen as interfering with the board's prerogatives under state corporate law to manage the corporation. However, the precatory nature of the election is generally thought to eliminate this problem. *See* David Webber, The Rise of the Working-Class Shareholder: Labor's Last Best Weapon 138 (2018).

110. Dodd-Frank Act, Pub. L. No. 111-203, § 951, 124 Stat. 1376, 1899–900 (2010).

111. Jill E. Fisch, *Leave It to Delaware: Why Congress Should Stay Out of Corporate Governance*, 37 Del. J. Corp. L. 731, 758 (2013) ("Federalism thus directly interferes with Delaware's private ordering approach.").

112. Jeffrey N. Gordon, *"Say on Pay": Cautionary Notes on the U.K. Experience and the Case for Shareholder Opt-in*, 46 HARV. J. ON LEGIS. 323, 327 (2009) (arguing that a "one size fits all" approach may not be best).

113. Fisch, *supra* note 111, at 758.

114. Stephen M. Bainbridge, *Dodd-Frank: Quack Federal Corporate Governance Round II*, 95 MINN. L. REV. 1779, 1815 (2011) (arguing that Dodd-Frank's say-on-pay provisions are "inconsistent with the board-centric model that has been the foundation of the U.S. corporate governance system's success").

115. WEBBER, *supra* note 109, at 138.

116. *Id.* at 141.

117. *Id.* at 140–41.

118. *Id.*

119. *See, e.g.*, LUCIAN BEBCHUK & JESSE FRIED, PAY WITHOUT PERFORMANCE: THE UNFULFILLED PROMISE OF EXECUTIVE COMPENSATION (2004); MICHAEL B. DORFF, INDISPENSABLE AND OTHER MYTHS: WHY THE CEO PAY EXPERIMENT FAILED AND HOW TO FIX IT (2014).

120. *See, e.g.*, Bebchuk, *supra* note 56.

121. *Id.*; *The Bebchuk Bylaw: Devilish . . . but Brilliant*, 6 M&A J., no. 10, 2006, at 1.

122. *See, e.g.*, Bainbridge, *Director Primacy*, *supra* note 103; Bainbridge, *Director Primacy II*, *supra* note 103.

123. Kevin Drawbaugh, *CEOs' Group Hits US Bill on Shareholder Pay Votes*, REUTERS (Mar. 8, 2007), https://www.reuters.com/article/congress-ceo-pay/update-1-ceos-group-hits-us-bill-on-shareholder-pay-votes-idUSN0833667220070308 (quoting John Castellani, president of the Business Roundtable). This sentiment has been repeated by late corporate law professor Larry Ribstein. *See* Larry Ribstein, *Shareholder Democracy vs. Democracy*, FORBES (Oct. 25, 2010), http://www.forbes.com/sites/larryribstein/2010/10/25/shareholder-democracy-vs-democracy/ ("Corporations are not democracies.").

124. *See, e.g.*, Bainbridge, *Director Primacy*, *supra* note 103; Bainbridge, *Director Primacy II*, *supra* note 103.

125. eBay Domestic Holdings, Inc. v. Newmark, 16 A.3d 1 (Del. Ch. Ct. 2010).

126. *Id.* at 34.

127. Christopher M. Bruner, *The Enduring Ambivalence of Corporate Law*, 59 ALA. L. REV. 1385, 1386 (2008) (arguing that "corporate law is, and will remain, deeply ambivalent – both doctrinally and morally – with respect to each of three fundamental and related issues: the locus of ultimate corporate governance authority, the intended beneficiaries of corporate production, and the relationship between corporate law and the achievement of the social good").

128. Revlon, Inc. v. MacAndrews & Forbes Holdings, Inc., 506 A.2d 173, 182 (Del. 1986); Paramount Commc'ns Inc. v. Time Inc., 571 A.2d 1140, 1151 (Del. 1990).

129. Honorable Leo E. Strine, Jr., *The Dangers of Denial: The Need for a Clear-Eyed Understanding of the Power and Accountability Structure Established by the Delaware General Corporation Law*, 50 WAKE FOREST L. REV. 761, 763–66 (2015). *See also* Leo E. Strine, Jr., *Our Continuing Struggle with the Idea That For-Profit Corporations Seek Profit*, 47 WAKE FOREST L. REV. 135, 135–36 (2012) ("[T]he continued failure of our societies to be clear-eyed about the role of the for-profit corporation endangers the public interest.").

4. The Corporation as Contract

1. *See* D. Gordon Smith, *The Shareholder Primacy Norm*, 23 J. CORP. L. 277, 277 (1998) ("The structure of corporate law ensures that corporations generally operate in the interests of shareholders.").

2. The classic example of this perspective is Milton Friedman, *The Social Responsibility of Business Is to Increase Its Profits*, N.Y. TIMES MAG., Sept. 13, 1970, at 32–33, 122–26.

3. *See, e.g.*, Lynn A. Stout, *Bad and Not-So-Bad Arguments for Shareholder Primacy*, 75 S. CAL. L. REV. 1189, 1190–92 (2002) ("The claim that shareholders own the public corporation simply is empirically incorrect.").

4. *See* Joel Seligman, *Equal Protection in Shareholder Voting Rights: The One Common Share, One Vote Controversy*, 54 GEO. WASH. L. REV. 687, 694 (1986) (discussing the practice of selling shares without the right to vote).

5. Martin Lipton & William Savitt, *The Many Myths of Lucian Bebchuk*, 93 VA. L. REV. 733, 754 (2007).

6. The same is true of closely held corporations, although the roles overlap to a great extent.

7. Michael C. Jensen & William Meckling, *Theory of the Firm: Managerial Behavior, Agency Costs and Capital Structure*, 3 J. FIN. ECON. 305 (1976).

8. *Id.* at 310–11.

9. *See, e.g.*, William W. Bratton, Jr., *The "Nexus of Contracts" Corporation: A Critical Appraisal*, 74 CORNELL L. REV. 407 (1989) (defining the nexus of contracts approach as "the firm is a legal fiction that serves as a nexus for a set of contracting relations among individual factors of production").

10. Frank H. Easterbrook & Daniel R. Fischel, *The Corporate Contract*, 89 COLUM. L. REV. 1416, 1444 (1989).

11. Lewis A. Kornhauser, *The Nexus of Contracts Approach to Corporations: A Comment on Easterbrook and Fischel*, 89 COLUM. L. REV. 1449, 1449 (1989) ("Critics and advocates agree that a revolution, under the banner 'nexus of contracts,' has in the last decade swept the legal theory of the corporation."); Stephen M. Bainbridge, *The Board of Directors as Nexus of Contracts*, 88 IOWA L. REV. 1, 9 (2002) ("The dominant model of the corporation in legal scholarship is the so-called nexus of contracts theory."); Thomas S. Ulen, *The Coasean Firm in Law and Economics*, 18 J. CORP. L. 301, 303 (1993) (arguing that "the nexus-of-contracts view of the modern corporation and the principal-agent explanation of some important aspects of the firm . . . have had profound implications for some of the most important issues of corporation law").

12. Melvin Eisenberg, *The Conception That the Corporation is a Nexus of Contracts, and the Dual Nature of the Firm*, 24 J. CORP. L. 819, 824 (1999) ("Unfortunately, it has proved easy to confuse the positive proposition that the corporation is a nexus of reciprocal arrangements with the normative proposition that the persons who constitute a corporation should be free to make whatever reciprocal arrangements they choose, without the constraints of any mandatory legal rules.").

13. Jensen & Meckling, *supra* note 7, at 310–11.

14. Michael Klausner, *The Contractarian Theory of Corporate Law: A Generation Later*, 31 J. CORP. L. 779, 780 (2006) (describing Easterbrook and Fischel as "the primary expositors of the contractarian theory").

15. *Id.* at 783 ("Easterbrook and Fischel's theory of corporate law is both normative and positive: that corporate law *should* take this form; and that it 'almost always' does.").

16. Jensen & Meckling, *supra* note 7, at 310 (italics omitted).

17. *Id.* at 310–11.

18. *Id.* at 311.

19. *Id.* (italics omitted).

20. *Id.* at 312–57.

21. *See, e.g.*, Oliver Hart, *An Economist's Perspective on the Theory of the Firm*, 89 COLUM. L. REV. 1757, 1759 (1989) ("Principal-agent theory . . . fails to answer the vital questions of what defines a firm and where the boundaries of its structure are located."); Thomas F. McInerney, *Implications of High Performance Production and Work Practices for Theory of the Firm and Corporate Governance*, 2004 COLUM. BUS. L. REV. 135, 137–38 ("Scholars working in this paradigm do not offer theories of the firm so much as theories of who controls the firm."); Edward B. Rock & Michael L. Wachter, *Islands of Conscious Power: Law, Norms, and the Self-Governing Corporation*, 149 U. PA. L. REV. 1619, 1624 (2001) ("Jensen and Meckling, despite the title, did not really offer a full-fledged theory of the firm. Rather, they offered a theory of agency costs within firms . . . .").

22. It is sometimes difficult to parse the language of the theory to determine what is actually being claimed. *See* Bainbridge, *supra* note 11, at 11 ("I have come around to the view that the corporation is a nexus of contracts in a literal sense, albeit a very limited one."); Julian Velasco, *Shareholder Ownership and Primacy*, 2010 U. ILL. L. REV. 897, 919 ("[A]lthough it may be technically accurate to describe a corporation as a nexus of contracts, it is entirely inadequate.").

23. Stephen M. Bainbridge, *Community and Statism: A Conservative Contractarian Critique of Progressive Corporate Law Scholarship*, 82 CORNELL L. REV. 856, 860 (1997) ("The nexus of contracts model has important implications for a range of corporate law topics, the most obvious of which is the debate over the proper role of mandatory legal rules."); Lucian Arye Bebchuk, *Foreword: The Debate on Contractual Freedom in Corporate Law*, 89 COLUM. L. REV. 1395, 1397 (1989) (noting that corporate law contractarians argue "that the contractual view of the corporation implies that the parties should be totally free to shape their contractual arrangements").

24. A more nuanced version of this would be: having the parties choose their terms is the system most likely to lead to an efficient result over time, as there is no other system likely to result in greater efficiency.

25. This fact is acknowledged by contractarian theorists. *See* Easterbrook & Fischel, *supra* note 10, at 1444–45 (acknowledging that statutory corporate law is necessary to create a corporation).

26. *Cf.* William W. Bratton, Jr., *The "Nexus of Contracts" Corporation: A Critical Appraisal*, 74 CORNELL L. REV. 407, 445 (1989) ("If the corporation really 'is' contract, as the new economic theory tells us, then the last doctrinal vestiges of state interference should have withered away by now . . . . But the sovereign presence persists.").

27. *See* Larry E. Ribstein, *Why Corporations?*, 1 BERKELEY BUS. L.J. 183, 208 (2004) ("This state-creation characterization effectively sets a presumption in favor of regulating corporations that does not apply to other business associations or contracts.").

28. *See, e.g.*, Paul G. Mahoney, *Contract or Concession? An Essay on the History of Corporate Law*, 34 GA. L. REV. 873, 893 (2000) ("The 'concession' theory of the corporation in the English-speaking world owes its lineage to two aggressive assertions of the sole right of government to create legal persons: Coke's decision in 1615 and the Bubble Act in 1720.").

29. Stefan J. Padfield, *Rehabilitating Concession Theory*, 66 OKLA. L. REV. 327, 329 (2014) (looking "to 'rehabilitate' concession theory, which views the corporation as fundamentally a creature of the state and thus presumptively subject to broad state regulation").

30. *See, e.g.*, STEPHEN M. BAINBRIDGE & M. TODD HENDERSON, LIMITED LIABILITY: A LEGAL AND ECONOMIC ANALYSIS 68–69 (2016) ("[I]t has been over half-a-century since corporate legal theory, of any political or economic stripe, took the concession theory seriously."); Henry N. Butler & Larry E. Ribstein, *The Contract Clause and the Corporation*, 55 BROOK. L. REV. 767, 775 (1989) ("There is no longer any justification for regarding the corporation as a concession of the state.").

31. *See* LARRY E. RIBSTEIN, THE RISE OF THE UNCORPORATION 11 (2010).

32. *Id.* at 66.

33. *Id.* at 99.

34. *Id.* at 79. Although he recognizes that there may have been (cumbersome) contractual methods for limiting liability for contractual claimants, it would have been "impossible" to secure limited liability against tort claimants without the government's help. *Id.* This thinking is a departure from Ribstein's earlier contentions that limited liability could somehow be rendered contractual. *See also* Henry N. Butler & Larry E. Ribstein, *The Contract Clause and the Corporation*, 55 BROOK. L. REV. 767, 775 (1989) ("Nor does state concession status flow from limited liability of shareholders as against involuntary creditors. Limited liability is merely a consequence of the shareholders' contract, just as it is of participants in other arrangements, such as non-partner creditors.").

35. RIBSTEIN, *supra* note 31, at 138. The importance of limited liability is a theme Ribstein turns to over and over again in the book. *See id.* at 5, 8, 10–11, 25, 37, 43–44, 72, 79–85, 95–97, 99–101, 120–21, 127, 138–47, 153, 162, 164–65, 256.

36. Discussing the characteristics that are specific to corporations, Ribstein notes that "partnerships long have been able to contract for such corporate-type features, with one critical exception – limited liability." *Id.* at 76.

37. Mahoney, *supra* note 28, at 874 (arguing that "the state, far from facilitating organizational development, often tries to thwart it").

38. DEL. CODE tit. 8 § 141(a) (2018) (emphasis added).

39. Klausner, *supra* note 14, at 784, 786–91.

40. *Id.* at 784.

41. John C. Coates IV & Bradley C. Faris, *Second-Generation Shareholder Bylaws: Post-Quickturn Alternatives*, 56 BUS. LAW. 1323, 1353 (2001) ("A bylaw is impermissible if its primary purpose is to prevent or interfere with the board's discretion under section 141(a) to manage the business and affairs of the corporation . . . .");

Lawrence A. Hamermesh, *Corporate Democracy and Stockholder-Adopted By-Laws: Taking Back the Street?*, 73 TUL. L. REV. 409, 428–44 (1998).

42. 17 C.F.R. § 240.14a-8 (2018).

43. Sarbanes-Oxley Act of 2002, Pub. L. No. 107-204, 116 Stat. 745 (codified in scattered sections of 11, 15, 18, 28, and 29 U.S.C.).

44. For example, Rule 14a-8 gives shareholders the authority to propose actions to the board at the annual meeting, and Sarbanes-Oxley puts independence requirements on audit committees, which are subcommittees of the board. Sarbanes-Oxley Act § 301, 15 U.S.C. § 78j-1 (Supp. III 2003).

45. RIBSTEIN, *supra* note 31, at 67 (arguing that "only a corporation *must* have a board of directors that is separate from the executives and appointed directly by the owners").

46. *Id.* at 68–75.

47. *See id.* at 26–27.

48. These reasons include: the complexity of drafting LLC or LLP charters; tax treatment of LLCs can be more difficult for many investors to manage; the unavailability of tax-deferred stock swaps for LLCs; the difference in treatment of equity compensation for executives and employees; and differences in state tax treatment.

49. *See* Dieter Sadowski et al., *The German Model of Corporate and Labor Governance*, 22 COMP. LAB. & POLY J. 33, 36–40 (2000). We will spend much more time on this and related issues in Chapter 11.

50. It is difficult to measure the extent to which contractarians shift their metaphor into the realm of literal truth. Certainly, most contractarians will admit that a corporation cannot be formed through contract. However, the theory is often described in shorthand as a positive description. *See, e.g.,* JONATHAN R. MACEY, CORPORATE GOVERNANCE: PROMISES MADE, PROMISES KEPT 22 (2008) ("It has long been recognized . . . that the corporation . . . should be viewed as a 'nexus of contracts' or a set of implicit and explicit contracts."); Stephen M. Bainbridge, *Unocal at 20: Director Primacy in Corporate Takeovers*, 31 DEL. J. CORP. L. 769, 781 (2006) ("[I]t is commonplace and correct to say that the corporation is a nexus of contracts . . . .").

51. Fred McChesney, for example, stated: "Admittedly, as a descriptive matter state corporation codes and other sources of law contain many mandatory terms that parties cannot contract around. . . . [T]o claim that contractarians would deny the existence of coercive legal rules is to accuse them of blindness or stupidity." Fred S. McChesney, *Economics, Law, and Science in the Corporate Field: A Comment on Eisenberg*, 89 COLUM. L. REV. 1530, 1537 (1989).

52. FRANK H. EASTERBROOK & DANIEL R. FISCHEL, THE ECONOMIC STRUCTURE OF CORPORATE LAW 34 (1991).

53. *Id.*

54. *See also* Stephen M. Bainbridge, *Community and Statism: A Conservative Contractarian Critique of Progressive Corporate Law*, 82 CORNELL L. REV. 856, 865 n.31 (1997) (explaining that "corporate default rules . . . [are not] entitlements but . . . our best guess as to what parties would rationally agree to in the absence of any pre-existing set of imposed terms"); Bernard S. Black, *Is Corporate Law Trivial?: A Political and Economic Analysis*, 84 NW. U.L. REV. 542, 544 (1990) (claiming that many features of noncontractual corporate law were trivial because

they represented terms that would have been in corporate charters or bylaws anyway).

55. EASTERBROOK & FISCHEL, *supra* note 52, at 15 ("The rhetoric of contract is a staple of political and philosophical debate. Contract means voluntary and unanimous agreement among affected parties. It is therefore a powerful concept.").

56. *Id.* at 34.

57. And, as we'll see in Chapter 11, when corporations were formed under conditions somewhat like this (in the periods following the wars in Germany), labor and capital bargained for shared representation on corporate boards.

58. EASTERBROOK & FISCHEL, *supra* note 52, at 23.

59. For a critique, *see* Oliver Hart & Luigi Zingales, *Companies Should Maximize Shareholder Welfare Not Market Value*, 2 J.L. FIN. & ACCT. 247, 248 (2017).

60. *Id.*

61. There is evidence from Germany, for example, that employees with board representation tend to trade wages for better job security. *See* E. Han Kim, Ernst Maug & Christoph Schneider, *Labor Representation in Governance as an Insurance Mechanism*, 2018 REV. FIN. 1251, 1279, 1286. This, too, will be discussed in more detail in Chapter 11.

62. MACEY, *supra* note 50, at 29.

63. DEL. CODE tit. 8, § 102 (2018) (describing the contents of a certificate of incorporation).

64. *Id.* § 109(b) ("The bylaws may contain any provision, not inconsistent with law or with the certificate of incorporation, relating to the business of the corporation, the conduct of its affairs, and its rights or powers or the rights or powers of its stockholders, directors, officers or employees."). In Delaware, the charter is more difficult to amend, as it requires both shareholder and board approval. *Id.* § 242. Bylaws, in contrast, can be created and amended by the board or by shareholders. *Id.* § 109(a).

65. *See, e.g.*, Airgas, Inc. v. Air Prods. & Chems., Inc., 8 A.3d 1182, 1188 (Del. 2010) (describing bylaws as "contracts among a corporation's shareholders"); Robert Borowski, *Combatting Multiforum Shareholder Litigation: A Federal Acceptance of Forum Selection Bylaws*, 44 SW. L. REV. 149, 150 (2014) (finding that "bylaws are generally treated as contracts between corporations and their shareholders"). *See generally* Verity Winship, *Litigation Rights and the Corporate Contract, in* THE CORPORATE CONTRACT IN CHANGING TIMES 273, 273 (Stephen D. Solomon & Randall S. Thomas eds., 2019) (describing the corporate contract as "the agreement or set of agreements that articulate the terms of the relationship among shareholders, directors and the corporation itself").

66. Boilermakers Local 154 Ret. Fund v. Chevron Corp., 73 A.3d 934, 939 (Del. Ch. 2013). *See also id.* at 955 ("In an unbroken line of decisions dating back several generations, our Supreme Court has made clear that the bylaws constitute a binding part of the contract between a Delaware corporation and its stockholders.").

67. D. Gordon Smith et al., *Private Ordering with Shareholder Bylaws*, 80 FORDHAM L. REV. 125, 127 (2011) (proposing to "empower shareholders in public corporations by facilitating their ability to contract" through bylaws).

68. For a discussion of these bylaw controversies, see Jill E. Fisch, *Governance by Contract: The Implications for Corporate Bylaws*, 106 CALIF. L. REV. 373 (2018).

69. *Boilermakers*, 73 A.3d at 939.

70. ATP Tour, Inc. v. Deutscher Tennis Bund, 91 A.3d 554, 558 (Del. 2014).

71. *Id.* ("But it is settled that contracting parties may agree to modify the American Rule and obligate the losing party to pay the prevailing party's fees. Because corporate bylaws are 'contracts among a corporation's shareholders,' a fee-shifting provision contained in a nonstock corporation's validly-enacted bylaw would fall within the contractual exception to the American Rule."); *Boilermakers*, 73 A.3d at 955.

72. CA, Inc. v. AFSCME Emps. Pension Plan, 953 A.2d 227, 229 (Del. 2008).

73. *Id.* at 232.

74. *Id.* at 236; *Boilermakers*, 73 A.3d at 951 (noting that "bylaws typically do not contain substantive mandates, but direct how the corporation, the board, and its stockholders may take certain action").

75. *See, e.g.*, Brett H. McDonnell, *Bylaw Reforms for Delaware's Corporation Law*, 33 DEL. J. CORP. L. 651, 651–52 (2008) (describing shareholder bylaw proposals as "an increasingly important part of battles over corporate governance" and "a useful way for shareholders to guard against board opportunism without going too far in usurping board authority"); Ben Walther, *Bylaw Governance*, 20 FORDHAM J. CORP. & FIN. L. 399, 404 (2015) (stating that under the bylaw governance model, "shareholders may exert authority over corporate affairs by promulgating bylaws that circumscribe the board's exercise of its authority").

76. At times, the language in Delaware opinions seems to be referencing the idea of a "social contract" to justify governance by the consent of the governed. *See Boilermakers*, 73 A.3d at 955–56 ("Stockholders are on notice that, as to those subjects that are subject of regulation by bylaw under 8 Del. C. § 109(b), the board itself may act unilaterally to adopt bylaws addressing those subjects. Such a change by the board is not extra-contractual simply because the board acts unilaterally; rather it is the kind of change that the overarching statutory and contractual regime the stockholders buy into explicitly allows the board to make on its own.").

77. Fisch, *supra* note 68, at 375 ("The contractual approach has become particularly influential in supporting deference to the participants' agreed-upon governance terms on both autonomy and efficiency grounds.").

78. 73 A.3d at 955–56 (emphasis added) (footnotes omitted).

79. *Id.* at 956.

80. One is reminded of Grant Gilmore's astonishment at Oliver Wendell Holmes: "The magician who could 'objectify' *Raffles v. Wichelhaus* . . . could, the need arising, objectify anything." GRANT GILMORE, THE DEATH OF CONTRACT 45 (Ronald K. L. Collins ed., 2d ed. 1995).

81. Fisch, *supra* note 68, at 389 (citing Kidsco Inc. v. Dinsmore, 674 A.2d 483, 490 (Del. Ch. 1995)).

82. *See, e.g.*, Salazar v. Citadel Commc'ns Corp., 90 P.3d 466, 469 (N.M. 2004) ("Under general New Mexico contract law, an agreement that is subject to unilateral modification or revocation is illusory and unenforceable . . . . The party that reserves the right to change the agreement unilaterally, and at any time, has not really promised anything at all and should not be permitted to bind the other party.").

83. *See, e.g.*, Fisch, *supra* note 68, at 374.

84. *Cf. id.* at 382–83 (noting the inconsistency).

85. Jensen & Meckling, *supra* note 7, at 311.

86. *Id.* at 308.

87. Oliver Hart, *Incomplete Contracts and Control*, 107 AM. ECON. REV. 1731, 1735 (2017); Michael J. Meurer, *Law, Economics, and the Theory of the Firm*, 52 BUFF. L. REV. 727, 732 (2004); Edward B. Rock & Michael L. Wachter, *Norms & Corporate Law: Introduction*, 149 U. PA. L. REV. 1607, 1624 (2001).

88. David A. Westbrook, *Corporation Law After Enron: The Possibility of a Capitalist Reimagination*, 92 GEO. L.J. 61, 105 n.277 (2003) ("So for Coase, in the first instance, the firm is *anything but* a nexus of contracts. Instead the firm is a site where the costs of continuous contracting (forming a market) outweigh the costs of forming the entity. Ironies abound in the legal academy's appreciation of the great economist.").

89. Meurer, *supra* note 87, at 731–32 (citing Harold Demsetz, *The Theory of the Firm Revisited, in* THE NATURE OF THE FIRM: ORIGINS, EVOLUTION, AND DEVELOPMENT (Oliver E. Williamson & Sidney G. Winter eds., 1991)).

90. Bainbridge's theory was developed over time through a series of articles on the subject. *See* Stephen M. Bainbridge, *Director Primacy: The Means and Ends of Corporate Governance*, 97 NW. U.L. REV. 547, 573 (2003) [hereinafter Bainbridge, *Director Primacy*]. *See generally* Stephen M. Bainbridge, *The Case for Limited Shareholder Voting Rights*, 53 UCLA L. REV. 601 (2006); Stephen M. Bainbridge, *Director Primacy and Shareholder Disempowerment*, 119 HARV. L. REV. 1735 (2006); Stephen M. Bainbridge, *Director Primacy in Corporate Takeovers: Preliminary Reflections*, 55 STAN. L. REV. 791 (2002). He synthesized his research into a book on the subject: STEPHEN M. BAINBRIDGE, THE NEW CORPORATE GOVERNANCE IN THEORY AND PRACTICE (2008).

91. Bainbridge, *Director Primacy*, *supra* note 90, at 547–50.

92. *Id.* at 563.

93. *Id.* at 550–51, 560 (also referring to the board as a *"sui generis* body"); Bainbridge, *supra* note 11, at 33.

94. Bainbridge, *Director Primacy*, *supra* note 90, at 554–60.

95. *Id.* at 555.

96. *Id.*

97. *Id.* at 556 (citing to the "Coasean theory of the firm").

98. KENNETH J. ARROW, THE LIMITS OF ORGANIZATION (1974).

99. Bainbridge, *Director Primacy*, *supra* note 90, at 557–58.

100. Brett H. McDonnell, *Professor Bainbridge and the Arrowian Moment: A Review of The New Corporate Governance in Theory and Practice*, 34 DEL. J. CORP. L. 139, 143 (2009).

101. *Id.* at 161. McDonnell considers various arguments for Bainbridge's allocation of power but ultimately finds none of them able to solve the dilemma. *Id.* at 162–85.

102. *Id.* at 143.

103. *See generally* Tamara Belinfanti & Lynn Stout, *Contested Visions: The Value of Systems Theory for Corporate Law*, 166 U. PENN. L. REV. 579 (2018).

104. *Id.* at 599. The management system "holacracy" applies an analogous approach. BRIAN J. ROBERTSON, HOLACRACY: THE NEW MANAGEMENT SYSTEM FOR A RAPIDLY CHANGING WORLD 158–59 (2015).

5.   Shareholder Homogeneity

1. Frank H. Easterbrook & Daniel R. Fischel, The Economic Structure of Corporate Law 70 (1991).

2. Robert B. Thompson & Paul H. Edelman, *Corporate Voting*, 62 Vand. L. Rev. 129, 152 (2009). Of course, using stock price (as opposed to, say, wage rates or consumer satisfaction) as the principal measure of corporate success tends to predetermine who should ultimately be given voting rights. That is, Thompson and Edelman may be right that shareholder voting largely serves as an error-correction device, but that doesn't tell us much about who *should* be voting in the first place. They seem to acknowledge this point in a later article, explaining that "we are not making normative claims about the merits of shareholder voting. We are agnostic on the question of whether shareholder voting leads either to social or corporate efficiency. We offer a positive theory that explains what we observe in the world about the role of the shareholder franchise." Paul H. Edelman, Randall S. Thomas & Robert B. Thompson, *Shareholder Voting in an Age of Intermediary Capitalism*, 87 S. Cal. L. Rev. 1359, 1370 (2014).

3. Shaun Martin & Frank Partnoy, *Encumbered Shares*, 2005 U. Ill. L. Rev. 775, 778 (2005) (quoting Frank H. Easterbrook & Daniel R. Fischel, *Voting in Corporate Law*, 26 J.L. & Econ. 395, 405 (1983)) (alteration in original).

4. Colleen Dunlavy, *Social Conceptions of the Corporation: Insights from the History of Shareholder Voting Rights*, 63 Wash. & Lee L. Rev. 1347, 1351–52, 1351 fig.1 (2006).

5. *See* James D. Cox & Thomas Lee Hazen, Corporations 348–51 (2d ed. 2003).

6. *See* Jeffrey N. Gordon, *Institutions as Relational Investors: A New Look at Cumulative Voting*, 94 Colum. L. Rev. 124 (1994).

7. Note that this is different from the "agency costs" problem that seems to (pre)-occupy most corporate law scholars.

8. *See* Kahn v. Lynch Commc'n Sys., Inc., 638 A.2d 1110, 1115 (Del. 1994) ("A controlling or dominating shareholder standing on both sides of a transaction . . . bears the burden of proving its entire fairness.").

9. *See, e.g.*, Del. Code Ann. tit. 8, § 144 (2010).

10. *Id.* § 144(a)(3) ("The contract or transaction is fair as to the corporation as of the time it is authorized, approved or ratified, by the board of directors, a committee or the shareholders."). For a discussion of the entire fairness test, see Cinerama, Inc. v. Technicolor Inc., 663 A.2d 1156, 1178–79 (Del. 1995).

11. Model Bus. Corp. Act § 8.30 (Am. Bar Ass'n 2016).

12. For an example of the discretion given to directors under the business judgment rule, see Shlensky v. Wrigley, 237 N.E.2d 776 (Ill. App. Ct. 1968).

13. *See, e.g., In re* Caremark Int'l Inc. Derivative Litig., 698 A.2d 959 (Del. Ch. 1996).

14. Donahue v. Rodd Electrotype Co., 328 N.E.2d 505, 515 (Mass. 1975).

15. *See* Robert B. Thompson, *The Shareholder's Cause of Action for Oppression*, 48 Bus. Law. 699, 711–12 (1993) (noting that minority oppression has been defined as "burdensome, harsh and wrongful conduct," "a visible departure from the standards of fair dealing," and "frustration of the reasonable expectations of the shareholders").

16. *In re* Kemp & Beatley, Inc., 473 N.E.2d 1173, 1179 (N.Y. 1984).

17. D. Gordon Smith, *The Shareholder Primacy Norm*, 23 J. CORP. L. 277 (1998).

18. 170 N.W. 668 (Mich. 1919).

19. Smith, *supra* note 17, at 315–20.

20. *Id.* at 322–23. Smith argued that ultimately the shareholder primacy norm is largely irrelevant to corporate law and corporate business decisions. *Id.*

21. *See, e.g.*, Nixon v. Blackwell, 626 A.2d 1366, 1376, 1380–81 (Del. 1993) (noting that it is "well established in our jurisprudence that stockholders need not always be treated equally for all purposes" and arguing it is "inappropriate judicial legislation . . . to fashion a special judicially-created rule for minority investors"); Wilkes v. Springside Nursing Home, Inc., 353 N.E.2d 657, 663 (Mass. 1976) (noting that the minority oppression doctrine should not "unduly hamper [the majority's] effectiveness in managing the corporation in the best interests of all concerned"); Lawrence E. Mitchell, *The Death of Fiduciary Duty in Close Corporations*, 138 U. PA. L. REV. 1675, 1688 (1990) ("The application of strict fiduciary standards to close corporations deprives controlling shareholders of the ability to manage the corporation – to use their own property – as they see fit.").

22. EASTERBROOK & FISCHEL, *supra* note 1, at 72.

23. *Id.*

24. Martin & Partnoy, *supra* note 3, at 784–85 (noting that Easterbrook and Fischel derived this conclusion from a "relatively stable period" in which the New York Stock Exchange refused to list companies with nonvoting shares).

25. 17 C.F.R. § 240.19c-4 (1988), *invalidated by* Bus. Roundtable v. SEC, 905 F.2d 406 (D.C. Cir. 1990).

26. At the time, some companies had issued, as a dividend to current shareholders, a new class of stock that provided an abnormally large number of votes per share. However, these new shares were not transferable, and could be sold only if they were converted to regular one-vote shares of common stock. The effect of such an issuance was to provide "lock in" power for long-term shareholders and/or managers. *See* Stephen M. Bainbridge, *The Short Life and Resurrection of SEC Rule 19c-4*, 69 WASH. U. L.Q. 565, 566 (1991).

27. *See Bus. Roundtable*, 905 F.2d at 406.

28. *See, e.g.*, NYSE, Listed Company Manual § 313(B), https://nyse.wolterskluwer.cloud/listed-company-manual; NASDAQ Initial Listing Guide § 5640, https://listingcenter.nasdaq.com/assets/initialguide.pdf.

29. *See, e.g.*, Troy A. Paredes, *A Systems Approach to Corporate Governance Reform: Why Importing U.S. Corporate Law Isn't the Answer*, 45 WM. & MARY L. REV. 1055, 1153 (2004) (arguing that dual-class voting structures could be prohibited as a way of protecting minority shareholder interests).

30. Dorothy S. Lund, *Nonvoting Shares and Efficient Corporate Governance*, 71 STAN. L. REV. 687 (2019).

31. This is still true of the New York Times. The Bancroft family, however, gave up control of the Wall Street Journal in 2007. Frank Ahrens, *Murdoch Seizes Wall St. Journal in $5 Billion Coup*, WASH. POST, Aug. 1, 2007, at A1.

32. *See, e.g.*, Lucian A. Bebchuk & Kobi Kastiel, *The Perils of Small-Minority Controllers*, 107 GEO. L.J. 1453 (2019); Robert J. Jackson, Jr., Commissioner, U.S. Sec. & Exch. Comm'n, Speech, Perpetual Dual-Class Stock: The Case Against Corporate Royalty (Feb. 15, 2018), https://www.sec.gov/news/speech/perpetual-dual-class-stock-case-against-corporate-royalty.

33. *See, e.g.*, Lund, *supra* note 30, at 700 ("The key implication of this analysis is that the use of nonvoting stock should not be discouraged. When issued alongside high-voting stock, nonvoting stock can make corporate governance more efficient.").

34. Preferred-stock shareholders do have the right to vote on any charter amendment that alters or changes "the powers, preferences, or special rights" of their shares. Del. Code Ann. tit. 8, § 242(b)(2); *see also* Model Bus. Corp. Act § 10.04(a)(3) (giving the holders of a separate class of stock the right to vote, as a group, on amendments that would "change the rights, preferences, or limitations of all or part of the shares of the class").

35. *See, e.g.*, Lehman Brothers Holdings Inc. and T. Rowe Price High Yield Fund, Inc., et al v. Spanish Broadcasting System, Inc., 39 Del. J. Corp. L. 575 (2014) ("If the dividend was not paid for four consecutive quarters, the Certificate of Designation in connection with the stock provided that a 'Voting Rights Triggering Event' (a 'VRTE') had occurred, conferring upon the Plaintiffs certain rights, including a right to fill seats on the company board, and to constrain the company from acquiring certain additional debt during the period the dividend arrearage continued.").

36. *See* William W. Bratton & Michael L. Wachter, *A Theory of Preferred Stock*, 161 U. Pa. L. Rev. 1815, 1826–27 (2013) (providing an example of the conflict).

37. Hall v. Isaacs, 146 A.2d 602 (Del. Ch. 1958).

38. *See, e.g.*, Commonwealth Assocs. v. Providence Health Care, Inc., 641 A.2d 155, 158 (Del. Ch. 1993) (expressing "doubt whether, in a post record-date sale of corporate stock, a negotiated provision in which a beneficial owner/seller specifically retained the 'dangling' right to vote as of the record date, would be a legal, valid and enforceable provision, unless the seller maintained an interest sufficient to support the granting of an irrevocable proxy with respect to the shares").

39. *See, e.g.*, Cone's Ex'rs v. Russell, 21 A. 847, 849 (N.J. Ch. 1891).

40. 447 A.2d 17 (Del. Ch. 1982).

41. *Id.* at 24. The court cited *Cone's* for the proposition that "the security of the small stockholders is found in the natural disposition of each stockholder to promote the best interests of all, in order to promote his individual interests." *Cone's Ex'rs*, 21 A. at 849.

42. Schreiber v. Carney, 447 A.2d 17, 20 (noting that the other shareholders "voted overwhelmingly in favor of the proposal").

43. *Id.* at 24.

44. *Id.* at 25 (quoting 5 Fletcher Cyclopedia Corporations § 2066 (perm. ed.)); *see also id.* ("[A] shareholder may exercise wide liberality of judgment in the matter of voting, and it is not objectionable that his motives may be for personal profit, or determined by whims or caprice, so long as he violates no duty owed his fellow stockholders.").

45. *Id.*

46. Del. Code Ann. tit. 8, § 218(c) (2014).

47. *Id.* § 218(a).

48. Martin & Partnoy, *supra* note 3, at 778 n.14.

49. Henry T.C. Hu & Bernard Black, *The New Vote Buying: Empty Voting and Hidden (Morphable) Ownership*, 79 S. Cal. L. Rev. 811, 828 (2006).

50. *Id.* at 832.

51. *Id.* at 834 (discussing share borrowing in the case of British Land, including the role of one fund manager who unknowingly lent stock to an opponent in the contest).

52. *See* Matthew T. Bodie, *Workers, Information, and Corporate Combinations: The Case for Nonbinding Employee Referenda in Transformative Transactions*, 85 WASH. U. L. REV. 871 (2008) (discussing employee interests in merger and acquisition decisions).

53. Martin & Partnoy, *supra* note 3, at 792.

54. Since stock options offer the chance for the holder to buy the stock at a certain strike price, the options are worth the same (nothing) whether the stock drops to $1 below the strike price or $100 below the strike price. This incentive scheme may have led to management and employees undervaluing excessive downside risk, including the risk that financial misreporting would come to light. *See* Matthew T. Bodie, *AOL Time Warner and the False God of Shareholder Primacy*, 31 J. CORP. L. 975, 995–97 (2006).

55. Matthew T. Bodie, *Aligning Incentives with Equity: Employee Stock Options and Rule 10b-5*, 88 IOWA L. REV. 539, 546–50 (2003).

56. These pension funds have been given extensive treatment in DAVID WEBBER, THE RISE OF THE WORKING-CLASS SHAREHOLDER: LABOR'S LAST BEST WEAPON (2018).

57. *See* Stephen M. Bainbridge, *Director Primacy and Shareholder Disempowerment*, 119 HARV. L. REV. 1735, 1755 (2006) ("Union pension funds reportedly have also tried to use shareholder proposals to obtain employee benefits they could not get through bargaining."); Joseph A. Grundfest, *The SEC's Proposed Proxy Access Rules: Politics, Economics, and the Law*, 65 BUS. LAW. 361, 382–83 (2010); Larry E. Ribstein, *The "Shareholder Democracy" Scam*, IDEOBLOG (Oct. 27, 2006, 07:35 AM), http://busmovie.typepad.com/ideoblog/2006/10/theshareholder.html [https://web.archive.org/web/20120224130605/https://busmovie.typepad.com /ideoblog/2006/10/the_shareholder.html] ("It should be obvious to anybody who cares to look past the rhetoric that the unions are seeking bargaining leverage on behalf of their members, and to ensure their own survival. They are not seeking to represent the interests of investors generally.").

58. Editorial, *Conflicted in California*, WALL ST. J., May 11, 2004, at A18 (complaining about labor's efforts to "hijack" corporate governance for their own ends).

59. *See* CalPERS, *Structure and Responsibilities* (Apr. 4, 2011), http://www.calpers.ca .gov/index.jsp?bc=/about/organization/board/structure-responsibilities.xml [https://web.archive.org/web/20110719033447/http://www.calpers.ca.gov/index .jsp?bc=/about/organization/board/structure-responsibilities.xml].

60. CalPERS, *Reform Focus List Companies* (Mar. 16, 2011), http://www.calpers-governance.org/alert/focus/ [https://web.archive.org/web/20140227005823/http:// www.calpers-governance.org/focuslist/reform-companies].

61. Grundfest, *supra* note 57, at 382 ("Safeway Corporation's 2003–2004 proxy fight with institutional investor CalPERS serves as an example of megaphone extern-alities and attempted electoral leverage."); *Conflicted in California*, *supra* note 58 ("Ostensibly Calpers is upset about underperformance, but the real problem seems to be the tough stance the grocery chain took against labor during a recent strike.").

62. Bainbridge, *supra* note 57, at 1755; Iman Anabtawi & Lynn Stout, *Fiduciary Duties for Activist Shareholders*, 60 STAN. L. REV. 1255, 1285–86 (2008); Jill E. Fisch,

Securities Intermediaries and the Separation of Ownership from Control, 33 SEATTLE U. L. REV. 877, 883 (2010); Grundfest, *supra* note 57, at 382–83; John F. Olson, *Reflections on a Visit to Leo Strine's Peaceable Kingdom*, 33 J. CORP. L. 73, 76–77 (2007); Mark J. Roe, *Delaware's Politics*, 118 HARV. L. REV. 2493, 2524–25 (2005); J.W. Verret, *Defending Against Shareholder Proxy Access: Delaware's Future Reviewing Company Defenses in the Era of Dodd-Frank*, 36 J. CORP. L. 391, 397 (2011); David H. Webber, *Is "Pay-to-Play" Driving Public Pension Fund Activism in Securities Class Actions? An Empirical Study*, 90 B.U. L. REV. 2031, 2071 (2010).

63. Michael C. Jensen & Kevin J. Murphy, *CEO Incentives – It's Not How Much You Pay, But How*, HARV. BUS. REV., May–June 1990, at 138.

64. Robert M. Kimmitt, *Public Footprints in Private Markets: Sovereign Wealth Funds and the World Economy*, FOREIGN AFFAIRS, Jan.–Feb. 2008, at 119 (discussing Kuwait's creation of the Kuwait Investment Board to invest its surplus oil revenue in 1953).

65. Ronald J. Gilson & Curtis J. Milhaupt, *Sovereign Wealth Funds and Corporate Governance: A Minimalist Response to the New Mercantilism*, 60 STAN. L. REV. 1345, 1354 n.44 (2008). Thus, the Norway Government Pension Fund is character-ized as an SWF because it is financed through the sale of oil, while CalPERS is not, since it is financed by employee and state contributions.

66. *Id.* at 1359.

67. *See* Peter Molk & Frank Partnoy, *Institutional Investors as Short Sellers?*, 99 B. U. L. REV. 837, 845 (2019).

68. 50 U.S.C. § 4565 (b)(2)(E) (2019); Interim Directive Regarding Disposition of Certain Mergers, Acquisitions, and Takeovers, 53 Fed. Reg. 43,999 (Oct. 26, 1988).

69. 50 U.S.C. § 4565 (2019).

70. Steve Lohr, *U.S. Moves to Ban Huawei from Government Contracts*, N.Y. TIMES (Aug. 7, 2019), https://www.nytimes.com/2019/08/07/business/huawei-us-ban.html.

71. Eric Dash & Andrew Ross Sorkin, *Abu Dhabi Buys $7.5 Billion Stake in Citigroup*, N.Y. TIMES, Nov. 27, 2007.

72. Keith Bradsher & Joseph Kahn, *In China, a Stake in Blackstone Stirs Uncertainty*, N.Y. TIMES, May 29, 2007, at C2.

73. Laurie J. Flynn, *Abu Dhabi Takes 8% Stake in Advanced Micro*, N.Y. TIMES, Nov. 17, 2007, at C4.

74. As Ronald Gilson and Curtis Milhaupt have put it, "national security concerns anchor one end of a continuum of issues concerning when the interests of a foreign government may differ from those of an ordinary shareholder." Gilson & Milhaupt, *supra* note 65, at 1351.

75. Kimmitt, *supra* note 64, at 128 ("SWFs are public-sector entities managing public funds, and profit maximization may not be considered the primary objective.").

76. Gilson & Milhaupt, *supra* note 65, at 1364.

77. *Id.* at 1364–68.

78. Bob Davis, *U.S. Pushes Sovereign Funds to Open to Outside Scrutiny*, WALL ST. J., Feb. 26, 2008, at A1 (discussing U.S. Treasury Assistant Secretary Clay Lowery's suggestion that "sovereign-wealth funds that choose to vote their shares when they take noncontrolling stakes in U.S. companies should disclose how they voted").

79. *See* Richard A. Epstein & Amanda M. Rose, *The Regulation of Sovereign Wealth Funds: The Virtues of Going Slow*, U. CHI. L. REV. 111, 127 (2009) (noting that "SWFs are not the only investors who may invest 'strategically'").

80. *See* Gilson & Milhaupt, *supra* note 65, at 1363 (using the theoretical example of an SWF trying to get the company to authorize favorable technology transfers to companies in the SWF's jurisdiction). However, as Gilson and Milhaupt concede, "to be sure, no one can point to a reported incidence of such behavior." *Id.* at 1362.

81. Gilson and Milhaupt acknowledge that if their plan were put into place, other countries would likely take steps to limit the rights of U.S. government funds, including state pension funds. These restrictions would limit "the positive impact that shareholder activism by U.S. state pension funds, most vocally by CalPERS, has had on corporate governance standards in other countries." *Id.* at 1368.

82. Paul Rose, *Sovereign Investing and Corporate Governance: Evidence and Policy*, 18 FORDHAM J. CORP. & FIN. L. 913, 915 (2013) ("[P]assive SWFs are not simply a non-factor in corporate governance, but may also have a negative effect by holding large, inert share blocks that could be held by more engaged shareholders who would be more vigilant in containing managerial agency costs.").

83. Henry Hansmann & Reinier Kraakman, *The End of History for Corporate Law*, 89 GEO. L.J. 439, 439 (2001).

84. *See* Iman Anabtawi, *Some Skepticism About Increasing Shareholder Power*, 53 UCLA L. REV. 561, 579–83 (2006) (discussing the different financial interests of short-term and long-term shareholders).

85. And they want to get the option at the stock's lowest point. In 2007, companies were accused of gaming the system by backdating the option's strike date to a day with a lower price. For a discussion of the backdating scandal, see David I. Walker, *Unpacking Backdating: Economic Analysis and Observations on the Stock Option Scandal*, 87 B.U. L. REV. 561 (2007).

86. Index funds track a particular index; they must manage the fund to mirror the composition of the index. They have been significantly more popular in the past decade. Lucian Bebchuk & Scott Hirst, *The Specter of the Giant Three*, 99 B. U. L. REV. 721, 723 (2019) (discussing the "steady rise of the 'Big Three' index fund managers – Blackrock, Vanguard, and State Street Global Advisors" and concluding that "the Big Three will likely continue to grow into a 'Giant Three,' and that the Giant Three will likely come to dominate voting in public companies").

87. Margaret M. Blair, *Directors' Duties in a Post-Enron World: Why Language Matters*, 38 WAKE FOREST L. REV. 885, 890 (2003).

88. Bodie, *supra* note 52, at 997–98.

89. Anabtawi, *supra* note 84, at 583–85.

90. JAMES P. HAWLEY & ANDREW T. WILLIAMS, THE RISE OF FIDUCIARY CAPITALISM 3, 21 (2000).

91. Robert G. Hansen & John R. Lott, Jr., *Externalities and Corporate Objectives in a World with Diversified Shareholder/Consumers*, 31 J. FIN. & QUANTITATIVE ANALYSIS 43, 44 (1996).

92. *Id.*

93. Bruce H. Kobayashi & Larry E. Ribstein, *Outsider Trading as an Incentive Device*, 40 U.C. DAVIS L. REV. 21, 44–45 (2006) (noting that such "costly manipulation" may be useful in overcoming "interference from self-interested managers or undiversified shareholders").

94. *See, e.g.*, Oliver Hart & Luigi Zingales, *Companies Should Maximize Shareholder Welfare Not Market Value*, 2 J.L. FIN. & ACCT. 247 (2017).

95. *See, e.g.*, Frank Ahrens, *Roy Disney's Quest*, WASH. POST, Feb. 21, 2004, at A1 (noting that Disney stock "is widely held by individual shareholders"); Peter J. Howe, *Shareholders Hold Key to the Kingdom*, BOSTON GLOBE, Mar. 3, 2004, at D1 (describing "hundreds of thousands of Disney fanatics who also own stock"); Sarah McBride, *Mice That Roar: Obsessive Fans Join Disney Proxy Fight*, WALL ST. J., Mar. 2, 2004, at A1 ("Hardcore Disney fans own stock in the object of their devotion. Those stakes may be just a few shares apiece, but multiplied by thousands of fans across the county, they help make Disney one of the most widely held stocks on Main Street.").

96. JAMES B. STEWART, DISNEY WAR 508 (2005) (discussing the thousands of shareholders who attended the 2004 shareholders' meeting).

97. Kenneth N. Gilpin, *Disney Dissidents Rebuke Eisner, Denying Him 43% of Vote*, N.Y. TIMES, Mar. 2, 2004. Eisner had angered some traditionalists by diversifying Disney's holdings and failing to continue Disney's animation successes of the 1990s. *See id.* ("During the course of his remarks, Roy Disney suggested that under Mr. Eisner's direction the Disney name and its products had lost their luster and unique character.").

98. *See* Henry Blodget, *The Conscientious Investor*, ATLANTIC MONTHLY, Oct. 2007, at 78.

99. Mark Miller, *Bit by Bit, Socially Conscious Investors Are Influencing 401(k)'s*, N.Y. TIMES, Sept. 29, 2019, at BU-5; Tine Thygesen, *Everyone Is Talking About ESG: What Is It And Why Should It Matter To You?*, FORBES (Nov. 8, 2019), https://www.forbes.com/sites/tinethygesen/2019/11/08/everyone-is-talking-about-esgwhat-is-it-and-why-should-it-matter-to-you/#78833be632e9.

100. Miller, *supra* note 99 ("For the 12 months ended April 30, for example, such funds investing in big-company stocks returned 11.63 percent, compared with 12.28 percent for all big-stock funds. For funds investing in mid-size companies, socially minded versions returned 7.65 percent over the period, compared with 10.24 percent for all funds.").

101. *Id.*; *see also* Blodget, *supra* note 98, at 80–82 (discussing the categorization difficulties of socially responsible investing).

102. Hart & Zingales, *supra* note 94.

103. *Id.*

104. Larry E. Ribstein, *Accountability and Responsibility in Corporate Governance*, 81 NOTRE DAME L. REV. 1431, 1433 (2006) ("Managers can promote shareholders' interests without maximizing profits to the extent the shareholders have some objective other than profit maximization.").

105. Much of the thinking in this subsection draws upon the thinking of Stephen Ellis, *Market Hegemony and Economic Theory*, 38 PHIL. SOC. SCI. 513 (2008).

106. *See, e.g.*, Norman P. Barry, *Do Corporations Have Any Responsibility Beyond Making a Profit?*, 3 J. MARKETS & MORALITY 100 (2000); Patrick Primeaux & John Steiber, *Profit Maximization: The Ethical Mandate of Business*, 13 J. BUS. ETHICS 287 (1994).

107. *See, e.g.*, Sandra E. Black & Elizabeth Brainerd, *Importing Inequality? The Impact of Globalization on Gender Discrimination*, 57 INDUS. & LAB. REL. REV. 540 (2004); Ann Schwartz-Miller & Wayne K. Talley, *Motor Bus Deregulation and the Gender Wage Gap: A Test of the Becker Hypothesis*, 26 E. ECON. J. 145 (2000).

108. *See* Ellis, *supra* note 105.
109. Lois A. Mohr, Deborah J. Webb & Katherine E. Harris, *Do Consumers Expect Companies to be Socially Responsible? The Impact of Corporate Social Responsibility on Buying Behavior*, 35 J. CONSUMER AFF. 45, 67 (2001).
110. *See* KENNETH J. ARROW, SOCIAL CHOICE AND INDIVIDUAL VALUES (2d ed. 1970).
111. *See* Ellis, *supra* note 105.
112. *See id.*
113. *See* MILTON FRIEDMAN, CAPITALISM AND FREEDOM 109–10 (2d ed. 1982).
114. *See* Ellis, *supra* note 105.
115. *See* Grant M. Hayden & Stephen E. Ellis, *Law and Economics After Behavioral Economics*, 55 U. KAN. L. REV. 629 (2007).
116. *See id.*
117. *See id.*

6.   The Argument from the Residual

1. FRANK H. EASTERBROOK & DANIEL R. FISCHEL, THE ECONOMIC STRUCTURE OF CORPORATE LAW 35–39 (1991).
2. *Id.*
3. *Id.* at 36–37.
4. *Id.* at 68.
5. *Id.* at 70.
6. Shaun Martin & Frank Partnoy, *Encumbered Shares*, 2005 U. ILL. L. REV. 775, 776 (2005) (noting that the notion of "one share, one vote" is based on "agency costs considerations"); Robert H. Sitkoff, *Corporate Political Speech, Political Extortion, and the Competition for Corporate Charters*, 69 U. CHI. L. REV. 1103, 1121 (2002) (noting that any rule other than one share, one vote "wastefully increases the agency costs associated with the corporate form").
7. EASTERBROOK & FISCHEL, *supra* note 1, at 69–70; *see also* HENRY HANSMANN, THE OWNERSHIP OF ENTERPRISE 62 (1996) ("Investor-owned firms have the important advantage that their owners generally share a single well-defined objective: to maximize the net present value of the firm's earnings.").
8. Grant M. Hayden, *The False Promise of One Person, One Vote*, 102 MICH. L. REV. 213, 236–47 (2003).
9. For example, an investor who owns $50,000 in stock in company A and has $100,000 overall in their portfolio will have different risk preferences for the firm than will a shareholder who has $50,000 in stock in company A and has $10 million overall in their portfolio. The declining marginal utility of wealth also means that the performance of company A has less effect on the utility of the second shareholder, even though both shareholders have the same number of shares.
10. For example, Hewlett-Packard shareholders battled over the wisdom of the merger between Hewlett-Packard and Compaq. Steve Lohr, *Hewlett's Shareholders Meet Today on Compaq Merger*, N.Y. TIMES, Mar. 19, 2002, at C4. Hewlett-Packard director Walter Hewlett fought the rest of the company's board and management over the merger, ultimately losing in a close election. Both sides agreed that the merger should be judged on its impact on Hewlett-Packard's success, but they

disagreed about whether the merger would help accomplish that goal. Hewlett and the company spent an estimated $100 million in their efforts to persuade shareholders. *Id.*

11. Oliver Hart & Luigi Zingales, *Companies Should Maximize Shareholder Welfare Not Market Value*, 2 J.L. FIN. & ACCT. 247 (2017).

12. *See, e.g.*, Benjamin Means, *Family Business Disputes*, BUS. L. TODAY, February 2015, at 1.

13. *See* ADOLF A. BERLE, JR. & GARDINER C. MEANS, THE MODERN CORPORATION AND PRIVATE PROPERTY (1932).

14. *See, e.g.*, Yair Listokin, *Management Always Wins the Close Ones*, 10 AM. L. & ECON. REV. 159, 171 (2008) (noting that "management sponsored proposals typically pass easily," with a mean approval rate of 85 percent).

15. Daniel J.H. Greenwood, *Fictional Shareholders: For Whom Are Corporate Managers Trustees, Revisited*, 69 S. CAL. L. REV. 1021, 1052 (1996) ("For fictional shareholders, whatever else the people behind them may want, all want to maximize the value of their shares.").

16. *See* EASTERBROOK & FISCHEL, *supra* note 1, at 69–70.

17. D. Gordon Smith, *The Shareholder Primacy Norm*, 23 J. CORP. L. 277 (1998).

18. *Id.*

19. Stephen M. Bainbridge, *Director Primacy and Shareholder Disempowerment*, 119 HARV. L. REV. 1735, 1750 (2006) ("Like many intracorporate contracts, however, the shareholder wealth maximization norm does not easily lend itself to judicial enforcement except in especially provocative situations. Instead, it is enforced indirectly through a complex and varied set of extrajudicial accountability mechanisms, of which shareholder voting is one.").

20. Greenwood, *supra* note 15, at 1052 ("It follows, then, that the separation of ownership and control is not a vaguely illegitimate deprivation of the rightful prerogatives of ownership, but rather a supremely sensible application of the division of labor."); *id.* at 1053 ("We have come then to a solution to the shareholder puzzle. The fictional shareholder reduces politics to administration.").

21. *Id.* at 1052–53 ("If the corporation were run by and for real people, it would be a hotbed of political controversy . . . . If the real people disagree with the fictional representation, the real people may simply be disregarded as not real shareholders.").

22. *See, e.g.*, Bainbridge, *supra* note 19.

23. *Id.* at 1749 ("Active investor involvement in corporate decisionmaking seems likely to disrupt the very mechanism that makes the widely held public corporation practicable: namely, the centralization of essentially nonreviewable decisionmaking authority in the board of directors. The chief economic virtue of the public corporation is . . . that it provides a hierarchical decisionmaking structure well-suited to the problem of operating a large business enterprise with numerous employees, managers, shareholders, creditors, and other constituencies.").

24. *Id.* at 1750. According to Bainbridge, this limited right is negotiated through contract. *Id.* ("Shareholders have certain contractual rights, which include the requirement that directors maximize shareholder wealth as their principal decisionmaking norm."). However, to the extent that corporations are creatures of state law, Bainbridge's contractual analysis fails to justify shareholders as the sole participants in the corporate franchise as set by state law.

25. Stephen M. Bainbridge, *The Case for Limited Shareholder Voting Rights*, 53 UCLA L. REV. 601, 626 (2006).

26. *See* Stephen M. Bainbridge, *Director Primacy: The Means and Ends of Corporate Governance*, 97 NW. U. L. REV. 547, 560 (2003); Stephen M. Bainbridge, *The Board of Directors as Nexus of Contracts*, 88 IOWA L. REV. 1, 33 (2002).

27. Armen A. Alchian & Harold Demsetz, *Production, Information Costs, and Economic Organization*, 62 AM. ECON. REV. 777 (1972).

28. *Id.* at 784.

29. *Id.* at 789 n.14.

30. *Id.*

31. Steven Davidoff Solomon, *Snap's Plan Is Most Unfriendly to Outsiders*, N.Y. TIMES (Feb. 3, 2017), https://www.nytimes.com/2017/02/03/business/dealbook/snap-ipo-plan-evan-spiegel.html.

32. Lucian Bebchuk & Kobi Kastiel, *The Untenable Case for Dual-Class Stock*, 103 VA. L. REV. 585 (2017).

33. Dorothy Shapiro Lund, *Nonvoting Shares and Efficient Corporate Governance*, 71 STAN. L. REV. 687 (2019).

34. Lucian Bebchuk & Scott Hirst, *The Specter of the Giant Three*, 99 B.U. L. REV. 721, 721 (2019) (discussing the "large, steady, and continuing growth of the Big Three index fund managers – BlackRock, Vanguard, and State Street Global Advisor").

35. *See* Lund, *supra* note 33, at 698.

36. Sean J. Griffith, *Opt-In Stewardship: Toward an Optimal Delegation on Mutual Fund Voting Authority*, 98 TEXAS L. REV. 983, 990 (2020) (questioning when mutual funds have a comparative informational advantage over the individual shareholders).

37. *See also* Franklin A. Gevurtz, *Saying Yes: Reviewing Board Decisions to Sell or Merge the Corporation*, 44 FLA. ST. U. L. REV. 437, 502 (2017) ("[T]ermination fees and asset and stock lock-ups can punish shareholders for a negative vote, thereby potentially coercing shareholders into voting for a merger or sale they would otherwise reject.").

38. *See, e.g.*, Basic, Inc. v. Levinson, 485 U.S. 224, 234–35 (1988) (discussing the importance of keeping merger negotiations secret).

39. State law generally impose on corporations a duty to disclose the facts material to their stockholders' decisions to vote on a merger. *See, e.g.*, Arnold v. Soc'y for Sav. Bancorp., Inc., 650 A.2d 1270, 1277 (Del. 1994). The test is generally stated as follows: "[A]n omitted fact is material if there is a substantial likelihood that a reasonable shareholder would consider it important in deciding how to vote. . . . Put another way, there must be a substantial likelihood that the disclosure of the omitted fact would have been viewed by the reasonable investor as having significantly altered the 'total mix' of information made available." Zirn v. VLI Corp., 621 A.2d 773, 778–79 (Del. 1993) (quoting TSC Indus., Inc. v. Northway, Inc., 426 U.S. 438, 449 (1976)). Two cases by the former Delaware vice chancellor Leo Strine, Jr., have highlighted the company's disclosure obligation to shareholders. The vice chancellor enjoined a shareholders' vote in *In re Lear Corp. Shareholders Litigation*, 926 A.2d 94 (Del. Ch. 2007), because the company had failed to disclose the CEO's financial situation that made a buyout personally favorable to him. *See id.* at 98 (concluding that shareholders were "entitled to know that the CEO harbored material economic motivations that differed from their own that could have influenced his negotiating posture"). In *In re Topps Co. Shareholders*

Litigation, 926 A.2d 58 (Del. Ch. 2007), Vice Chancellor Strine held that the company had failed to disclose several critical factors to shareholders about its proposed merger, such as the willingness of the acquirer to retain current management and the seriousness of a competing bid. In both cases, the shareholders' vote was enjoined until shareholders received the appropriate disclosures.

Federal securities regulations provide for more uniform disclosure through § 14 of the 1934 Securities Exchange Act. 15 U.S.C. § 78n (2000). Specific disclosures are provided for in the regulations. *See* 17 C.F.R. §§ 240.14a-3, 240.101 (2007) (Schedule 14A).

40. *See, e.g.,* Bernard S. Black, *Shareholder Passivity Reexamined,* 89 MICH. L. REV. 520, 522 (1990) (attempting, from "within the law-and-economics tradition, to resurrect shareholder voice as a constraint on corporate managers").

41. Jeffrey N. Gordon, *The Rise of Independent Directors in the United States, 1950–2005: Of Shareholder Value and Stock Market Prices,* 59 STAN. L. REV. 1465, 1469 (2007) (arguing that the function of the board changed over the past fifty years from the advising board to the monitoring board, and that director independence became "correspondingly critical").

42. Leo E. Strine, Jr., *Who Bleeds When the Wolves Bite?: A Flesh-and-Blood Perspective on Hedge Fund Activism and Our Strange Corporate Governance System,* 126 YALE L.J. 1870, 1872 (2017) ("[T]he most vocal and active stockholders tend to be the ones with the investment strategies most in tension with the efficient market hypothesis, and often involve hedge funds who only became stockholders after deciding to change the company and who have no prior interest in the company's well-being . . . .").

43. Shareholders may also make money from stock buybacks, where the company pays them for some portion of their stock.

44. *See* ROBERT C. CLARK, CORPORATE LAW § 14.1, at 594 (1986) ("It is often said that the directors' decision to declare dividends is a matter of business judgment.").

45. EASTERBROOK & FISCHEL, *supra* note 1, at 68.

46. *Id.* at 67 ("Creditors have fixed claims, and employees generally negotiate compensation schedules in advance of performance.").

47. And, in fact, many European companies have financial structures that lean more heavily on credit than on equity.

48. 26 U.S.C. § 206(a)(1) (minimum wage); MARK A. ROTHSTEIN ET AL., EMPLOYMENT LAW § 4.13, at 364 (3d ed. 2005) (noting that state wage and hour laws "generally require the payment of wages on a regular periodic basis, either monthly, semi-monthly, or weekly").

49. Thomas Heath, *A Year After Their Tax Cuts, How Have Corporations Spent the Windfall?,* WASH. POST, Dec. 14, 2018 (discussing how the corporations spent their tax cut savings on investments, research, and stock buybacks).

50. EASTERBROOK & FISCHEL, *supra* note 1, at 68.

51. RESTATEMENT OF EMPLOYMENT LAW § 2.01 (AM. LAW INST. 2015) (finding that the contract-law default rule for the employment relationship is that "either party may terminate the relationship with or without cause").

52. As Henry Hansmann and Reinier Kraakman note, this inability to withdraw protects other members of the firm from attacks on the firm by creditors of the individual shareholders. Henry Hansmann & Reinier Kraakman, *The Essential Role of Organizational Law,* 110 YALE L.J. 387, 390 (2000) ("The truly essential aspect of

asset partitioning is, in effect, the reverse of limited liability – namely, the shielding of the assets of the entity from claims of the creditors of the entity's owners or managers.").

53. Margaret M. Blair, *Locking in Capital: What Corporate Law Achieved for Business Organizers in the Nineteenth Century*, 51 UCLA L. REV. 387, 392 (2003) (citing the importance of "resource commitment" or capital lock-in as a critical reason for the success of the corporation as a private enterprise).

54. David G. Yosifon, *Consumer Lock-in and the Theory of the Firm*, 35 SEATTLE U. L. REV. 1429, 1441–42 (2012) ("Our highly robust securities markets, with professional, cheap broker-intermediaries, make stocks a highly liquid investment. In practice, it is not difficult to 'cash-in' an investment in a large, publicly held company, even though one cannot 'cash-in' directly with the corporate treasury."). *See also* Henry G. Manne, *Mergers and the Market for Corporate Control*, 73 J. POL. ECON. 110, 110–11 (1965) (championing the market for corporate control as a check against managerial opportunism).

55. Surveys have shown that only around 5 percent of employees work in more than one job at a time. Andy Puzder, *Does Everyone Have Two Jobs?*, WALL ST. J., July 25, 2018, at A17 ("Bureau of Labor Statistics data show only a small minority of Americans work multiple jobs. That percentage has been around 5% of working Americans since 2010, though it was higher before then.").

56. *See* Lund, *supra* note 33, at 716.

57. Gregory Dow & Louis Putterman, *Why Capital (Usually) Hires Labor: An Assessment of Proposed Explanations, in* EMPLOYEES AND CORPORATE GOVERNANCE 17, 39 (Margaret M. Blair & Mark J. Roe eds., 1999) (contrasting employees, who generally hold only one job at a time, with shareholders, who not only can sell their shares but are also extensively diversified).

58. Norman D. Bishara, Kenneth J. Martin & Randall S. Thomas, *An Empirical Analysis of Noncompetition Clauses and Other Restrictive Postemployment Covenants*, 68 VAND. L. REV. 1, 3 (2015) (noting that "most employment contracts are not publicly available" but that the use of such covenants in CEO contracts has been increasing).

59. The theory of human capital – namely, the value of ongoing knowledge, skill, and abilities to do a particular job well – was first developed by Gary Becker. *See* GARY S. BECKER, HUMAN CAPITAL: A THEORETICAL AND EMPIRICAL ANALYSIS, WITH SPECIAL REFERENCE TO EDUCATION (1964).

60. Margaret M. Blair, *Firm-Specific Human Capital and Theories of the Firm, in* EMPLOYEES AND CORPORATE GOVERNANCE, *supra* note 57, at 58, 62.

61. MARGARET M. BLAIR, OWNERSHIP AND CONTROL: RETHINKING CORPORATE GOVERNANCE FOR THE TWENTY-FIRST CENTURY 257 (1995) ("Employees therefore are also 'residual claimants,' who share in the business risk associated with the enterprise.").

62. For example, a capital investment could be valued at the original contribution plus some inflation/appreciation rate, or it could be valued as a percentage of the value of the ongoing enterprise.

63. *See, e.g.*, Joe Holleman, *Local Walgreens Cashier Surprised in Store by Ellen DeGeneres*, ST. LOUIS POST-DISPATCH (Jan. 4, 2018), https://www.stltoday.com /news/local/columns/joe-holleman/local-walgreens-cashier-surprised-in-store-by -ellen-degeneres/article_b73acb94-2058-53e2-820d-a21ca5e241e7.html.

64. *See, e.g.*, TONY HSIEH, DELIVERING HAPPINESS: A PATH TO PROFITS, PASSION, AND PURPOSE (2010).

65. Matthew Bodie, *The Internet Wants You to Lose Your Job*, Quartz.com (Feb. 3, 2016), https://qz.com/608697/the-internet-wants-you-to-lose-your-job/ (noting that employee misfires on social media affect brand reputation).

66. Mark Anderson, *Entity Exit: Rights, Remedies, and Bounded Rationality*, 17 Hous. Bus. & Tax L.J. 1, 2 (2016) ("A single partner in a partnership at will can cause the dissolution of the partnership by merely expressing her will to cease to be associated with a partnership." (citing Unif. P'ship Act § 31(1)(b) (1914) (superseded 1992))).

67. Econ. Policy Inst., *The Productivity–Pay Gap* (July 2019), https://www.epi.org/productivity-pay-gap/ ("From 1979 to 2018, net productivity rose 69.6 percent, while the hourly pay of typical workers essentially stagnated – increasing only 11.6 percent over 39 years (after adjusting for inflation).").

68. Matthew Yglesias, *Corporate Profit Share of GDP Reaches All-Time High Despite Sharia Socialism*, Slate.com (Dec. 3, 2012), https://slate.com/business/2012/12/profit-share-of-gdp-corporate-profits-after-tax-are-at-an-all-time-high.html (noting that "after-tax corporate profits are at an all-time high as a share of GDP").

69. *See* Dalia Tsuk, *Corporations Without Labor: The Politics of Progressive Corporate Law*, 151 U. Pa. L. Rev. 1861, 1864 (2003) (exploring "how, in the course of the twentieth century, legal scholars and political theorists helped remove the interests of workers (as differentiated from shareholders, officers, and directors) from the core concerns of corporate law and theory").

7. The Argument from Arrow's Theorem

1. *See* Kenneth J. Arrow, Social Choice & Individual Values (2d ed. 1963); *see also* Norman Frohlich & Joe A. Oppenheimer, Modern Political Economy 19–23 (1978) (summarizing the assumptions, conditions, and conclusions of the theorem); Peter C. Ordeshook, Game Theory and Political Theory: An Introduction 62–65 (1986) (providing a concise outline of a proof of the theorem).

2. *See* Frank H. Easterbrook & Daniel R. Fischel, *Voting in Corporate Law*, 26 J.L. & Econ. 395 (1983).

3. *Id.* at 405.

4. *Id.*

5. Frank H. Easterbrook & Daniel R. Fischel, The Economic Structure of Corporate Law 70 (1991). Because the arguments in the article and book are identical, we will refer to the earlier article, Easterbrook & Fischel, *supra* note 2.

6. Easterbrook & Fischel, *supra* note 2, at 405 (citing Kenneth J. Arrow, Social Choice & Individual Values (2d ed. 1963); Duncan Black, The Theory of Committees and Elections (1958)).

7. *Id.*

8. *Id.* This, they mention, is also the reason why the law makes little effort to require firms to pursue goals other than profit maximization. *Id.* at 405–06.

9. Social choice theory and Arrow's theorem have mainly come into legal scholarship under the guise of public choice theory. For summaries of the literature, see Saul Levmore, *Foreword* to Maxwell L. Stearns, Public Choice and Public Law: Readings and Commentary, at xii–xiv (1997); Daniel A. Farber & Philip P. Frickey, Law and Public Choice: A Critical Introduction 38–42 (1991).

10. *See* FROHLICH & OPPENHEIMER, *supra* note 1, at 16.

11. ARROW, *supra* note 1, at 22–23, 51–60.

12. *See id.* (laying out the logical foundations and conclusions for the theorem); *see also* FROHLICH & OPPENHEIMER, *supra* note 1, at 19–23; ORDESHOOK, *supra* note 1, at 62–65. This chapter will borrow terminology from WILLIAM H. RIKER, LIBERALISM AGAINST POPULISM: A CONFRONTATION BETWEEN THE THEORY OF DEMOCRACY AND THE THEORY OF SOCIAL CHOICE 293–98 (1982). For a good summary of the state of social choice theory and Arrow's theorem, see 1 HANDBOOK OF SOCIAL CHOICE AND WELFARE, at ix (Kenneth J. Arrow et al. eds., 2002).

13. *See* RIKER, *supra* note 12, at 295.

14. *Id.* at 117–18.

15. *See id.* at 116–17, 297.

16. *See id.* at 118. The term "irrelevant" is not pejorative, but instead refers to an alternative outside the set from which a group must choose that does not alter the desirability of the other alternatives relative to each other. Grant M. Hayden, *The Limits of Social Choice Theory: A Defense of the Voting Rights Act*, 74 TULANE L. REV. 87, 101 (1999).

17. *See* RIKER, *supra* note 12, at 119, 297.

18. *See* Hayden, *supra* note 16, at 101–02 (describing intransitivity as a voting cycle and explaining the problems with a system displaying this characteristic); Grant M. Hayden, Note, *Some Implications of Arrow's Theorem for Voting Rights*, 47 STAN. L. REV. 295, 299 (1995) (defining intransitivity and stating that it may in essence lead to dictatorial power being exercised in a social choice function by way of agenda control).

19. Easterbrook & Fischel, *supra* note 2, at 405.

20. *See id.*

21. *Id.* at 405–06.

22. HENRY HANSMANN, THE OWNERSHIP OF ENTERPRISE 44 (1996).

23. *Id.* at 41–42.

24. *Id.* at 42.

25. Gregory K. Dow, *The New Institutional Economics and Employment Regulation, in* GOVERNMENT REGULATION OF THE EMPLOYMENT RELATIONSHIP 57, 69 (Bruce E. Kaufman ed., 1997).

26. *Id.* Though he relies on Arrow's theorem as part of a general argument against opening up corporate elections to additional constituencies, Dow seems most worried about cycling in connection with board-level decision-making. *See id.*

27. *See, e.g., id.*

28. Margaret M. Blair & Lynn A. Stout, *A Team Production Theory of Corporate Law*, 85 VA. L. REV. 247 (1999). In their model, people who hope to profit from team production give up some of their rights to the corporation and, in return, the corporation coordinates the activities of the team members and allocates the resulting production in a way that minimizes shirking and rent-seeking. *Id.* at 250–51.

29. *Id.* at 253.

30. *Id.* at 312–15.

31. *Id.* at 313. For their other arguments, see *id.* at 314–15.

32. *See* Kotaro Suzumura, *Introduction, in* 1 HANDBOOK OF SOCIAL CHOICE AND WELFARE, *supra* note 12, at 1, 18–25 (describing decades of work attacking Arrow's theory, but reiterating its continued vitality).

33. *See* Henry Hansmann & Reinier Kraakman, *The Basic Governance Structure, in* THE ANATOMY OF CORPORATE LAW: A COMPARATIVE AND FUNCTIONAL APPROACH 33, 64 (Reinier Kraakman et al. eds., 2004); Henry Hansmann & Reinier Kraakman, *The End of History for Corporate Law*, 89 GEO. L.J. 439, 447–49 (2001).

34. The arguments are drawn, somewhat confusingly for our purposes, from Kenneth Arrow's other work on institutional design, KENNETH J. ARROW, THE LIMITS OF ORGANIZATION (1974).

35. *See* Stephen M. Bainbridge, *Participatory Management Within a Theory of the Firm*, 21 J. CORP. L. 657, 725 (1996).

36. Blair & Stout, *supra* note 28, at 313.

37. This is certainly understandable, since both arguments are related to potential breakdowns in collective decision-making. This is not to say that the authors are conflating the two arguments, just that it is difficult to see whether and to what degree they are relying upon the argument from Arrow's theorem when discussing reasons for limiting the franchise to shareholders.

38. *See* Bainbridge, *supra* note 35, at 725 n.409, 667 n.51.

39. *See* DEL. CODE ANN. tit. 8, § 141(b) (2019) ("The vote of the majority of the directors present at a meeting at which a quorum is present shall be the act of the board of directors unless the certificate of incorporation or the bylaws shall require a vote of a greater number.").

40. *See* Hayden, Note, *supra* note 18, at 305.

41. *See* ORDESHOOK, *supra* note 1, at 56–57 (discussing the Condorcet paradox and its argument that journalistic shorthand such as "the public interest" or "community goals" has no proper place in any adequate theory of political processes); RIKER, *supra* note 12, at 119.

42. Easterbrook & Fischel, *supra* note 2, at 405. One assumes this means choices that are inconsistent with each other, as opposed to inconsistent with some hypothetically "correct" choice (which, as we now know, would not be possible to discern).

43. Or subject to dictatorial control, a state of affairs that is no better in this context. *See* Allan Gibbard, *Manipulation of Voting Rules: A General Result*, 41 ECONOMETRICA 587, 587 (1973); Mark A. Satterthwaite, *Strategy-Proofness and Arrow's Conditions: Existence and Correspondence Theorems for Voting Procedures and Social Welfare Functions*, 10 J. ECON. THEORY 187, 188 (1975).

44. *See* HANSMANN, *supra* note 22, at 41–42.

45. Jeffrey N. Gordon, *Shareholder Initiative: A Social Choice and Game Theoretic Approach to Corporate Law*, 60 U. CIN. L. REV. 347, 351–52 (1991).

46. *Id.* at 359–60.

47. *See id.* at 359–63.

48. *See id.* at 363.

49. *Id.* at 373.

50. Indeed, Gordon makes some of these distinctions between the cycling problem with initiatives and the potential cycling problem that may arise in board elections with a more heterogeneous shareholder electorate. *See id.* at 372–73.

51. *See* Bainbridge, *supra* note 35, at 665 (discussing various explanations, such as investment time and tax bracket, for disagreement over how best to achieve the goal of wealth maximization). If there was complete agreement, there would, of course, be no reason to have board elections in the first place, since we could just ask one of the shareholders to report the shared preference ranking.

52. If it was a cash-out merger offering the highest current cash value of the three options, this preference set would correlate with shareholders interested in short-term profit maximization.

53. This is not to say that it would be difficult to put together a scenario in which an expanded corporate electorate (including constituencies other than shareholders) had a preference profile that led to an intransitive outcome. The point here is that devising such a scenario with shareholders alone is relatively easy, even assuming an identical interest in wealth maximization, and the burden is on those who advance the argument from Arrow's theorem to show that there is a marked difference in the probability of acyclic outcomes with an expanded electorate.

54. *See* Hayden, Note, *supra* note 18, at 299–304 (providing examples of how the Condorcet method, the amendment procedure, the Borda count, and cumulative voting systems all fall prey to Arrow's theorem).

55. *See, e.g., id.* at 312 (arguing that the racial bloc voting requirements of certain claims under the Voting Rights Act may represent a case of "naturally occurring" spectrum agreement that decreases the incidence of cycling); Hayden, *supra* note 16, at 109–32 (arguing that the level of spectrum agreement required in Voting Rights Act claims, while not complete, is sufficient to reduce the incidence of cycling to near zero). As will be discussed, many groups of people associated through a polity or a corporation may have sufficiently common reference points to greatly reduce the incidence of intransitivities.

56. *See* Scott L. Feld & Bernard Grofman, *Partial Single-Peakedness: An Extension and Clarification*, 51 PUB. CHOICE 71, 71 (1986) (explaining that "empirical observations of a wide variety of actual collective decision-making processes indicate that cyclical majorities are very rare"); Bernard Grofman, *Public Choice, Civic Republicanism, and American Politics: Perspectives of a "Reasonable Choice" Modeler*, 71 TEX. L. REV. 1541, 1553 (1993) (noting that cycles are much harder to find than early social choice models have predicted).

57. *See* Richard G. Niemi & Herbert F. Weisberg, *A Mathematical Solution for the Probability of the Paradox of Voting*, 13 BEHAV. SCI. 317, 321 (1968).

58. *See id.* at 322 & tbl.2.

59. *See* Hayden, Note, *supra* note 18, at 306–07; Hayden, *supra* note 16, at 107–08. Although the term spectrum agreement seems to imply some express understanding between voters, it is enough that voter preferences may be arrayed on a common continuum, regardless of whether the voters agreed ahead of time or, indeed, even know about the continuum.

60. Hayden, *supra* note 16, at 107.

61. *See* RIKER, *supra* note 12, at 123–28.

62. *Id.* at 126.

63. *See* DUNCAN BLACK, THE THEORY OF COMMITTEES AND ELECTIONS 19–25 (1958) (discussing proofs of theorems and examples involving single-peaked preference curves); DUNCAN BLACK & R.A. NEWING, COMMITTEE DECISIONS WITH COMPLEMENTARY VALUATION 19–28 (1951) (discussing group voting on two separate issues and proving there can be at most one majority decision); Duncan Black, *On the Rationale of Group Decision-Making*, 56 J. POL. ECON. 23, 23–24 & fig.1 (1948) (explaining and depicting a single-peaked preference profile for a voter with one most desired alternative).

64. *See* BLACK, *supra* note 63, at 125–29.

65. *Id.*

66. *See* Amartya K. Sen, *A Possibility Theorem on Majority Decisions*, 34 ECONOMETRICA 491, 492–95 (1966).

67. *Id.* at 492.

68. *See* Feld & Grofman, *supra* note 56, at 72–73 ("*[I]f even one* individual has non-single-peaked preferences then there can be a paradox of cyclical majorities."); Richard G. Niemi, *Majority Decision-Making with Partial Unidimensionality*, 63 AM. POL. SCI. REV. 488, 488 (1969) ("[T]he preference ordering of every individual must be single peaked" for "majority voting [to] yield a transitive social ordering.").

69. *See* Hayden, *supra* note 16, at 125–26 (providing an example of a preference profile where sixteen of seventeen preference orders are single-peaked, yet a majority vote produces an intransitive outcome).

70. Gerald H. Kramer, *On a Class of Equilibrium Conditions for Majority Rule*, 41 ECONOMETRICA 285, 285 (1973).

71. *See* Niemi, *supra* note 68, at 488.

72. *Id.* at 493–94; Hayden, *supra* note 16, at 127–28 (discussing Niemi's findings). This is counterintuitive, because the likelihood of transitive outcomes decreases as you increase the number of individuals in a profile, assuming an impartial culture. *See* Niemi, *supra* note 68, at 493–94.

73. *See, e.g.*, Dean Jamison & Edward Luce, *Social Homogeneity and the Probability of Intransitive Majority Rule*, 5 J. ECON. THEORY 79, 84–86 (1972); Peter C. Fishburn, *Voter Concordance, Simple Majorities, and Group Decision Methods*, 18 BEHAV. SCI. 364, 371–72 (1973); Hayden, *supra* note 16, at 128–30 (discussing these two studies).

74. *See* Feld & Grofman, *supra* note 56, at 73–79 (extending Niemi's result and finding that a social preference order will be transitive if there is more than a 50 percent probability that a randomly chosen individual would align the alternatives along one existing continuum); Hayden, *supra* note 16, at 130–31 (discussing Feld & Grofman's findings).

75. Niemi, *supra* note 68, at 494.

76. *See* FROHLICH & OPPENHEIMER, *supra* note 1, at 19–20.

77. This is not the way the German system of codetermination is structured. There, shareholders and employees elect their own representatives to the supervisory board in separate elections. This system is discussed more fully in Chapter 11.

78. Easterbrook & Fischel, *supra* note 2, at 405.

79. As should be apparent from the rest of this chapter, however, we are not making that argument.

80. Easterbrook & Fischel, *supra* note 2, at 405.

81. *See* Grofman, *supra* note 56, at 1552.

82. Joshua R. Mourning, Note, *The Majority-Voting Movement: Curtailing Shareholder Disenfranchisement in Corporate Director Elections*, 85 Wash. U. L. Rev. 1143, 1144 (2007). Some shareholders have pressed corporations to change their voting rules so that a director must win a majority of the votes cast in order to win the seat. *See generally id.* at 1143–46 (discussing this movement). However, even under such a "majority-vote" regime, a director who fails to get a majority will stay on until a replacement is chosen or until the majority of shareholders vote to remove the person. *See* Del. Code Ann. tit. 8, § 141(b) (2019) (stating that "[e]ach director shall hold office until such director's successor is elected and qualified or until such director's earlier resignation or removal"). However, some companies have established resignation policies that require directors to resign if they are not elected by the shareholders. *See* Mourning, *supra*, at 1182–85. For criticism of majority voting as an ineffective reform, see Vincent Falcone, Note, *Majority Voting in Director Elections: A Simple, Direct, and Swift Solution?*, 2007 Colum. Bus. L. Rev. 844, 881–82.

83. *See, e.g.*, Del. Code Ann. tit. 8, § 141(d) (2019) (allowing such a staggered election procedure).

84. For some background on structure-induced equilibria, see, *e.g.*, Riker, *supra* note 12.

85. Grofman, *supra* note 56, at 1561–62.

86. *See* Gordon, *supra* note 45, at 372–73.

87. Adolf A. Berle & Gardiner C. Means, The Modern Corporation and Private Property 119–52 (1932).

88. For an empirical examination of the power of incumbent boards to influence elections, see Yair Listokin, *Management Always Wins the Close Ones*, 10 Am. L. & Econ. Rev. 159 (2008).

8.   The Shareholder Franchise and Board Primacy

1. In the early 1990s, for example, a group of scholars rallied around the progressive banner in their critiques. *See, e.g.*, Progressive Corporate Law (Lawrence E. Mitchell ed., 1995).

2. *See* Bernard Grofman, *Public Choice, Civic Republicanism, and American Politics: Perspectives of a "Reasonable Choice" Modeler*, 71 Tex. L. Rev. 1541, 1547–51 (1993). This is not the only way of describing this basic distinction. As we will see later, it may also be at the heart of the difference between direct and representative democracy, and Kenneth Arrow's distinction between consensus and authority decision-making structures.

3. *Id.* at 1549 (citing Cass A. Sunstein, *Beyond the Republican Revival*, 97 Yale L.J. 1539, 1554–55 (1988)).

4. *See id.* For a brief historical survey of republicanism, see Brett H. McDonnell, *Employee Primacy, or Economics Meets Civic Republicanism at Work*, 13 Stan. J. L. Bus. & Fin. 334, 344–47 (2008).

5. Grofman, *supra* note 2, at 1549–50.

6. *Id.* at 1549.

7. *See id.*

8. *See id.* at 1551.

9. These categorizations are our own; we do not mean to imply that the members of each group have adopted these labels or are working in concert.

10. *See, e.g.,* Lucian A. Bebchuk, *The Myth of the Shareholder Franchise*, 93 VA. L. REV. 675, 676 (2007).

11. Stephen M. Bainbridge, *Director Primacy: The Means and Ends of Corporate Governance*, 97 NW. U. L. REV. 547, 560 (2003) [hereinafter Bainbridge, *Director Primacy*]; Stephen M. Bainbridge, *The Board of Directors as Nexus of Contracts*, 88 IOWA L. REV. 1, 33 (2002) [hereinafter Bainbridge, *Nexus*].

12. Bainbridge, *Director Primacy, supra* note 11, at 560 ("[T]o the limited extent to which the corporation is properly understood as a real entity, it is the board of directors that personifies the corporate entity.").

13. Margaret M. Blair & Lynn A. Stout, *A Team Production Theory of Corporate Law*, 85 VA. L. REV. 247, 280 (1999).

14. Bainbridge, *Director Primacy, supra* note 11, at 591–92.

15. Stephen M. Bainbridge, *Director Primacy and Shareholder Disempowerment*, 119 HARV. L. REV. 1735, 1754–57 (2006).

16. Bainbridge, *Director Primacy, supra* note 11, at 572–73.

17. Bainbridge, *supra* note 15, at 1749.

18. Bainbridge, *Director Primacy, supra* note 11, at 563.

19. Blair & Stout, *supra* note 13, at 254 (stating that the team production approach is "consistent with the 'nexus of contracts' approach").

20. *Id.* at 251.

21. *Id.* at 293–94.

22. *Id.*

23. *Id.* at 250 (stating that along with shareholders, other corporate contributors include "[e]xecutives, rank-and-file employees, and even creditors or the local community"); *id.* at 278 (describing participants in the corporation as "share-holders, employees, and perhaps other stakeholders such as creditors or the local community").

24. *Id.* at 250.

25. *Id.* at 280–81.

26. Bainbridge, *supra* note 15; Lynn A. Stout, *The Mythical Benefits of Shareholder Control*, 93 VA. L. REV. 789, 791–92 (2009).

27. Lynn Stout argued in later articles for greater constraints on shareholders. *See, e.g.,* Iman Anabtawi & Lynn Stout, *Fiduciary Duties for Activist Shareholders*, 60 STAN. L. REV. 1255, 1256 (2008) (arguing that corporate law should impose a duty of loyalty on shareholders). She has also echoed the concerns about shareholders' short-term time horizons that drive the proposals of Mitchell and Lipton, and Rosenblum.

28. LAWRENCE E. MITCHELL, CORPORATE IRRESPONSIBILITY: AMERICA'S NEWEST EXPORT (2001); Lawrence E. Mitchell, *A Critical Look at Corporate Governance*, 45 VAND. L. REV. 1263, 1272 (1992).

29. MITCHELL, *supra* note 28, at 112.

30. *Id.*

31. *Id.* at 119.

32. *Id.* at 129 (settling on the quinquennial plan as a "middle ground" proposal that is a "good idea" and "a little less scary to contemplate" than the self-perpetuating board).

33. *See* Martin Lipton & Steven A. Rosenblum, *A New System of Corporate Governance: The Quinquennial Election of Directors*, 58 U. CHI. L. REV. 187, 205–14 (1991).

34. *Id.* at 225; *see also id.* at 229–30.

35. *Id.* at 244–45.

36. *Id.* at 233–40.

37. *Id.* at 235–36.

38. *Id.* at 231. However, the proposal would also eliminate shareholder proposals under SEC Rule 14a-8, as the authors believe that such proposals are "the tool of gadflies who seek to promote special interests." *Id.* at 231–32.

39. Mitchell, *supra* note 28, at 1303.

40. *Id.*

41. MITCHELL, *supra* note 28, at 112.

42. *Id.* at 131. However, Mitchell frames this change as a potential change, rather than an essential one, and he acknowledges that his proposed change to the electorate is not "thoroughly develop[ed]." *Id.* at 130–31.

43. Lawrence E. Mitchell, *The Legitimate Rights of Public Shareholders*, 66 WASH. & LEE L. REV. 1635, 1677 (2009). Again, however, Mitchell acknowledges that the ramifications of this change are "beyond the scope of my task here." *Id.* n.139 (citing again to the quinquennial election proposal of Lipton & Rosenblum, *supra* note 33). In another article, Mitchell also developed an entirely different policy proposal: direct election of the chief executive officer by shareholders, creditors, and employees, each voting as a class. Lawrence E. Mitchell, *On the Direct Election of CEOs*, 32 OHIO N.U. L. REV. 261, 263 (2006). Mitchell argues that the addition of creditors and employees to the voting pool would provide a better-informed, more balanced electorate. *Id.* at 280–82.

44. *See* Iman Anabtawi, *Some Skepticism About Increasing Shareholder Power*, 53 UCLA L. REV. 561, 577–93 (2006) (cataloging the ways in which shareholder interests diverge); Grant M. Hayden & Matthew T. Bodie, *One Share, One Vote and the False Promise of Shareholder Homogeneity*, 30 CARDOZO L. REV. 445, 477–98 (2008) (same).

45. Henry T.C. Hu & Bernard Black, *The New Vote Buying: Empty Voting and Hidden (Morphable) Ownership*, 79 S. CAL. L. REV. 811, 815 (2006); Shaun Martin & Frank Partnoy, *Encumbered Shares*, 2005 U. ILL. L. REV. 775, 778.

46. For example, some shareholders may be in a control group and others may not. *See* Hayden & Bodie, *supra* note 44, at 477–80. Employee and pension-holding share-holders have different interests than nonemployee shareholders. *See id.* at 486–88. And even traditional shareholders may have different time horizons for wealth maximization that cannot be costlessly equalized through existing financial instruments. *See id.* at 492–94.

47. *See* Grant M. Hayden & Matthew T. Bodie, *Arrow's Theorem and the Exclusive Shareholder Franchise*, 62 VAND. L. REV. 1217, 1230–32 (2009).

48. *See* Martin & Partnoy, *supra* note 45, at 778 ("It is simply not true that the 'preferences of [shareholders] are likely to be similar if not identical.'" (quoting Frank H. Easterbrook & Daniel R. Fischel, *Voting in Corporate Law*, 26 J.L. & ECON. 395, 405 (1983))); *see also* Daniel J.H. Greenwood, *Fictional Shareholders: For Whom Are Corporate Managers Trustees, Revisited*, 69 S. CAL. L. REV. 1021, 1052 (1996) ("For fictional shareholders, whatever else the people behind them may want, all want to maximize the value of their shares."); Hayden & Bodie, *supra* note 44, at 477–99.

49. Anabtawi & Stout, *supra* note 27, at 1290–92.

50. Ronald J. Gilson & Curtis J. Milhaupt, *Sovereign Wealth Funds and Corporate Governance: A Minimalist Response to the New Mercantilism*, 60 STAN. L. REV. 1345, 1362–65 (2008).

51. *See* MITCHELL, *supra* note 28, at 99; Bainbridge, *Director Primacy*, *supra* note 11, at 563–74; Blair & Stout, *supra* note 13, at 290–92; Lipton & Rosenblum, *supra* note 33, at 205–14.

52. *See* Bainbridge, *Director Primacy*, *supra* note 11, at 572–73.

53. For an early discussion of the strengths and weaknesses, see THE FEDERALIST NO. 10 (James Madison).

54. For an argument against shareholder proxy proposals on grounds of inefficiency, see Roberta Romano, *Less Is More: Making Institutional Investor Activism a Valuable Mechanism of Corporate Governance*, 18 YALE J. ON REG. 174 (2001).

55. *See* STEPHEN M. BAINBRIDGE, THE NEW CORPORATE GOVERNANCE IN THEORY AND PRACTICE 46–49 (2008). Arrow's models of consensus and authority decision-making are another way of describing this difference between more and less responsive systems of governance. *See* KENNETH J. ARROW, THE LIMITS OF ORGANIZATION 63–79 (1974).

56. *See* Stephen M. Bainbridge, *Participatory Management Within a Theory of the Firm*, 21 J. CORP. L. 657, 725 (1996) ("The resulting conflicts of interest inevitably impede consensus-based decisionmaking within the board."); *see also* BAINBRIDGE, *supra* note 55, at 40–41.

57. *See* Bainbridge, *Director Primacy*, *supra* note 11, at 557–59.

58. *See* BAINBRIDGE, *supra* note 55, at 56.

59. *See id.* at 57.

60. Jeffrey N. Gordon, *Shareholder Initiative: A Social Choice and Game Theoretic Approach to Corporate Law*, 60 U. CIN. L. REV. 347, 351–53, 359–61 (1991).

61. *See* Bainbridge, *supra* note 56, at 667 & n.51, 725 & n.409.

62. *See* BAINBRIDGE, *supra* note 55, at 228–32; Anabtawi, *supra* note 44, at 574–77.

63. *See* Blair & Stout, *supra* note 13, at 291–92.

64. *Id.* at 277.

65. *Id.* at 281.

66. *Id.* at 291.

67. Lipton & Rosenblum, *supra* note 33, at 205–13.

68. *Id.* at 227.

69. *Id.*

70. MITCHELL, *supra* note 28, at 118.

71. *Id.* at 119.

72. *See* BAINBRIDGE, *supra* note 55, at 50–53; Blair & Stout, *supra* note 13, at 313–14; Lipton & Rosenblum, *supra* note 33, at 225–26.

73. *See* Blair & Stout, *supra* note 13, at 313.

74. BAINBRIDGE, *supra* note 55, at 50.

75. *See* Blair & Stout, *supra* note 13, at 313.

76. Indeed, if preferences were completely homogeneous, we could just poll one member of the electorate and skip the rest of the process.

77. For a discussion of the structure of the codetermined board, see Mark J. Roe, *Codetermination and German Securities Markets, in* EMPLOYEES AND CORPORATE GOVERNANCE 194 (Margaret M. Blair & Mark J. Roe eds., 1999).

78. *See* DEL. CODE ANN. tit. 8, § 141(b) (2019) ("The vote of the majority of the directors present at a meeting at which a quorum is present shall be the act of the board of directors unless the certificate of incorporation or the bylaws shall require a vote of a greater number.").

79. In his review of organizational structure, Henry Hansmann placed significant weight on the value of board homogeneity and the corresponding increased costs of decision-making when a board of directors includes nonshareholder directors. *See* HENRY HANSMANN, THE OWNERSHIP OF ENTERPRISE 89–92 (1996). Hansmann was primarily concerned with the potential for long-running conflict between directors who represented different groups of employees. *Id.* at 91–92 & 319 n.5. Scholars have argued that Hansmann's homogeneity theory, like Bainbridge's reliance on the value of authority, is underdeveloped, lacks empirical support, and proves too much. Brett McDonnell, *ESOPs' Failures: Fiduciary Duties when Managers of Employee-Owned Companies Vote to Entrench Themselves,* 2000 COLUM. BUS. L. REV. 199, 232 (suspecting that "Hansmann overestimates the problem"); Justin Schwartz, *Where Did Mill Go Wrong?: Why the Capital-Managed Firm Rather Than the Labor-Managed Enterprise Is the Predominant Organizational Form in Market Economies,* 73 OHIO ST. L.J. 219, 257 (2012).

80. *See* Lynne L. Dallas, *The New Managerialism and Diversity on Corporate Boards of Directors,* 76 TUL. L. REV. 1363, 1388–405 (2002) (documenting the many ways in which increasing board diversity would promote better decision-making); Lisa M. Fairfax, *The Bottom Line on Board Diversity: A Cost-Benefit Analysis of the Business Rationales for Diversity on Corporate Boards,* 2005 WIS. L. REV. 795, 831–33 (documenting studies that link greater diversity with better decision-making); Kristin N. Johnson, *Banking on Diversity: Does Gender Diversity Improve Financial Firms' Risk Oversight?,* 70 SMU L. REV. 327, 330 (2017) ("Scholars have long posited that introducing greater diversity among decision-making authorities, such as the board of directors and senior executives, could lead to superior outcomes."). *See also* Troy A. Paredes, *Too Much Pay, Too Much Deference: Behavioral Corporate Finance, CEOs, and Corporate Governance,* 32 FLA. ST. U. L. REV. 673, 681 (2005) (arguing that boards should appoint a "chief naysayer" whose job is to be a devil's advocate, "punching holes in proposals before the company commits to them").

81. *See* BAINBRIDGE, *supra* note 55, at 45–49.

82. *See id.* at 50.

83. *See* ARROW, *supra* note 55, at 69. This dichotomy roughly follows our earlier discussion of the degree of responsiveness of governance systems.

84. Brett H. McDonnell, *Professor Bainbridge and the Arrowian Moment: A Review of "The New Corporate Governance in Theory and Practice,"* 34 DEL. J. CORP. L. 139, 142–43 (2009) (book review).

85. *See id.*

86. Bainbridge asserts that there is great diversity among different classes of employees but provides little evidence that the asserted diversity is any greater than among shareholders. *See* BAINBRIDGE, *supra* note 55, at 48.

87. *See id.* at 50–52.

88. *See* Hayden & Bodie, *supra* note 47, at 1235–38.

89. *See id.* at 1238.

90. This assumes that the various constituencies would elect their board representatives in separate elections, which is how the German system of codetermination works. *See*

Jean J. du Plessis & Otto Saenger, *The Supervisory Board as Company Organ, in* GERMAN CORPORATE GOVERNANCE IN INTERNATIONAL AND EUROPEAN CONTEXT 105, 133–53 (Jean J. du Plessis et al. eds., 3d ed. 2017). But the point here would be equally applicable in an election in which all constituencies vote in the same election and we need to decide how much weight to assign to each vote.

91. *See* Hayden & Bodie, *supra* note 44, at 453.

92. *See id.* at 453–54.

93. *See id.* at 454–56.

94. *See id.* at 460–62.

95. *See id.* at 447–48.

96. This depends, of course, on the type of corporation. The customers of a utility company, for example, are clearly interested in the corporation and would be relatively easy to identify. *See* HANSMANN, *supra* note 79, at 168–76 (making the case that a consumer-owned electric cooperative could allow consumers to avoid both the costs of monopoly and the costs of rate regulation); *see also* Debra C. Jeter, Randall S. Thomas & Harwell Wells, *Democracy and Dysfunction: Rural Electric Cooperatives and the Surprising Persistence of the Separation of Ownership and Control*, 70 ALA. L. REV. 361, 367 (2018) (drawing upon Hansmann's work).

97. James Madison described this as the danger of majority factions. THE FEDERALIST NO. 10 (James Madison).

98. In the United States, this meant, among other things, dividing the government into three branches with checks on each other, dividing the federal legislature into two chambers, and making one of those chambers (the Senate) less responsive to the people. The substantive protections are embodied in the Bill of Rights and some of the subsequent amendments to the Constitution. *See, e.g.,* Gerhard Casper, *An Essay in Separation of Powers: Some Early Versions and Practices*, 30 WM. & MARY L. REV. 211, 211–24 (1989).

99. For a discussion of protections for corporate minority shareholders, see Anupam Chander, *Minorities, Shareholder and Otherwise*, 113 YALE L.J. 119, 119–65 (2003).

100. *See id.* at 143–45.

101. *See id.* at 130.

102. *See* BAINBRIDGE, *supra* note 55, at 228–30.

103. *See* Bainbridge, *Director Primacy, supra* note 11, at 563.

104. *See* Blair & Stout, *supra* note 13, at 288.

105. *See id.*

106. *See id.*

107. *See id.* at 313.

108. *See id.* at 313–14.

109. *See* Roberta Romano, *The States as a Laboratory: Legal Innovation and State Competition for Corporate Charters*, 23 YALE J. ON REG. 209, 215 tbl.1 (2006) (finding that thirty-one states have constituency statutes).

110. New York, for example, provides that when considering a change or potential change in the control of the corporation, a director "shall be entitled to consider" the effects that the corporation's actions may have upon the corporation's various stakeholders, including current employees, retired employees, customers, creditors, and the communities in which it does business. N.Y. BUS. CORP. LAW § 717(b) (McKinney 2019).

111. For a summary of the arguments for and against constituency statutes, see Brett H. McDonnell, *Corporate Constituency Statutes and Employee Governance*, 30 Wm. Mitchell L. Rev. 1227, 1232–36 (2004).

112. Lawrence E. Mitchell, *A Theoretical and Practical Framework for Enforcing Corporate Constituency Statutes*, 70 Tex. L. Rev. 579 (1992).

113. *See, e.g., id.* at 581.

114. *See, e.g.*, N.Y. Bus. Corp. Law § 717(b) (McKinney 2019) ("Nothing in this paragraph shall create any duties owed by any director to any person or entity to consider or afford any particular weight to any of the foregoing or abrogate any duty of the directors, either statutory or recognized by common law or court decisions.").

115. Mitchell, *supra* note 112, at 580 n.4; *see also id.* at 581 ("The principal criticism of rejecting this traditional relationship is that authorizing the board to consider constituencies that have no monitoring or enforcement powers would leave the board accountable to nobody."); Mark J. Roe, *The Shareholder Wealth Maximization Norm and Industrial Organization*, 149 U. Pa. L. Rev. 2063, 2065 (2001) ("[A] stakeholder measure of managerial accountability could leave managers so much discretion that managers could easily pursue their own agenda, one that might maximize neither shareholder, employee, consumer, nor national wealth, but only their own.").

116. *See* David Millon, *Communitarianism in Corporate Law: Foundations and Law Reform Strategies*, in Progressive Corporate Law, *supra* note 1, at 1, 30 ("However attractive [the constituency] model might be in theory, communitarian scholars have yet to show persuasively that it could function effectively in practice."); Katherine Van Wezel Stone, *Employees as Stakeholders Under State Non-Shareholder Constituency Statutes*, 21 Stetson L. Rev. 45, 70 (1991) (noting that constituency statutes provide "very little" actual protection to employees and other constituents). Some have applied this criticism more broadly to progressive communitarian efforts as a whole. David Millon, *New Game Plan or Business as Usual? A Critique of the Team Production Model of Corporate Law*, 86 Va. L. Rev. 1001, 1040 (2000) [hereinafter Millon, *New Game Plan*] ("[P]rogressives have yet to devise a sufficiently rigorous analytical framework to structure director decisionmaking in cases in which shareholder and nonshareholder interests conflict.").

117. *See, e.g.*, Blair & Stout, *supra* note 13, at 286–87, 298.

118. *Id.* at 312.

119. *See id.* at 313–14.

120. *Id.* at 313.

121. *Id.*

122. *Id.* at 314.

123. *See id.* at 314–15.

124. *Cf.* Millon, *New Game Plan*, *supra* note 116, at 1019 ("At the very least, under a [team production model]-based conception of the board's role, one might expect the board to have the power and duty to veto shareholders' decisions that harm nonshareholder constituencies.").

125. Shareholder primacists themselves would dispute that the model is shortsighted. For example, Reinier Kraakman and Henry Hansmann characterize the goal of shareholder primacy as "striv[ing] to increase long-term shareholder value."

Henry Hansmann & Reinier Kraakman, *The End of History for Corporate Law*, 89 Geo L.J. 439, 439 (2001).

126. Lipton & Rosenblum, *supra* note 33, at 215.

127. *Id.* at 227–28 (arguing that "[t]he quinquennial system would benefit the corporation's other constituencies, which prosper if the enterprise's business operations prosper over the long term").

128. *Id.* at 228.

129. *See* MITCHELL, *supra* note 28, at 3, 111–12.

130. *See, e.g., id.* at 4–6.

131. *Id.* at 20–27.

132. *Id.* at 47–48 (comparing corporations to the sharks from the film *Deep Blue Sea* and noting that "the sharks ran amok threatening anyone that might come in their path").

133. *Id.* at 132.

134. *Id.* at 112.

135. *Id.* at 130–31.

136. *Id.*

137. Stephen M. Bainbridge, *In Defense of the Shareholder Wealth Maximization Norm: A Reply to Professor Green*, 50 WASH. & LEE L. REV. 1423, 1423–25, 1442–43 (1993).

138. Bainbridge, *Director Primacy*, *supra* note 11, at 557–58, 574 (noting the difficulty of shareholder collective action when disagreements exist as to what maximizes value, and contrasting this difficulty with the ease of director primacy when the directors are bound to seek shareholder wealth maximization alone).

139. *Id.* at 579 (arguing that, given the opportunity in a hypothetical negotiation to choose default rules for corporations, a shareholder would choose shareholder wealth maximization as the ideal option).

140. *See* Bainbridge, *supra* note 15, at 1749.

141. Bainbridge, *Nexus*, *supra* note 11, at 28–29.

142. *See* Blair & Stout, *supra* note 13, at 280–81.

143. Bainbridge, *Nexus*, *supra* note 11, at 33 (emphasis omitted).

144. ADOLF A. BERLE & GARDINER C. MEANS, THE MODERN CORPORATION AND PRIVATE PROPERTY 278 (1932).

9.   A Firm-Based Approach to Corporate Voting Rights

1. Oliver Hart, *An Economist's Perspective on the Theory of the Firm*, 89 COLUM. L. REV. 1757, 1757–65 (1989) (discussing various theories of the firm).

2. ERIC W. ORTS, BUSINESS PERSONS: A LEGAL THEORY OF THE FIRM (2013); Scott E. Masten, *A Legal Basis for the Firm*, 4 J.L. ECON. & ORG. 181 (1988).

3. Friedrich A. Hayek, *The Use of Knowledge in Society*, 35 AM. ECON. REV. 519, 520 (1945).

4. Ronald H. Coase, *The Nature of the Firm*, 4 ECONOMICA 386, 388 (1937) (quoting D.H. ROBERTSON, THE CONTROL OF INDUSTRY 85 (1930)).

5. Reza Dibadj, *Reconceiving the Firm*, 26 CARDOZO L. REV. 1459, 1462 (2005) ("The predominant model of microeconomics, neoclassical price theory, assumes simply that the firm is a black box that maximizes profitability.").

6. Edward B. Rock & Michael L. Wachter, *Islands of Conscious Power: Law, Norms, and the Self-Governing Corporation*, 149 U. PA. L. REV. 1619, 1631 (2001).

7. Coase, *supra* note 4.

8. *Id.* at 388.

9. *Id.* at 390–92.

10. *Id.* at 387.

11. *Id.* at 403.

12. *Id.*

13. *Id.* at 404.

14. *Id.*

15. *See* Eric W. Orts, *Shirking and Sharking: A Legal Theory of the Firm*, 16 YALE L. & POLY REV. 265, 296–97 (1998).

16. Armen A. Alchian & Harold Demsetz, *Production, Information Costs, and Economic Organization*, 62 AM. ECON. REV. 777, 777 (1972) ("When a lumber mill employs a cabinetmaker, cooperation between specialists is achieved within a firm, and when a cabinetmaker purchases wood from a lumberman, the cooperation takes place across markets (or between firms).").

17. *Id.* ("To speak of managing, directing, or assigning workers to various tasks is a deceptive way of noting that the employer continually is involved in renegotiation of contracts on terms that must be acceptable to both parties.").

18. *Id.*

19. *Id.* ("Long-term contracts between employer and employee are not the essence of the organization we call a firm.").

20. *Id.* at 779.

21. *Id.* at 780.

22. *Id.* at 782–83.

23. Alchian and Demsetz set forth the following characteristics of the firm: "(a) joint input production, (b) several input owners, (c) one party who is common to all the contracts of the joint inputs, (d) who has rights to renegotiate any input's contract independently of contracts with other input owners, (e) who holds the residual claim, and (f) who has the right to sell his central contractual residual status." *Id.* at 783.

24. *Id.* at 789 n.14.

25. OLIVER E. WILLIAMSON, THE ECONOMIC INSTITUTIONS OF CAPITALISM: FIRMS, MARKETS, RELATIONAL CONTRACTING (1985); Jeffrey T. Macher & Barak D. Richman, *Transaction Cost Economics: An Assessment of Empirical Research in the Social Sciences*, 10 BUS. & POL. 1 (2008) (discussing the transaction costs approach).

26. Oliver E. Williamson, *Why Law, Economics, and Organization?*, 1 ANN. REV. L. & SOC. 369, 373 (2005) ("Governance problems are posed when incomplete contracts (to include unforeseen contingencies) are combined with opportunism.").

27. George S. Geis, *The Space Between Markets and Hierarchies*, 95 VA. L. REV. 99, 153 (2009) ("Oliver Williamson has significantly expanded upon Coase's initial insight by discussing the importance of bundling relationship-specific assets into a firm to avoid counterparty opportunism, and, more generally, by showing how a proper conception of transaction costs should include both the direct costs of managing relationships and the opportunity costs of suboptimal governance decisions.").

28. *See* WILLIAMSON, *supra* note 25, at 114–15; OLIVER E. WILLIAMSON, THE MECHANISMS OF GOVERNANCE 47–48 (1996).

29. *See* OLIVER HART, FIRMS, CONTRACTS, AND FINANCIAL STRUCTURE (1995); Sanford Grossman & Oliver Hart, *The Costs and Benefits of Ownership: A Theory of Vertical and Lateral Integration*, 94 J. POL. ECON. 691 (1986); Oliver Hart & John Moore, *Incomplete Contracts and Renegotiation*, 56 ECONOMETRICA 755 (1988); Oliver Hart & John Moore, *Property Rights and the Nature of the Firm*, 98 J. POL. ECON. 1119 (1990).

30. D. Gordon Smith, *The Critical Resource Theory of Fiduciary Duty*, 55 VAND. L. REV. 1399, 1404–05 (2002) ("The central insight of the property rights theory of the firm is that an appropriate allocation of ownership rights over the assets of a firm reduces the likelihood that one party will unfairly take advantage of the other participants within the firm.").

31. Indeed, Margaret Blair offers the following critique: "The tendency in the transactions cost literature has been to recognize that firm-specific human capital raises similar questions, but then to sidestep the implications of these questions for corporate governance." Margaret M. Blair, *Firm-Specific Human Capital and Theories of the Firm, in* EMPLOYEES AND CORPORATE GOVERNANCE 58, 66 (Margaret M. Blair & Mark J. Roe eds., 2000).

32. Raghuram G. Rajan & Luigi Zingales, *Power in a Theory of the Firm*, 113 Q.J. ECON. 387, 390 (1998).

33. *Id.* at 388.

34. *Id.*

35. Smith, *supra* note 30, at 1404 ("[T]the critical resource theory reveals that the beneficiary's vulnerability emanates from an inability to protect against opportunism by the fiduciary with respect to the critical resource.").

36. *See* Érica Gorga & Michael Halberstam, *Knowledge Inputs, Legal Institutions, and Firm Structure: Towards a Knowledge-Based Theory of the Firm*, 101 NW. U. L. REV. 1123 (2007); Sarah Kaplan et al., *Knowledge-Based Theories of the Firm: A Review and Extension*, 23 ACAD. MGMT. REV. 242 (2002). *See also* Katherine V.W. Stone, *Knowledge at Work: Disputes Over the Ownership of Human Capital in the Changing Workplace*, 34 CONN. L. REV. 721 (2002) (discussing legal conceptions that govern the ownership of human capital within the workplace).

37. For a discussion of explicit versus tacit knowledge, see Ikujiro Nonaka et al., *A Theory of Organizational Knowledge Creation: Understanding the Dynamic Process of Creating Knowledge, in* HANDBOOK OF ORGANIZATIONAL LEARNING & KNOWLEDGE 491, 494 (Meinolf Dierkes, et al. eds., 2001). Gorga and Halberstam classify knowledge into three types: knowledge embedded in physical assets, knowledge embedded in the organizational structure or the group of individuals that constitute the firm, and specialized knowledge embedded in the individual. Gorga & Halberstam, *supra* note 36, at 1141–42. As they explain, "[t]he way the firm develops the knowledge it will use in its production process and the extent that firm can bind this knowledge to its structure will influence its organizational structure." *Id.* at 1140.

38. Gorga & Halberstam, *supra* note 36, at 1137 (criticizing the property rights theory for failing to account for the importance of employees as assets).

39. *Id.* at 1173–83.

40. *Id.* at 1183–92. *Cf.* Oren Bar-Gill & Gideon Parchomovsky, *Law and Boundaries of Technology Intensive Firms*, 157 U. Pa. L. Rev. 1649, 1686–88 (2009) (discussing the role of covenants not to compete in managing innovation within the firm).

41. Thomas McInerney, *Theory of the Firm and Corporate Governance*, 2004 Colum. Bus. L. Rev. 135.

42. *See, e.g.*, Rajan & Zingales, *supra* note 32, at 424–25 (arguing that there is "ample opportunity for gains from trade" between economics and sociology, as sociologists have studied the role of power within organizations "in some detail"); D. Gordon Smith & Brayden G. King, *Contracts as Organizations*, 51 Ariz. L. Rev. 1 (2009) (comparing organizational theories with the traditional legal and economic theories of contract and firm).

43. *See, e.g.*, Alfred D. Chandler, Jr., The Visible Hand: The Managerial Revolution in American Business 1–12 (1977) (discussing the role of middle- and upper-management in coordinating large firms and their employees).

44. *See* Paul S. Adler & Charles Heckscher, *Towards Collaborative Community, in* The Firm as a Collaborative Community: Reconstructing Trust in the Knowledge Economy 11 (Charles Heckscher & Paul S. Adler eds., 2006).

45. *Id.* at 39–44, 54–59.

46. *Id.* at 64–65 (discussing the Walmart approach).

47. *See* D. Gordon Smith & Cynthia A. Williams, Business Organizations 53 (2004) ("[N]o formalities are required to form a partnership."); Christine Hurt, *Partnership Lost*, 53 U. Rich. L. Rev. 491, 497 (2019) ("Partnerships existed at common law in England and in the United States before partnership acts were promulgated in the 1800s.").

48. *See, e.g.*, Bass v. Bass, 814 S.W.2d 38, 41 (Tenn. 1991) (holding that "it is not essential that the parties actually intend to become partners").

49. Unif. P'ship Act § 6(1), 6 U.L.A. 526 (1995); Rev. Unif. P'ship Act § 202(a) (amended 1997).

50. *See, e.g.*, Ingram v. Deere, 288 S.W.3d 886, 891 (Tex. 2009); Holmes v. Lerner, 88 Cal. Rptr. 2d 130 (Ct. App. 1999); Smith v. Redd, 593 So. 2d 989, 991 (Miss. 1991).

51. Unif. P'ship Act § 18(e), 6 U.L.A. 526 (1995); Rev. Unif. P'ship Act § 401(f) (amended 1997).

52. *See* Unif. P'ship Act § 18(h), 6 U.L.A. 526 (1995); Rev. Unif. P'ship Act § 401 (j) (amended 1997).

53. *See, e.g.*, Day v. Sidley & Austin, 394 F. Supp. 986, 992 (D.D.C. 1975) (discussing how "statutory rules governing the rights and duties of the partners are 'subject to any agreement between them'").

54. *See* Rev. Unif. Ltd. P'ship Act § 303 (amended 1985), 6A U.L.A. 144–45 (1995). However, under the original Uniform Limited Partnership Act, limited partners could be subject to liability as managing partners if they participated in governance. Unif. Ltd. P'ship Act § 7 (1916), 6A U.L.A. 336 (1995) ("A limited partner shall not become liable as a general partner unless . . . he takes part in the control of the business.").

55. Larry E. Ribstein, *The Evolving Partnership*, 26 J. Corp. L. 819, 843 (2001).

56. *See* Donahue v. Rodd Electrotype Co. of New England, 328 N.E.2d 505, 511 (Mass. 1975) (defining closely held corporations as having "(1) a small number of stockholders; (2) no ready market for the corporate stock; and (3) substantial majority

stockholder participation in the management, direction and operations of the corporation").

57. Preferred stock is particularly common in start-up corporations. Venture capital investors prefer to invest with preferred stock, which converts into common stock with multiple voting shares if certain triggers are reached. William W. Bratton, *Venture Capital on the Downside: Preferred Stock and Corporate Control*, 100 MICH. L. REV. 891, 892 (2002) (noting that "[c]onvertible preferred stock is the dominant financial contract in the venture capital market").

58. *See, e.g.,* FRANKLIN A. GEVURTZ, CORPORATION LAW 486–96 (2000).

59. Perhaps the most famous example of such a trust involves the Ringling family of circus fame. *See* Ringling Bros.-Barnum & Bailey Combined Shows, Inc. v. Ringling, 53 A.2d 441, 447 (Del. 1947) (upholding such a trust).

60. *See, e.g.,* Wilkes v. Springside Nursing Home, Inc., 353 N.E.2d 657 (Mass. 1976) (finding "no legitimate business purpose" in the majority's decision to suspend a minority shareholder's salary, fail to reelect him as a director, and fail to appoint him as an officer); Leslie v. Boston Software Collaborative, Inc., 14 Mass. L. Rptr. 379 (Mass. Super. Ct. 2002) (minority shareholder terminated from his position as treasurer by majority shareholders).

61. *See* Douglas K. Moll, *Shareholder Oppression & Dividend Policy in the Close Corporation*, 60 WASH. & LEE L. REV. 841 (2003); Douglas K. Moll, *Shareholder Oppression v. Employment at Will in the Close Corporation: The Investment Model Solution*, 1999 U. ILL. L. REV. 517 (1999). For further discussion on the protection of minority shareholders vis-à-vis the protection of political minorities, see Anupam Chander, *Minorities, Shareholder and Otherwise*, 113 YALE L.J. 119 (2003).

62. Dorothy S. Lund, *Nonvoting Shares and Efficient Corporate Governance*, 71 STAN. L. REV. 687 (2019).

63. STEPHEN M. BAINBRIDGE, CORPORATION LAW & ECONOMICS 66–67 (2002) ("[P]referred stock may have a preference over common stock with respect to dividends and/or liquidation."). Preferred shares have often been ignored in the debate about shareholder wealth maximization, with the assumption that the shareholders in question are the holders of common stock. *See id.* at 66 (noting that preferred stock is "an odd beast, neither wholly fish nor wholly fowl"); William W. Bratton & Michael L. Wachter, *A Theory of Preferred Stock*, 161 U. PA. L. REV. 1815, 1820 (2013) ("Preferred stock sits on a fault line between two great private law paradigms, corporate law and contract law. It is neither one nor the other; rather, it draws on both.").

64. *See* Zohar Goshen & Richard Squire, *Principal Costs: A New Theory for Corporate Law and Governance*, 117 COLUM. L. REV. 767, 773 (2017) ("ecause the impact of a given governance structure on control costs is firm-specific, there is no particular governance structure that can be described as intrinsically good, bad, welfare enhancing, or inefficient.").

65. *See, e.g.,* Accountable Capitalism Act, S. 3348, 115th Cong. (2018); Reward Work Act, S. 2605, 115th Cong. (2018).

66. Hon. Leo E. Strine, Jr., *The Dangers of Denial: The Need for a Clear-Eyed Understanding of the Power and Accountability Structure Established by the Delaware General Corporation Law*, 50 WAKE FOREST L. REV. 761, 763–66 (2015); *see also* Hon. Leo E. Strine, Jr., *Our Continuing Struggle with the Idea*

That For-Profit Corporations Seek Profit, 47 WAKE FOREST L. REV. 135, 135–36 (2012) ("[T]he continued failure of our societies to be clear-eyed about the role of the for-profit corporation endangers the public interest.").

67. Smith, *supra* note 30, at 1458 (contemplating that "the key residual ownership right in the corporation is the right to elect directors").

68. LARRY E. RIBSTEIN, THE RISE OF THE UNCORPORATION 4 (2010) ("The corporation undeniably has driven business growth in the United States since the Industrial Revolution.").

69. William A. Klein, *The Modern Business Organization: Bargaining Under Constraints*, 91 YALE L.J. 1521, 1521 (1982) (suggesting that "the most useful way to analyze the modern business enterprise is to interpret the terms of the economic arrangements of a firm (partnership, corporation, cooperative) and the terms of the related economic arrangements that should not be analyzed separately from the firm (distributorship, loan agreement, employment contracts) as a series of bargains subject to constraints and made in contemplation of a long-term relationship").

70. For the beginnings of the debate over the separation of ownership and control, see ADOLF A. BERLE & GARDINER C. MEANS, THE MODERN CORPORATION AND PRIVATE PROPERTY (1932). *See also* Michael C. Jensen & William H. Meckling, *Theory of the Firm: Managerial Behavior, Agency Costs and Ownership Structure*, 3 J. FIN ECON. 305 (1976) (discussing the problem of agency costs in light of the separation of ownership and control).

71. *See, e.g.*, Lucian Bebchuk, *The Case for Increasing Shareholder Power*, 118 HARV. L. REV. 883 (2005).

72. *See, e.g.*, Stephen M. Bainbridge, *Director Primacy: The Means and Ends of Corporate Governance*, 97 NW. U. L. REV. 547, 550 (2003); Martin Lipton & William Savitt, *The Many Myths of Lucian Bebchuk*, 93 VA. L. REV. 733, 754 (2007); Lynn A. Stout, *The Mythical Benefits of Shareholder Control*, 93 VA. L. REV. 789, 804–05 (2007).

73. *See, e.g.*, Margaret M. Blair & Lynn A. Stout, *A Team Production Theory of Corporate Law*, 85 VA. L. REV. 247, 313 (1999).

74. *See* Grant Hayden & Matthew T. Bodie, *Shareholder Democracy and the Curious Turn Toward Board Primacy*, 51 WM. & MARY L. REV. 2071, 2113 (2010) (discussing the "strange turn" against stakeholder board representation).

75. *See* Bengt Holmstrom, *The Firm as a Subeconomy*, 15 J.L. ECON. & ORG. 74, 80 (1999) ("When contracts are incomplete in the sense that they cannot incorporate all future contracting opportunities, governance becomes consequential.").

76. *See, e.g.*, FRANK H. EASTERBROOK & DANIEL R. FISCHEL, THE ECONOMIC STRUCTURE OF CORPORATE LAW 67–69 (1991); Benjamin Means, *A Contractual Approach to Shareholder Oppression Law*, 79 FORDHAM L. REV. 1161, 1197 (2010) (discussing the problem of "shareholder oppression" and vulnerability, and the inability of contracts to unequivocally protect such shareholders).

77. *See* Margaret M. Blair, *Locking in Capital: What Corporate Law Achieved for Business Organizers in the Nineteenth Century*, 51 UCLA L. REV. 387, 392 (2003) (citing the importance of "resource commitment" or capital lock-in as a critical reason for the success of the corporation as a private enterprise).

78. *See* Kent Greenfield, *The Place of Workers in Corporate Law*, 39 B.C. L. REV. 283, 302 (1998) (noting that firm-specific skills "make a worker more valuable to her present employer, but also make her more vulnerable to a firm's opportunistic behavior"); Andrew Keay, *Stakeholder Theory in Corporate Law: Has It Got What It Takes?*, 9 RICH. J. GLOBAL L. & BUS. 249, 368 (2010) ("For instance, employees may make an investment in corporations by way of undergoing specialised training that might not be able to be used elsewhere in other employment.").

79. As late as the nineteenth century, employees worked for terms as long as a year and were not entitled to any contractual payment if they left before the end. *See, e.g.*, Stark v. Parker, 19 Mass. (2 Pick.) 267, 292–94 (1824) (denying any contractual recovery for an employee who left after nine months of a twelve-month job); Britton v. Turner, 6 N.H. 481, 491–92 (1834) (denying contractual recovery but allowing for recovery under restitution). Now, however, wage and hour laws require payment for time worked and periodic payments made to the employee. *See generally* Fair Labor Standards Act of 1938, Pub. L. No. 75-718, 52 Stat. 1060 (codified as amended at 29 U.S.C. §§ 201–219 (2012)).

80. There may be certain exceptions in unusual situations. *See* HENRY HANSMANN, THE OWNERSHIP OF ENTERPRISE 149–223 (1996) (discussing specific instances of customer-owned enterprises); David G. Yosifon, *The Consumer Interest in Corporate Law*, 43 U.C. DAVIS L. REV. 253 (2009) [hereinafter Yosifon, *Consumer Interest*] (arguing that consumers are inadequately represented in corporate governance); David G. Yosifon, *Consumer Lock-in and the Theory of the Firm*, 35 SEATTLE U. L. REV. 1429, 1430 (2012) [hereinafter Yosifon, *Lock-in*] (concluding that "a departure from the shareholder wealth maximization norm and an embrace of a multi-stakeholder corporate governance regime may be necessary to overcome agency problems associated with consumer lock-in").

81. *See generally* Coase, *supra* note 4, at 401–05.

82. *See id.* at 403 ("We can best approach the question of what constitutes a firm in practice by considering the legal relationship normally called that of 'master and servant' or 'employer and employee'.").

83. *See* Alchian & Demsetz, *supra* note 16, at 778 (describing the firm as a "centralized contractual agent in a team production process").

84. *Id.* at 780.

85. *See* Blair & Stout, *supra* note 73, at 275 (analyzing the "team production problem" arising "when a number of individuals must invest firm-specific resources to produce a nonseparable output").

86. *See id.* at 249 ("If the team members' investments are firm-specific . . . and if output from the enterprise is nonseparable, . . . serious problems can arise in determining how any economic surpluses generated by team production . . . should be divided.").

87. *See id.* at 277 ("Providers of financial capital – shareholders and even, potentially, some creditors – are, by this agreement, just as 'stuck' in the firm as are providers of specialized human capital.").

88. *Id.* at 261.

89. *See id.* at 269 (arguing that "employees, shareholders, and executives" are the main players on the corporate "team").

90. *But cf.* Alan J. Meese, *The Team Production Theory of Corporate Law: A Critical Assessment*, 43 WM. & MARY L. REV. 1629, 1652–55 (2002) (arguing that "[t]here is no doubt that creditors who loan money to publicly held corporations thereby make a team-specific investment" but that they are "less vulnerable to opportunism when trading with publicly held corporations" when compared to other team members).

91. The California Supreme Court changed its definition of employment to focus on whether the worker is engaged in the primary business of the firm. Using the so-called ABC test, the court held that a worker is an independent contractor only if (A) the workers is not controlled by the hiring entity in the performance of the work, (B) the worker "performs work that is outside the usual course of the hiring entity's business," and (C) that the worker is "customarily engaged in an independently established trade, occupation, or business." Dynamex Operations W. v. Superior Court, 416 P.3d 1, 40 (Cal. 2018). The change has now been codified. Cal. Assemb. B. 5, Sept. 18, 2019 (amending CAL. LAB. CODE § 2750.3).

92. *See* Yosifon, *Consumer Interest, supra* note 80, at 259 (discussing the cabined role of some consumers in the transacting process).

93. *See id.* at 265 ("If the activities and inputs of those participants are adequately coordinated, their collective output can be qualitatively different and vastly larger than the sum of what each individual could produce separately.").

94. Some skeptics of shareholder primacy have advocated specifically for employee governance rights. KENT GREENFIELD, THE FAILURE OF CORPORATE LAW: FUNDAMENTAL FLAWS AND PROGRESSIVE POSSIBILITIES 112 (2006) (advocating for a special role for employees in corporate law, including the possibility of board representation); Brett H. McDonnell, *Strategies for an Employee Role in Corporate Governance*, 46 WAKE FOREST L. REV. 429, 430–31 (2011) (evaluating "a number of possible strategies for creating a role for employees in corporate governance"); *see also* Brett H. McDonnell, *Employee Primacy, or Economics Meets Civic Republicanism at Work*, 13 STAN. J.L. BUS. & FIN. 334, 334 (2008) (promoting employee primacy); Marleen A. O'Connor, *Restructuring the Corporation's Nexus of Contracts: Recognizing A Fiduciary Duty to Protect Displaced Workers*, 69 N. C. L. REV. 1189 (1991); Marleen O'Connor, *Labor's Role in the American Corporate Governance Structure*, 22 COMP. LAB. L. & POLY J. 97 (2000). Others have noted that employees have a stronger or the strongest case among stakeholders for participation in governance. David Millon, *Communitarianism in Corporate Law: Foundations and Law Reform Strategies, in* PROGRESSIVE CORPORATE LAW 1, 14 (Lawrence E. Mitchell ed., 1995) (noting that "[t]he most compelling theoretical arguments for nonshareholder protection have focused on employees," and that "the relative inadequacy of bargaining power and other disadvantages may more seriously impede bargained-for protection for employees than for other nonshareholder groups").

95. *See* Blair & Stout, *supra* note 73, at 275 ("[T]he public corporation is not so much a 'nexus of contracts' (explicit or implicit) as a 'nexus of firm-specific investments,' in which several different groups contribute unique and essential resources to the corporate enterprise, and who each find it difficult to protect their contribution through explicit contracts.").

96. *See, e.g.*, Robert P. Bartlett III, *Shareholder Wealth Maximization as Means to an End*, 38 SEATTLE U. L. REV. 255, 296 (2015) ("[C]ourts should revert to their

traditional focus on policing against the bargaining failures that can occur when investors use directors to address the incomplete contracting challenges that are replete in corporate finance."); Frederick Tung, *Leverage in the Board Room: The Unsung Influence of Private Lenders in Corporate Governance*, 57 UCLA L. Rev. 115, 119 (2009) [hereinafter Tung, *Leverage*] (arguing that "bank creditors and other private lenders often enjoy significant oversight and influence over managerial decisions"). For a discussion of the possible expansion of fiduciary duties to creditors, see Frederick Tung, *The New Death of Contract: Creeping Corporate Fiduciary Duties for Creditors*, 57 Emory L.J. 809, 814–15 (2008) [hereinafter Tung, *Fiduciary Duties*].

97. *See* Hansmann, *supra* note 80, at 149–68 (discussing consumer ownership); Yosifon, *Lock-In*, *supra* note 80, at 1449–59 (discussing types of lock-in situations).

98. *See* Tung, *Fiduciary Duties*, *supra* note 96, at 842 ("By the time the firm is in distress, its creditors will enjoy differing rights (including payment and priority rights), differing stakes in the continuation of the borrower firm, and differing contract protections.").

99. *Cf.* Mark E. Budnitz, *The Development of Consumer Protection Law, the Institutionalization of Consumerism, and Future Prospects and Perils*, 26 Ga. St. U. L. Rev. 1147, 1169 (2010) ("Despite the many state and federal statutes that have been enacted in the last forty years to regulate consumer transactions, the underlying contract between the company and the consumer remains crucial in determining the rights and liabilities of the parties.").

100. Individual shareholders at individual companies can no doubt use corporate law and governance to advance environmental concerns. *See* Sarah E. Light, *The Law of the Corporation as Environmental Law*, 71 Stan. L. Rev. 137, 140 (2019) ("In light of the significant impact that firms can have on the environment (often, though not always, when they are organized as publicly traded corporations), this Article argues that the law governing the corporation throughout its life cycle – corporate law, securities regulation, antitrust law, and bankruptcy law – should be understood as a fundamental part of environmental law.").

101. *See* Blair & Stout, *supra* note 73, at 250 ("[P]ublic corporation law can offer a second-best solution to team production problems because it allows rational individuals who hope to profit from team production to overcome shirking and rent-seeking by opting into an internal governance structure we call the 'mediating hierarchy.'").

102. Note that a shared governance structure for the firm would still align with William Bratton's description of the corporate purpose: "corporate law should facilitate corporate attempts to maximize productive output (and hence wealth) in a competitive economy, encouraging long-term investment at the lowest cost of capital, subject to exterior regulations that control externalities." William W. Bratton, *Framing a Purpose for Corporate Law*, 39 J. Corp. L. 713, 723–24 (2014).

103. Zohar Goshen & Richard Squire, *Principal Costs: A New Theory for Corporate Law and Governance*, 117 Colum. L. Rev. 767, 770 (2017).

104. Lund, *supra* note 62.

105. *Union Members Summary*, Bureau L. Stat. (Jan. 18, 2019), https://www.bls.gov /news.release/union2.nr0.htm (finding that 6.4 percent of private-sector employees are unionized).

106. Employers need only to bargain about terms and conditions of employment; they need not discuss areas within the "core of entrepreneurial control." NLRB v. Wooster Div. of Borg-Warner Corp., 356 U.S. 342, 349 (1958) (discussing the mandatory subjects of collective bargaining); SAMUEL ESTREICHER & MATTHEW T. BODIE, LABOR LAW 134–39 (2016).

107. For a sampling of the legal academic literature – much of it involving employee ownership – see MARGARET M. BLAIR, OWNERSHIP AND CONTROL (1995); THE NEW RELATIONSHIP: HUMAN CAPITAL IN THE AMERICAN CORPORATION (Margaret M. Blair & Thomas A. Kochan eds., 2000); JOSEPH R. BLASI, EMPLOYEE OWNERSHIP: REVOLUTION OR RIPOFF? (1988); HANSMANN, *supra* note 80, at 66–119; SAUL A. RUBENSTEIN & THOMAS A. KOCHAN, LEARNING FROM SATURN: POSSIBILITIES FOR CORPORATE GOVERNANCE AND EMPLOYEE RELATIONS (2001); PAUL WEILER, GOVERNING THE WORKPLACE (1990); Alan Hyde, *In Defense of Employee Ownership*, 67 CHI.-KENT L. REV. 159, 160 (1991).

108. *See, e.g.*, ROBERT E. COLE, WORK, MOBILITY, AND PARTICIPATION: A COMPARATIVE STUDY OF AMERICAN AND JAPANESE INDUSTRY (1980); Jon Gertner, *From 0 to 60 to World Domination*, N.Y. TIMES, Feb. 18, 2007 (Magazine), at 34.

109. *See, e.g.*, JOSEPH M. JURAN, QUALITY BY DESIGN (1992); DAVID I. LEVINE, REINVENTING THE WORKPLACE: HOW BUSINESS AND EMPLOYEES CAN BOTH WIN (1995); PAUL LILLRANK & NORIAKI KANO, CONTINUOUS IMPROVEMENT: QUALITY CONTROL CIRCLES IN JAPANESE INDUSTRY (1989); Erin White, *How a Company Made Everyone a Team Player*, WALL ST. J., Aug. 13, 2007, at B1.

110. *See* Katherine V.W. Stone, *Labor and the Corporate Structure: Changing Conceptions and Emerging Possibilities*, 55 U. CHI. L. REV. 73, 143–46 (1988) (discussing Taylorism in the workplace).

111. New managerial methodologies providing for participatory management and employee voice are increasingly popular around the globe. *See, e.g.*, FREDERIC LALOUX, REINVENTING ORGANIZATIONS: A GUIDE TO CREATING ORGANIZATIONS INSPIRED BY THE NEXT STAGE OF HUMAN CONSCIOUSNESS (2014); BRIAN J. ROBERTSON, HOLACRACY: THE NEW MANAGEMENT SYSTEM FOR A RAPIDLY CHANGING WORLD (2015).

112. *See, e.g.*, Basic, Inc. v. Levinson, 485 U.S. 224, 234–35 (1988) (discussing the importance of keeping merger negotiations secret).

113. *See, e.g.*, MICHAEL J. PIORE & CHARLES F. SABEL, THE SECOND INDUSTRIAL DIVIDE: POSSIBILITIES FOR PROSPERITY 231–36 (1984) (discussing the practice of "flexible specialization" on the shop floor). *See also* MIKE ROSE, THE MIND AT WORK: VALUING THE INTELLIGENCE OF THE AMERICAN WORKER xxxiv (2004) (discussing the various intelligences of different types of workers). For an exploration of a nonbinding employee referendum on mergers and acquisitions, see Matthew T. Bodie, *Workers, Information, and Corporate Combinations: The Case for Nonbinding Employee Referenda in Transformative Transactions*, 85 WASH. U. L. REV. 871 (2007).

114. *See* Lewis v. Vogelstein, 699 A.2d 327, 331–33 (Del. Ch. 1997) (discussing the issues surrounding a stock option grant to directors); Afra Afsharipour & J. Travis Laster, *Enhanced Scrutiny on the Buy-Side*, 53 GA. L. REV. 443, 453 (2019) ("Numerous studies provide evidence that acquisitions offer significant benefits

to bidder management – particularly bidder CEOs – in the form of increased compensation, power, and prestige.").

115. LUCIAN BEBCHUK & JESSE FRIED, PAY WITHOUT PERFORMANCE: THE UNFULFILLED PROMISE OF EXECUTIVE COMPENSATION 25–31 (2004).

116. Brian G.M. Main, Charles A. O'Reilly III & James Wade, *The CEO, the Board of Directors, and Executive Compensation: Economic and Psychological Perspectives*, 4 INDUS. & CORP. CHANGE 292 (1995).

117. *See* BEBCHUK & FRIED, *supra* note 115, at 37–39. *See also In re* Walt Disney Co. Derivative Litig., 907 A.2d 693, 704–11 (Del. Ch. 2005), *aff'd* 906 A.2d 27 (Del. 2006) (discussing the process through which Michael Ovitz was hired by Walt Disney in 1995). Despite denying the duties of care and good faith challenge against the Ovitz hiring, Chancellor Chandler acknowledged that "the compensation committee met *for one hour*" to discuss the terms of Michael Ovitz's compensation along with the compensation packages for various Disney employees, 121 stock option grants, top-level executive Robert Iger's employment agreement, and board member and compensation committee chair Irwin Russell's $250,000 compensation for negotiating the Ovitz deal. *Id.* at 708.

118. *See* Stewart J. Schwab & Randall S. Thomas, *Realigning Corporate Governance: Shareholder Activism by Labor Unions*, 96 MICH. L. REV. 1018 (1998).

119. *Id.* at 1036.

120. *Id.* at 1045. ("The amazing thing about these union-sponsored shareholder proposals is how ordinary they are, from the perspective of any institutional investor."). *See generally* DAVID WEBBER, THE RISE OF THE WORKING-CLASS SHAREHOLDER: LABOR'S LAST BEST WEAPON (2018).

121. WEBBER, *supra* note 120, at 45–78, 111–51, 164–80.

122. *See, e.g.*, Dynamex Operations W. v. Superior Court, 416 P.3d 1, 40 (Cal. 2018) (requiring independent contractors to be "customarily engaged in an independently established trade, occupation, or business").

123. *See* Ronald J. Gilson, Charles F. Sable & Robert E. Scott, *Braiding: The Interaction of Formal and Informal Contracting in Theory, Practice, and Doctrine*, 110 COLUM. L. REV. 1377, 1382 (2010); *see also* Geis, *supra* note 27, at 100.

124. *See* Simone M. Sepe, *Directors' Duty to Creditors and the Debt Contract*, 1 J. BUS. & TECH. L. 553, 561 (2007) (noting that "communitarians . . . advocate a multifiduciary model where all corporate stakeholders benefit from the attribution of directors' fiduciary duties"); *see also* Millon, *supra* note 94, at 11–12 (discussing the use of the multifiduciary model by communitarian corporate law scholars).

125. *See* Millon, *supra* note 94, at 11–12 (discussing efforts to provide protections to nonshareholder constituencies); Blair & Stout, *supra* note 73, at 293–94 (arguing that directors owe a duty to the corporation and that the corporation consists of all of the stakeholders who are responsible for the business of the enterprise).

126. *See* Millon, *supra* note 94, at 11 (noting especially those whose interests may be negatively affected by the pursuit of shareholder interests and welfare).

127. *See id.* (rejecting the principles underlying shareholder primacy); Blair & Stout, *supra* note 73, at 280–81 (describing directors as "trustees for the corporation itself – mediating hierarchs whose job is to balance team members' competing interests in a fashion that keeps everyone happy enough that the productive coalition stays together").

128. *See* Joseph Heath, *Business Ethics Without Stakeholders*, 16 Bus. Ethics Q. 533, 543 (2006) (arguing that stakeholder theory creates "extraordinary agency risks" because of the potential for conflicts); Eric W. Orts & Alan Strudler, *Putting a Stake in Stakeholder Theory*, 88 J. Bus. Ethics 605, 611 (2009) (arguing that stakeholder theory fails to provide a system of mechanisms for governance, other than "balancing" stakeholder concerns).

129. Instead, many stakeholder theorists also ascribe to the entity view of the corporation, which argues for treating the corporation as a state-created separate entity. *See* Martin Petrin, *Reconceptualizing the Theory of the Firm: From Nature to Function*, 118 Penn. St. L. Rev. 1, 24 (2013) ("[O]ther CSR scholars and stakeholder theorists have justified consideration of broader stakeholder interests by characterizing the firm as not merely a legal fiction but rather as a moral organism with social and ethical responsibilities, or built upon the view of the corporation as an entity existing in time and as a distinct person.") (internal quotations and citation omitted).

130. *See* Hayden & Bodie, *supra* note 74, at 2113 (discussing the "strange turn" from stakeholder theory to the exclusive shareholder franchise). Stakeholder theorists have acknowledged this difficulty. *See* Blair & Stout, *supra* note 73, at 312 ("Recognizing that shareholder voting rights can act as a safety net to protect against extreme misconduct poses something of a problem for the mediating hierarchy approach, as it suggests that shareholders enjoy more control over how the firm is run than do other members of the coalition.").

10.   Democratic Participation and Shared Governance

1. *See also* Grant M. Hayden, *The False Promise of One Person, One Vote*, 102 Mich. L. Rev. 213, 251–61 (2003); Melvyn R. Durchslag, Salyer, Ball, *and* Hold: *Reappraising the Right to Vote in Terms of Political "Interest" and Vote Dilution*, 33 Case W. Res. L. Rev 1, 38–39 (1982).

2. These two questions are not unrelated, but in order to think through some of the issues here, we think it helps to keep them separated.

3. For example, this is the intuition that underpins Kenneth Arrow's condition of democratic fairness typically referred to as universal admissibility. *See* Grant M. Hayden, *Some Implications of Arrow's Theorem for Voting Rights*, 47 Stan. L. Rev. 295, 298 (1995); *see also* William H. Riker, Liberalism Against Populism: A Confrontation Between the Theory of Democracy and the Theory of Social Choice 217 (1982).

4. *See* Herbert Hovenkamp, *The Limits of Preference-Based Legal Policy*, 89 Nw. U. L. Rev. 4, 4–6 (1994).

5. *See, e.g.*, Louis Kapow & Steven Shavell, Fairness Versus Welfare (2002). For a discussion of this feature of law and economics, see Stephen E. Ellis & Grant M. Hayden, *The Cult of Efficiency in Corporate Law*, 5 Va. L. & Bus. Rev. 239, 252–53 (2010).

6. *See* Hayden, *supra* note 1, at 248.

7. For a summary of the problem of making interpersonal utility comparisons, see Hayden, *supra* note 1, at 236–47. For more general background on the subject, see Interpersonal Comparisons of Well-Being (Jon Elster & John E. Roemer eds.,

1991); James Griffin, WELL-BEING: ITS MEANING, MEASUREMENT, AND MORAL IMPORTANCE 113–20 (1986); Peter Hammond, *Interpersonal Comparisons of Utility: Why and How They Are and Should Be Made, in* INTERPERSONAL COMPARISONS OF WELL-BEING 200, 238–54 (Jon Elster & John E. Roemer eds., 1991).

8. *See* Hayden, *supra* note 1, at 255–59.

9. *See* Chapter 2. For an extended discussion, see Grant M. Hayden & Matthew T. Bodie, *One Share, One Vote and the False Promise of Shareholder Homogeneity*, 30 CARDOZO L. REV. 445, 460–62 (2008).

10. Of course, we could stitch together more than one underinclusive marker and better capture voter interest.

11. *See* Hayden & Bodie, *supra* note 9, at 460–62.

12. *See, e.g.*, Kramer v. Union Free Sch. Dist., 395 U.S. 621, 626–27 (1969).

13. FRANK H. EASTERBROOK & DANIEL R. FISCHEL, THE ECONOMIC STRUCTURE OF CORPORATE LAW 72 (1991) ("The most basic statutory voting rule is the same in every state. It is this: all common shares vote, all votes have the same weights, and no other participant in the venture votes, unless there is some agreement to the contrary. Such agreements are rare.").

14. *Cf.* Matt Phillips, *Belly-Flop by Facebook Puts Investors on Edge*, N.Y. TIMES, July 26, 2018, at B1.

15. *See* Henry T.C. Hu & Bernard Black, *The New Vote Buying: Empty Voting and Hidden (Morphable) Ownership*, 79 S. CAL. L. REV. 811, 816 (2006); Shaun Martin & Frank Partnoy, *Encumbered Shares*, 2005 U. ILL. L. REV. 775, 780 (discussing "economically encumbered" and "legally encumbered" shares).

16. Benjamin Means, *Nonmarket Values in Family Businesses*, 54 WM. & MARY L. REV. 1185, 1185 (2013).

17. *See* Einer Elhauge, *Sacrificing Corporate Profits in the Public Interest*, 80 N.Y. U. L. REV. 733 (2005).

18. *See* Max M. Schanzenbach & Robert H. Sitkoff, *Reconciling Fiduciary Duty and Social Conscience: The Law and Economics of ESG Investing by a Trustee*, 72 STAN. L. REV. 381 (2020).

19. *See* Ronald J. Gilson & Curtis J. Milhaupt, *Sovereign Wealth Funds and Corporate Governance: A Minimalist Response to the New Mercantilism*, 60 STAN. L. REV. 1345 (2008).

20. *See* Tom C.W. Lin, *The New Investor*, 60 UCLA L. REV. 678, 680 (2013).

21. *See* Dorothy S. Lund, *The Case Against Passive Shareholder Voting*, 43 J. CORP. L. 493, 497 (2018) (proposing that lawmakers should restrict truly passive funds from voting at shareholder meetings because of their lack of interests in voting).

22. William K. Sjostrom, Jr., *The Case Against Mandatory Annual Director Elections and Shareholders' Meetings*, 74 TENN. L. REV. 199, 201 (2007) (discussing the "mandatory requirement under state corporate law and stock exchange listing standards that public corporations hold annual shareholders' meetings for the election of directors").

23. Hon. Leo E. Strine, Jr., *Toward Common Sense and Common Ground? Reflections on the Shared Interests of Managers and Labor in a More Rational System of Corporate Governance*, 33 J. CORP. L. 1, 6–7 (2007) (discussing the "separation of ownership from ownership," namely that "the equity of public corporations is often owned, not by the end-user investors, but by another form of agency, a mutual fund, or other institutional investor").

24. Marcel Kahan & Edward Rock, *The Hanging Chads of Corporate Voting*, 96 GEO. L.J. 1227, 1231 (2008) ("The inescapable complexity combined with the already well-studied issues of shareholders' rational apathy and free rider problems detract from the case for shareholder voting.").

25. George Geis, *Traceable Shares and Corporate Law*, 113 NW. U. L. REV. 227, 228–29 (2019) (noting the failure to connect particular shares with their owners in the context of electronic trading).

26. RESTATEMENT (SECOND) OF AGENCY § 220(1) (AM. LAW. INST. 1958) (defining a servant/employee as "a person employed to perform services in the affairs of another and who with respect to the physical conduct in the performance of the services is subject to the other's control or right to control").

27. *Id.* § 220 cmt. c (noting that the employment relationship is "one not capable of exact definition"); Matthew T. Bodie, *Participation as a Theory of Employment*, 89 NOTRE DAME L. REV. 661, 682–83 (2013) ("Courts and commentators continue to bemoan [the control test's] inability to deliver clear answers.").

28. Firms are expected to differentiate between employees and independent contractors over a host of provisions, including whether taxes need to be withheld, 26 U.S.C. §§ 3401 (c), 3402 (2018); whether the firm must pay a share of Social Security and Medicare (FICA), *id.* §§ 3101, 3121(d), and unemployment (FUTA) taxes, *id.* §§ 3301, 3306(i), for the worker; and whether the workers count as employees for benefit plan purposes, *id.* § 410(a). The IRS defines employees based on the common law control test, *i.d.* § 3121(d) (2) (defining an employee as, among other definitions, "any individual who, under the usual common law rules applicable in determining the employer-employee relationship, has the status of an employee").

29. HENRY HANSMANN, THE OWNERSHIP OF ENTERPRISE 89–91, 97–98 (1996); Henry Hansmann, *Employee Ownership and Unions: Lessons from the Airline Industry, in* EMPLOYEE REPRESENTATION IN THE EMERGING WORKPLACE: ALTERNATIVES/SUPPLEMENTS TO COLLECTIVE BARGAINING 573–80 (Samuel Estreicher ed., 1998).

30. *See* Dorothy S. Lund, *Nonvoting Shares and Efficient Corporate Governance*, 71 STAN. L. REV. 687 (2019) (discussing the benefits of a disproportionate voting structure).

31. Recent innovations in employee participatory governance structures include holacracy and other participatory (or "evolutionary") management structures. *See* FREDERIC LALOUX, REINVENTING ORGANIZATIONS: A GUIDE TO CREATING ORGANIZATIONS INSPIRED BY THE NEXT STAGE OF HUMAN CONSCIOUSNESS (2014); BRIAN J. ROBERTSON, HOLACRACY: THE NEW MANAGEMENT SYSTEM FOR A RAPIDLY CHANGING WORLD (2015).

32. Andreas Rühmkorf, *Company Law and Corporate Governance in Germany: From Stakeholder Value to Corporate Sustainability?, in* CAMBRIDGE HANDBOOK OF CORPORATE LAW, CORPORATE GOVERNANCE AND SUSTAINABILITY (Beate Sjåfjell & Christopher Bruner eds., 2019); Ewan McGaughey, *The Codetermination Bargains: The History of German Corporate and Labor Law*, 23 COLUM. J. EUR. L. 135, 136 (2016).

33. *See, e.g.*, Accountable Capitalism Act, S. 3348, 115th Cong. (2018); Reward Work Act, S. 2605, 115th Cong. (2018).

34. *Cf.* Accountable Capitalism Act, S. 3348, 115th Cong. (2018) (granting employees voting rights to 40 percent of the board).

35. HANSMANN, *supra* note 29, at 168–76 (discussing how rural electrical cooperatives involve ownership by customers); David G. Yosifon, *The Consumer Interest in Corporate Law*, 43 U.C. DAVIS L. REV. 253 (2009) (arguing that consumers may have ongoing interests through lock-in purchases).

36. *See, e.g.*, Oglebay Norton Co. v. Armco, Inc., 556 N.E.2d 515, 517 (Ohio 1990) (discussing a long-standing business relationship between a shipper and an iron ore producer, which included a seat for the producer on the shipper's board of directors); Ronald J. Gilson et. al., *Braiding: The Interaction of Formal and Informal Contracting in Theory, Practice, and Doctrine*, 110 COLUM. L. REV. 1377 (2010) (discussing formal governance structures in certain braided contracts between firms).

11.   The German Codetermination Experience

1. Anthony Bisconti, Note, *The Double Bottom Line: Can Constituency Statutes Protect Socially Responsible Corporations Stuck in Revlon Land?*, 42 LOY. L.A. L. REV. 765, 768 (2009) (noting that constituency statutes have been adopted by a majority of the states).

2. *See* David Gelles & David Yaffe-Bellany, *Feeling Heat, C.E.O.s Pledge New Priorities*, N.Y. TIMES, Aug. 19, 2019, at A1.

3. For information about codetermination or employee governance participation in other countries, see Klas Levinson, *Codetermination in Sweden: Myth and Reality*, 21 ECON. & INDUS. DEM. 457 (2000); Caspar Rose, *The Challenges of Employee-Appointed Board Members for Corporate Governance: The Danish Evidence*, 9 EUR. BUS. ORG. L. REV. 215 (2008); Milan Utroša, *Works Councils and Co-Determination in Slovenia*, 1 S.E. EUR. REV. 23 (1998); Eivind Falkum, Inger M. Hagen & Sissel C. Trygstad, Participation and Codetermination Among Norwegian Employees: State of the Art 2009, Conference Paper, 9th IIRA European Congress, June–July 2010, Copenhagen, https://faos.ku.dk/pdf/iirakongres2010/track2/38.pdf/.

4. For a comprehensive rundown, see Ewan McGaughey, *Democracy in America at Work: The History of Labor's Vote in Corporate Governance*, 42 SEATTLE U. L. REV. 697 (2019).

5. MASS. GEN. LAWS ch. 156, § 23 (2018); *see* McGaughey, *supra* note 4, at 718.

6. *See* McGaughey, *supra* note 4, at 736–37. This representation was usually adopted in the context of an employee stock ownership plan (ESOP). For a discussion of the United Airlines ESOP, see Jeffrey N. Gordon, *Employee Stock Ownership in Economic Transitions: The Case of United Airlines*, 10 J. APPLIED CORP. FIN. 39, 54 (1998) ("The board consist[ed] of [twelve] members: five 'public directors,' four 'independent directors,' two 'union directors,' and one 'salaried and management' director (the latter three directors known collectively as 'employee directors').").

7. *See, e.g.*, Accountable Capitalism Act, S. 3348, 115th Cong. § 6 (2018) (requiring 40 percent of boards in large companies to be elected by employees); Reward Work Act, S. 2605, 115th Cong. § 3(c)(2) (2018) (requiring one-third of listed board to be elected by employees); H.R. 6096, 115th Cong. § 3(c)(2) (2018) (same); *see also* McGaughey, *supra* note 4, at 698–99.

8. For a recent list of countries, see Ewan McGaughey, *Votes at Work in Britain: Shareholder Monopolisation and the "Single Channel,"* 47 INDUS. L. J. 76, 79–80, 79 n.17, 80 fig.1 (2018).

9. *See* Robert Scholz & Sigurt Vitols, *Board-Level Codetermination: A Driving Force for Corporate Social Responsibility in German Companies?*, 25 EUR. J. IND. REL. 233, 233–34 (2019).

10. Here we are using the terminology from Otto Sandrock & Jean J. du Plessis, *The German System of Supervisory Codetermination by Employees, in* GERMAN CORPORATE GOVERNANCE IN INTERNATIONAL AND EUROPEAN CONTEXT 167, 169 (Jean J. du Plessis et al. eds., 3d ed. 2017).

11. *See id.* at 169–71.

12. *See* JOHN T. ADDISON, THE ECONOMICS OF CODETERMINATION: LESSONS FROM THE GERMAN EXPERIENCE 16–19 (2009).

13. *See* Sandrock & du Plessis, *supra* note 10, at 169.

14. *See id.* at 172–78.

15. *See* Jean J. du Plessis et al., *An Overview of German Business or Enterprise Law and the One-Tier and Two-Tier Board Systems Contrasted, in* GERMAN CORPORATE GOVERNANCE IN INTERNATIONAL AND EUROPEAN CONTEXT, *supra* note 10, at 1, 8–13.

16. *See* Jean J. du Plessis & Otto Saenger, *The Supervisory Board as Company Organ, in* GERMAN CORPORATE GOVERNANCE IN INTERNATIONAL AND EUROPEAN CONTEXT, *supra* note 10, at 105, 133–53 [hereinafter du Plessis & Saenger, *Supervisory Board*]; Jean J. du Plessis & Otto Saenger, *The General Meeting and the Management Board as Company Organs, in* GERMAN CORPORATE GOVERNANCE IN INTERNATIONAL AND EUROPEAN CONTEXT, *supra* note 10, at 63, 73 [hereinafter du Plessis & Saenger, *General Meeting*].

17. Generally speaking, the two-tiered boards are probably better at supervising top employees because there are fewer of the conflicts of interest that occur when managers are on the corporate board; without those managers, though, information may flow to the supervisory board more sluggishly.

18. Depending on the level of codetermination (discussed below), the personnel director has the support of the employee representatives on the supervisory board. For full-parity codetermination governed by the 1952 law, employee representatives have veto power over the appointment of the personnel director; for companies with quasi-parity codetermination, personnel directors are usually not appointed unless they enjoy the support of the employee representatives. *See* Otto Sandrock, *German and International Perspectives of the German Model of Codetermination*, 26 EUR. BUS. L. REV. 129, 131–32 (2015).

19. Thilo Kuntz, *German Corporate Law in the 20th Century, in* RESEARCH HANDBOOK ON THE HISTORY OF CORPORATE AND COMPANY LAW 205 (Harwell Wells ed., 2018) (discussing how supervisory directors were traditionally part-time positions somewhat removed from day-to-day governance, but have recently stepped up their oversight roles).

20. *See* Sandrock & du Plessis, *supra* note 10, at 182–83.

21. *See* Jean J. du Plessis & Ingo Saenger, *An Overview of the Corporate Governance Debate in Germany, in* GERMAN CORPORATE GOVERNANCE IN INTERNATIONAL AND EUROPEAN CONTEXT, *supra* note 10, at 17, 48–49; Sandrock & du Plessis,

supra note 10, at 173–78; ADDISON, *supra* note 12, at 103; Sandrock, *supra* note 18, at 131–32.

22. *See* Sandrock & du Plessis, *supra* note 10, at 173–76. The threshold at which this applies to companies in this sector is lower – 1,000 instead of 2,000 employees. Volkswagen is a special case. Along with 50 percent representation for the workers, the government of Lower Saxony also has seats on the board, which gives the workers a de facto majority (because of traditional government support for the workers). In addition, the voting rights of individual shareholders are limited to a maximum of 20 percent for any particular shareholder. Gesetz über die Überführung der Anteilsrechte an der Volkswagenwerk Gesellschaft mit beschränkter Haftung in private Hand [Law on the Privatization of Equity in the Volkswagenwerk Limited Company], July 21, 1960, B G Bl I at 585, B G Bl III at 641-1-1; JACK EWING, FASTER, HIGHER, FARTHER: THE INSIDE STORY OF THE VOLKSWAGEN SCANDAL 57 (2017).

23. *See, e.g.,* CORPORATE LAW AND ECONOMIC ANALYSIS 295–96 (Lucian Arye Bebchuck ed., 1990) (one passing reference to codetermination); FRANK H. EASTERBROOK & DANIEL R. FISCHEL, THE ECONOMIC STRUCTURE OF CORPORATE LAW 69 (1991) (again, one passing reference to codetermination); HENRY HANSMANN, THE OWNERSHIP OF ENTERPRISE 110–12 (1996) (a few pages); STEPHEN M. BAINBRIDGE, THE NEW CORPORATE GOVERNANCE IN THEORY AND PRACTICE 47–49 (2008) (a few pages); JONATHAN R. MACEY, CORPORATE GOVERNANCE: PROMISES KEPT, PROMISES BROKEN 230 (2008) (some passing references to the German system).

24. One refreshing exception is EMPLOYEES AND CORPORATE GOVERNANCE 163–235 (Margaret M. Blair & Mark J. Roe eds., 1999).

25. Stephen M. Bainbridge, *Privately Ordered Participatory Management: An Organizational Failures Analysis,* 23 DEL. J. CORP. L. 979, 1054 (1998) (noting that "German codetermination was created by sweeping statutory mandates" and concluding that it was unlikely to be adopted through private ordering).

26. *See* George W. Dent, Jr., *Stakeholder Governance: A Bad Idea Getting Worse,* 58 CASE W. RES. L. REV. 1107, 1115 (2008).

27. *See* Henry Hansmann & Reinier Kraakman, *The End of History for Corporate Law,* 89 GEO. L.J. 439, 445 (2001) ("The growing view today is that meaningful direct worker voting participation in corporate affairs tends to produce inefficient decisions, paralysis, or weak boards, and that these costs are likely to exceed any potential benefits that worker participation might bring."); Luca Enriques, Henry Hansmann, Reinier Kraakman & Mariana Pargendler, *The Basic Governance Structure: Minority Shareholders and Non-Shareholder Constituencies, in* THE ANATOMY OF CORPORATE LAW: A COMPARATIVE AND FUNCTIONAL APPROACH 79, 106 (John Armour et al. eds., 3d ed. 2017).

28. *See* ROBERTA ROMANO, THE GENIUS OF AMERICAN CORPORATE LAW 129–30 (1993).

29. This argument in a broader theoretical context is also discussed in ADDISON, *supra* note 12, at 104–08.

30. *See* Michael C. Jensen & William H. Meckling, *Rights and Production Functions: An Application to Labor-Managed Firms and Codetermination,* 52 J. BUS. 469, 473–75, 503–04 (1979).

31. *Id.* at 473.

32. *See id.* at 503.

33. *See id.*

34. *Id.* at 504.

35. *See* Ewan McGaughey, *The Codetermination Bargains: The History of German Corporate and Labor Law*, 23 COLUM. J. EUR. L. 135 (2016).

36. *Id.* at 155.

37. *See id.* at 157.

38. *See id.* at 162.

39. *See id.* at 163–67.

40. *See id.* at 174.

41. *See id.* at 170.

42. *See id.* at 136–37, 155–56, 168.

43. This is discussed more extensively in Chapter 4. *See also* Grant M. Hayden & Matthew T. Bodie, *Shareholder Voting and the Symbolic Politics of Corporation as Contract*, 53 WAKE FOREST L. REV. 511, 531, 533, 541–42 (2018).

44. For discussions of the legal impediments to systems of worker participation, see Matthew T. Bodie, *Holacracy and the Law*, 42 DEL. J. CORP. L. 619, 662–71 (2018); Jeffrey M. Hirsch, *Labor Law Obstacles to the Collective Negotiation and Implementation of Employee Stock Ownership Plans: A Response to Henry Hansmann and Other "Survivalists,"* 67 FORDHAM L. REV. 957 (1998).

45. *See* David I. Levine & Laura D. Tyson, *Participation, Productivity, and the Firm's Environment, in* PAYING FOR PRODUCTIVITY: A LOOK AT THE EVIDENCE 183 (Alan S. Blinder ed., 1990).

46. *See id.* at 214–19.

47. *See id.* at 214. Under the prisoner's dilemma framework, individual players make less-than-optimal choices because of the interdependency of outcomes and the inability to trust their partner/opponent.

48. *See* ADDISON, *supra* note 12, at 2.

49. *See id.*

50. *See* Sandrock, *supra* note 18, at 131.

51. *See* du Plessis & Saenger, *supra* note 21, at 49.

52. *See id.*

53. *See* Sandrock & du Plessis, *supra* note 10, at 186.

54. *See id.* at 184; du Plessis & Saenger, *General Meeting, supra* note 16, at 66.

55. *See* Scholz & Vitols, *supra* note 9, at 235 tbl.1. The numbers add up to more than thirty-seven because some studies had multiple subjects, but the overall skew toward shareholder interests is still clear, with only five studies involving wages and not a single study analyzing the effect of codetermination on any measures of corporate social responsibility.

56. *See id.*

57. *See id.* at 235.

58. Jill E. Fisch, *Measuring Efficiency in Corporate Law: The Role of Shareholder Primacy*, 31 J. CORP. L. 637, 639–40 (2006) ("Indeed, most studies do not expressly consider the implications of using shareholder wealth as a measure of firm value, despite the fact that they purport to be conducting a general efficiency analysis in which the primary goal should be maximizing the size of the corporate surplus, while considerations of the appropriate division of the corporate surplus should be secondary."). *See also* Oliver Hart & Luigi Zingales, *Companies Should*

Maximize Shareholder Welfare Not Market Value, 2 J.L. FIN. & ACCT. 247, 248 (2017) (discussing the difference between shareholder utility maximization and shareholder wealth maximization).

59. Making a similar point on the range of possibilities, John Addison explains, "Worker representation on company boards arouses strong feelings. At one extreme it is viewed as tantamount to wealth confiscation with palpably adverse consequences for firm performance. At another, it is viewed as helping guarantee cooperative labor relations, with long-term gains in terms of productivity and improved worker morale. Intermediate positions would recognize the joint occurrence of allocative and distributive effects, permitting either increases or decreases in overall welfare . . . ." ADDISON, *supra* note 12, at 119 (citation omitted). On this question of economic performance, we take the intermediate position.

60. For the best summary of the literature through 2008 and a discussion of the three initial phases of research detailed below, see ADDISON, *supra* note 12, at 108–21; *see also* UWE JIRJAHN, ÖKONOMISCHE WIRKUNGEN DER MITBESTIMMUNG IN DEUTSCHLAND: EIN UPDATE (Hans Böckler Stiftung, Arbeitspapier 186, Feb. 2010).

61. *See, e.g.,* Jan Svejnar, *Relative Wage Effects of Unions, Dictatorship, and Co-determination: Econometric Evidence from Germany*, 63 REV. ECON. & STATS. 188 (1981) (finding codetermination associated with higher earnings in the iron and steel industry but not in the coal mining industry); Giuseppe Benelli et al., *Labor Participation in Corporate Policy-Making Decisions: West Germany's Experience with Codetermination*, 60 J. BUS. 553 (1987) (finding no real differences between firms with codetermination and without codetermination across a variety of measures of performance); Michael A. Gurdon & Anoop Rai, *Codetermination and Enterprise Performance: Empirical Evidence from West Germany*, 42 J. ECON. & BUS. 289 (1990) (finding codetermination led to higher profitability but lower productivity).

62. *See* ADDISON, *supra* note 12, at 109. Those early studies were criticized for reasons that included "sample size, data frequency (in the case of stock returns), lack of controls for other relevant economic or organizational variables, focus on a single event, and narrow reach." *Id.*

63. *See, e.g.,* Felix FitzRoy & Kornelius Kraft, *Economic Effects of Codetermination*, 95 SCAND. J. ECON. 365 (1993) (finding that the shift to quasi-parity codetermination in 1976 had a negative effect on productivity); Theodor Baums & Bernd Frick, *Co-determination in Germany: The Impact of Court Decisions on the Market Value of Firms*, 1 ECON. ANALYSIS 143 (1998) (finding that court rulings that expanded or restricted codetermination had no real effect on share prices); Gary Gorton & Frank A. Schmid, *Capital, Labor, and the Firm: A Study of Codetermination*, 2 J. EURO. ECON. ASSN 863 (2004) (finding that moving from one-third to quasi-parity codetermination negatively affected shareholder wealth).

64. *See, e.g.,* Felix FitzRoy & Kornelius Kraft, *Co-determination, Efficiency, and Productivity*, 43 BRIT. J. IND. REL. 233 (2005); *see also* ADDISON, *supra* note 12, at 115–16, 120. The negative findings in the second phase of studies may have been artefacts of the cross-section estimation they used, which (by definition) did not control for firm heterogeneity or firm-specific effects. *Id.* at 115, 120.

65. *See, e.g.,* Kornelius Kraft et al., *Codetermination and Innovation*, 35 CAMBRIDGE J. ECON. 145 (2011); *see also* ADDISON, *supra* note 12, at 116.

66. *See* Larry Fauver & Michael E. Fuerst, *Does Good Corporate Governance Include Employee Representation? Evidence from German Corporate Boards*, 82 J. FIN. ECON. 673 (2006); *see also* Simon Renaud, *Dynamic Efficiency of Supervisory Board Codetermination in Germany*, 21 LABOUR 689 (2007).

67. *See* JIRJAHN, *supra* note 60, at 52.

68. *See* Jean J. du Plessis et al., *Preface* to GERMAN CORPORATE GOVERNANCE IN INTERNATIONAL AND EUROPEAN CONTEXT, *supra* note 10, at vii; Sandrock, *supra* note 18, at 136. For some brief comparisons between the German recovery and that of other countries, see Michael Burda & Jennifer Hunt, *What Explains the German Labor Market Miracle in the Great Recession?* 273–75 (Brookings Institution, Brookings Papers on Economic Activity, Spring 2011).

69. *See* Sandrock, *supra* note 18, at 134.

70. *See id.*; Sandrock & du Plessis, *supra* note 10, at 188–89, 193.

71. *See* Lutz Bellman et al., *The German Labour Market Puzzle in the Great Recession, in* PRODUCTIVITY PUZZLES ACROSS EUROPE 187, 187–88 (Philippe Askenazy et al. eds., 2016); Sandrock, *supra* note 18, at 134; Sandrock & du Plessis, *supra* note 10, at 188–89, 193.

72. Bellman et al., *supra* note 71, at 229.

73. *See id.* at 187.

74. *Id.*

75. Indeed, by the end of 2009, Paul Krugman had already devoted an entire column to "Germany's jobs miracle." Paul Krugman, *Free to Lose*, N.Y. TIMES, Nov. 13, 2009, at A31.

76. *See* Simon Jäger, Benjamin Schoefer & Jörg Heining, Labor in the Boardroom 29, http://economics.mit.edu/files/17273 (unpublished manuscript) (emphasis added).

77. *See id.*

78. E. Han Kim, Ernst Maug & Christoph Schneider, *Labor Representation in Governance as an Insurance Mechanism*, 2018 REV. FIN. 1251, 1286.

79. *Id.* at 1279, 1286. The benefit of this employment insurance was really only experienced by white-collar and skilled blue-collar employees; unskilled blue-collar workers do not receive much in the way of job security protections. *Id.* at 1286. The authors of the study attribute this finding to the lack of real representation of unskilled workers on supervisory boards. *Id.*

80. *Id.* at 1286.

81. Jäger et al., *supra* note 76, at 25.

82. *See* Kim et al., *supra* note 78, at 1286.

83. Chen Lin, Thomas Schmid & Yuhai Xuan, *Employee Representation and Financial Leverage*, 127 J. FIN. ECON. 303, 321 (2018).

84. *Id.*

85. *See id.*

86. *See id.*

87. *See id.* at 322.

88. *See* Scholz & Vitols, *supra* note 9.

89. *See id.* at 34–37.

90. *See id.* at 39–44.

91. *See id.* at 43–44.

92. *See id.*

93. *See id.*

94. *See* Sandrock & du Plessis, *supra* note 10, at 188.
95. *See id.* at 237; Otto Sandrock, *The Impact of European Developments on German Codetermination and German Corporate Law, in* GERMAN CORPORATE GOVERNANCE IN INTERNATIONAL AND EUROPEAN CONTEXT, *supra* note 10, at 243, 320.
96. *See* Sandrock & du Plessis, *supra* note 10, at 168.
97. *See id.* at 196–233; Sandrock, *supra* note 18, at 137–45.
98. *See* du Plessis et al., *supra* note 15, at 8–13.
99. In a process that may cost hundreds of thousands of euros, individual employees elect members of an electoral college, who in turn elect the employee representatives to the supervisory board. *See* Sandrock & du Plessis, *supra* note 10, at 205; Sandrock, *supra* note 18, at 138.

12.   Conclusion

1. Taylor Telford, *Income Inequality in America Is the Highest It's Been Since Census Bureau Started Tracking It, Data Shows*, WASH. POST (Sept. 26, 2019), https://www.washingtonpost.com/business/2019/09/26/income-inequality-america-highest-its-been-since-census-started-tracking-it-data-show/.
2. Thomas Piketty, Emmanuel Saez & Gabriel Zucman, *Distributional National Accounts: Methods and Estimates for the United States*, 46 fig.5 (NBER Working Paper No. 22945, Dec. 2016), https://www.nber.org/papers/w22945.pdf.
3. *Id.*
4. Dylan Matthews, *Are 26 Billionaires Worth More Than Half the Planet? The Debate, Explained.*, VOX.COM (Jan. 26, 2019), https://www.vox.com/future-perfect/2019/1/22/18192774/oxfam-inequality-report-2019-davos-wealth; *Global Inequality*, INEQUALITY.ORG, https://inequality.org/facts/global-inequality/ (last visited Nov. 18, 2019).
5. INTERNATIONAL MONETARY FUND, WORLD ECONOMIC OUTLOOK: GLOBAL MANUFACTURING DOWNTURN, RISING TRADE BARRIERS 65 (2019).
6. Alexia Fernández Campbell, *CEOs Made 287 Times More Money Last Year Than Their Workers Did*, VOX.COM (June 26, 2019), https://www.vox.com/policy-and-politics/2019/6/26/18744304/ceo-pay-ratio-disclosure-2018.
7. Dave Jamieson & Paul Blumenthal, *Labor Unions Spent A Record Amount On The Elections. But Not As Much As These 5 People*, HUFFINGTON POST (Nov. 8, 2016), https://www.huffingtonpost.com/entry/labor-union-election-2016_us_58223b92e4b0e80b02cd7259.
8. *Id.*
9. For deeper qualitative examinations of working-class alienation, see BEN BRADLEE JR., THE FORGOTTEN: HOW THE PEOPLE OF ONE PENNSYLVANIA COUNTY ELECTED DONALD TRUMP AND CHANGED AMERICA (2018); ARLIE RUSSELL HOCHSCHILD, STRANGERS IN THEIR OWN LAND: ANGER AND MOURNING ON THE AMERICAN RIGHT (2016); RICK WARTZMAN, THE END OF LOYALTY: THE RISE AND FALL OF GOOD JOBS IN AMERICA (2017).
10. Paul H. Edelman, Randall S. Thomas & Robert B. Thompson, *Shareholder Voting in an Age of Intermediary Capitalism*, 87 S. CAL. L. REV. 1359, 1370 (2014).

11. *Our Commitment*, BUSINESS ROUNDTABLE (emphasis added), https://opportunity
.businessroundtable.org/ourcommitment/ (last visited Oct. 27, 2019).
12. Leo E. Strine, Jr., *Toward Fair and Sustainable Capitalism: A Comprehensive
Proposal to Help American Workers, Restore Fair Gainsharing Between Employees
and Shareholders, and Increase American Competitiveness by Reorienting Our
Corporate Governance System Toward Sustainable Long-Term Growth and
Encouraging Investments in America's Future* 2 (John M. Olin Ctr. for Law,
Econ., & Bus., Discussion Paper No. 1018, 2019), https://papers.ssrn.com/sol3/
papers.cfm?abstract_id=3461924.
13. *Id.*
14. Accountable Capitalism Act, S. 3348, 115th Cong. (2018); Reward Work Act,
S. 2605, 115th Cong. (2018).
15. Elizabeth Warren, *Plans: Empowering Workers Through Accountable Capitalism*,
ELIZABETH WARREN FOR PRESIDENT, https://elizabethwarren.com/plans/accoun
table-capitalism ("Her Accountable Capitalism plan . . . [e]mpowers workers at big
American corporations to elect no less than 40% of the company's board members:
Borrowing from the successful approach in Germany and other developed economies, Elizabeth's plan gives workers a big voice in all corporate decisions, including
those about outsourcing, wages, and investment.").
16. Bernie Sanders, *Issues: Corporate Accountability and Democracy*, BERNIE SANDERS
FOR PRESIDENT, https://berniesanders.com/issues/corporate-accountability-and-
democracy/ ("Under this plan, 45 percent of the board of directors in any large
corporation with at least $100 million in annual revenue, corporations with at least
$100 million in balance sheet total, and all publicly traded companies will be
directly elected by the firm's workers – similar to what happens under 'employee
co-determination' in Germany, which long has had one of the most productive and
successful economies in the world.").
17. Noam Scheiber, *Google Workers Reject Silicon Valley Individualism in Walkout*,
N.Y. TIMES (Nov. 6, 2018), https://www.nytimes.com/2018/11/06/business/goo
gle-employee-walkout-labor.html (noting that Google workers demanded "a
worker representative on the board of Google's parent company, Alphabet").
18. *See generally* ALLAN A. KENNEDY, THE END OF SHAREHOLDER VALUE:
CORPORATIONS AT THE CROSSROADS (2000).
19. Henry Hansmann & Reinier Kraakman, *The End of History for Corporate Law*, 89
GEO. L.J. 439 (2001) ("There is no longer any serious competitor to the view that
corporate law should principally strive to increase long-term shareholder value.").
20. Roberta Romano, *After the Revolution in Corporate Law*, 55 J. LEGAL EDUC. 342,
356 (2005) (finding that "there is consensus on ends, as there is among most
U.S. corporate law scholars since the field was transformed with the application
of finance and the theory of the firm (a consensus that the objective of public, for-
profit corporations is to maximize shareholder wealth)").
21. Stephen M. Bainbridge, *Dodd-Frank: Quack Federal Corporate Governance Round
II*, 95 MINN. L. REV. 1779 (2011); Roberta Romano, *The Sarbanes-Oxley Act and
the Making of Quack Corporate Governance*, 114 YALE L.J. 1521 (2005).
22. Romano, *supra* note 20, at 343 ("In the 1960s, corporate law was an ossified,
stagnant field.").

INDEX